Aristophanes 1

Clouds, Wasps, Birds

Aristophanes 1

Clouds, Wasps, Birds

Translated, with Notes, by Peter Meineck

Introduced by Ian C. Storey

Hackett Publishing Company, Inc.
Indianapolis/Cambridge

Printed in the United States of America

05 04 03 02 01 00 99 98 1 2 3 4 5 6 7 8 9

For further information, please address
Hackett Publishing Company, Inc.
PO Box 44937
Indianapolis, IN 46244-0937

Cover design by Brian Rak and John Pershing.
Interior design by Meera Dash and Dan Kirklin.

Library of Congress Cataloging-in-Publication Data

Aristophanes.
[Selections. English. 1999]
Aristophanes / translated, with notes, by Peter Meineck : introduced by Ian C. Storey.
p. cm.
Includes bibliographical references
Contents: Clouds—Wasps—Birds
ISBN 0-87220-361-1 (alk. paper). — ISBN 0-87220-360-3 (pbk. : alk. paper)
1. Aristophanes—Translations into English. 2. Greek drama (Comedy)—Translations into English. I. Meineck, Peter, 1967– . II. Title.
PA3877.A2 1999 98-37824
882'.01—dc21 CIP

The paper used in this publication
meets the minimum requirements of
the American National Standard for Information Sciences—
Permanence of Paper for Printed Library Materials,
ANSI Z39.48 1984.

Contents

General Introduction

Old (and Aristophanic) Comedy

Aristophanic comedy is not the sort of comedy with which we are familiar: situation comedy, comedy of errors and manners, plot and subplot, romance, with an emphasis on the familial and domestic. I would rather ask the reader to imagine a dramatic combination of the slapstick of the Three Stooges, the song and dance of a Broadway musical, the verbal wit of W. S. Gilbert or of a television show like *Frasier*, the exuberance of Mardi Gras, the open-ended plot line of *The Simpsons*, the parody of a Mel Brooks movie, the political satire of Doonesbury (or your favorite editorial cartoonist), the outrageous sexuality of *The Rocky Horror Picture Show*, and the fantasy of J. R. R. Tolkien, wrapped up in the format of a Monty Python movie.

Aristophanic comedy is "fantasy" or "farce" rather than pure "comedy." It depends not on complicated plot or subtle interaction of characters, but on the working out of a "great idea," the more bizarre the better (e.g., the sex-strike that stops the war in *Lysistrata*, or the establishment of Cloudcuckooland in *Birds*). Imagine a fantastic idea, wind it up and let it run, watch the logical (or illogical) conclusions that follow, and let the whole thing end in a great final scene. "Plot" is not a useful term here; of the eleven extant comedies of Aristophanes, only *Thesmophoriazusae* has anything like the linear plot of a modern comedy. The background is always topical and immediate, the city of Athens in the present, although in *Plutus* we can detect a shift from the local problems of Athens to those of Greece as a whole.

The comedy often features a central character—avoid the term "hero" here—who is responsible for the creation and execution of the great idea. Whitman attempted to create a type of "comic hero" in whose nature was a wide streak of *poneria* ("villainy"), but Aristophanes' heroes are not all cut from the same cloth. Some are old men (Dicaeopolis, Strepsiades, Trygaeus, Peithetaerus, Chremylus, "relative" in *Thesm.*); two are mature women (Lysistrata, Praxagora). In *Frogs* the protagonist is a god, Dionysus, a familiar character in comedy, and in *Wasps* the great idea is devised by a younger man (Contracleon) for the good of his elderly and cantankerous father (Procleon), a younger man who has much in common with the poet. These protagonists stand up against a situation they find intolerable, create a brilliant and fanciful solution, and keep the comic pot bubbling to the end of the drama. Not all are wholly sympathetic; Strepsiades can be stupid and tiresome in the teaching scene with Socrates (*Cl.* 627–804), and more than one critic has seen Peithetaerus, "Makemedo," of *Birds* as a comic portrait of megalomania.

Despite Aristotle's attempt (*Poetics* 1447a35) to defend an etymology of "village song," comedy (*komoidia*) is "revel-song" (*komos* + *ode*), the celebration of exuberant release that was inherent in the worship of Dionysus. Songs and dancing must have been common to every Greek state, but formal comic drama is attested for Sicily in the early fifth century and then for Athens, where the genre would reach its greatest heights, in the fifth and fourth centuries.[1] As early as 330 B.C.E., Aristotle (*Ethics* 1128a 21–24) can distinguish "old" (*palaia*) comedy, where "indecency" (*aischrologia*, the closest the Greeks get to "obscenity") provided the humor, from "new" (*kaine*) comedy, where humor is derived by "innuendo" (*hyponoia*). Later in the age of Alexandrian scholarship (the last three centuries B.C.E.),

---

[1] There are hints of something called "Megarian comedy," but whether the Megara meant is the city to the northwest of Athens or that in Sicily is uncertain (Aristotle *Poetics* 1448a29). Athenian comedians would make jokes at Megarian comedy as poor trash in comparison with their own—one such joke occurs at *Wasps* 56ff., "you shouldn't expect anything too high-brow from us, but you're not going to get any of that disgusting stuff lifted off the Megarians either." It is uncertain whether this indicates a formal genre of comic drama at Megara.

comedy was subdivided formally into a trinity of Old (*archaia*, although Aristotle's term *palaia* is sometimes found), Middle (*mese*), and New (*nea*). For Old Comedy the canonical starting date was 487–86, the first official state-sponsored production, while the death of Aristophanes in the late 380s provides a reasonable closing point. For New Comedy the début of its best known exponent, Menander (325 or 321), is a useful place to start. It is doubtful if "Middle Comedy" means anything more than "between Aristophanes and Menander" (i.e., c.380–c. 320); it seems to be comedy in transition with no Aristophanes or Menander to dominate the comic stage.[2]

Old Comedy lasted for just about a hundred years, and thus what was first enacted in 487–86, or what Magnes, the first comedian about whom we know anything, produced for his victory in 472, is hardly going to be the same as what Aristophanes was creating at the end of the century. Old Comedy is not a monolithic art form, and Aristophanic comedy is not necessarily typical or perhaps even representative of Old Comedy. As I will outline, his comedy was very topical, "political" in the best sense of the word, but we can detect themes and subjects in the other Old Comic poets that are not to be found in Aristophanes. One such is the comic parody of myth. The best example here is Cratinus' lost *Dionysalexandros*, of which the hypothesis and some fragments remain; in this comedy Paris cannot be found to adjudicate his famous Judgment, and Dionysus must be pressed into service by Hermes. Aristophanes does not seem to have written this sort of comedy at the height of his career. He does write parody, but usually of specific tragedies by Euripides.[3] Or we find fragments in Pherecrates from comedies about women, domestic comedy, or the *hetaira*-play ("prostitute"). Aristophanes does write about women, but about women who have invaded the male public space. Only in his last two plays do we get women in domestic scenes. Aristotle tells us (*Poetics* 1449b7–9) that Crates (a contemporary of Aristophanes) "was the first to abandon the abusive style

---

2 For studies of Middle Comedy see W. G. Arnott, "From Aristophanes to Menander," *Greece & Rome* 19 (1972):65–80; H.-G. Nesselrath, *Die attische Mittlere Komödie* (Berlin 1990); and G. Dobrov (ed.), *Beyond Aristophanes* (Atlanta 1995).

3 His *Phoenissae* ("Phoenician Women") is based on Euripides' late play of that title, and his *Lemniae* ("Women of Lemnos") on Euripides' *Hypsipyle* (also a late play).

and write general plots," while another ancient source tells us that Pherecrates followed Crates in abstaining from personal abuse.[4] Thus it is clear that Old Comedy featured much more than the personal and political "satire" of Aristophanes, Eupolis, and Cratinus, but through the circumstances of survival we must depend on Aristophanes' eleven extant comedies for a play-length view of Old Comedy.

Aristophanes

We do not have biographies for ancient writers in the same way that a curious reader can open an encyclopedia and find the biographical details about Dante or Jane Austen or Tennessee Williams. There does exist a *Life of Aristophanes*, originating from the Alexandrian period, but it is hardly serious biography.[5] Rife with expressions such as "some say" or "according to others" that do not give the reader much confidence, most of the information is anecdotal and based on deductions (usually faulty) from what Aristophanes or other comedians have said in their plays. Every so often, however, we get an intriguing nugget that cannot be traced back to a comic source, for instance, the assertion that Plato sent Dionysius of Syracuse a copy of the plays of Aristophanes so that "he might learn about the government of Athens" (*Life* 42 ff.). We must use the *Life* with care, seeking material that does not seem to have come from comedy itself.

Similarly the *scholia* (ancient commentaries transmitted along with the comic texts) attempt to explain various references in Aristophanes, but on what evidence is uncertain, and the scholiasts have a strong tendency to be literally minded and to seek external and political compulsions on comedy.[6] There is also considerable information to be had from the various aspects of the later encyclopedic

---

4 Anon. *peri komodias* III (Koster):29–32.

5 The Greek text of the *Life of Aristophanes* may be found at K-A III.2 nr. 1 (pp. 1–4), a translation at M. Lefkowitz, *The Lives of the Greek Poets* (London 1981), pp. 169–72. Lefkowitz argues (pp. 105–16) that the *Life* contains little of historical value.

6 On the value of the comic scholia, especially for personal allusions, see S. Halliwell, "Ancient interpretations of ὀνομαστὶ κωμῳδεῖν in Aristophanes," *Classical Quarterly* 34 (1984):83–88.

tradition (entries in the *Suda*, the lexicon of Photius, certain anonymous writers "on comedy"), and the ancient writers themselves have much to contribute, such as Plato's inclusion of Aristophanes in the company of his *Symposium* (c.380) or Aelian's story of Aristophanes' complicity in the "witch-hunt" against Socrates (*Varia Historia* 2.13). But again the evidence is of varying value.

All but one of the surviving comedies have come down with hypotheses that summarize the plays and provide intriguing details about the comedy and information about production; from the first hypothesis to *Birds*, for example, "it was produced in the archonship of Charias [415/4] at the City Dionysia through Callistratus; he was second with *Birds*, while Ameipsias won with *Komastai* ("Revellers"), and Phrynichus third with *Monotropos* ("The Hermit")." It is these that make possible the chronology listed below. Finally there are the comments of Aristophanes himself in the eleven plays that we have. These occur most often in the parabases (for which term see below), but also in the prologues and in certain choral interludes. From these we learn that Aristophanes had some connection with the island of Aegina (*Ach.* 652–54), made his comic début at an early age (*Cl.* 530), and could describe himself while no older than thirty as "the bald one" (*Peace* 767–74).

These last present a particular danger, however, in that there exists a great temptation to take Aristophanes at face value and to build a biography based on what he and other comedians allege. Much the same sort of thing happened with Roman poets such as Catullus, Propertius, and Ovid, whose personal poetry was used to reconstruct a biography of the poet's life without considering that we were being given the *persona* of a poet in love, not an accurate biographical picture. In the parabases of his first five plays, as well as in the prologues and at other points in the episodes and choral songs, Aristophanes gives us a picture of the young and innovative comic poet, and again this may be his face to the world rather than a real and accurate self-portrait. Obviously some truth must lurk beneath the comic front—Aristophanes and Cleon must have had some encounter in 426 and again later (cf. *Ach.* 377–82, 502 ff., 630 ff.; *Wasps* 1284–91), but we must not take the comedian as an impeccable source. We may think of modern comedians such as Jack Benny and Dean Martin, who propagated their self-myths of the miserly tightwad or the lovable drunk; Aristophanes cultivates the image of the unappreciated and brilliant artist. The biographical truth need not be the same.

The following biographical details can be accepted with reasonable confidence. Although there lurks a persistent tradition that he was charged on one or more occasions with *xenia* ("not being a citizen"), he was born an Athenian, son of Philippus, of the deme of Cydathenaeum. Attica was subdivided politically into 139 demes ("ridings," "parishes"), and Cydathenaeum was a wealthy city deme on the northwestern slopes of the Acropolis. Aristophanes' deme may indicate just that this was where his grandfather was living when the deme structure was put in place in the last years of the sixth century, but he clearly did have a good education and very likely belonged to the privileged classes. Although some have seen in his plays a real love of the countryside, as opposed to the *asty* ("town"), Aristophanes is very much a man of the city of Athens. His comedies are full of allusions to the people and issues and places of the city. Thus I can see him as a resident of this affluent city deme. Cydathenaeum was a deme of the tribe Pandionis. Thus, when the chorus at *Peace* 1173 describes a man seeing his name on the military list posted beside the statue of Pandion, we may detect a personal experience.

We should date his birth around the middle of the fifth century B.C.E. Some critics have interpreted *Clouds* 528 ff., referring to the production of his first play, *Banqueters*, in 427:

> It was here in this very theatre,
> that my tale of the righteous boy and the little bugger was so very well received.
> It is true that I was not of age to mother properly such a child, and so I exposed
> my prodigy to be adopted by another in my stead

as indicating that Aristophanes was not of legal age in 427, that is, younger than eighteen, and thus dated his birth c. 444. But this seems too literal a reading, and we should be content with a birthdate around 450; this would make him, incidentally, almost an exact contemporary of the infamous Alcibiades.[7]

---

[7] Cartledge, however, makes the interesting point (xvi) that on a birthdate of 444, Aristophanes would have come of age in 426, that same year as Cleon's first attack on him. Given the tradition of Aristophanes accused of *xenia*,

Aristophanes was one of four major figues of Old Comedy who came upon the scene in the 420s (Eupolis and Phrynichus in 429, Aristophanes in 427, Platon [not the philosopher] in 424). His dramatic career began in 427 with the production of his *Banqueters*. It enjoyed success, probably the second prize; if it had won, we would have expected Aristophanes to have trumpeted his success. His early plays (*Banqueters, Babylonians, Acharnians*) were all staged through other men as producers, Philonides and Callistratus, but this does not necessarily reflect his novice status. Aristophanes continued this practice, which is known for other poets, in his maturity (e.g., *Frogs* [405] through Philonides). His first comedy in his own name was *Knights* at the Lenaea of 424.

His early career has been the subject of considerable study in the last twenty years.[8] At the core of the debate is a passage from the parabasis of *Wasps* (1016–37) which was usually considered to suggest two stages in his early career as a poet: (i) "in secret, unseen, playing second fiddle to other dramatists" as indicating his comedies produced through others, i.e. 427–424L, and (ii) "then on that great day he ventured forth, alone into the fray, riding his own chariot of comedy" meaning his production of *Knights* at 424L; this will be picked up at 1029 "when he produced his own great plays." But others have made a plausible, if not totally persuasive, case for a three-fold division: (i) "in secret, unseen, playing second fiddle to other dramatists" as indicating his helping other poets *before* his own début in 427, (ii) "then on that great day he ventured forth . . ." as denoting his plays produced through others from 427-424, and (iii) a new stage indicated at 1029, "when he produced his own great plays," his "open" career beginning with *Knights* in 424. Another passage (*Kn*. 541–44) also suggests that Aristophanes saw his early career in more than two stages. On this reading Aristophanes will

---

Cartledge wonders if Cleon (of the same deme as Aristophanes) was making some trouble over the poet's citizenship as he came of age.

[8] See S. Halliwell, "Aristophanes' 'Apprenticeship,'" *Classical Quarterly* 30 (1980):33–45; D. Welsh, "*IG* ii^2 2343, Philonides and Aristophanes' *Banqueters*," *Classical Quarterly* 33 (1983):51–55; N. W. Slater, "Aristophanes' apprenticeship again," *Greek, Roman and Byzantine Studies* 30 (1989):67–82; MacDowell (1995) chap. 3.

have cooperated with other poets and contributed to their comedies, and it gives an interesting glimpse of life behind the comic scenes.[9]

Two figures from his early career deserve mention. First there is Cleon, a political leader of the 420s, with whom the young poet seems to have two personal encounters and whom he attacks fiercely in several plays. Cleon has come down to us as the archdemagogue of late-fifth-century Athens. Etymologically, "demagogue" is an inoffensive term (*demos* = "people" + *agein* = "lead"), but in both ancient Greek and modern English it acquired the pejorative overtones that "politician" possesses today. Cleon and his like were the "new men" of Athens in the 420s, members of the commercial middle class who had prospered during the period of Athenian supremacy, having made their money rather than inherited it, and who were seeking political power and challenging the authority of the traditional aristocratic leaders. In 426 Aristophanes put on his *Babylonians* at the Dionysia, and the three passages in *Acharnians* cited before plus the scholia *ad loc* show that Cleon took some official action against him, probably an *eisangelia* to the *Boule* (the Council of 500 that with the *ekklesia* ran the affairs of state) on the grounds of insulting the people in the presence of foreigners. The play turned in part, as far as we can gather from its meager remains, on the relationship between Athens and her allies ("the Cities").[10] It is equally likely that Aristophanes made fun of Cleon and that Cleon could not take a joke. The charge was probably rejected by the Council, but Aristophanes is very careful in *Acharnians* to stress that "I do not mean the city, just certain worthless individuals" (515 ff.). A second

---

[9] The core of the debate is between G. Mastromarco, "L' esordio 'segreto' di Aristofane," *Quaderni di Storia* 5 (1979):153–92 and Halliwell (see note 8) against D. M. MacDowell, "Aristophanes and Kallistratos," *Classical Quarterly* 32 (1982):21–26 and F. Perusino, *Dalla commedia antica alla commedia di mezzo* (Urbino 1986). Slater, Sommerstein (*Wasps*) 215 ff., and S. Halliwell, "Authorial collaboration in the Athenian comic theatre," *Greek, Roman and Byzantine Studies* 30 (1989):515–28, pursue the tripartite division further.

[10] Many assumptions have been made concerning *Babylonians,* especially that Aristophanes was defending the allied cities against Athenian domination. On the play (which had Dionysus as a character) see MacDowell (1995), pp. 30–45, D. Welsh, "The chorus of Aristophanes' *Babylonians,*" *Greek, Roman and Byzantine Studies* 24 (1983):137–50, and I. C. Storey, "The politics of 'angry Eupolis,'" *Ancient History Bulletin* 8 (1994):109–11.

attack by Cleon took place in 423 and is reflected in some autobiographical lines in *Wasps* (1284–91), from which we can see that Aristophanes came to some agreement with Cleon (not to caricature him in comedy?), an agreement that he emphatically breaks in *Wasps*.[11] Cleon was one of Aristophanes' major targets in his comedy. *Knights* (424L) is a play-length attack on him, disguised thinly by the name "Paphlagon"; a section from the original version of *Clouds* (575–94) calls on the Athenians to "un-elect" Cleon as general; and he lurks beneath the whole of *Wasps*, in the names of the characters ("Procleon" and "Contracleon") and as a dog in the trial of the dogs (lines 891–1008).[12] His death in 422–21 effectively robbed the comedian of his favorite target. Hyperbolus, Cleon's successor as "leader of the people," was just not the same.

Then there is Eupolis, another of the new comedians of the 420s. A rather romantic picture has emerged of two young, new poets, friends and contemporaries arm in arm against the establishment, collaborators in the creation of new and sophisticated comedy.[13] Cratinus makes fun of Aristophanes for "using material from Eupolis" (fr. 213), and there seems to have been a public exchange in which Aristophanes accused Eupolis of plagiarizing his *Knights* in his *Maricas* (421L)—see *Cl.* 551–56—and Eupolis (fr. 89) retorted, "I helped the bald poet write those *Knights*, and made him a present of them." But all this comes from exchanges in comedy; Eupolis is a rival and a player in the great game involving poets and audiences. The rivalry and bitterness are probably thus overrated. The relationship between poets need not have been hostile and competitive, and one suspects that there is a great deal of intertextual material in the comedies that we simply just do not get.[14]

---

11 See I. C. Storey, "*Wasps* 1284–91 and the portrait of Kleon in *Wasps*," *Scholia* 4 (1995):3–23.

12 On the picture of Cleon in *Knights*, see L. Edmunds, *Cleon, Knights, and Aristophanes' Politics* (Lanham MD 1987); in *Wasps*, see Storey 1995.

13 The testimonia and fragments of Eupolis are collected at K–A V 294–539. See also my articles, "Dating and Re-dating Eupolis," *Phoenix* 44 (1990): 1–30, and "*Notus est omnibus Eupolis?*" in Sommerstein et al. (1993), pp. 373–96.

14 Consult Halliwell (see note 9) and Hubbard on the relationship between the poets. K. Sidwell has also been advancing some interesting and controversial theories on the comic personae of the poets.

Aristophanes was credited with forty-four plays in antiquity, although four were attributed by the author of the *Life* to Archippus instead. Over a career of at least forty years he produced forty comedies, of which eleven have survived—the best survival rate of any Greek dramatist. The following dates can be presented with confidence—lost plays in [...]; the letters L and D designate the festival, Lenaea or Dionysia:

427	[*Daitales*]	"Banqueters"	2nd prize?
426D	[*Babylonioi*]	"Babylonians"	1st prize
425L	*Acharnes*	"Acharnians"	1st prize
424L	*Hippeis*	"Knights"	1st prize
423L	[play unknown]—see *Wasps* 1038		
423D	[*Nephelai*]	"Clouds"	3rd prize
422L	*Sphekes*	"Wasps"	2nd prize
	Proagon	"Preview"	1st prize[15]
421D	*Eirene*	"Peace"	2nd prize
c.418	*Nephelai*	"Clouds" [partly revised]	
414L	[*Amphiaraus*]		
414D	*Ornithes*	"Birds"	2nd prize
411L(?)	*Lysistrata*	"Lysistrata"	
411D(?)	*Thesmophoriazusae*	"Women at the Thesmophoria"	
408	[*Plutus*]	"Wealth"	
405L	*Batrachoi*	"Frogs"	1st prize
393-391	*Ecclesiazusae*	"Assembly-women"	
388	*Plutus*	"Wealth"	
after 388	[*Cocalus*][16]		
	[*Aiolosikon*]		

[15] The hypothesis to *Wasps* gives the second prize to Aristophanes' *Wasps* and the first to Philonides' *Proagon*, but Philonides is a known producer of Aristophanes' plays, and whenever *Proagon* is cited, it is attributed to Aristophanes. Aristophanes, it seems, found a way to win two prizes at the same festival.

[16] An inscription (*IG* ii2 2318.196) gives Araros a Dionysia-victory in 387; if the hypothesis to *Plutus* is correct that after 388 Aristophanes produced *Cocalus* and *Aiolosikon* through Araros, we can assign a victory with *Cocalus* to Aristophanes in 387.

Some of the lost plays can be dated to a year or so. For example, *Georgoi* ("Farmers") with its allusion to Nicias' behavior in 425 and a clear background of war (frr. 102, 111) must belong to the years 424–22, while *Holkades* ("Merchantships") is attested as a peace-play (Hypothesis I *Peace*) and as an attack on Cleon, thus also from the 420s—it *may* be the unknown comedy of 423L.

Aristophanes burst upon the scene with a vengeance. He may have hidden his light by assisting other poets before his début in 427, but from 427–21 he produced at least ten plays, an indication of this great new talent. He had his share of victories, at the Lenaea at least, inasmuch as we can identify victories at that festival in 425, 424, 422, and 405, but for the Dionysia things are less certain. An inscription (*IG* ii2 2325.58) suggests strongly that he and then Eupolis won their first Dionysia-victories before 423; if his *Babylonians* did not win in 426, then he must have won at 425D. What I find peculiar is that we are never given a victory total for Aristophanes. For just about every other major poet of Old Comedy and also the "Big Three" of tragedy, we get victory totals; for example, for Eupolis, we get seven victories (of fourteen or fifteen plays), but for Aristophanes, silence. Is it possible that this greatest of Old Comic poets did not have an impressive victory total? We do know of four Lenaea-victories, but were these all there were? Perhaps the Dionysia-victory of 426 (or 425) was his only one, or one of just a few. He may have started off with several successes, perhaps enough to justify his claim at *Wasps* 1024 "And he won great honor, the likes of which had never before been awarded to any one man," but his later career may not have fulfilled these early expectations. Perhaps like Euripides, his reputation came later. Did Plato's attractive portrait of Aristophanes in *Symposium* make him the leading Old Comedian in the eyes of later antiquity?

About other details of his life we have little secure information. He seems not to have had a political career or to have held any elected office—here contrast Sophocles, the tragedian, who served Athens in a number of public capacities. An Aristophanes of Cydathenaeum is known to have served as a *bouleutes* (member of the Council of 500) early in the fourth century,[17] but this was not an elected magistracy. This may be our Aristophanes, or conceivably a

---

[17] See B. D. Meritt and J. S. Traill, *The Athenian Agora: vol. XV, Inscriptions: The Athenian Councillors* (Princeton 1974) nr. 12, pp. 32 ff.

grandson. In 405 his *Frogs*, produced at the height of his career and just months before the war would end disastrously for Athens, won a crown of leaves from the sacred olive tree and the unprecedented honor of a second production; this was due, according to Dicaearchus, to the parabasis.[18]

He had three sons, Araros, Philippus, and a third whose name is given variously as Philetaerus or Nicostratus.[19] They are all described as comic poets, but only Araros seems to have made any mark, and if Alexis fr. 184 is to believed, he did not live up to his father ("I have a very deep well inside, more frigid than the comedy of Araros"). Aristophanes is said to have produced his last two plays, *Cocalus* and *Aiolosikon*, through Araros (Hypothesis IV *Plutus*). His last play in his own name was *Plutus* (388), and we know of the two produced through his son. Thereafter Aristophanes disappears from view, and we may reasonably date his death in the period 385–80. Plato's *Symposium* dates from about 380, and if Aristophanes had died in the recent past, the brilliant picture created by Plato may be seen as a posthumous tribute to him. Webster thought that an elegant grave relief of a comic poet dating to the late 380s might be that of Aristophanes, but more recent opinion dates this relief to the middle of the century, too late to be that of Aristophanes.[20]

Comic Festivals and Production

Comedy, along with the older dramatic genres of tragedy and satyr-play, was produced at public festivals in honor of the god Dionysus. Too often we think of Dionysus as "jolly Bacchus," whom the Romans in particular portrayed as the god of drinking and sexual orgies. But he was far more, a god of the dark side of humanity, of passions and the life force, companion of the Mother, a dying and rising god of the year cycle, god of the mountain rather than the city, whose followers were mainly male satyrs and female maenads ("the

---

[18] *Life* 32–39 and Hypothesis I *Frogs*. The date of the restaging of *Frogs* has been the subject of much recent discussion. See Sommerstein (*Frogs*), 21.

[19] For the testimonia and fragments see K–A II 524–31 (Araros), VII 322–32 (Philetaerus), VII 353–5 (Philippus), VII 74–92 (Nicostratus).

[20] See T. B. L. Webster, *Monuments Illustrating Old and Middle Comedy*, BICS Supp. 39, 3rd ed. (London 1978), p. 117.

mad women"), who dressed in animal skins, wreathed their hair with ivy, wielded *thrysoi* (poles tipped with foliage), hunted their prey on the mountainside, tore it apart, and ate the flesh raw.[21] Euripides' *Bacchae* (c.407) gives the best picture of this god and his rites as seen through fifth-century eyes. His main festival at Athens was the City Dionysia, held in late March or early April. A "city" Dionysia may seem like a contradiction in terms, and what the Athenians seem to have done is to tame Dionysia by diverting the wild festivals more suited to the mountain to a context within the city. And part of this worship was drama, in part perhaps the replacement of the savage reality with a controlled reenactment.

The canonical date for the beginning of Old Comedy is 487–86 (*Suda* χ 318, s.v. Chionides), that is, the first formal inclusion of comedy at the City Dionysia. This was the major festival of Dionysus and of the dramas produced in his honor, but from the late 440s comedies were staged formally at the Lenaea also, a festival in late January or early February.[22] Tragedies also were performed at the Lenaea, but this was comedy's festival. There is some evidence that the Lenaea was a lesser festival; an ancient source speaks of Platon "being bumped back to the Lenaea" after a fourth-place finish at the Dionysia, but this may just be a faulty deduction by the ancient source.[23]

For the Dionysia, we know that it lasted five days, 10–14 Elaphebolion, that the first day was devoted to the formal parade (*pompe*) of the god, and that contests for tragedy, comedy, and dithyrambs (songs with a chorus of fifty) took place during these days. The exact order of events is in dispute, but a reasonable reconstruction is found in Csapo and Slater (103–8): Day 1 —*pompe* + dithyrambs; Day 2—five comedies, one by each poet; Day 3—three tragedies + satyr-play by a tragedian; Day 4—three tragedies + satyr-

---

21 On the cult of Dionysus see E. R. Dodds, *Euripides' Bacchae* (Oxford 1960), and R. Seaford, *Euripides Bacchae* (Warminster 1996).

22 For translations of and commentary on the ancient evidence see Csapo and Slater, pp. 103–85.

23 *P.Oxy*. 2737, fr. i, col. ii 1–17 says that Platon did well when he produced through others, but when he produced *Rhabdouchoi* ("Ushers") on his own, he finished fourth and was bumped back to the Lenaea; see Csapo and Slater nr. 71.

play by the second tragedian; Day 5—three tragedies + satyr-play by the third tragedian. Five comedies are attested for the years 434 and 388, but the hypotheses to several of Aristophanes' comedies list only three prizes. It has often been assumed that during the war the comedies were reduced from five to three, and that they followed the tragedians, one on each of days 3 to 5. But this was challenged by Luppe and others, and the number may have remained at five throughout.[24] The passage at *Birds* 786–89 about flying off during a boring tragedy and then flying "back in plenty of time to see us" does not have to refer to comedy; it just means "to the theatre."[25]

These occasions were religious festivals; drama was part of the ritual ceremonies of the god, and several recent critics have read the comedies with a ritual subtext.[26] But even more significant is that they were public and civic occasions. There was a political side to the festivals. One of the nine archons was responsible for the dramatic contests; poets were "granted choruses" by that official, a *misthos* ("stipend") was paid to the poet, and a *choregos* ("sponsor") appointed to pick up the costs of production as part of his public responsibility ("liturgy"). These were state-sponsored productions, and considerable debate attends the question of why the Athenian democracy ran these dramatic festivals essentially at state expense. Especially at the City Dionysia the role of the city loomed large—no public business was transacted, the ten elected generals would enter formally and pour the opening libation, the *phoros* ("tribute") from the cities would be paraded formally through the theatre, benefactors of the city would be honored, and those whose fathers had died in battle would receive a suit of armor from the city when they came of age.[27] Theatres in ancient Greece were large—that at Athens is estimated to have held fifteen thousand to seventeen thousand spectators—and thus the tragedies and comedies played to the state as au-

---

[24] W. Luppe, "Die Zahl der Konkurrenten an den komischen Agonen zur Zeit des peloponnischen Krieges," *Philologus* 116 (1972):53–76; against this view see G. Mastromarco, "Guerra peloponnesiaca e agoni comici in Athene," *Belfagor* 30 (1975):469–73. See also Csapo and Slater 107.

[25] See Dunbar (*Birds*), p. 481.

[26] See Storey 1992: 3 ff.

[27] See Csapo and Slater, p. 107 ff., and an important study by S. Goldhill, "The Great Dionysia and Civic Ideology," *Journal of Hellenic Studies* 107 (1987):58–76.

dience. Drama was not the province of a few in a covered theatre; it was for the people as a larger body. We need to imagine a combination of the faithful gathered in Vatican Square on Easter Day, the crowds that fill the Mall on the Fourth of July, and the audiences on the opening night of a great summer blockbuster. Drama was intensely alive and intensely important to the people of Athens.

We are used to "theatre of illusion"—the three-sided box and special effects make us believe that we are there, watching what goes on. But Greek drama is "theatre of convention," or, in Taplin's phrase, "theatre of the mind." The audience will do a great deal of the work in allowing the drama (tragic or comic) to work. Notice the opening of Menander's *Dyskolos* (the speaker is the god Pan):

> Imagine the setting to be Phyle in Attica, and the shrine that I am coming out of is that of the people of Phyle ... a well-known place. In the house on the right lives Knemon, a thoroughly unpleasant man ...

The audience is told in the prologue what the program notes provide today.

The theatrical space in the time of Aristophanes was located on the southeastern slope of the Acropolis, in an area that had long been sacred to Dionysus (Thuc. 2.15.4). All one really needs for a Greek theatre is a hill and a flat space at the bottom, a circular dancing-place (*orchestra*) for the chorus, and an acting-space for the actors.[28] Aristophanes operated with a flat *orchestra* (about sixty-five feet across), two passages from each side that allowed the entrance of chorus and actors (*eisodoi*), and a stage building (*skene* = "tent," "shack") with at least one door. The flat roof of this building could also be used for scenes above ground level—at *Wasps* 68 Contracleon is "sleeping up there on the roof." Certain scenes from comedy show that there was a window in the *skene* so that actors inside could be seen and heard outside (e.g., Procleon's appearance at *Wasps* 155–70).

Two points are the subject of debate: the number of doors and the presence of a low stage in front of the *skene*. By the time of Menander's

---

28 The physical aspect is well presented for the student by Csapo and Slater, pp. 79–88, and by G. Ley, *A Short Introduction to the Ancient Greek Theater* (Chicago 1991). A more technical study is that of Dearden.

Dyskolos (317) there are clearly three doors in the *skene*-building, but this play postdates the great rebuilding of the theatre by Lycurgus in the third quarter of the fourth century. Critics claim that certain scenes demand more than one door, but given the minimalist nature of the Greek theatre, the audience would not be bothered when the door changed its identity within a comedy.[29] In *Frogs* a single door could be that of Heracles' house and later the entry to the palace of Hades. There is good humor also to be had from a single door representing two houses, for example, the houses of Lamachus and Dicaeopolis at *Ach.* 1069–1142 as delicacies are brought out for the latter and the items of war for the former. But there are places where two doors seem to be needed, for example, at *Cl.* 125 where Pheidippides says "I'm going inside" and then Strepsiades proceeds to knock at the door of Socrates' Pondertorium. A similar staging is needed at lines 800 ff. *Wasps* and *Birds*, on the other hand, can be played with a single door throughout.

The matter of the raised stage is equally problematic. Ewans and Wiles insist that the focus of the playing-space is the center of the orchestra, where an altar was placed, which could be used in the play (at *Thesm.* 689 ff., Euripides' kinsman takes refuge from the women), or the line connecting that center to the main door, and that a raised stage is useless in a high theatre where much of the audience is well above the playing-area.[30] But there are indications in the text of a raised area, for instance, at *Kn.* 149 "come up here," and vase-paintings of comic scenes do show a raised structure.[31] If there was a "stage," it was low and provided no impediment to the actors operating in the orchestra and interacting with the chorus or even with the audience.

Physical effects are not prominent in the Greek theatre. The *skene* could be painted or decorated to suit its use as a palace, house, cave, or temple, and the opening scene of *Wasps* shows that a net has been

---

[29] See Dearden, pp. 20–30.

[30] M. Ewans, *Aischylos. The Oresteia* (London 1995), xx–xxii (esp. n. 14 for bibliography); D. Wiles, *Tragedy in Performance* (London 1997) chap. 3.

[31] See Taplin plates 9.1, 11.3, 12.5, 12.6, 14.12, 15.13. These are from the fourth century, and thus later than the plays that inspired the vase-painters; they may reflect the presence of a stage in fourth-century Italian comedy or just be a convention to communicate the fact that this is a dramatic performance.

placed over the front and that the door has been barred. For special effects there was the *ekkyklema* ("roll-out"), which was some sort of wheeled platform allowing an interior scene or tableau to be displayed. The most famous instances are in Aeschylus' *Oresteia*, where first Clytemnestra and then Orestes are shown standing over the bodies of their victims, but in comedy the students inside Socrates' Pondertorium are so displayed at 185 ff., and two tragic poets, Euripides and Agathon, are wheeled out in the process of composition at *Ach.* 409 and *Thesm.* 96. Then there is the *machina*, a cranelike device that would allow actors to hover in the air and deliver their lines or to swing from behind to the front of the *skene*. The most striking example is the opening of *Peace* where Bellerophon's famous ride to Olympus on Pegasus is transformed into an elderly Athenian riding the world's largest dung-beetle, but it is also used for the entry of Socrates at *Cl.* 218, suspended in some fashion from the crane.

Props in tragedy are rare, and when they occur, for instance, the purple carpet in *Agamemnon*, or the bow of Heracles in Sophocles' *Philoctetes*, they are significant items. Comedy uses physical items much more often; the austerity of tragedy is definitely lacking. *Wasps* in particular is a very visual comedy—we have the house besieged at the start, the chorus costumed as Wasps, the creation of a trial space at home with all the necessary paraphernalia, the procession of the household vessels, and the dressing-up of father in fine cloak and elegant footwear.

A rule of three actors seems to have operated for both tragedy and comedy.[32] It is usually assumed that it was an external restriction, designed to assure a level playing-field among competitors, and for the most part Aristophanic comedy can be performed with three actors only. Sometimes there seem to be four speaking parts, for example, in the scene with the ambassadors at *Birds* 1565–1693 (Makemedo, Poseidon, Heracles, and the Triballian), but the last speaks only three lines of pidgin Greek (1615, 1628, 1678), and these would be spoken by one of the other actors. Actors took multiple roles, for instance in *Clouds* the actors playing Strepsiades and Socrates play the two *Logoi*, and in *Birds* Euelpides "Goodhope" is

---

[32] See D. M. MacDowell, "The Number of Speaking Actors in Old Comedy," *Classical Quarterly* 44 (1994):325–35, and C. W. Marshall, "Comic Technique and the Fourth Actor," *Classical Quarterly* 47 (1997):77–84.

given a formal sendoff at 846–50, because his actor is needed for other parts in the episodes. In a theatre with fifteen thousand spectators and with masked actors, it would be difficult for a spectator to discern who was speaking in a multiple scene; hence three-actor scenes need to be well choreographed and the roles sharply distinguished.

The costumes of the comic actors were bizarre, intended to be ridiculous—Aristotle (*Poet.* 1449a33) identifies *to geloion* ("the ridiculous") as the aim of comedy—involving grotesque masks, padding, and a dangling phallus. Taplin has some instructive illustrations of the comic actor—that of the intriguing "*Choregoi*" vase shows both comic and tragic actors on stage.[33] The difference in dress and mask is arresting.

Tragic choruses had twelve members, whereas comedy seems to have had twice that number. The prominence of the chorus in fifth-century drama suggests that Aristotle was right to trace both tragedy and comedy to choral performances, from which actors gradually spun off. The archon's phrase for accepting a poet's submission was "to grant a chorus," and for much of the fifth century a chorus is a necessary part of the drama, although in the tragedies of Euripides we sometimes feel its marginality. In comedy, however, the chorus has an essential role. The chorus can oppose or support the great idea and its proponent; carry much of the imagery of the drama (Clouds for lofty, insubstantial ideas; Wasps are old jurors with a sting; Birds for the flight of fancy that creates Cloudcuckooland); speak for the poet on various occasions; and provide a song-and-dance to fill the interludes. Only in the last two plays does the chorus begin to lose its importance, and the breaks between scenes are now filled in the manuscripts and papyri with <*chorou*> ("of the chorus"), that is, with songs not written for the occasion. By the time of Menander and the development of the five-act structure, the chorus comes on stage only to fill the gaps and has no dramatic or thematic role in the comedy. Sometimes we get double choruses, as in *Lysistrata* where two half-choruses oppose each other (old women versus old men) and in Eupolis' lost *Maricas* (421L) where half-choruses of rich and poor each champion a political antagonist.

---

[33] See Taplin plates 9.1 (the "*Choregoi*" vase), 10.2, 11.3, 11.4, 12.5, 12.6 (particularly expressive), and 16.16.

The chorus is usually a homogenous body, but we do have places where each *choreutes* could have been individually represented (and costumed), such as the twenty-four different birds at *Birds* 297–304 and the chorus in Eupolis' lost *Poleis* where the *choreutai* were twenty-four cities of the empire.

The festivals were also competitions; prizes were given for the best comic poet and for the best actor. Thus to the atmosphere described before we might perhaps add the excitement of Oscar night. Judges were selected from each of the ten tribes; five of these votes were selected at random, and the decision made on this basis. Thus the festivals would be rife with the spirit of competition and rivalry, and often we get hints of the great game involving poets, rivals, judges, and audience, as in the prologue of *Wasps*:

> Now you shouldn't expect anything too high-brow from us ...
> what we've got here is just a little story, but with a moral,
> something we can all understand. Don't worry, it won't go
>   over your heads,
> but it will still be on a higher level than those other disgusting,
>   obscene farces. (56, 64–66)

Or see the second parabases of *Clouds* (1116–30) and *Birds* (1102–17) where the chorus threatens and cajoles the judges for a favorable verdict. One of the best exchanges took place in 424 and 423 when Aristophanes made fun of his competitor, Cratinus, as a drunken old playwright, well past his prime (*Kn.* 526–36), and Cratinus responded with his *Pytine* at 423D, in which he put himself into his own play, as the poet who had deserted his true wife, Comedy, for another woman, Pytine or "the Wine Flask." The revised parabasis of *Clouds* (518–62) shows Aristophanes' reaction to his third-place finish that year—and like the woman in Hamlet's play, I think he "doth protest too much."

The extant remains of the Theatre of Dionysus show an elaborately paved marble floor, well-cut marble seats, and a high raised stage, but all this is postclassical. In the fifth century the orchestra was flat earth, and the seats wooden benches (*ta ikria*). The audience consisted principally, but not exclusively, of Athenian male citizens; the resident-aliens (*metoikoi*) attended at both festivals, and *xenoi* and allies from the cities were certainly present at the Dionysia. Boys were in the audience, but could women attend? This has been the subject of much discussion, with much of the evidence coming from comedy itself.[34] The debate rests on the dominant nature of the dramatic festival; if it were primarily a religious occasion, why would the women be barred from this one festival only, when women were so involved in the religious life of the city? But if drama is essentially a civic occasion, then women as noncitizens might well have been excluded or strongly discouraged. Perhaps the question is not "could women attend?" but "did women attend?" Perhaps the presence of women was a class-based matter, with the upper classes more secluded than the women who lived and worked in the agora. But Henderson is certainly right that whether women were there in any numbers, "the notional audience was male." Thus at *Peace* 51–53 the servant announces, "And I will explain the plot to the kids, to the young men, and the grown men, to the important men, and to the super-important men over there." The audience is thought of and addressed as "gentlemen," not as "ladies and gentlemen." One major difference between tragedy and comedy lies in its relationship to the audience.[35] Tragedy very rarely admits its own existence and does not call attention to itself—this is frequently referred to as "meta-theatre"—whereas comedy does all it can to destroy the theatrical illusion. Comedy pulls its audience into the drama, both in the direct addresses in the prologue and the parabasis and in such scenes as at *Clouds* 1094 ff., where Superior Argument, invited to look at the audience, agrees that the perverts are in the majority.

Structure of an Old Comedy

The eleven plays of Aristophanes display certain common structural features that seem also to occur in the fragments of the other comedians. Clearly the poets and their audience expected certain re-

---

[34] Three recent articles take differing stances: A. Podlecki, "Could Women Attend the Theater in Ancient Athens?" *Ancient World* 21 (1990):27–43; J. Henderson, "Women in the Athenian Dramatic Festivals," *Transactions of the American Philological Association* 121 (1991): 133–47; and S. Goldhill, "Representing Democracy: Women at the Great Dionysia," in R. Osborne and S. Hornblower, eds., *Ritual, Finance, Politics* (Oxford 1994):347–69. See also Csapo and Slater, pp. 286–93, for the ancient evidence.

[35] See O. Taplin, "Fifth-century Tragedy and Comedy: a *synkrisis*," *Journal of Hellenic Studies* 106 (1986):163–74.

peated and familiar features in comedy, but Aristophanes (and presumably his rivals as well) varies these features so much that there is no "typical" or "normal" comedy among the extant eleven. It is fair, however, to say that *Knights* and *Wasps* come the closest to a standard form.[36]

1. **Prologue:** Comedy, unlike tragedy, has to create and introduce its own plots and characters, and also must warm up its audience for a sympathetic and favorable reception. Prologues usually run for two hundred or so lines, and thus consist of several scenes, and can include singing by the actors. The meter is the usual iambic trimeter ("the closest to ordinary speech"—Aristotle *Poetics* 1449a25). In *Wasps* we have a dream sequence, a direct exposition to the audience, a guessing game about the plot, the jack-in-the-box scenes with the old man, and finally the introduction of the chorus.
2. **Parodos:** This is the entry of the chorus.[37] The identity of the chorus is usually divulged in the prologue (as at *Wasps* 214–29) so that the audience will have some idea of what to expect. The chorus may enter to assist the main character (as in *Knights, Peace, Plutus*), or to oppose him (as in *Acharnians, Wasps, Birds,* and the chorus of old men in *Lysistrata*); sometimes they watch and observe (as in *Frogs*). This section is sung, that is, it tends to be in lyric meter rather than in the iambic trimeters so prevalent elsewhere. The entry of the chorus must have been one of the awaited moments of the play. Its members can rush violently onstage, ready to do battle (*Ach., Kn.*), but *Clouds, Wasps,* and *Birds* show interesting variations. The chorus members of *Wasps* can barely walk, let alone rush onstage; they have also a supporting chorus of boys. In *Birds* the spectacle is the wonderful variation of bird costumes and the choreography; there must have been the same gush of enthusiasm as when the curtain rises on a particularly gorgeous set in the theatre. In *Clouds* Aristophanes plays games with the audience; for instance, Strepsiades cannot see the

---

[36] The fullest study of comic structure is in A.W. Pickard-Cambridge, *Dithyramb, Tragedy, and Comedy*, 2d ed. (Oxford 1962), pp. 194–229; Sommerstein (*Ach.*) 9–11 has a useful summary.

[37] See Zimmermann on the parodos.

Clouds until they are "there, in the wings!" (326)—comedy again calling attention to itself. As with the prologue, the parodos may consist of a string of scenes.

3. **Agon:** Often the comedy will turn on the result of a formal contest between two speakers, the agon.[38] A symmetrical pattern exists in the agon, for each side outlines his or her argument. The chorus sets the terms; with the *agon* in *Wasps* as a model, they begin with a song (ode—540–45), then introduce the first speaker (546–47), who then states his case in a tetrameter (usually anapestic or iambic),[39] with interjections by opponent, chorus, or a third party (548–620). The first speaker ends with a *pnigos* ("choking-song"—621–30), in which the tetrameter is cut in half to a dimeter. The same format is repeated for the second side: antode (same metrical pattern as the ode—644–47), introduction (648–49), second speaker (tetrameter—650–718), *pnigos* (719–24). Some plays contain two formal agons (*Knights* and *Clouds*), some have the formal pattern, but only one speaker who outlines his case in an exposition (*Birds, Eccl.*); three plays lack an agon of the formal sort just outlined (*Ach., Peace, Thesm.*—they do have important speeches by the main character, and, interestingly enough, the first and last are concerned with tragedy). In *Frogs* the structure is inverted, the episodes coming before the agon, and the agon itself (between Euripides and Aeschylus) does not resolve the larger contest. When there is a formal debate, the second speaker is the victor, except for *Plutus* where Penia ("Poverty") speaks second and should win, but the play proceeds with the first speaker victorious. Much scholarly blood has been spilled in the debate whether this means that the comedy should be taken as ironic rather than as straight fantasy.[40]

---

[38] Gelzer (1960) is the standard study of the comic agon.

[39] The anapestic tetrameter catalectic is a more elegant and loftier metre, the iambic tetrameter catalectic more down-to-earth and informal; in *Clouds* the older antagonist (Superior Argument) speaks in anapests, whereas his modern counterpart (Inferior) uses iambics. The same thing happens in *Frogs*, Aeschylus (anapests) v. Euripides (iambics).

[40] For a good summary of the problem and a controversial interpretation see A. H. Sommerstein, "Aristophanes and the Demon Poverty," *Classical Quarterly* 34 (1984):314–33. MacDowell (1995) 292 doubts whether the audience were even aware of Aristophanes' technique of the second speaker's winning; this I do not find convincing.

4. **Parabasis:** This is perhaps the most curious and formal feature of Old Comedy. It is sung by the chorus with the actors offstage, directed to the audience, and comes at a natural break in the action, often just before or just after an agon. As with the agon, a formal pattern can be detected, although Aristophanes' parabases vary from comedy to comedy. The full structure is best found in the parabases of *Wasps* and *Birds*. I will use the former as a model: [a] song, often directed to the departing actors (1009–14); [b] parabasis proper (1015–50), in a fifteen-syllable meter, most commonly the anapestic tetrameter catalectic,[41] although in *Clouds* Aristophanes sharpens his attack on other poets by usurping the eupolidean meter of his rival Eupolis; [c] a *pnigos* in the same meter, reduced to a dimeter; this rounds off the parabasis proper (1051–59); [d] ode (1060–70); [e] epirrhema (1071–90)—an address (probably by the chorus leader) to the audience, usually in trochaic tetrameter catalectic or the rarer paeonic tetrameter (*Wasps* 1275–83); [f] antode (1091–1100); [g] antepirrhema (1101–21). The last four, [d]–[g], are known collectively as the "epirrhematic syzygy," and can be found on their own without [a]–[c]; this happens in *Frogs* where the anapests of [b] occur in the parodos at 354–71 and the syzygy in the break at 674–737, and also in second parabases (see following).

Not all plays have parabases with such a neat format. In *Ach.* the song [a] is reduced to a pair of anapestic tetrameters; in *Peace* we get only [b] + [c], and the ode/antode [d] + [f]; in *Lysist.* with its two semichoruses, the parabasis takes the form of two syzygies, with no parabasis proper. *Thesm.* has a very stripped-down parabasis, possessing [b] + [c] and only one epirrhema [f]. There is no formal parabasis in *Eccl.* or *Plutus*.

The chorus sometimes speaks of "stripping off for our anapests" (*Ach.* 627); this may be meant metaphorically, but if the parabasis were accompanied by vigorous dancing, it may well have removed outer cloaks for this purpose. The chorus stays in its character (as wasps or birds), except for the parabasis proper and *pnigos* of the first five extant comedies, where the chorus becomes the poet himself, developing his comic persona (the young, brilliant,

[41] The anapestic tetrameter catalectic was in fact called the "aristophanean" by the ancients.

and unappreciated poet), praising his own art, running down his rivals, and tweaking the audience for their lack of support. But in *Birds* the chorus members are birds throughout. In the syzygy of the principal parabasis the chorus reverts to (or maintains) its dramatic role, explaining why jurors should be wasps or what clouds and birds can do for humanity.

It is frequently supposed that these formal and repeated features indicate that the parabasis is an old element in comedy, dating from the early history of comedy. Aristophanes and his contemporaries may well have found the parabasis as an established and expected feature of comedy, but studies by Bowie and Hubbard have demonstrated that it is thematically essential to the play and not just a venerable appendage maintained by conservatively minded poets for a similarly traditional audience.[42]

5. **Episodes:** These are scenes dominated by the actors, normally in iambic trimeter, but interspersed with choral elements. Very often they follow the agon and reveal the dramatic consequences of the great idea. The best of these, perhaps the best scene in all Aristophanes, is the trial of the dogs in *Wasps* (891–1008) which proceeds from Contracleon's victory in the agon and the decision to try cases at home. In the second half of comedies such as *Ach.*, *Peace*, *Birds*, *Eccl.*, and *Plutus* we get series of "intruders" who enter to be part of the great idea now implemented and who are usually driven off with slapstick violence. *Frogs* is an interesting exception, in that the episodes precede the agon and occupy the first half of the comedy. What can be observed is how Aristophanes varies these scenes with great finesse; in *Birds* we get three distinct sets of episodes which might stretch out this longest of extant comedies, but they succeed admirably in maintaining the interest and attention of the audience.

6. **Choral songs (*kommatia*):** The episodes are separated by choral interludes in which the chorus may address the audience again or engage in extended personal humor. Some in fact are parabatic in form and are usually described as "second" parabases (*Cl.* 1116–30, *Wasps* 1265–91—this lacks the antode—and *Birds*

[42] Hubbard passim; A. M. Bowie, "The Parabasis in Aristophanes: Prolegomena, *Acharnians*," *Classical Quarterly* 32 (1982):27–40.

1058–1117); *Ach.* has a second and even a third parabasis (971–99, 1143–72). One particular sequence deserves note: the trochaic songs at *Birds* 1470–92, 1553–64, 1694–1705, where the chorus of birds reflects on certain strange sights who turn out to be notorious denizens on the Athenian scene.

7. **Exodos:** The formal conclusion to the play. Aristophanes' plays end in a number of ways: reconciliation of the semichoruses in *Lysistrata*, the marriages in *Peace* and *Birds*, the party at the end of *Acharnians*, the sense of victory and general rejoicing in *Knights* and *Frogs*. Two endings are worth mentioning: the dancing contest at the close of *Wasps* where the old man dances all contenders into oblivion, including the actual figures of Carcinus and his sons (the poet claims that he is the first to send a chorus off dancing), and the finale of *Clouds* where the entire action of the comedy is reversed with the burning down of Socrates' Pondertorium. Such a "down" ending is rare and must be explained by the revision of the play. In any case, the *exodos* must have been the equivalent of the final number that climaxes a Broadway musical or a Gilbert & Sullivan operetta.

Interpreting Aristophanes

Aristophanes is a challenging poet for critics, and the twentieth century has seen much debate over how we should appreciate his comedies. The fundamental question is, "How serious is Aristophanes?" He makes fun of people and institutions, of issues and ideas; it is often assumed, and not just by students coming to Aristophanes for the first time, that if he makes fun of someone (or something), he must be opposed to it, that he is making a statement; in short, his comedy is satire or propaganda. This was how critics in the early part of the century approached Aristophanes—he was writing from a certain viewpoint and aiming to get that point across. The problem was that whatever standpoint was accepted (partisan of peace, champion of the people or of country folk or of city dwellers, conservative traditionalist), one had to ignore other parts of his comedy to make one's case.[43] Perhaps the extreme instance of

---

[43] Whitman, chap. 1, has a very good summary of such early views of Aristophanes.

this approach was Norwood's (210) suggestion that Cleon's rivals had suborned Aristophanes to write his *Knights* against Cleon.

The poles of the debate about comedy versus satire/propaganda are the studies of Gomme and de Ste Croix. The former argues in a landmark article that Aristophanes is serious only about his art, that his claim to be a new and sophisticated poet is what we should take at face value, that there is very little that is serious politically in his comedy. Gomme provided a useful corrective to the theory that comedy is essentially propaganda, and his thesis that we should give primacy to his claims as a comic poet led to several good studies during the 1950s and 1960s of comic structure and fantasy. In 1972 de Ste Croix provided the counterpoint to Gomme; while not denying the primacy of humor, he argued that a comedian may also be serious, that we should seek passages where there is no obvious humor, where we seem to glimpse the poet behind his plays, and that what he finds funny (in the case of *Wasps*, the jury system itself) is also significant. His conclusion was that a "Cimonian" bias could be found behind Aristophanes' comedy, that is, a conservative right-of-center leaning that favored traditional values and leaders and that may have been democratic, but endorsed a democracy firmly led by the *kaloi k'agathoi* ("the good and noble"). This approach has won several adherents, most notably Sommerstein (1996), who has formed the same conclusion from a study of the *komodoumenoi* ("the people made fun of"); Edmunds, who in his study of *Knights* assumes a political crusade by the poet; MacDowell ("Aristophanes is not just trying to make the Athenians laugh but is making a serious point which is intended to influence them" [1995] p. 6); and Henderson (in Winkler & Zeitlin 1990), for whom Old Comedy was a sort of "unofficial opposition" to the democracy of the day.

Not all critics accept comedy as political satire. In the past fifteen years several other approaches have been followed, often dealing with *Acharnians*, where Aristophanes openly identifies himself with the main character on two occasions (377–82, 502 ff.) and the play is often read as an earnest plea for peace in 425. Heath argues that comedy was *never* taken seriously, either politically or even when Aristophanes makes claims about his comedy. Goldhill points to the many "voices" in a comedy, to the many stances and attitudes a comedian must adopt; how can one argue that one is the genuine Aristophanes that must take precedence over the rest? Carrière and Halliwell pay great attention to the cultural theories of Bakhtin, on which comedy is essentially "carnival," a release from the ordinary life of the city, and that it should not be taken as serious politics, but as the fulfilment of wish and escapism. Bowie has developed what has become a popular modern interpretation, ritual as a subtext for comedy, for instance, *Wasps* as a parody of the *ephebeia* (the coming of age of young men); the audience would appreciate the reversal of roles inherent in the concept. Taaffe and Muecke have brought feminist techniques into play in the plays of gender confusion (*Lysist.*, *Thesm.*, *Eccl.*), while Reckford downplays the importance of politics in comedy in favor of the healing powers of laughter and comedy.[44]

A safe middle ground needs to be found by the student trying to cope with this intensely topical comedy. One needs to resist the temptation that making fun of someone or something is the same as trying "to get" that target. Humor does not necessarily have to have a bite. On the other hand, de Ste Croix is quite right to insist that comedy can be serious, and the evidence adduced (the parabasis of *Frogs*, Lysistrata's speech at 1112–56, the return to the golden days of the past in the closing scenes of *Knights*, the frequent barbs at the jury system that was one of the pillars of the democracy, the attacks on the demagogues while politicians of traditional background are spared) is impressive. But another question can be raised: Does comedy lead or follow public opinion? The demagogues (Cleon, Cleophon, Hyperbolus, and their ilk) are caricatured with little mercy, but in the 420s they were a novelty and thus a comedian's dream. They were the natural target for the comic poet and his audience; Aristophanes' caricature of them may owe more to public taste than to political or personal animosity. The same may be said of the familiar antithesis in comedy of old = good/modern = bad (cf. the end of *Knights* and *Lysistrata* or the parabasis of *Frogs*); the poet may be giving vent to his own deeply held feelings or just catering to popular taste.

---

[44] M. Heath, *Political Comedy in Aristophanes* (Göttingen 1987), and "Some Deceptions in Aristophanes," in F. Cairns and M. Heath, eds., *Papers of the Leeds International Latin Seminar* 6 (1990):229–40; S. Goldhill, *The Poet's Voice* (London 1991):167–223; Halliwell (see note 6), and also "Comic satire and freedom of speech in classical Athens," *Journal of Hellenic Studies* 111 (1991):48–70; J. C. Carrière, *Le Carnaval et la Politique* (Paris 1979); F. Muecke, "A portrait of the artist as a young woman," *Classical Quarterly* 32 (1982):41–55; L. Taaffe, *Aristophanes and Women* (London 1993).

One of the most striking features of Old Comedy was personal humor, jokes against real people who were probably sitting in the audience at the time.[45] Later antiquity would fasten on *to onomasti komodein* ("to make fun of by name") as the quintessence of Old Comedy. The origins of comedy are explained by outlining how personal jokes came to be part of public festivals; the end of Old Comedy is explained by laws on personal humor or the rise of oligarchy ("fear fell on the poets"). Comedy thus acquired its redeeming social value, marking out those deserving of ridicule; for Horace (*Satires* I.4.1–7) comedy is the literary ancestor of his own satire:

> The poets Eupolis, Cratinus, and Aristophanes, indeed all the poets of Old Comedy, if there was any man deserving to be singled out as a bad man or a thief, because he was an adulterer, a pick-pocket or notorious in some way, they would attack them with great freedom.

It is interesting to speculate on the sequence in which the Alexandrian critics worked. Did they fasten on the best-known threesome of Old Comedy (Cratinus, Eupolis, Aristophanes) and from their works deduce a political and satirical essence for the genre? This is the usual assumption among critics, but the opposite is possible, that the critics, proceeding perhaps on the same lines as Aristotle, first defined Old Comedy as political satire and then sought a comic threesome whose comedy fit that model.

Again, care must be used in assessing such jokes. Because Aristophanes makes fun of someone, does that indicate personal animosity or just the recognition that here was good humor? Was anyone ever hurt by comedy? Comedy is usually blamed for the Athenian hostility against Socrates (see Plat. *Apol.* 19c, *Phd.* 70b), but Plato is writing well after the fact and looking for someone to blame. Was there even a sense of having arrived if one was prominent enough to be the target of comedy? In other words, could Athenians take a joke? Cleon, it appears, could not, but Lucian's words (second century A.D.) in the mouth of Philosophy are intriguing:

> Is that all you're worried about? A few rude remarks? You know the way that Comedy treats me at the Dionysia, but we're still

---

[45] Consult Halliwell (see note 6) and Storey (1998) here.

> the best of friends. I've never taken her to court or even complained privately to her. I just let her enjoy the fun that's all part and parcel of the festival. For I know that no harm can come from a joke. (*Halieus* 14)

In the case of the three great caricatures in Aristophanes (Euripides, Cleon, and Socrates), I see the first as essentially complimentary with the proviso that by the time of *Frogs,* Aristophanes recognized that Euripides' tragedy was wonderful but fundamentally subversive, the second as hostile with more than a little malice, and the last a joke that got away from its creator.

So what does one say in the end about Aristophanes? He is, I think, a traditionalist, a supporter of the "good old days," a democrat who would prefer leaders from the *kaloi k'agathoi* rather than these upstarts from the mercantile class—Aristophanes is something of a snob—but above all a poet who possesses the same qualities that he attributes to Euripides: *sophos* ("wise"), *dexios* ("clever"), and *gonimos* ("creative"). He excels at comedy of the imagination, the creation of wonderful fantasies, the development and execution of these ideas, and a great variety of humors. He can take us to Olympus on the back of a dung-beetle, into the war between the sexes with brilliant effect, to the Underworld in search of a poet "who can save our city." Aeschylus and Euripides duel for the throne of tragedy and for the salvation of Athens, and they agree that the criteria for good art are "technical skill and making the people better citizens" (*Frogs* 1009). Aristophanes, I think, is saying in *Frogs* that for a poet who combines both and whose theme is *ta dikaia* ("what is right"), you need look no further than the comedian you are watching.

Ian C. Storey

Diagram of the Stage

Schematic reproduced courtesy of Courtney/Collins Studio. Copyright 1998

Hypothetical reconstruction of the Theatre of Dionysus, c. 458 B.C.E. *(according to Meineck). In the orchestra are uncostumed blocking mannequins, as seen from approximately ten tiers above the first seating row (seating not shown). Scholars are divided both on whether there was a raised stage at this period, and, if so, its height.*

Translator's Preface

The three translations in this volume began their creative lives as play texts for performance, and are a result of eight years of work on ancient comedy with the Aquila Theatre Company and before that, the London Small Theatre Company. I have had the pleasure of staging them in the United Kingdom, Canada, the United States, Holland, and Greece in a variety of theatres—from intimate black boxes, to large performing arts centers, to the ancient stadium at Delphi. My aim has been to create texts that serve both as tools for the effective execution of onstage comedy and as accurate reflections of the Greek. I have benefited enormously from the work of scholars and translators such as Alan Sommerstein, Sir Kenneth Dover, Douglass Parker, William Arrowsmith, and others who have contributed to our understanding of the genius of Aristophanic comedy, and have based my translation primarily on the Greek texts edited by Sommerstein (*Clouds* 1982, *Wasps* 1983) and Dunbar (*Birds* 1995).

That sound scholarship is essential to any translation of an ancient play goes without saying, but what about the lessons learned from performance? A play is only created for performance, and its existence as a written text is subordinate to its primary form and function as a live, shared experience between actors and audience. But can a contemporary, English-language production of an Aristophanes play, any more than a script that gives directions for one, still be called an experience of Aristophanes? True, there are as many differences between contemporary theatre and that of late fifth century B.C.E. as there are similarities, but the essential aim of Aristophanes to provoke, poke fun at, celebrate, analyze, and criticize the society around him can still manifest itself as a potent dramatic force today: fathers and sons still battle across the generation gap, legal systems are still perceived as ineffective, politicians are still accused of corruption, new ideas and intellectual movements still provoke laughter and cause misunderstandings. People are still in debt, still trying to escape the hustle and bustle of everyday life, still looking for their own Cloudcuckoolands.

I have chosen not to update the contemporary references in these translations. A joke about a politician's errant behavior in the news today will seem as out of date to an audience or reader in five years as will a reference to Cleon or Alcibiades. It never ceases to amaze me how the combined creativity of a well informed director and actor can take what seem to be obscure and inappropriate ancient references and communicate them directly and immediately on stage, with a facial expression, a movement, or the manipulation of body language. An understanding of the times in which the plays were produced is essential to this approach. With this in mind, I have employed two types of notes to help the reader gain a better understanding of these plays. The footnotes on the page are intended quickly to inform while not distracting from the flow of the play, while the endnotes provide more detailed discussion of certain subjects and point to ancient evidence and supporting scholarship. These notes may also help provide insight into some of my translation choices. In the instances where I have adapted a phrase or reference into a contemporary form to keep its sense or humor, I have included a closer translation of the Greek in the notes.

Theatre is, of course, a Greek word that means "Seeing Place"; thus I have tried to bring a visual dimension to these translations with detailed stage directions and references in the endnotes to pictorial evidence for many of the stage properties and costumes found in the plays. Aristophanes gets enormous comic mileage out of common household utensils and everyday objects, and it is important to provide the interested reader with information as to where representations can be found. I have attempted to keep the number of supporting works to a minimum, drawing most examples from John Boardman's Thames and Hudson series on Greek vase painting and sculpture.

The Greek texts have come down to us without stage directions, and sometimes we cannot say for certain which line should be assigned to which character. Some sense of the structure of the play can be gleaned from textual indications, and I have made decisions on entrances and exits based on my own sense of dramatic structure and knowledge of the physical staging conditions of the Greek theatre. Although I have had the opportunity to work extensively with masks and stage live performances at both Epidaurus and Delphi (as well as in hundreds of modern stages), it is impossible to know for certain the exact stage movements of these plays.

My overall aim has been to produce translations that are understandable, performable, accessible, and entertaining. I have not attempted to replicate the meter of the Greek, but I have adopted the same basic line divisions to assist text referencing. One of the most satisfying parts of my work has been to hear an audience in Athens, Georgia, still laughing at the same joke 2500 years after it was first delivered in Athens, Greece. Aristophanes is undoubtedly one of the world's greatest comic dramatists; his work offers us a direct connection with our past, and I hope this volume of plays will in some small way help further our understanding and appreciation of this daring, provocative, and hilarious genius.

I would like to thank some of the many people who have inspired and helped these translations come to fruition. The contribution and expertise of the many actors who worked on these plays was invaluable: in particular, Robert Richmond, Anthony Cochrane, Peter Hilton, John Williams, David Caron, Nick Hardy, Nina Lucking, Karen Mann, Steve Owen, Adrian Schiller, Anthony James, and Daniel York. Many classicists throughout the United States and Canada worked hard to bring these plays to their campuses, convincing skeptical deans that Aristophanes sells: particularly, Mary Kay Gamel at University of California Santa Cruz, Rick Lafleur at the University of Georgia, Karelisa Hartigan at the University of Florida, Susan Ford Wiltshire at Vanderbilt University, Tim Moore at University of Texas Austin, Tony Edwards and William Fitzgerald at University of California San Diego, John Fitch at the University of Victoria, Keith Nightenhelser at Depauw University, Robert Ketterer at the University of Iowa, Stewart and Marleen Florey and Pat and Will Freiert at Gustavus Adolphus College, Catherine Freis at Millsaps College, Helen Moritz at Santa Clara University, Peter Burian at Duke University, Stewart Wheeler and Dean Simpson at the University of Richmond, and John Fischer at Wabash College. Also thanks to many theatres and arts centers that have received and promoted this work in their communities.

The faculty and staff of the Department of Theatre, Speech and

Dance at the University of South Carolina welcomed Aquila with open arms as their company in residence, and their support and encouragement enabled *Birds* to take flight, especially, Jim O'Connor, Thorne Compton, and Arpina Markarian. Also Peter Sederberg, Dean of the South Carolina Honors College, and Ward Briggs, head of classics, allowed me to teach two of these translations at the Univeristy of South Carolina. The students of my Honors courses in Greek Drama and Classical Greece helped me to gain a greater understanding of these plays in the classroom; their enthusiasm and love for the subject was infectious. Ron Pearson and Mike Taylor at the Koger Center for the Arts in Columbia, South Carolina, gave Aquila a fantastic state-of-the-art U.S. home where our work has continued to develop and grow. Grateful thanks also go to Robert Richmond, Aquila's Artistic Director, for bringing these plays to life on stage and his undying dedication to performance of classical theatre; Robert Ketterer for his hard work reviewing these texts and his helpful suggestions; and Brian Rak, Meera Dash, and Jay Hullett at Hackett, who have provided excellent advice, consultation, and support.

Much of the work on *Clouds* was completed while I was a summer scholar at the Center for Hellenic Studies in Washington, D.C., where the staff proved so very helpful; and I was fortunate to gain the expert help and assistance of my fellow scholars, particularly, Ian Storey, Ken Kitchell, and Neil O'Sullivan. *Birds* was completed while I was a visiting scholar at University of Texas Austin where Tom Palaima, Tim Moore, Doug Parker, and the late, great Gareth Morgan made me so very welcome. Clairemonte Bourne and Tim Beale, the coproducers of *Wasps*, helped keep Aquila on track in the early days of the company in London, when life, more often than not, seemed to imitate art, particularly *Wasps*. This whole volume is dedicated to my wife Kelly for her love, support, and encouragement. This work would never have seen the light of day without her particularly Texan ability to force me back to my desk from time to time and continually inspire me with her passion for the ancient world.

Peter Meineck

Clouds

Strepsiades (center) and characters from *Clouds*. The London Small Theatre Company, Amsterdam 1990

Clouds: Introduction

Clouds is certainly Aristophanes' best-known comedy. If modern readers know one of his plays, it is usually this one, although in the late years of the twentieth century, *Lysistrata* may run a close second. The manuscript tradition and the accompanying scholia are by far the fullest for *Clouds,* and the anecdotal tradition in ancient authors concerning this play is equally large.[1] This is of course due to the presence of the august (dare one say "saintly"?) figure of Socrates in the comedy. Plato and Xenophon created a character of legendary importance in classical culture, and Aristophanes' contemporary caricature of him attracted a huge amount of attention.

The play revolves around an old country farmer, Strepsiades ("Twister"), whose son, Pheidippides, has run him deeply into debt through an upper-class lifestyle and a passion for horses. His "great idea": for his son to enter the *phrontisterion* ("Pondertorium") of Socrates where he will learn the Inferior Argument, which "can debate an unjust case and win" (115), and thus talk his way out of his father's debts. When the son refuses to obey, Strepsiades goes himself to learn from Socrates. The play proceeds in four movements: (a) 1–509, his introduction and initiation to the Pondertorium, and meeting with the chorus of Clouds, new deities who preside over the "new learning,"[2]

[1] These are collected (in Greek) at K–A III.2 11–16.

[2] On the chorus and its identity in the comedy see Segal, Dover (*Cl.*) lxv–lxx, and Bowie (1993) 124–30.

(b) the parabasis (510–626), a choral digression, (c) a teaching scene (627–803) in which the old man fails miserably at learning and remembering anything at all, a brief scene (814–888) in which the son is dragooned into attending after all, and then quite a good agon (889–1113) between the Inferior and Superior Arguments—Pheidippides will study with the winner (who turns out to be the Inferior), and (d) the consequences of the "new learning" (1131–end), which do result in Strepsiades' avoiding his debts but with results that he could not have foreseen—the "new learning" will lead one to prefer Euripides over Aeschylus and to beat one's parents. In a strange *volte-face* the clouds reveal themselves as agents of the traditional gods (1457-61), and after admitting the error of his ways, Strepsiades proceeds to burn down the Pondertorium.

Whitman argued that Aristophanic comedy featured a recurring type of comic hero, the old countryman who achieves his great idea and comes out on top through a streak of *poneria* ("knavery," "roguishness") at the heart of his personality, and Strepsiades certainly fits this model. Much is made in the prologue of his country roots and attitudes, as opposed to the luxury (decadence?) of the town, and while he may lack the grandiose imagination of Dicaeopolis (*Acharnians*) or Makemedo (*Birds*), the earnestness of Trygaeus (*Peace*) or Lysistrata, or the irrepressibility of Procleon (*Wasps*), he does possess a down-to-earth cunning, a simplicity that the spectator will find appealing. Simply put, he is the ideal sort to "take the piss" out of sophistic pretensions. The teaching scene (627–804) shows Aristophanes at his comic best where the less-than-bright Strepsiades foils every attempt by Socrates to teach him anything. Yet the scene depends on stretching the spectator's reactions in two opposite directions: he wants to be a *sophos* like Socrates, for (unlike Strepsiades) he knows about measures and rhythms, and at the same time wants to see the *sophos* taken down a rung or two. We admire Strepsiades' low cunning and desire not to pay his debts, but at the same time we wince at his essential dishonesty and insistence at learning the Inferior Argument.[3] It can be observed that the "great idea" is undone at the end, that Strepsiades repents of what he has

---

[3]If a modern parallel be sought, we need look no further than Homer Simpson (*The Simpsons*), whose essential character trait must be *poneria* and who elicits both exasperation and sympathy from millions of viewers.

done (1462–4), that the play ends with destruction rather than jubilation or reconciliation. But the ending is one place that we know was altered in the revision, and the original may well have ended differently.

Clouds may be less "political" than other plays of the 420s—if it were not for the passing reference at line 7, we would not know that Athens was at war at this time—but it is no less topical. *Clouds* dramatizes a contact with what we call the "Enlightenment," the intellectual fervor that burst on the Greeks in the fifth century. Beginning with the Ionian physical scientists of the sixth century, it went far beyond inquiries on the physical nature of the universe; the thinkers of the fifth century raised the great questions of ethics, being, political science, anthropology, language, and even of the nature of knowledge itself.[4] These included the great philosophers such as Parmenides, Heraclitus, and Anaxagoras, but of more importance for this comedy were the sophists, the professional teachers who traveled from city to city claiming to teach knowledge and skills, including public oratory, making the weaker case appear the stronger (112–15). The most familiar are Protagoras ("man is a measure of all things"), Hippias, Prodicus (see line 361), and Gorgias; Plato's dialogues (especially *Protagoras* and *Gorgias*) present a somewhat unflattering picture of these men, who at times are portrayed as "con artists" or "snake-oil salesmen." And then there is Socrates, the only Athenian among these intellectuals, who was especially interested in knowledge and ethics, who was anything but a sophist, at least if Plato and Xenophon are to be trusted.[5] Physically distinctive (with a face like a satyr) and given to strange habits (walking barefoot with a distinctive gait, wearing light clothing, rolling his eyes), he was a comedian's godsend, and what Aristophanes has done is take this familiar Athenian, now in his 40s, who moved in important company, and turn him into an itinerant sophist.

---

[4]The literature here is immense. I refer the interested student to W. K. C. Guthrie, *A History of Greek Philosophy*, vol. 2 and 3 (Cambridge 1965/1969), and to G. Kerferd, *The Sophistic Movement* (Cambridge 1981).

[5]Socrates left no written works, and we depend on the portraits drawn by Plato in his dialogues, who did not begin to write until after Socrates' death in 399, and by Xenophon in his *Memoirs*, also later than 399. One well-known saying sums up Socrates' ethical belief, "no-one does wrong knowingly."

At line 1399 Pheidippides speaks for so many of the "Enlightenment" when he exclaims, "How pleasurable it is to be acquainted with modern ways and intelligent notions." The wave of fresh thought, of questioning traditional views, of challenging the status quo must have been much like the spirit of change that flowed through the 1960s. The key word is "new," for we see new gods and deities (Clouds and Vortex), new words (943, 1397), new principles and techniques (480, 897), the new education (936), and even new laws (1423). *Clouds* deals with the encounter by the old and unsophisticated Strepsiades with the new world of thoughts and thinkers. There is one other reference to newness, or innovation, in this play, at line 547, but this is the innovation of Aristophanes, part of his new and clever comedy—at *Wasps* 1044 referring to *Clouds* he "sowed a crop of new concepts"—and this should give us pause before we assume that for Aristophanes "old" was good and "new" bad. "Clever," "new," and "wise" are words that apply to the "new learning" and also to Aristophanes' own comedy.[6]

The principal problem in dealing with *Clouds* is the portrait of Socrates and what this says about Aristophanes' personal and comic intentions. The Socrates in the comedy and the Socrates that we know from Plato and Xenophon are simply not the same. The comic Socrates teaches in a school, charges fees for instruction, gives lessons in the physical sciences, grammar, music, and rhetoric, and disbelieves in the traditional gods, all of which are expressly denied in various places in the works of Plato and Xenophon. The comic portrait agrees with the real Socrates on physical details only (his gait, bare feet, rolling eyes, etc.). After an exhaustive examination of the evidence, Dover concludes that "Plato and Xenophon tell the truth: Ar. attaches to Socrates the characteristics which belonged to the sophists in general but did not belong to Socrates" (xlix). Socrates was an attractive target—he was Athenian and physically distinctive, the perfect focus for a comedy about ideas and intellectuals.

This leads to the larger question—what was Aristophanes' purpose in this? A number of approaches have been followed, which can be summarized briefly as (a) hostility and malice, (b) pure comedy with more than a hint of appreciation for Socrates, and (c) an "us against them" mentality. The first approach has commended it-

---

[6]See Cartledge 22–31 and Bowie (1993) 132.

self to those who see Aristophanes as a traditionalist who hated anything new (demagogues, Euripides, intellectuals), as a man who saw new ideas, in art or in science, as essentially dangerous. The main problem here is that the old men in the play, Strepsiades and Superior Argument, are hardly paragons of virtue or intellect; and if the new is being compared unfavorably to the old, then the old fails to live up to any standard.[7] There is much to be said for (b), most eloquently stated by Murray. I have mentioned that both Socrates and Aristophanes have newness, wisdom, and cleverness in common, and the sympathetic picture of Aristophanes in Plato's *Symposium* reveals a comedian with affinities to the Socratic circle. At one point (221b) Alcibiades even refers to the picture of Socrates in *Clouds* with no hint of rancor. Some have objected that this requires a cynical disregard on Aristophanes' part, that he would knowingly caricature falsely a man known to him, but Aristophanes' skill is precisely that, willful distortion and exaggeration. A passage in Plutarch records Socrates' alleged reaction to *Clouds*, "I feel that I am being made fun of by friends at a great party" (Plutarch *Moralia* 10c–d). This may be how the joke was intended and taken.

I have less sympathy with (c). It argues for an Aristophanes who really did not understand the difference between Socrates and a sophist, or if he did, that it did not concern him a great deal.[8] On this view Aristophanes is the spokesman for "us" against "them," where "them" includes poets, philosophers, politicians, etc. Socrates is a representative of the abnormal and thus good comic material; whether the caricature is fair or not is not really the point. My problem here is that Aristophanes is hardly the "average man," but rather a superior poet who saw himself as the brilliant teacher and savior of the city. He is really one of "them," one of the *sophoi*, not one of *hoi polloi*. He belongs with Euripides and Socrates, not against

---

[7]Norwood 219ff. saw the Superior Argument as essentially attractive and positive, but Dover (*Cl.*) lxiv provides a useful corrective, "apart from the inability to meet reasonable argument with anything better than an outburst of bad temper . . . the most striking characteristic of Right ["Superior Argument"] is his obsession with boys' genitals." Both Arguments have their moments, and good comedy will allow the spectator to sympathize with and laugh at both.

[8]See Dover (*Cl.*) xxxii–lvii and J. Henderson in Sommerstein et al. (1993) 307–19.

them. We must assume, I think, that he knew the difference between Socrates and a sophist, and that as a comedian he could not pass up the opportunity that Socrates provided. He was the obvious target for a caricature of the intellectual movement.

The play itself was produced at the Dionysia of 423, and gained the third prize—the winner being Cratinus with *Pytine* ("Wine Flask") and second place going to Ameipsias' *Connus*.[9] But the text we have is not that of the original production; this becomes abundantly clear at 518ff., when the chorus talks of the previous failure of "this comedy" and at 553 mentions Eupolis' *Maricas*, which was not produced until 421, at the Lenaea. This part of the parabasis certainly belongs to a revision. The actual details of the lost first *Clouds* and the implications for production will be considered in the appendix, but it is clear that what we have is a partial and not completed revision that was never produced on stage. Thus, the student should use care in treating this text as an organic whole, which it is not, and refrain from drawing conclusions about Aristophanes' technique and attitudes, since we do not know either what was in the original or what the completed revision would have looked like. The critical judgment that one brings to *Birds* or *Wasps* or *Frogs* should be suspended here.

I.C.S.

---

[9]*Pytine* was a brilliant piece of metatheatre, which I have discussed in the general introduction. Ameipsias' play seems to have focused on a musician (Connus) and had a chorus of *phrontistai* ("thinkers").

Clouds: Cast of Characters

STREPSIADES	a rural Athenian
PHEIDIPPIDES	son of Strepsiades
HOUSEBOY	of Strepsiades
STUDENTS	of Socrates
SOCRATES	a philosopher
CHORUS	of Clouds
SUPERIOR ARGUMENT	
INFERIOR ARGUMENT	
FIRST CREDITOR	
SECOND CREDITOR	
CHAEREPHON	a philosopher
XANTHIAS	servant to Strepsiades

Clouds was first produced by Aristophanes in 423 B.C.E., at the Dionysia Festival in the city of Athens. This translation was inspired by a production by the London Small Theatre Company, which received its first U.K. public performance at the Shaw Theatre, London, in January 1990 and its first U.S. public performance at the Judith Anderson Theatre, New York, in May 1990, directed by Fiona Laird and produced by Peter Meineck.

* refers to an endnote (found at the end of the play).
Each footnote is preceded by the line number to which it refers.

Clouds

SCENE: *A house in Athens.*

*(An old man named Strepsiades and his son Pheidippides are asleep. Strepsiades is tossing and turning and muttering to himself until he finally wakes up with a start.)**

STREPSIADES:
Oh! Oh!
Oh, Zeus almighty! What a night!
It's never-ending! It must be morning soon.
I thought I heard the cock crow hours ago.
Just listen to those blasted servants, snoring away,
back in my day they'd have never dared to sleep in.
Damn this stupid war! It'll ruin us. I can't even beat my own slaves anymore
in case they sneak off and hide out in enemy territory!*

(Pointing to Pheidippides)

Just look at him, the "refined young gentleman," he'll never see the sunrise,
he'll just carry on, blissfully farting away under his five fluffy blankets.

8: For more than seven years Athens and Sparta had been engaged in the Peloponnesian War.

It's all right for some! Oh, I'll just try and bury my head and ignore the snoring.

(Strepsiades tries to go back to sleep, he tosses and turns and then angrily throws off the covers in frustration.)

It's no good, I just can't sleep!
I'm being bitten by debts and eaten away by stable bills.
Why? Because of this long-haired son of mine,
and all his riding events and chariot races.
He lives, breathes and dreams horses!
It's already the 20th day of the month,
and the interest is due on the 30th. I'm finished!

(He calls out to a slave.)

Boy! light a lamp and fetch my ledger!
I need to count up my debts and calculate the interest.

(A slave hurries from the stage right door with some tablets and a lamp. He hands the tablets to Strepsiades and holds the lamp so he can read the accounts.)

Now then, let's have a look at these debts:
"Twelve hundred drachmas owed to Pasias." Twelve hundred drachmas!
What on earth was that for? Oh, gods, I remember now, a horse for Pheidippides!
Twelve hundred drachmas? Ouch! I think I was the one taken for a ride.*

(Pheidippides, dreaming of chariot races, mutters in his sleep.)

PHEIDIPPIDES:
Philon, you cheat, keep to your own lane!

STREPSIADES:
You hear that! That's the problem right there.
He's constantly at the races, even in his sleep!

14: Long hair was considered a Spartan fashion and was worn by aspiring young aristocrats with antidemocratic sentiments (see *Wasps* 476).

PHEIDIPPIDES:
How many turns must the war chariots make?

STREPSIADES:
Enough to turn your father into a pauper!
"What terrible debt shall strike after Pasias' bills?
Three hundred drachmas owed to Amynias
for a running board and a new set of wheels!"

PHEIDIPPIDES:
Make sure my horse has a roll before he goes home!

STREPSIADES:
It's my money those damned horses are rolling in!
While I am saddled with lawsuits and debts
and my creditors can't wait to seize my property.

(Pheidippides wakes up.)

PHEIDIPPIDES:
What is it, father? Is it really necessary to spend
the entire night twisting and writhing about?

STREPSIADES:
I'm being bitten to death . . . by bed bailiffs!*

PHEIDIPPIDES:
Please, father. I am trying to get some sleep!

(Pheidippides settles down back to sleep.)

STREPSIADES:
Go on then, sleep away, soon enough all this will be yours.
My debts will be on your head one day! Sleep away, my boy.
Oh, I wish I had never met your mother, and I hope whoever it was

---

31: Amynias was lampooned in comedy as an upper-class, long-haired, good for nothing (see *Wasps* line 74).

32: These lines are adapted from a lost Euripides play (fr. 1011) "What terrible thing will strike the house?"

who introduced us dies a horribly cruel death!
Ah yes, those were the days, a lovely country life,
full of simple rustic pleasures. An unwashed, unshaven heaven,
abounding with honey bees, shaggy sheep, lashings of olive oil . . .
then I married the niece of Megacles, son of Megacles.
I was just a plain country boy, but she was from the city
and had all these refined and delicate ways. A proper little lady.*
And when we were joined together as man and wife, I went to bed
smelling fresh and fruity, like ripe figs and new wool.
She smelled of fine perfume, golden saffron, sexy kisses,
extravagance and luxury. Aphrodite all over and everywhere Eros.*
Mind you, I can't say that she's lazy, not at all, she knew how to weave,
If you know what I mean. In-out, in-out, she loved to poke the thread!
It got to the point that I had to hold up my gown, show the evidence,
and tell her that it would wear out if she kept on whacking it like that!*

(Strepsiades lifts his gown to reveal a limp phallus.)

HOUSEBOY:
There's no oil left in the lamp.

STREPSIADES:
Why did you use the thirstiest lamp in the house?
You've earned a beating. Come here.

HOUSEBOY:
Why should I?

46: Megacles was a common name of the prominent aristocratic Alcmaeonid clan. Both Pericles and Alcibiades were related.

51: Saffron was the traditional golden yellow color of female festive robes and a bride's wedding veil.

56: A reference to Strepsiades' lack of sexual prowess in old age. See *Wasps* (note on line 252) and *Birds* (line 1589).

STREPSIADES:

Because you inserted a thick wick, that's why!

(The houseboy exits through the stage right door.)

Where was I? Oh yes. Well, soon enough we had a son,
and then my troubles really began. The wife and I could not agree
on a name for the boy. She wanted something upper-class and horsy,
a name with *hippus* in it, like "Xanthippus," "Chaerippus," or "Callippides."
But I wanted to name him Pheidonides after his grandfather,
a good old-fashioned thrifty name.
We argued for ages, then eventually we reached a compromise
and gave him the name Pheidippides.
When he was little she used to take him in her arms and say,
"When you grow up, you'll be a rich man like uncle Megacles
and drive a chariot through the city wearing a beautiful golden robe."*
But I would tell him, "When you're big you'll be just like your father
and drive goats down from the mountains, wearing a lovely leather jerkin."
But he never listened to a single word I said,
it was like flogging a dead horse, and now the household accounts
have a severe case of "galloping consumption."
I've been up all night trying to concoct a plan to get me out of this mess,
and I have found one drastic course, an extraordinary, supernatural trail.
If I can only persuade the lad to take it, I'll be saved!

63: Names containing *hippus* ("horse") were popular with the Athenian upper classes. Aristophanes' father was named Phillippus.

64: Pheidonides means "son of thrifty."

66: The name means something like "Spare the horses."

70: A victory in the Panathenaic games won the charioteer the right of riding in the procession to the Acropolis wearing a golden cloak (***70 Drive a chariot**).

Now then, let me think what would be the gentlest way to wake him up . . .?

(Strepsiades leans over and whispers in Pheidippides' ear.)

Pheidipoo, little Pheidipoo . . .

(There is no response from Pheidippides, Strepsiades becomes frustrated and shouts.)

PHEIDIPPIDES!

(Pheidippides wakes with a start.)

PHEIDIPPIDES:
What! What do you want, father?

STREPSIADES:
Give me a kiss and take my hand.

(He does so.)

PHEIDIPPIDES:
All right. What is it?

STREPSIADES:
Tell me son, do you love me?

PHEIDIPPIDES:
By Poseidon, god of horses, of course I do!

STREPSIADES:
I don't want to hear about the god of horses!
He's the very reason that I'm in this mess.
Listen son, if you really love me, will you do what I ask?

PHEIDIPPIDES:
What would you like me to do?

83: Poseidon was the second patron deity of Athens after Athena, God of the sea, "Earthshaker," and father of horses (***83 God of horses**).

STREPSIADES:
Turn your life around, right now,
do what I say, and go and learn.

PHEIDIPPIDES:
Learn what?

STREPSIADES:
Will you do it?

PHEIDIPPIDES:
(Exasperated) I'll do it, by Dionysus!

STREPSIADES:
Great! Now look over there *(he points to the stage left door).*
Can you see that tiny doorway and that funny little house?

PHEIDIPPIDES:
I see it, what are you showing me, father?

STREPSIADES:
That, my boy, is the house of clever souls, the Pondertorium.
The men who live there are able to talk us into believing
that the universe is a casserole dish that covers us all
and we are the hot coals, nestling inside.*
What's more, for a small fee, these gentleman they will teach you
how to successfully argue any case, right or wrong.

PHEIDIPPIDES:
Who are these people?

STREPSIADES:
I'm not sure I know their names, but they are all gentlemen,
good and true, and fine philosophers of the finite.

PHEIDIPPIDES:
Ughh! I know who you mean, that godforsaken bunch

91: Dionysus was the god of wine, revelry, and the theatre.

of pasty looking frauds, going around barefoot!*
You're talking about Socrates and Chaerephon!

STREPSIADES:
Shut up! Stop talking like a baby.
Consider your father's daily bread, there'll be none left,
unless you give up horse racing and sign up for classes.

PHEIDIPPIDES:
No, by Dionysus, no! Not even if you gave me
a pair of Leogoras' finest pheasants!

STREPSIADES:
Please! My darling little boy, I beg you. Go and be taught.

PHEIDIPPIDES:
But what do I need to learn?

STREPSIADES:
I have heard it said, that in this house reside two different
kinds of argument, one is called the Superior Argument,
whatever that is, and the other, is known as the Inferior Argument.*
Some men say that the Inferior Argument can debate an unjust case
and win. All you have to do is learn this Inferior Argument for me,
then you can talk your way out of all the debts I've incurred
on your behalf, and I won't have to repay a single obol!

PHEIDIPPIDES:
No, I won't do it! How could I bear to show my pallid face
to all my friends in the cavalry? Wild horses couldn't drag me in
there!

104: A philosopher-colleague of Socrates (***104 Chaerephon**).

109: Leogoras came from an old, established Athenian family and was known for his expensive tastes (see *Wasps* line 1269). Pheasants were a rare species in Greece and an expensive luxury.

118: An obol was a small Athenian coin. Six obols were equal to one drachma.

120: The Athenian cavalry (*hippeis*) was an exclusive corps of around a thousand wealthy young upper-class citizens who could afford the expense of a horse and armor.

STREPSIADES:
Then get out of my house, by Demeter! You'll not get another crumb out of me. And that goes for your chariot stallion and your branded thoroughbred. I've had enough of your horsing around!

PHEIDIPPIDES:
I'll just go to uncle Megacles. He'll make sure
that I'm not without horse and home!

(Exit Pheidippides through the stage right door.)

STREPSIADES:
I'm not down and out yet! With the help of the gods,
I'll enroll at the Pondertorium and learn it all myself!

(Strepsiades strides off towards the stage left door, then slows down and stops.)

Oh, I'm just a stupid old fool. How on earth can I be expected
to learn all those hair-splitting arguments at my age?
I'm far too old, and my mind's certainly not what it used to be.

(He turns around and sets off for the stage right door, then suddenly stops.)

No! I have to do it! It's my one and only chance.
No more delaying, I'm going to walk right up and knock on the door!

(He marches purposefully up to the stage left door, knocks hard, and shouts out.)

Boy! Boy! Where are you? Boy!

(The stage left door-hatch opens suddenly.)

STUDENT:
Go to Hell!

(The student slams the hatch shut. Strepsiades knocks on the door again, and the hatch reopens.)

Who's there?

121: Demeter was the goddess of the harvest.

STREPSIADES:
Strepsiades, son of Pheidon, from Cicynna.

STUDENT:
Obviously an uneducated idiot! Don't you realize that you thoughtlessly
banged away at the door with such force that you may well have caused
the miscarriage of a brilliant new idea on the verge of discovery!

STREPSIADES:
I'm very sorry, I'm from far away, in the country.
What was it that may have "miscarried"?

(The student furtively looks around, then leans in to whisper.)

STUDENT:
Only students may be told such things. It is the sacred law.

(Strepsiades mimics the student's movements and also whispers.)

STREPSIADES:
It's quite all right, you can tell me,
I've come to sign up as a student in the Pondertorium.

(The stage left door opens, and the student breaks into normal speech.)

STUDENT:
Very well, but remember these things are holy mysteries and must
be kept secret. Just now, Socrates asked Chaerephon how many
feet a flea could jump, calculating the equation of one flea foot for a foot.
This question came to Chaerephon's mind, as the flea in question
had just bitten his eyebrow and leapt onto Socrates' head.*

134: The exact location of Cicynna is not known, but it was probably a rural Attic *deme* (district).

143: Secret initiation rites such as those at Eleusis that promised life after death were called "The Mysteries."

STREPSIADES:
How did he measure the distance?

STUDENT:
Expertly. He dipped the flea's feet in some melted wax,
and when it had dried, he carefully removed the molds,
producing a pair of Persian booties in miniature.
He was halfway through measuring the distance when you . . .

STREPSIADES:
Zeus almighty! What a delicate, subtle intellect!

STUDENT:
You should have heard the new concept that Socrates recently announced.

STREPSIADES:
What concept? Tell me, I beg you!

STUDENT:
Chaerephon of Sphettus asked Socrates to pronounce
his opinion on an important scientific matter.

STREPSIADES:
What was that?

STUDENT:
Whether the hum of a gnat is generated via its mouth or its anus.

STREPSIADES:
Really? And what did he find out about the gnat?

STUDENT:
He said that the intestine of a gnat is extremely constricted
and that air is pressed through this narrow conduit to the anus,
then the sphincter, acting as an oscillating cavity in close proximity

---

151: These were soft calf-length leather boots (***151 Booties**).

156: Sphettus was an Attic deme. Aristophanes may be continuing the insect gags with a pun based on *sphex* ("wasp").

to a compressed channel, is forced to issue a vibrating sound
as a direct result of the wind acting upon it.

STREPSIADES:
So a gnat's arse is a trumpet! Who'd have thought it?
What an amazing display of rectumology; really gutsy stuff!
I'm sure Socrates could easily fend off hostile legal actions
with such a deep understanding of arseholes.

STUDENT:
Yesterday he was robbed of a stupendous new idea by a speckled gecko.

STREPSIADES:
What? Tell me more.

STUDENT:
He was preoccupied studying the lunar revolutions,
and as he stood there gaping at the night sky,
a speckled gecko on the roof shat right on his head.

STREPSIADES:
(Laughing) A speckled gecko shitting on Socrates, I like that.

STUDENT:
Then, last evening there was nothing for supper.

STREPSIADES:
Really? So how did he think he was going to get some oats?

STUDENT:
First, he laid the table by sprinkling a thin layer of ash over it,
then he bowed a skewer to form a pair of compasses, picked up
the bent legs . . . from the wrestling school and stole his cloak!

174: The Turkish gecko has a spotted skin that resembles stars; hence its Latin name *Stellio* **(*174 Speckled gecko)**.

179: This joke hinges on the word *diabêtês,* which can mean both a pair of compasses or "bestrider." The wrestling schools were popular places for meeting young men, and Socrates often taught there. Both Plato's "Academy" and Aristotle's "Lyceum" were wrestling schools (***179 Wrestling school**).

STREPSIADES:
Amazing! And to think, some people still think highly of Thales!
Come on, open, open the Pondertorium!
Quickly, I want to see *him*. I want to meet Socrates!
I can't wait any longer, I'm dying to learn. Open the door!

(The central doors open and the ekkyklema is rolled out onstage. A group of four pallid, barefooted and shabbily dressed students are revealed busy with various activities.)

By Heracles! What on earth are these creatures!

STUDENT:
You seem surprised. What do you think they are?

STREPSIADES:
They look like a bunch of half-starved walking wounded to me.*

(Pointing to a group of the students)

Why are they staring at the ground?

STUDENT:
They are seeking to know what lies beneath the earth.

STREPSIADES:
I see, they're looking for onions to eat. They don't need to waste time pondering about that, I know just where the can find some lovely big ones.
(Pointing to another group) Why are they bending over like that?

STUDENT:
They are probing the nether regions of Erebus deep beneath Tartarus.

180: Thales (c.625–c.545) was one of the "Seven Sages" and was regarded as the father of natural philosophy.

188: The study of subterranean phenomena was considered heretical by many Athenians as an affront to the realm of Hades (***188 What lies beneath**).

192: Erebus and Tartarus were the darkest and bleakest regions of the underworld (see *Birds* line 661).

STREPSIADES:
Really? So why are their arses pointing at the sky?

STUDENT:
They are simultaneously studying "arse-stronomy!"
(To the students) Back inside! He must not find you out here.

STREPSIADES:
Hold on! Not so fast. Let them stay a while,
I'd like to probe them with a penetrating point.

(Exit the students on the ekkyklema, which moves back behind the doors.)

STUDENT:
Sorry. It's against all the rules. It's not good for them
to spend too much time outside, exposed to the fresh air.

(Strepsiades notices a strange array of ludicrous scientific instruments.)

STREPSIADES:
What, in the name of the gods, might these be?

STUDENT:
This is for astronomy.*

STREPSIADES:
What's this for?

STUDENT:
Geometry.

STREPSIADES:
Geometry? What's that?

STUDENT:
It is the science of measuring the land.

STREPSIADES:
I see, to measure out plots for the landlords?*

STUDENT:
No, to measure land generally.

STREPSIADES:
Lovely! What a very democratic mechanism.

(The student shows Strepsiades a large map.)

STUDENT:
This is a map of the entire world. Look, here is Athens.

STREPSIADES:
Don't be stupid, that can't be Athens!
Where are all the jurors and the law courts?

STUDENT:
I'm telling you, this area is clearly the region of Attica.

STREPSIADES:
So where's my deme then? Where's Cicynna?

STUDENT:
I don't know! Over there somewhere. You see here, that is Euboea,
the long island lying off the coast.

STREPSIADES:
Yeah, me and Pericles really laid those revolting bastards out!
Where's Sparta then?

STUDENT:
Right here.

STREPSIADES:
That's far too close! You need to move it immediately!
You had better reponder that one, mate!

208: For the fondness of Athenians for litigation and law courts see the introduction to *Wasps*, pp. 127–28.

213: Euboea, which lay off the cost of Boeotia, rebelled against Athenian control in 446. It was reconquered by Pericles, who divided up much of the land and awarded it to Athenian citizens.

STUDENT:
But it's simply not possible just to . . .

STREPSIADES:
Then you'll get a beating, by Zeus . . .

*(Enter Socrates suspended over the stage on a rack by the stage crane.)**

Who on earth is that man hanging about up there?

STUDENT:
Himself.

STREPSIADES:
Who's "Himself"?

STUDENT:
Socrates.

STREPSIADES:
Socrates! Call him over for me, will you?

STUDENT:
You call him! I'm, eh . . . very busy.

(Exit the student scurrying off through the stage left door.)

STREPSIADES:
Socrates! Oh Socrates!

SOCRATES:
Why do you call me, ephemeral creature?*

STREPSIADES:
Socrates! What are you doing up there?

SOCRATES:
I walk the air in order to look down on the sun.

225: The Greek *periphronô* can mean "contemplate" or "hold in contempt" (***225 Look down on the sun**).

STREPSIADES:
But why do you need to float on a rack to scorn the gods?
If you have to do it, why not do it on the ground?

SOCRATES:
In order that I may make exact discoveries of the highest nature!
Thus, my mind is suspended to create only elevated notions.
The grains of these thoughts then merge with the similar
atmosphere of thin air! If I had remained earthbound
and attempted to scrutinize the heights, I would have found
nothing; for the earth forces the creative juices to be drawn
to its core, depriving one of the all important "water on the brain!"

STREPSIADES:
Eh?
You mean, you need a good brainwashing to think such thoughts?*
Oh my dear Socrates, you must come down at once.
You must teach me all the things that I have come to learn.

(Socrates is lowered to the ground.)

SOCRATES:
And just why have you come?

STREPSIADES:
I want to learn to debate.
I'm being besieged by creditors, all my worldly goods
are under threat of seizure, the bailiffs are banging on my door!

SOCRATES:
Did you fail to realize you were amassing such enormous debts?

STREPSIADES:
Oh, I tried to keep things on a tight rein, but it was like closing

---

234: A parody of one of the main theories of the philosopher Diogenes of Apollonia, who believed that intellectual ability was influenced by moisture in the air. The dryer the air, the purer the thoughts. Because the earth held moisture, the nearer the ground a creature lived, the less intelligent it would be.

the stable door after the horse had bolted. I want you to teach me that other Argument of yours, the one that never pays its dues. Name your price, whatever it takes, I swear by the gods to pay you!*

SOCRATES:
(Laughing) "Swear by the gods"? We don't give credit to the gods here.

STREPSIADES:
Then how do you make oaths? This all sounds very Byzantine to me.*

SOCRATES:
Do you really want to know the truth regarding matters of religion?

STREPSIADES:
I do, by Zeus! Is that possible?

SOCRATES:
And do you wish communion with the Clouds, to actually speak to our divinities?

STREPSIADES:
Oh, yes please!

SOCRATES:
Then lie down on this sacred couch.

STREPSIADES:
(He does so.) I'm lying down.

SOCRATES:
Here, take this ritual wreath.

(Socrates hands him a shabby-looking wreath.)

247: The Greek *nomisma* has the sense of both "belief" and "currency."

254: Being ceremonially seated or "enthronement" was part of the initiation rites of the Corybantes and the Eleusinian Mysteries.

256: Wreaths were worn at many religious occasions, including initiation rites and sacrificial ceremonies.

STREPSIADES:
A wreath? Gods no! Socrates, I don't want to be sacrificed!
You're not going to make a meal out of me!*

SOCRATES:
Don't worry, it's just a part of the initiation rites, everyone has to do it.

STREPSIADES:
What do I get out of it?

SOCRATES:
Why, you will become a polished public speaker, a rattling castanet,*
the "flour" of finest orators. Now hold still . . .

(Socrates sprinkles flour over Strepsiades.)

STREPSIADES:
By Zeus, I'm no powder puff! I know when I'm getting a good dusting!*

SOCRATES:
Silence! Speak no ill words, old man, and heed my invocation.
O master, our lord, infinite Air, upholder of the buoyant earth.
O radiant Ether, O reverend thunder-cracking Clouds, ascend!
Reveal yourselves, sacred ladies, emerge for those with higher thoughts!

STREPSIADES:
Wait, wait! I need to wrap myself up first so I don't get soaked.
Dammit! I knew I shouldn't have left home without a hat.

SOCRATES:
Come, you illustrious Clouds, come and reveal yourselves to this mortal.
From the sacred snow-capped crests of Olympus, from the festive spiraling

---

264: The philosopher Diogenes believed that the earth was kept in position by a surrounding cushion or a pedestal of air.

dances of the Sea-Nymphs in the lush gardens of the Ocean father;
from the shimmering waters of the Nile where you dip your golden goblets;
from lake Maeotis or the icy heights of Mount Mimas. Hear my prayer!
Receive our sacrifice and bless our sacred rites.

(The Clouds are heard offstage.)

CHORUS:
Arise, appear, ever-soaring Clouds,
The shape of shimmering drops assume.
From mountain slopes, where forests crowd,
From ocean depths where breakers boom.

Look down upon the vales and hills,
See sacred earth where showers splash.
The holy rivers where rainfall spills,
The roaring sea's rush and dash.

Shake off the rain and misty haze,
A shining radiance warms the sky.
Upon this earth the Clouds will gaze
Under the tireless gleam of heaven's eye.

SOCRATES:
Oh, magnificent, revered Clouds, you heard my summons. You came!
Did you hear that sound? Those bellowing godlike thunderclaps?*

STREPSIADES:
I revere you too, oh illustrious Clouds! Let me answer your rumbling part

---

271: Poseidon's garden of the Hesperides was said to lie on the western shore of the ocean beyond the pillars of Heracles.

273: Lake Maeotis was the Greek name for the sea of Azov to the north of the Black Sea in the Crimea. Mt. Mimas was the name for a a mountain in Ionia (the west coast of modern day Turkey) that stood opposite the island of Chios.

with a rumbling fart! You've put the wind up me all right, I'm all a jitter!
I don't know if it's right or wrong, but I need to take a thundering crap!

SOCRATES:
Will you stop messing about and behaving like one of those wretched comic playwrights!
Speak no ill words, a mighty flurry of goddesses is on the move, singing as they go.

(The chorus begins to enter the orchestra from left and right. Strepsiades still cannot see them.)

CHORUS:
On to Athens, maidens bearing rain,
The hallowed land of Cecrops' race,
Where the initiates seek to attain
Acceptance to a sacred place.

The house of Mysteries for holy rites
And massive temples with statues grand.
The godly processions to sacred sites,
The splendid sacrifices that crown the land.

Celebrations held throughout the year
Then sweet Dionysus comes in spring.
And the resonant tone of the pipes we hear
As the joyous chorus dance and sing.

STREPSIADES:
Zeus! Socrates, you must tell me, who are these ladies singing this amazing song? Are they some new breed of female idols?

300: Cecrops was the mythical original king of Athens and was born from the earth of Attica (***300 Cecrops**).

305: This is the Attic cult sanctuary to Demeter and Persephone at Eleusis, where the initiations into the Mysteries were held.

SOCRATES:

No, no, no. They are the heavenly Clouds, magnificent goddesses for men
of leisure. They grace us with our intellect, argumentative skills, perception,
hyperbolization, circumlocution, pulverization, and predomination!

STREPSIADES:

That's why my spirit has soared at the sound of their voices!
I'm raring to split hairs, quibble over windy intricacies, set notion
against notion, and strike down arguments within counterarguments!
Oh, Socrates, I can't wait any longer, I've just got to see them!

SOCRATES:

Then look over here, up at Mount Parnes. Here they come, delicately wafting down.

STREPSIADES:

Where? Where? I can't see! Show me.

SOCRATES:

There, there. Can you see them all? Floating down over hill and dale,
Look, there wafting towards us, to the left and right.*

STREPSIADES:

What on earth are you talking about! I can't see anything!

SOCRATES:

Look there, in the wings!

STREPSIADES:

Yes, I think I . . . I can just about make something out.

SOCRATES:

Are you completely blind! Surely you can see them now?

(The chorus is now assembled in the orchestra.)

323: The highest peak in Attica lying directly to the north of Athens.

STREPSIADES:
By Zeus! The Illustrious ones themselves, they're everywhere, all around us!

SOCRATES:
And to think that you never knew they were goddesses, you had no faith.

STREPSIADES:
I thought they were just a load of old vapor, all drizzle and fog!

SOCRATES:
Exactly, because you were unaware that they cultivate a slew of sophisticated scholars;
Prophets from the colonies, atmospheric therapists, long-haired loungers with jangling jewelry,
creators of complex, convoluted compositions, ethereal, immaterial, vacuous visionaries!
Intangible, insubstantial idleness sustained by waxing lyrical about the Clouds!

STREPSIADES:
Oh, I see! That's why they utter things like "the menacing storm clouds advance, edged
with silver linings" and then call them "the billowing locks of hundred-headed Typhon,"
"furious gusts," "sky-borne cisterns," "jagged clawed birds soaring through the air,"
and sing about "torrents pouring down from rain filled clouds," and for that load
of hot air they get rewarded with beautiful fillets of fish and lovely little roasted thrushes!

334: Aristophanes may be describing Lampon the Prophet, Hippocrates of Cos, the wealthy young students of the sophists and dithyrambic poets (***331–34 Sophisticated scholars**).

336: Typhon was a mythological hundred-headed monster associated with violent storm winds.

339: A victorious poet was given a festive banquet by his producer following the performances.

SOCRATES:
Just think, it's all due to the Clouds.

STREPSIADES:
But if they are supposed to be Clouds, why do they look like women?
What happened? The Clouds up in the sky don't look like that.

SOCRATES:
Well, what do they look like?

STREPSIADES:
I don't really know just how to describe them exactly. Like a flock of woolly sheepskin rugs,
certainly not like women. I've never seen a Cloud with a nose before.

SOCRATES:
Really? Then answer this one question.

STREPSIADES:
Ask away.

SOCRATES:
Have you ever looked up at the Clouds and thought that they seemed
to assume the shape of, say a centaur, perhaps a leopard, or even a bull?

STREPSIADES:
I have, but so what?

SOCRATES:
The Clouds can assume any form they please. If they should happen to look down and spy
some long-haired, unkempt uncivilized type, say the son of Xenophantus, for example,
then they assume the form of a centaur in recognition of his true heart's desire.

350: This probably refers to the poet Hieronymus, ridiculed in *Acharnians* (lines 388–90) for his long hair. Centaurs, the half-man, half-horse creatures of mythology, were often portrayed as possessing rampant sexual appetites.

STREPSIADES:
Ha! Then what if they see that fraudster, Simon, who robbed the public funds?

SOCRATES:
Then they assume his true likeness and turn into wolves.

STREPSIADES:
Oh! Now I know why they looked like a herd of deer the other day.
They must have recognized Cleonymus, the shield-shedder, for the cowardly bastard that he is.

SOCRATES:
Precisely, and now they have obviously just seen Cleisthenes, hence they become women!

STREPSIADES:
Oh, hail divine ladies! Please do for me what you do for others,
sing a song to reach the very heights of heaven.

CHORUS:
(To Strepsiades) Hail, O geriatric one, you who quest for artful words.
(To Socrates) Hail priest of pedantic prattle, what would you bid us do?
There are only two ethereal experts we hearken to:
Prodicus for his sheer wisdom and knowledge,
and you, for the way you strut around like a grand gander,*
roll your eyes, go barefoot, endure all, and hold such high opinions.

351: Probably a corrupt minor politician in the circle of Cleon (***351 Simon**).

354: A minor Athenian politician nicknamed the "shield-dropper" by Aristophanes for alleged cowardice in battle (see *Wasps* ***19 Cleonymus**).

355: Cleisthenes was frequently ridiculed in Aristophanic comedy for his effeminate manner and lack of a beard. He appears as a character in Aristophanes' *Thesmophoriazusae* (lines 575–654).

361: A renowned sophist known for his teachings on the intricacies of language and their effective use in argument. He was operating in Athens around the same time as Socrates and held radical views concerning the birth of the cosmos (see *Birds* lines 690–92).

STREPSIADES:
Good Earth! What vocals! Wondrous, sacred, marvelous!

SOCRATES:
You see, these are the only true gods, everything else is utter nonsense.

STREPSIADES:
What about Zeus? How can Olympian Zeus not be a god?

SOCRATES:
Zeus? Don't be absurd! Zeus doesn't exist.

STREPSIADES:
What are you saying? Who is it that makes rain, then?

SOCRATES:
Why, the Clouds of course! I'll prove it to you. Does it ever rain without Clouds? No, and you would have thought that Zeus could have made rain on his own if he so desired, without the help of the Clouds.

STREPSIADES:
And I always thought it was Zeus pissing through a sieve!
You certainly have a way with words, that makes complete sense.
But hold on, who makes the thunder that makes me shake in teror?

SOCRATES:
It is just the Clouds rocking in the sky.

STREPSIADES:
Is nothing sacred! How do they do that?

368: Zeus was known as the Sky Father. He was said to cause the rain, thunder, and lightning, and many of his rituals originated in a desire to control the weather and pray for rain.

375: Similar theories were held by the earlier philosophers, Heraclitus and Anaxagoras.

SOCRATES:
Simple. When they become completely saturated with moisture, they are forced
by Necessity to begin to oscillate to and fro. Every now and again they ram each other
and of course, being packed with precipitation, CRASH! A cloudburst!

STREPSIADES:
But surely someone must force them to move in the first place. That must be Zeus.

SOCRATES:
Not at all, it is the whirling of the Celestial Basin!

STREPSIADES:
Basin? So Zeus is no more and Basin is king now, is he?
But you haven't explained who it is that makes the thunder.

SOCRATES:
Listen! The Clouds become full of water and crash into each other,
thus they emit a thundering sound because of their sheer density.

STREPSIADES:
Do you seriously expect me to believe that?

SOCRATES:
Then allow me to demonstrate, using you as my example. Have you ever been
at the Panathenaea Festival, and eaten too much soup? What happened?

378: "Necessity" is *anankê*, the personification of the compelling force of nature (***378 Necessity**).

380: The Greek has *dinos*, a large bowl used for mixing wine and also a term that means "vortex" (***380 Celestial Basin**).

381: Zeus became king of the gods by overthrowing his father Cronus (see *Birds* ***467 Heavenly succession**).

387: A public festival held in honor of Athena each year with the Great Panathenaea occurring once every four years.

Your stomach suddenly became upset and started to rumble, yes?

STREPSIADES:

Yes, by Apollo. It grumbles and groans with all that soup sloshing around,
and then it makes a noise that sounds just like thunder. First of all
it's just a little splutter . . . Phuurrrt! Then it gets a bit louder . . . PHHUuuuurrtt!
And when I finally get to take a shit, it really thunders just like those clouds . . .
. . . PHHHAAAARRRRAAARRRAAATTT!

SOCRATES:

My dear old fellow, if a tiny stomach such as yours can emit such a fart,
just think what a colossal thunder the vast atmosphere can produce.

STREPSIADES:

Yes, thunder and farter, they even sound the same.
But what about those flashing, fiery shafts of lightning that can burn
us to a crisp or at the least give us a good grilling every now and then?
Surely that is Zeus' instrument against oath-breakers.

SOCRATES:

You blithering, prehistoric, pre-cronian old fool!
If Zeus smites oath-breakers, why has he not incinerated Simon,
Cleonymus, or Theorus? They couldn't break more oaths if they tried!
Instead he strikes the temple at Cape Sunium and turns his own oak trees to charcoal.

394: In Greek, *brontê* and *pordê*. Etymology was an area of interest for the sophists, reduced to cheap toilet humor by Strepsiades.

398: Cronus was the father of Zeus, and his name a byword for archaic times.

399: Theorus was a minor politician in the circle of Cleon; he is vilified as a flatterer in *Wasps* (lines 42–51).

400: A promontory on the southeastern point of Attica jutting out into the Aegean Sea.

Everyone knows that an oath as solid as oak can't be broken. What was he thinking?

STREPSIADES:

I don't know, but it all sounds very convincing. So what's a thunderbolt then?

SOCRATES:

When an arid gust is blown up above and becomes trapped inside the clouds,
it tends to inflate them rather like a bladder; the sheer volume of air causes
the clouds to explode, and the compressed hot wind is forced out with such
terrific energy that in the process it bursts into spontaneous flame.*

STREPSIADES:

The exact same thing happened to me once at the Diasia feast.
I was cooking a nice big sausage for the family, and I completely
forgot to prick it. Well, it swelled right up and suddenly BANG!
It blew up right in my face, and showered me with hot blood and fat!

CHORUS:

You come craving knowledge of the highest kind
So the Greeks will call you Athens' mastermind.
If you possess a brain fit for cogitation
And can suffer cold, stress, and deprivation.
If you can pace about and stand for hours
Not drink nor train by sheer willpower,
If you hold the clever soul in high regard,
Battling by the tongue will not be hard.

STREPSIADES:

My mind never rests, I'm as tough as old boots.

401: The oak tree was sacred to Zeus. The god's presence at his shrine in Dodona was represented by a holy oak tree.

408: A festival sacred to Zeus Meilichios ("the kindly one").

I've a mean, lean stomach, and I can live on roots.
Fear not, there's nothing that this body can't handle;
I'm ready to temper my spirit upon your anvil!

SOCRATES:
And do you repudiate all other gods, except those we venerate,
the holy trinity of Chaos, Clouds, and a confident tongue?

STREPSIADES:
I wouldn't even speak to a god if I met one, and you won't catch me
sacrificing, pouring libations, or burning incense on any of their altars.

CHORUS:
Then tell us, what is it you would like us to do for you? We will not fail you,
not if you pay us due honor and respect and come in search of knowledge.

STREPSIADES:
Reverend ladies! It's just a tiny little thing that I ask of you;
I wish to be the finest speaker in all of Greece, a hundred times over!

CHORUS:
So be it. From this day henceforth no man shall ever pass
more motions in the public assembly than you . . .

STREPSIADES:
No, no, no! I'm not interested in politics and carrying on in the assembly!
I want to twist Justice around and escape the clutches of my creditors.

CHORUS:
Then you will have your heart's desire, it is but a small thing you require.
Just place yourself into the hands of our leading devotees.

STREPSIADES:
I'll do it! I have to! I've got no choice, you see!
The horses and my marriage will be the death of me!

So here I am, take me now, I'm yours!
Beat me, bruise me, it's in a very good cause.
I'll starve, not bathe, shiver, shake, and freeze,
Feel free to tan my hide as often as you please!

I'll do anything to avoid the paying of my debts,
And men will come to realize my newly won assets.
I'll be dangerous, mad, and devil-may-care,
A low-down dirty liar, driven to despair!

A courthouse junkie blessed with the gift of gab,
A barrack-room lawyer and a filthy, oily rag!
A chiseler, a shyster, a bullshitter and cheat,
A miscreant, a twister, and a master of deceit!

Feed me on chop logic, I'll feast on your split hairs,
And all those who meet me, should take extra care.
So now I've told you what it is I yearn to be,
Serve me to your students and make mincemeat out of me!

CHORUS:
I can't help but admire
his sheer strength of character.
Let me tell you this,
If you learn your lessons well,
Your very name will reach up
to resound in the heights of heaven!

STREPSIADES:
Then what lies in store for me?

CHORUS:
For the rest of your days you will be
the most blessed and envied of all men.

STREPSIADES:
Really?

CHORUS:
Of course!
Crowds will gather at your door

clamoring for any opportunity
to actually get to talk to you.
They'll all come in supplication,
seeking your sage advice.
You'll help them to decide vitally important
and extravagantly expensive issues,
issues suited to such an intellect as yours.
Now to enroll this old man in our educational program;
it is time to stimulate his mind and test his knowledge.

SOCRATES:
So, tell me a little about yourself.
I need to understand your particular personality traits.
Then I can correctly determine the best tactics to deploy.

STREPSIADES:
Tactics? Are you planning to lay siege to me?

SOCRATES:
No, no, I just want to analyze you a little.
Now then, are you in possession of a powerful memory?

STREPSIADES:
Well, that all depends. If someone owes me money,
it is quite superb, but if, on the other hand, I owe money,
then I'm afraid it has a tendency to let me down.

SOCRATES:
Then perhaps you have a particular penchant for oral recitation?

STREPSIADES:
(Laughing) Me? I'm certainly reticent to pay my debts!

SOCRATES:
Look, how on earth do you expect to learn anything?

STREPSIADES:
Oh, don't be such a worrier, I'll get the hang of it.

SOCRATES:
All right then, make sure that whenever I throw out some juicy bits

of heavenly wisdom that you snatch them up right away.

STREPSIADES:
(Laughing) What do you take me for, a dog?

SOCRATES:
You utter, uneducated barbarian oaf!
We may well have to beat some sense into this old fool.
Tell me, what would you do if someone were to hit you?

STREPSIADES:
I'd fall over! And I'd stay down too, at least until a witness
came along. Then I'd go and file assault charges
and get a hefty out-of-court settlement or some nice damages!

SOCRATES:
Remove your outer garment.

STREPSIADES:
What for, am I in trouble already?

SOCRATES:
No, all new initiates must disrobe.

STREPSIADES:
But, I promise I won't steal anything inside.

SOCRATES:
Just take the damn thing off, will you!

(Strepsiades takes off his tunic and gives it to Socrates, leaving him naked except for a loincloth.)

STREPSIADES:
If I work really hard and attend to my studies,
which of your followers can I ever hope to be like?

499: Under Athenian law a citizen could search the house of a suspected thief. However, the person had to first remove his cloak to prove that he was not attempting to plant any incriminating evidence.

SOCRATES:
You should try to be like Chaerephon.

STREPSIADES:
Good gods no, I'll be as good as dead!

SOCRATES:
Will you please stop jabbering away.
Get a move on and follow me!

STREPSIADES:
All right, all right, but at least put a honey cake in my hand,
I'm scared, it's like descending into Trophonius' grotto.

SOCRATES:
Stop dilly-dallying at the door and come on!

(Enter Socrates and Strepsiades into the Pondertorium through the stage left door.)

CHORUS:
Good luck to this brave soul
Embarking on his quest,
Though he's old and gray
I know he'll do his best.
A dyed-in-the-wool spirit
Dipping into new ideas,
Such a radical education
For a man of advanced years.

[Parabasis]

(The chorus leader addresses the audience, speaking for Aristophanes.)

508: A legendary master builder who had an oracle near Lebadea in Boeotia. Visitors performed various initiation rites before descending into a mysterious subterranean passage armed with a honey cake to placate the serpents who were said to guard the cave (***508 Trophonius**).

CHORUS:

Dear audience, allow me to speak candidly for a moment.
It is time to hear the truth, sworn by Dionysus, the very deity
that nurtured my rare talent and raised me to win great dramatic victories.
I thought that you were an intelligent audience, I thought that you would
truly enjoy this, the most intellectual of all my comedies.
I sweated night and day over a hot script to serve up to you
the very first taste of the fruits of my labor. But look what happened.
I was utterly defeated, thwarted by those other vile, despicable hacks!
And it is you people who must bear the blame for this disgrace,
for you should have known better. I did it all for you, and just look how you chose
to repay me! But never fear, I will always be here for those with the good taste
to fully appreciate the quality of my work. It was here, in this very theatre,
that my tale of the righteous boy and the little bugger was so very well received.
It is true that I was not yet of an age to mother properly such a child, and so I exposed
my prodigy to be adopted by another in my stead. Then you, dear audience, you all
became its foster parents, it was you who nurtured it, you raised it.
Ever since then I have held you all in the highest esteem, and I always
swore by your sound judgment and prudent wisdom. And now like Electra,
this comedy comes searching, hoping, seeking an audience equal in wit and intelligence,

---

525: This text of *Clouds* seems to have been revised. The original production placed third at the festival of Dionysus in 421.

530: Probably *Banqueters* (427), Aristophanes' first play, which placed second.

535: Electra was the daughter of Agamemnon and Clytemnestra, a famous figure in both myth and drama. Aeschylus, Sophocles, and Euripides all produced plays about Electra longing for the return of her brother, Orestes.

and like the hair on Orestes' head, she'll know them when she sees them!
Contemplate for a moment, if you will, the value of her discreet sensibilities.
She does not dangle one of those huge, red-tipped appendages
between her legs to get cheap laughs from the children among you.*
She doesn't make rude jibes at the expense of bald men, and she categorically refuses*
to perform any kind of suggestive dances. You will never see her leading actor
dressed up as an old man, running around, hitting all and sundry with a stick
to divert your attention from the poor quality of the rotten old jokes! What's more
you will certainly not encounter anybody charging onstage with flaming torches,
shouting Oh! Oh! No, this play comes here today trusting only in itself and its poetry,*
and I, the playwright, am cast from the same mold. I have always been bold
(bold, not bald—I know I'm bald!), and I have never ever attempted to bamboozle you
by rehashing the same tired old material time and time again. No, I devote
every strain of my poetic fiber to the invention of brand new, cutting-edge comedy.
Every play has something different, something innovative, vivacious, and skillful.
When Cleon was at the peak of his powers, I slugged him in the stomach,
but I never hit the man when he was down. But just look at my rivals and how they
treated Hyperbolus, they walked all over him, not to mention the punishment they

---

537: Orestes proved his identity to Electra with a lock of hair in Aeschylus' *The Libation Bearers* (lines 229–30).

550: For the politician Cleon see *Wasps* ***39 Cleon**.

552: Hyperbolus became prominent in Athenian public life after the death of Cleon in 422.

dealt out to his poor old mother! It all started with Eupolis and that dreadful farce
of his, *Maricas*, blatant plagiarism! A disgusting imitation of my *Knights* with the totally
unnecessary addition of an inebriated old hag crudely gyrating in the dances.*
The very same character, might I add, that we saw Phrynichus present
in his comedy about the women being fed to the sea creature!
Then came Hermippus, and his vicious attacks on Hyperbolus.
Soon everyone jumped on the Hyperbolus band wagon and were happily
dishing out the dirt, and worst of all stealing all my best eel gags!
If you find that kind of drivel amusing, you will never fully appreciate my work,
but those who enjoy my comedic innovations will be considered wise in years to come.

Zeus the highest god of all,
Greatest ruler, hear our call.

Come, Poseidon, with trident flashing,
From salty depths with breakers crashing.

The sky-father that witnessed our birth
Most sacred nurturer of life on earth.

The charioteer who fills our days,
With the light, heat, and brilliant rays.

553: Eupolis was one of the most highly regarded Athenian comic poets. His work survives only in fragments, but he is known to have produced his first play in 429 and won at least seven victories. Hyperbolus' mother appeared in his *Maricas* of 421.

557: A comic dramatist and contemporary of Aristophanes. Evidently he had produced a comic farce based on the Andromeda myth.

558: The comic dramatist Hermippus had produced a play called *Bread Sellers* which featured Hyperbolus and his mother.

560: In *Knights* (lines 864–67) Aristophanes said Cleon's politics were like a fisherman stirring up the mud to get the eels to bite.

571: This is Helios, the sun god, who drives his chariot from the east to the west, bringing light.

To god and mortal, great power advance,
We call you all to join our dance!

(The Clouds address the audience.)

Attention please, audience! It is time to prick your collective conscience.
You have performed us a great disservice, and we are here to chastise you for it!
No deity gives more to this city than we, and yet you fail to pay us the slightest respect!
We are the ones who are ever-present, and we constantly have your best interests
at heart, but you never pour us any libations or even offer a single sacrifice!
When you are about to embark on some futile armed campaign, we bellow noisily
and send sheets of rain. When you were holding elections for general and chose
that damned Paphlagonian tanner, we frowned down and thundered our dissent.
"Such sheets of fire, such bursts of horrid thunder." Even the moon reversed*
her course, and the very sun in the sky snuffed his great wick and announced
that he would not rekindle his heavenly light if you nominated Cleon as General!
But in spite of everything, you still went ahead and voted for the man!
It has been said that bad decisions run rife in this city, and yet somehow the gods
always conspire to make everything turn out for the best. It is the same in this instance,

---

581: It seems from Aristophanes' *Acharnians* (lines 170–73) that a meeting of the assembly could be canceled due to rain. Thunder was also traditionally viewed as giving voice to the displeasure of the gods.

582: Aristophanes' nickname for Cleon as used in *Knights*. Cleon's family may have owned a tanning factory.

586: Cleon was elected as one of the ten generals around February 424, and an eclipse occurred in March (Thucydides 4.52.1).

for there is a simple solution to turn this terrible error of judgment to your advantage.
Just go ahead and indict that gannet Cleon on charges of fraud and embezzlement,
clap him in the stocks, and lock him up. Lo and behold, out of your previous folly
shall come your salvation, everything will be as before,
back the way things were, to the very great benefit of your city.

Come, Phoebus Apollo, lord of Delos,
Leave Cynthus' rocks and come to us.

Come, Artemis, leave your house of gold,
Worshipped by Lydian daughters age-old.

Goddess of the Aegis, protector of our city,
Lady Athena, held in highest sanctity.

From Parnassus' towering heights,
Setting ablaze his pine torch light,

The Bacchants of Delphi, wild and joyous,
Come, festive god, come, Dionysus.

LEADER:
When we were on our way here, we happened to meet the Moon,
who told us to relay her benedictions to the Athenians and their allies.
However, she also informed us that she is very cross with you
and that you have treated her with disrespect, despite all
the wonderful things she has done for you all. Just think, she saves
you at least a drachma a month for all the torches you have no need of.
She's heard you telling your houseboys, "Don't bother with the lamp
tonight, my lad, the moonlight's nice and bright."
She does that for you and a lot more besides! She also informed us
that she is most displeased with all this fiddling about with the lunar cycle,
she says it is playing absolute havoc with the calendar, and she has received numerous
complaints from angry gods who have been cheated out of their due festival days!*

To top it all, on sacred sacrificial days you are going around, torturing people
and sitting in court passing judgment when you should be worshipping.
There have even been times when the gods were partaking in a solemn memorial
service to Memnon or Sarpedon while you lot were pouring libations, drinking
and cavorting about all over the city—disgraceful! That is why Hyperbolus,
your elected religious remembrancer, had his wreath removed by the gods.
Now he knows that you should arrange your dates in concordance with the moon!

(Enter Socrates from the stage left door.)

SOCRATES:
By Breath, by Chaos, by Air!
I have never before encountered such a feeble-minded,
imbecilic, slow-witted country bumpkin in all my life!
He forgets the tiniest scraps of knowledge
before he's even had a chance to learn them!

(Calling into the Pondertorium)

Strepsiades! Come on out here, into the light,
Hurry up, and bring the couch with you.*

623: Both warriors from the Trojan War. Memnon was the king of the Ethiopians and the son of Eos (Dawn) and Tithonus. The morning dew was regarded as Dawn crying for her slain son who was killed by Achilles. Sarpedon was the son of Zeus and Laodamia and was killed by Patroclus. Zeus was so devastated by his son's death that he caused blood to rain down from the sky.

625: A remembrancer served on the Amphictyonic council, which decided sacred matters at Delphi. Perhaps a freak gust of wind had swept away Hyperbolus' official wreath at such an occasion.

627: The act of drawing breath was connected with the intellect by both Heraclitus and Diogenes of Apollonia.

(Enter Strepsiades, still seminaked, from the stage left door carrying a small couch. Like Socrates, he is now barefoot.)

STREPSIADES:
No need, the flea-infested thing can get up and walk out on its own!

SOCRATES:
Put it down over there and listen carefully.

STREPSIADES:
All right.

SOCRATES:
Good, let's get started. Which facet of your intellect do you wish to develop?
Perhaps you would like to use this opportunity to master a subject you never had
the opportunity to learn before? Meter? Rhythm? Scales?

STREPSIADES:
Scales! Only the other day that bastard grain merchant
fiddled me out of a full two measures!

SOCRATES:
Not those kind of scales, you idiot! I'm attempting to engage you in a discussion
on music and poetry. Now, consider which measure is more aesthetically pleasing,
the three-quarter beat or the four-quarter beat?

STREPSIADES:
Personally, I think the pint takes some beating!

SOCRATES:
Will you stop babbling such utter nonsense!

STREPSIADES:
It's not nonsense, everyone knows four quarts makes a pint!

SOCRATES:
Oh damn you! You illiterate uneducated peasant!

Let's at least see if you can learn something about rhythm.

STREPSIADES:
Rhythm? How is learning about rhythm going to buy me barley?

SOCRATES:
A detailed knowledge of rhythm enables you to socialize effectively in polite
company and seem refined and cultured. You'll know all about martial modes
and dactylic meter . . .

(Strepsiades looks confused.)

Beating the rhythm with your fingers!*

STREPSIADES:
I know how to beat with my fingers, by Zeus!

SOCRATES:
You do? Tell me about it.

STREPSIADES:
Well when I was a young lad it was this . . .

(Strepsiades grabs and shuffles his phallus.)

SOCRATES:
Gods! You are nothing but a village idiot!

STREPSIADES:
You're the idiot, I don't want to learn any of this stuff.

SOCRATES:
Well, what DO you want to learn?

STREPSIADES:
The other thing, you know *(whispering):* the Wrong Argument.

SOCRATES:
That's an advanced class, you can't just start there, you have to master the basics first,

such as the correct gender affiliation of certain types of quadrapedic livestock.*

STREPSIADES:
Livestock! I'm an expert. Let's see, masculine:
ram, billy-goat, bull, dog, chicken . . .

SOCRATES:
And the feminine?

STREPSIADES:
Ewe, nanny-goat, cow, bitch, chicken . . .

SOCRATES:
Aha! You called both the male and the female chicken.
You can't do that!

STREPSIADES:
What do you mean?

SOCRATES:
You said "chicken" and "chicken."

STREPSIADES:
By Poseidon, you're right! Well, what should I have said?

SOCRATES:
Chicken . . . and chickeness!

STREPSIADES:
Chickeness? That's a good one, by Air!
For just that single piece of learning
I should fill your meal-kneader with barley oats.

662: The Greek word *alektruôn* was used for both the cock and the hen.

669: A *cardopus* was a troughlike kneading tray with a large pestle that was used like a rolling pin (***671 Meal-kneader**). Barley was a cheap food but also part of many sacred festivals and initiation rites.

SOCRATES:
You've done it again, said another one. You used the masculine form for meal-kneader, but it really should be feminine.

STREPSIADES:
What? I made a meal-kneader masculine?

SOCRATES:
Yes, just like Cleonymus.

STREPSIADES:
What do you mean?

SOCRATES:
Meal-kneader and Cleonymus are treated in the same manner.

STREPSIADES:
But Socrates, Cleonymus doesn't even own a meal kneader.
His "needs" are met by having his oats delivered by the back door,*
if you, eh, know what I mean! What should I call it from now on?

SOCRATES:
The feminine form, that is "fe-meal kneader."

STREPSIADES:
So a meal-kneader needs a female to be a fe-meal kneader?

SOCRATES:
Exactly.

STREPSIADES:
I see, so I should have said, Cleonymus never needed a female?

SOCRATES:
Yes. Well then, we must still educate you on proper names.
You need to know which are masculine and which are feminine.

671: The word *cardopus* is feminine, although it appears to have a masculine ending.

STREPSIADES:
I know which are feminine all right.

SOCRATES:
Go on then.

(Strepsides lustfully imagines a group of well-known Athenian beauties.)

STREPSIADES:
Lysilla (*Wow wee!*), Philinna (*Oh yeah!*), Cleitagora (*Hubba, hubba*), and Demetria (*Ow!*).

SOCRATES:
And the masculine names?

(He imagines a collection of effeminate young men.)

STREPSIADES:
There's plenty: Philoxenus (*Luvvie!*), Melesias (*Big Boy!*), Amynias (*Hello sailor!*) . . .

SOCRATES:
Those are hardly masculine!

STREPSIADES:
You don't think they're masculine?

SOCRATES:
Absolutely not. If you saw Amynias, just how would you call out to him?

STREPSIADES:
Like this. "Coo-ee! Coo-ee! Amynia luvvie! Amynia darling!"

684: All of these seem to be fairly common women's names; however, the scholia cites them as prostitutes. Cleitagora is mentioned in this context in *Wasps* (lines 1245-47).

686: Philoxenus ("Guest-lover") was regarded by Old Comedy as a homosexual, Melesias is unknown, and Amynias is attacked several times in *Wasps* as a corrupt good-for-nothing and freeloader (see *Wasps* 74–76, 466, and 1267–70).

SOCRATES:
I rest my case. You are clearly calling out to him like a woman, and what's more, "Amynia" is feminine.

STREPSIADES:
That's what the old poof gets for dodging the draft.
But everyone knows Amynias is an old woman, I don't need to be taught that.

SOCRATES:
Be quiet by Zeus! Now lie down on the couch there.

STREPSIADES:
What for?

SOCRATES:
You need to concentrate on personal matters.

STREPSIADES:
No, I'm begging you! Don't make me lie down there. I can just as easily
do my personal concentrating on the bare earth!

SOCRATES:
I'm sorry, you simply have no choice.

STREPSIADES:
Oh no! Those fleas are going to have a field day feasting on me!

(Exit Socrates through the stage left door.)

CHORUS:
So philosophize and cogitate,
Intellectualize and ruminate.
Twist your thoughts, your mind must bend,
Through mental blocks and each dead end.
Let ideas jump and concepts fly,
Don't let sweet sleep close your eyes.

STREPSIADES:
Oh! Woe! Oh! Woe!

CHORUS:
What pains thee, art thou smitten?

STREPSIADES:
Misery! Agony! I'm being bitten!
They're leaping off this bed and biting
Like Corinthians fleeing from the fighting!
They've been gnawing on my bones all day,
They're sucking all my blood away!
They've champed my bollocks all red raw,
My poor old arse has never felt this sore!
These bugs will chew me half to death . . .

CHORUS:
I suggest you give that moaning a rest!

STREPSIADES:
Some hope you are, what bad advice!
I've lost money and health for a load of lice!
My very soul is bruised and beaten,
My clothes and shoes are all moth eaten.
So I sing to keep my spirits high,
But it's all over now, the end is nigh!

(Enter Socrates through the stage left door.)

SOCRATES:
What are you doing? You are supposed to be contemplating.

STREPSIADES:
I am, by Poseidon.

SOCRATES:
And just what, pray, have you been contemplating?

707: The high language is a parody from tragedy, perhaps Euripides' *Hecuba*, produced just a year earlier.

710: "Corinthians" seems to have been an Athenian slang term for "bedbugs" or "fleas," derived from a simple pun on *koreis* (bugs) and *Korinthioi* (Corinthians).

STREPSIADES:
I've been contemplating my future, once these bugs have finished me off!

SOCRATES:
Go to hell!

STREPSIADES:
Hell's right, chum! That's exactly what this is.

CHORUS:
Don't be so fainthearted, cover yourself up
and devise some fraudulent and illicit affair.

STREPSIADES:
Oh, if only instead of these lambskin covers,
I could get into an illicit affair!

(Strepsiades covers himself up and lies on the couch. He wriggles about, and then the covers rise, propped up by his phallus. Socrates reenters.)

SOCRATES:
All right, let's see how he's doing.
You there! Are you sleeping?

(Strepsiades pops his head out from under the fleece.)

STREPSIADES:
No, by Apollo, not me, no.

SOCRATES:
Have you been able to get a good grasp on anything?

STREPSIADES:
Eh . . . well, no, not really.

729: Veiling the head in a lamb's fleece was part of the initiation rites of the Eleusinian Mysteries.

SOCRATES:
Nothing whatsoever?

STREPSIADES:
Well, my right hand has a good grasp on my prick at the moment.

(Strepsiades removes the covers to reveal his erect phallus.)

SOCRATES:
Oh, by all the gods! Cover yourself up at once and think about something else!

STREPSIADES:
But what? Tell me, Socrates, please.

SOCRATES:
No, you must discover that for yourself, then tell me what it is you want.

STREPSIADES:
But you know very well what I want, I've told you a thousand times:
It's my debts, I want to get out of paying them off!

SOCRATES:
All right then, cover yourself up and dissect your suppositions
into microscopic elements. Then consider the matter in minute detail
thus arriving at a correct analysis derived from an orthodox methodology.

(Strepsiades pulls the fleece over his head and fidgets for a while before lying down.)

STREPSIADES:
Ohh! Ahh!

SOCRATES:
Stop fidgeting! Now, should your concept place you in a quandary
move on, free your mind, then the idea can be set in motion
once the innermost recesses of your intellect have been unlocked.

(Strepsiades uncovers himself.)

STREPSIADES:
My beloved Socrates!

SOCRATES:
What is it?

(Strepsiades gets up on his feet and runs toward Socrates.)

STREPSIADES:
I've thought of an illicit idea for avoiding my debts!

SOCRATES:
Do divulge.

STREPSIADES:
Tell me this . . .

SOCRATES:
What, what?

STREPSIADES:
What if I got hold of a witch from Thessaly
and made her magic the moon out of the sky.
I could put it away in a dressing case like a mirror,
and hide it where no one would ever find it.

SOCRATES:
But how would that help you?

STREPSIADES:
How? If I stopped the moon from rising, then I would never have to pay the interest on any of my debts.

750: The reputation of Thessalian women for sorcery was proverbial. Plato's *Gorgias* (513a) tells how they possess the power to "draw down the moon," and Menander produced a comedy, *Thettale*, dealing with the subject.

SOCRATES:
Why ever not?

STREPSIADES:
Because interest is always due at the end of the month, when the new moon appears!

SOCRATES:
I see, here's another situation to consider. What would you do
if a lawsuit was written up against you for five talents in damages?
How would you go about having the case removed from the record?

STREPSIADES:
Er, I've no idea, let me have a think about it.

(Strepsiades goes back under the fleece.)

SOCRATES:
Be sure not to constrict your imagination by keeping your thoughts wrapped up.
Let your mind fly through the air, but not too much. Think of your creativity
as a beetle on a string, airborne, but connected, flying, but not too high.

(He pops up from under the cover.)

STREPSIADES:
I've got it! A brilliant way of removing the lawsuit!
You're going to love this one.

SOCRATES:
Tell me more.

STREPSIADES:
Have you seen those pretty, see-through stones that the healers sell?*
You know, the ones they use to start fires.

763: In a popular child's game, a beetle would be tied to a stone or other heavy object and forced to fly while anchored by the string.

SOCRATES:
You mean glass.

STREPSIADES:
That's the stuff! If I had some glass, I could secretly position myself behind
the bailiff as he writes up the case on his wax tablet. Then I could aim the sun rays
at his docket and melt away the writing so there would be no record of my case!

SOCRATES:
Sweet charity! How "ingenious."

STREPSIADES:
Great! I've managed to erase a five-talent lawsuit.

SOCRATES:
Come on, then, chew this one over.

STREPSIADES:
I'm ready.

SOCRATES:
You're in court, defending a suit, and it looks like you will surely lose.
It's your turn to present your defense, and you have absolutely no witnesses.
How would you effectively contest the case and, moreover, win the suit itself?

STREPSIADES:
Easy!

SOCRATES:
Let's hear it then.

772: The "Charities" or "Graces" were female deities who personified beauty, charm, grace, the arts, and intellectual ability.

STREPSIADES:
During the case for the prosecution,
I would run off home and hang myself!

SOCRATES:
What are you talking about?

STREPSIADES:
By all the gods, it's foolproof! How can anybody sue me when I'm dead?

SOCRATES:
This is preposterous! I've had just about enough of this!
You'll get no more instruction from me.

STREPSIADES:
But Socrates, in the name of heaven, why not?

SOCRATES:
Because if I do manage to get something through to you, it is instantly
forgotten. Here, I'll prove it. What was the first thing I taught you?

STREPSIADES:
Mmmm, the first lesson, hang on, let me think, what was that, eh,
something female where we scatter our oats, oh I don't know!

SOCRATES:
You fossilized, forgetful old fool! Just piss off!

(Exit Socrates in disgust through the stage left door.)

STREPSIADES:
Oh no! I'm finished. This is terrible!
If I don't learn tongue-twisting, then I'm lost without a hope!
Clouds! You have to help me out. What can I do?

CHORUS:
You have a grownup son, don't you?
If you take our advice,
you will send him to take your place.

STREPSIADES:
Yes, I've a son, a refined, lovely lad, but he's not interested in higher education. What else can I do?

CHORUS:
He's your son, is he not? Who is master of your house?

STREPSIADES:
Well, he's a passionate, spirited boy from a fine family, the house of Coesyra, no less. But you're right, it's high time I set him straight, and if he says no, then he's out on his ear once and for all. Wait for me, I won't be long.

(Exit Strepsiades through the stage right door as the chorus serenades Socrates.)

CHORUS:
Now it is clear, once and for all
The great benefits we bring to you,
For this man is at your beck and call
To us alone, your prayers are due.

You've created one hysterical man,
His excitement cannot be contained.
Now quickly take him for all you can
For luck can change and drain away.

(Enter Pheidippides from the stage right door, chased by Strepsiades.)

STREPSIADES:
Get out! By Vapor, out of my house, once and for all.
Go and eat your uncle Megacles out of house and home!

PHEIDIPPIDES:
Father, whatever is the matter?
You are clearly insane, by Zeus!

814: Strepsiades' own version of Socrates' "by Air" (lines 627 and 667).

STREPSIADES:
Listen to you, "By Zeus!" How childish!
Fancy believing in Olympian Zeus at your age.

PHEIDIPPIDES:
What on earth is so funny?

STREPSIADES:
You are, a young child like you with such old-fashioned ideas, it's really quite ridiculous. But listen, come here, I want to reveal something to you. When you understand, then, and only then, my son will you truly be a man. But you must ensure that no one else knows this.

PHEIDIPPIDES:
Well, I'm here. Now what is it?

STREPSIADES:
Did you or did you not just swear to Zeus?

PHEIDIPPIDES:
I did.

STREPSIADES:
Now you'll see the benefits of education.
Pheidippides, there is no Zeus!

PHEIDIPPIDES:
What!

STREPSIADES:
Zeus is overthrown! Basin is king now!

PHEIDIPPIDES:
Ha! What rot!

STREPSIADES:
It's the truth.

PHEIDIPPIDES:
I don't believe you, who told you this nonsense?

STREPSIADES:
Socrates the Melian and Chaerephon,
and he's an expert in the true path of . . . fleas.

PHEIDIPPIDES:
Oh dear, your insanity is at a really advanced stage
if you have begun to follow the views of those maniacs.

STREPSIADES:
How dare you say such things! These are brilliant men
with superb minds. They live a simple frugal life and refuse
to cut their hair, use soap, or set foot in a bathhouse.
But you, you've been taking yourself and my money to the cleaners
for years, scrubbing away as if I was dead and buried!
Come on, hurry up, you have to go and learn in my place.

PHEIDIPPIDES:
What for? There's nothing even vaguely useful they could teach me.

STREPSIADES:
Nothing useful? What about all worldly knowledge, eh?
You could start off by learning what an imbecile you are.
Hang on, I've just had a thought. Wait here!

(Exit Strepsiades through the stage right door.)

PHEIDIPPIDES:
Dear me! Father is clearly completely deranged, what should I do?
I could have him tried in court and found legally incompetent,*
or perhaps I had better book the undertaker right away.

(Enter Strepsiades through the stage right door holding two identical chickens.)

STREPSIADES:
Now then, tell me what you would call this?

830: Strepsiades confuses Socrates with "the Melian," Diagoras of Melos, an atheist who openly scorned traditional religious views. He was eventually condemned to death (see *Birds* lines 1072–74).

(Strepsiades holds up one of the chickens.)

PHEIDIPPIDES:
A chicken.

STREPSIADES:
Very good. And what would you call this?

(Strepsiades holds up the other chicken.)

PHEIDIPPIDES:
A chicken.

STREPSIADES:
Really? You would call them both by the same name, eh?
Now you really are being stupid. Here let me show you
so you will know next time you are asked; this one here
is indeed called a "chicken". . . but this is a "chickeness."

PHEIDIPPIDES: *(Laughing)*
"Chickeness!" Is that an example of the "worldly knowledge"
that you learned in that house of stupid old clods?

(Strepsiades throws the chickens off and starts to lead Pheidippides to the stage left door.)

STREPSIADES:
It is, but son, I couldn't remember most of the stuff they taught,
every time I learned something I would forget it, I'm just too old
and . . .

PHEIDIPPIDES:
That's why you've lost the clothes off your back, is it?

STREPSIADES:
They're not lost, just donated to my educational endowment.

PHEIDIPPIDES:
And just where are your shoes, you gullible old idiot?

STREPSIADES:

To quote Pericles, "They were spent on necessary expenses." Come on, let's go. Do this one thing for your father, even if you don't agree with it. I remember when you were a little six year old, your little lisping voice begged me for a new toy cart as your festival* present, and I spent my first hard-earned obol of jury pay on you.

PHEIDIPPIDES:

Oh, all right then, but you'll regret this.

STREPSIADES:

Good lad, I knew you'd be persuaded. Socrates! Come out, come here!

(Enter Socrates from the stage left door.)

Here is my son, as promised. I persuaded him to come along though he was dead set against it at first.

SOCRATES:

No, no, no, he simply will not do, he's a mere child. He would never get the hang of the way we tackle things here. He just wouldn't grasp it.

PHEIDIPPIDES:

Grasp your own tackle and then go and hang yourself!*

STREPSIADES:

Pheidippides! Watch your language in front of the teacher!

SOCRATES:

"Graaasp?" Just listen to his infantile diction!
What ever do you expect me to do with such flaccid lips?
How could he learn prevarication, incrimination, and

859: Pericles had apparently used ten talents of state funds as a bribe for the Spartans to withdraw from Athenian territory in 445. He listed this in his annual accounts presented to the assembly as "payment for necessary expenses."

864: Jurors received three obols a day in payment for jury service (see the introduction to *Wasps*, pp. 127–28).

misrepresentation? Then again for the right course fees
it may be possible, just look what a talent bought for Hyperbolus!*

STREPSIADES:
You can do it! He'll learn, he's a natural, you'll find out!
You should have seen him when he was a little lad, gifted!
A boy genius! He'd build the most beautiful mud pies, carve
little boats, and make toy chariots out of old shoes, and you can't
even begin to imagine the inventive little frogs he made from
pomegranates. I want you to teach him those two Arguments,
the Superior, whatever that is, and the Inferior, you know, the one
that can argue a wrongful case and defeat the Superior Argument.
If you can't manage both, then at least make him learn the wrong one.

SOCRATES:
He can learn it from the Arguments themselves. I must be off.

(Exit Socrates through the stage left door.)

STREPSIADES:
Remember, he needs to argue his way out of all types
of legitimate lawsuits!

*(Enter the Superior Argument from the stage left door.)**

SUPERIOR:
Come out, let the audience have a look at you!
You know how much you like to show off.

(Enter the Inferior Argument from the stage left door.)

INFERIOR:
Oh, "get you hence" dear *(he sees the audience)*. Ohhh! What a crowd,
the more to witness your thrashing, the better. I just love it!

SUPERIOR:
And who are you to think you can thrash me?

891: A quote from Euripides' *Telephus,* where Agamemnon quarrels with Menelaus and tells him to "Go where you like."

INFERIOR:
Just an argument.

SUPERIOR:
An Inferior Argument.

INFERIOR:
Oh, aren't you the high and mighty one! That may be so darling,
but I'll still thrash you, all the same.

SUPERIOR:
Really? And just how do you plan to do that?

INFERIOR:
With innovative new ideas.

SUPERIOR:
Oh very chic, you're very fashionable aren't you,
thanks to these idiots *(indicating the audience).*

INFERIOR:
On the contrary, they are of the highest intelligence.

SUPERIOR:
I'm going to annihilate you.

INFERIOR:
I see, how?

SUPERIOR:
Simply by stating my just argument.

INFERIOR:
Then let me start by defeating it with a counterargument,
because it is quite clear that Justice doesn't exist.

SUPERIOR:
Don't be ridiculous!

INFERIOR:
Well, where is she then?

SUPERIOR:
She resides with the gods on Olympus, as well you know.

INFERIOR:
Well then, if Justice lives on Olympus,
why hasn't Zeus been punished for locking up his father, mmm?*

SUPERIOR:
You're just spewing venom. Urghh! Get me a bucket, someone!

INFERIOR:
You're a doddering old relic.

SUPERIOR:
And you're a filthy queer!*

INFERIOR:
Your words are strewn with roses!

SUPERIOR:
Freeloader!

INFERIOR:
You crown me with lilies!

SUPERIOR:
Father-beater!

INFERIOR:
You're completely unaware that you're showering me with gold.

SUPERIOR:
In my day, you'd be showered with lead!

904: Hesiod describes Justice seated at the feet of Zeus on Olympus (*Works and Days* 257–59).

906: Cronus, the father of Zeus, swallowed his children to prevent them usurping him. But Rhea, Zeus' mother, substituted her son for a stone, which proved indigestible for Cronus. He vomited up the stone and the other swallowed offspring.

INFERIOR:
Yes, I know but, my dear fellow, in these modern times we live in
all your worse name calling just pays me greater honor!

SUPERIOR:
You are completely contemptuous!

INFERIOR:
And you are absolutely archaic!

SUPERIOR:
It's your fault that the youth of today refuses
to attend school. You'll get your comeuppance,
you'll see, the Athenians will realize what fools
they've been to learn their lessons from the likes of you!

INFERIOR:
Pooh! You need to freshen up a bit.

SUPERIOR:
Oh, you've been busy all right, you worthless beggar.
You used to be the king of the scroungers,*
gnawing on old sycophantic sayings from a tatty old swag bag.*

INFERIOR:
How shrewd . . .

SUPERIOR:
How insane . . .

INFERIOR:
. . . all that you've said I've done.

SUPERIOR:
. . . the city is to support you,
as you corrupt its young.

INFERIOR:
Don't even think about trying to teach this boy,
you crusty old Cronus!

SUPERIOR:
It is my duty, he needs to be saved from
the threat of spouting senseless gibberish.

INFERIOR:
(To Pheidippides) Come over here and ignore this reactionary old maniac.

SUPERIOR:
Keep away from him or you'll be sorry!

CHORUS:
Oh, stop all this fighting and arguing!

(Addressing the Superior Argument)

Why don't you give an account of the schooling
you used to give in the old days,

(Addressing the Inferior Argument)

and then you
can tell us about your new educational methods.
Then this boy can hear your conflicting arguments,
make his own mind up, and enroll in the school of his choice.

SUPERIOR:
I see no reason why not.

INFERIOR:
I'm happy to do it.

CHORUS:
Good, who would like to speak first?

INFERIOR:
Oh, let him go first.
I want to hear what he has to say,
then I'm going let my innovative phraseology fly
and shoot down his arguments once and for all.
My penetrating insights are like hornets,
and they'll prick him blind.
And if I hear so much as a peep out of him,
he'll wish he was dead and buried!

CHORUS:
Now our two antagonists
Will decide which one is cleverest.
The cut and thrust of confrontation,
A war of words and machination.
This ideological contest
Will decide which one is best.
The end result of this demonstration
Is the very future of education!

You crowned the older generation with your morality,
now is your chance to proudly tell us exactly what you stand for.

SUPERIOR:
Then let me begin by explaining how education was run in the good old days
when my just cause was predominant and discretion was the aspiration of every man.
First, it was a given that boys should be seen and not heard and that students
should attend their district schools marching through the streets in orderly pairs
behind the lyre-master. Moreover, they were never allowed to wear cloaks,
even if the snow was falling as thick as porridge. These boys were then taught fine,
patriotic songs, and not to rub their thighs together while seated in the classroom!
Ah, yes what stirring hymns they would sing: "City-destroying Pallas" and "Hark I hear
a far-off tune," and they sung strong and proud like the manly fathers that raised them.
And if any boy engaged in classroom buffoonery or attempted to torture the music
by singing in the cacaphonic, newfangled style of that awful lyre-plucker, Phrynis,

---

971: Phrynis introduced modulations of harmony and rhythm into the traditional music of the *kithara* (lyre).

he was given a damned good thrashing for deliberately perverting the Muses!
Also, while sitting in the gymnasium the boys had to keep their legs closed in order
that they not expose the spectators to any inappropriate and offensive sights.
When they stood up, they had to smooth the sand down where they were sitting
so that they would not leave behind any untoward impressions of their manhood.
No boy was permitted to oil himself below the waist, and consequently each
had a lovely soft down on his balls like a pair of fresh, ripe apricots . . .
They were not permitted to entice older lovers with effeminate voices,
or seductive looks, nor mince around pimping themselves out to all and sundry!
No taking the radish head during dinner, not grabbing an elder's celery stick,
or pulling his parsley, no nibbling on tit-bits, no giggling at the table,
no sitting with legs crossed, no . . .

INFERIOR:
What a load of archaic claptrap! Your speech, sir, reeks of rotten old sacrificial beef,*
it is crawling with grasshoppers and hums to the antiquated strains of Cedeides!

SUPERIOR:
Clearly you are missing the point. It was my system of student tutoring that raised
the men who fought so bravely at Marathon. All you do is train our young to be ashamed

---

985: Golden representations of grasshoppers (cicadas) were worn in the hair of the older generation and were a symbol of the Athenians' origins as "born from the earth of Attica." Cedeides was a dithyrambic poet who composed in an "old-fashioned" style.

987: A famous Athenian victory over a vastly superior Persian force in 490 (*Wasps* ***711 Marathon**).

of themselves and hide behind their cloaks. It grieves me to watch the war dance
at the Panathenaea and to have to see these wimpy lads who can barely lift a shield,
embarrassed at the sight of their own manly meat! It's a disgrace to Athena herself!*
So come on young fellow, the choice is clear: choose me, the Superior Argument.
I'll teach you to detest hanging about in the marketplace, and to keep out of public baths.
You'll learn to be ashamed of the shameful and to burn with indignation when you are ridiculed.
You'll gracefully let your elders and betters have your seat, and you will always treat your
parents with the utmost respect, you will do nothing to harm your personal virtue.
No more chasing in and out of party girls' bedrooms and running the risk of ruining your
reputation because of some harlot's love tokens. No more arguing with your father,
nor insulting his status by calling him a "crusty old fart" or "Cronus' older brother."
No, you'll come to respect all those years he spent raising you from a tiny little chick.

INFERIOR:
Oh dear me, "young fellow," if you take his advice by Dionysus you'll turn out
like those dullard sons of Hippocrates, and be forever known as a little milksop.

SUPERIOR:
Don't listen to him, you'll be forever in the wrestling school, your bronzed body

---

1001: Hippocrates was elected to the Athenian generalship in 426–25. He died at the battle of Delium in 424, leaving three sons, Demophon, Pericles, and Telesippus, who were regarded as uneducated morons by the comic playwrights.

glistening and hard. No wasting precious time twittering away on absurd topics
in the marketplace, nor bickering in the courts, splitting hairs, arguing the toss
and wrangling over some insignificant little suit. We'll see you at the Academy,
bravely racing a friend under the boughs of holy olive-trees, your hair festooned
with fresh cut reeds, surrounded by sweet-scented wildflowers as the catkins
gently fall from the willows. There, you'll not have a care in the world, as the trees
rustle gently in the balmy breeze, and you partake of the joys of spring.
This is the right way for you, my lad, and if you do what I say
you'll be eternally blessed
with a strapping body, a gleaming complexion,
huge shoulders, a tiny little tongue,
big buttocks, and a small cock.*
Should you choose to follow the fashion currently
in vogue amongst the young men of this city,
then it'll be pasty skin, round shoulders,
concave chest, an enormous tongue,
no arse, a great hunk of meat, and a very long . . . turn of phrase!
He will have you believe that what should be shameful
is beautiful, and what should be beautiful is made shameful.
Worst of all, in no time at all he'll turn you into an arse bandit
like that lecherous old queen, Antimachus.

CHORUS:

(Addressing the Superior Argument)

Such elevated sentiments
Extolling high accomplishments,

1005: A public park about a mile from the city that was created for the citizens by Cimon in the 460s and dedicated to the god Academos. It was later to become famous as the site of Plato's school.

1023: This man is unknown and only mentioned here and in Aristophanes' *Acharnians* (line 1150), though the scholia insist that it is not the same person.

Presenting such a fine defense
In praise of pride and sound good sense.
What blessed men you once did raise
Before our time, in olden days.

(Addressing the Inferior Argument]

So be creative with your modern art.
This man has made a very good start.

If you want to avoid looking completely foolish and win this argument,
then I think you had better use some of your crafty techniques.

INFERIOR:
In point of fact, I've been standing here for quite some time
literally busting a gut to confound his ridiculous statements
with my "counterintelligence." Why else do you think the philosophers
named me the Inferior Argument? Because it was I who created
the concept of disputing entrenched ideals and ethics.
My dear boy, don't you see? To be able to take up the Inferior Argument and win
is worth far, far more than any number of silver coins you could care to count.
Let's examine these educational methods that he regards with such great confidence.
First of all, I clearly heard him say that he would abolish all bathing in warm water
Tell me, sir, if you will, the basis for your belief that hot baths are bad?

SUPERIOR:
That they are most reprehensible and make the men who take them effeminate!

INFERIOR:
I've got you! You're quite pinned down and there's no escape!
Now tell me this, which son of Zeus do you believe has the finest
spirit and had successfully undertaken the most labors?

SUPERIOR:
As far as I am concerned, there is no better man than Heracles.

INFERIOR:
Precisely! And have you ever seen a cold Heraclean bath?
And who could possibly be more manly than Heracles?

SUPERIOR:
That's exactly why the gymnasiums are empty, because the youth
of today are all at the bath houses spouting this kind of claptrap!

INFERIOR:
Next, you take exception to our youngsters frequenting the public marketplace,
whereas I wholeheartedly recommend it. After all, if meeting in public is so appalling,
why does Homer describe Nestor and other men of wisdom as "public speakers"?
Let me now take up the issue of the tongue, which he states is not seemly for
the young to exercise. I have to disagree, and am of the opposite opinion.
In addition, he pronounces that one must be discreet, a pair of fatal assumptions.
I would dearly love for you to tell me anyone who gained the slightest benefit
from behaving discreetly, just name them and prove me wrong.

SUPERIOR:
There's plenty. What about Peleus, he won a knife for his discretion.

INFERIOR:
A knife! What a delightful little thing to earn, by Zeus.
Even Hyperbolus, who's made a heap of cash swindling us all

1051: According to legend, natural warm springs were a gift from the craftsman god Hephaestus to Heracles.

1063: Peleus was falsely accused of rape by Hippolyta, the wife of the king of Iolcus, after he had refused her sexual advances. He was banished to Mt. Pelion, where he was left at the mercy of wild beasts. The gods took pity and sent him a knife for protection.

at the lamp market, can't boast that he ever earned a knife!

SUPERIOR:
Thanks to his discretion, Peleus won the right to marry Thetis.

INFERIOR:
Yes, a little too discreet between the sheets, I heard, that's why
she ran out on him, because he simply wasn't outrageous enough in bed.*
You know some women like it that way, you horny old Cronus stud!
Just consider, dear boy, what a life of discretion consists of,
and all the hedonistic delights you would miss out on—boys, girls,
drinking games, fancy food, fine wine, a good laugh.
How on earth could you endure life without these necessities?
Now, let us move on and discuss the needs of human nature.*
Suppose that you've been indulging in an illicit love affair. You are discovered!
A scandal! What will you do? You are finished, because you don't have the means
to argue your way out of trouble. But if you choose to make my acquaintance,
your nature can run free, with a spring in your step and a smile on your face,
and shameful thoughts will never even cross your mind. If the husband accuses you
of adultery, plead innocence and blame Zeus. Say that clearly he can't resist his lust
for women, so how can you, a mere mortal, be expected to have more strength than a god?

1066: Aristophanes calls Hyperbolus a "lamp maker" in *Peace* (line 690) and *Knights* (line 1315). His family may have once sold lamps in the market. Cleon is likewise called a "tanner" (see *Wasps,* note on line 39).

1067: A beautiful sea-nymph coveted by Zeus and Poseidon. She was married to the virtuous and mortal Peleus to nullify a prophecy that she would bear a son more powerful than his father. The son of Peleus and Thetis was Achilles.

1078: Athenian law acquitted a husband of murder if he caught an adulterer engaged in sexual relations with his wife.

SUPERIOR:
Yes, but what if he takes your advice and gets punished by pubic plucking, scrotal singeing,
and a jolly good rectal radish ramming. No argument of yours is going to help him after that!

INFERIOR:
You mean people might think that he was gay?

SUPERIOR:
Yes, what could possibly be worse than that?

INFERIOR:
Will you concede to me if I can prove this point to you?

SUPERIOR:
If you can, you'll not hear another peep out of me.

INFERIOR:
How would you describe most of our lawyers?

SUPERIOR:
They're gay.

INFERIOR:
Quite right, and what about our tragic dramatists?

SUPERIOR:
All gay.

INFERIOR:
Yes, indeed. And our politicians?

SUPERIOR:
Definitely gay.

1084: Adulterers were left at the mercy of the wronged husband. It seems that instead of killing the violator, it was more normal to accept a monetary payment and then inflict a degrading punishment.

1085: The Greek has *euruprôktos,* which means "wide-arse."

INFERIOR:
Then surely you must see that you are defending a lost cause.
I mean, take a good look at the audience,
what would you call most of them?

SUPERIOR:
I'm looking.

INFERIOR:
And what do you see?

SUPERIOR:
By all the gods, most of them are . . . gay!

(He starts pointing at individual members of the audience.)

Well I know he is, and he definitely is,
and that long-haired chap over there and . . . oh my!

INFERIOR:
Well then, what have you got to say for yourself now?

SUPERIOR:
I have to admit that you fuckers
have beaten me.
Here, take my cloak,
I think I might give it a try myself!

(Exit Superior Argument through the stage left door.)

INFERIOR:
(To Strepsiades) Well then, what do you think? Are you and your son going to run off home,
or are you going to leave the boy with me to learn my oratorical arts?

STREPSIADES:
He's all yours to teach, and you have my permission to beat him too.
Remember, I want him to have a razor-sharp tongue, and fully
adjustable too, with one edge honed for petty lawsuits and the other
sharpened for cutting to the chase on more serious matters.

INFERIOR:
Have no fear, he will return an expert in sophistry.

PHEIDIPPIDES:
I'll return a pasty-faced fiend, you mean!

CHORUS:
Go on, off you go.

(Exit Inferior Argument and Pheidippides through the stage left door into the Pondertorium.)

I think that one day you may well
rue the day you did this.

(Exit Strepsiades through the stage right door into his house.)

It's time to tell the judges why we should have first prize,
And why honoring this Cloud chorus will prove extremely wise.
When you're ploughing all your fields and you reach the sowing date,
We'll rain on your land first and make the others wait.
What's more, we'll watch your vines and carefully guard your crops.
We'll stop them getting parched and swamped by huge raindrops.
But if on the other hand you mortals treat us with disrespect
We goddesses will shower you with our malicious effects.
Your lands will yield you nothing, your wine cellars deplete,
For your olives and your grapes will be pelted by our sleet.
When we see you baking bricks and laying tiles of clay,
We'll crack them with our hail, then wash them all away.
Should a friend or family member happen to be wed,
We'll blow a gale all night and keep him from his bed.
You'd rather be in Egypt sizzling in the desert sun,
Than make an unfair judgment and not vote us number one!

(Enter Strepsiades from the stage right door.)

1115: Athenian plays were presented as part of a dramatic competition in honor of the god Dionysus and would have been judged by a panel of referees. The chorus also address the judges in *Birds* (lines 1102–17).

STREPSIADES:

Let's see now; five, four, three, two . . . oh no, only two more days
until the old-and-new day at the end of the month, the day I fear
the most, the day that makes me tremble, the day that gives me the jitters,
the day that debts are due! Every last one of my creditors will have
paid their court fees and are planning to destroy me, once and for all!
They won't listen: I've pleaded with them to give me more time, begged
to have my credit extended, implored them to write off my debts.
But nothing works, they all want paying, they just call me a criminal,
hurl abuse, and threaten me with the law! The unfeeling bastards!

(He walks toward the stage left door.)

Well, let them try it, that's what I say, they can take me to court
for all I care, they'll be sorry, if my Pheidippides has learned how
to talk the talk. Well there's only one way to find out, I'll give the
Pondertorium a knock and see if he's ready.

(Strepsiades knocks on the door.)

Boy! Boy! Open up! Boy!

(Enter Socrates.)

SOCRATES:

Ah, Strepsiades, good day to you.

STREPSIADES:

Likewise mate! I've brought you a little gift, here.

*(Strepsiades hands Socrates a small bag of barley.)**

It's right and proper to bring a present for the teacher.

1131: Days were counted forward until the twentieth, when, in accordance with the waning of the moon, they ran backward. The final day of the month was called the "old-and-new day" as there was said to be no moon until the first day of the next month.

1135: Due to the transitory nature of the "old-and-new day," it was set aside for the collection of debts, interest, and the placing of court deposits to register proceedings against a debtor.

Has my lad learned the argument, you know, the one
that did that little turn for us a while ago?

SOCRATES:
Indeed he has.

STREPSIADES:
Oh, Mistress of Misrepresentation, how marvelous!

SOCRATES:
Now you will be able to contest all the litigation you please.

STREPSIADES:
What? Even if a witness swore that they saw me borrow the cash?

SOCRATES:
Even if there were a thousand witnesses!

(Strepsiades breaks into a joyous song.)

STREPSIADES:
*Then be it known, let my shouts attest**
That all the moneylenders have cause to mourn,
For I banish your debts and compound interest.
I've no more need to endure your scorn.

For today my prodigy has sprung
From within these very walls
Armed with a glinting two-edged tongue
To save my house and foes forestall.

So run and fetch him with a shout,
He will relieve his father's woes.
Call my child, have him come out,
*Come forth my son, it is time to go.**

(Enter Pheidippides from the stage left door.)

1150: Strepsiades has already embraced "Basin" (*dinos*) as a god. It seems only natural that he would now be worshipping this fictitious goddess of fraud.

SOCRATES:
I believe this is the man you are looking for.

STREPSIADES:
My dear boy! My dear, dear boy!

SOCRATES:
Take him and be on your way.

(Exit Socrates through the stage left door.)

STREPSIADES:
My son! My child!
Hooray! Hooray!
Just let me look at you! What a lovely skin tone!
I can see the contention and the negation written all over your face.
You look like a true Athenian now, with our characteristic "I've no idea
what you're talking about" look blooming in your cheeks. Why, you've even
picked up the look-of-righteous-indignation-even-when-you're-in-the-wrong expression.
Now you can save me, since it was you who got me into this mess in the first place.

PHEIDIPPIDES:
What are you are so afraid of?

STREPSIADES:
Why, the old-and-new day, of course!

PHEIDIPPIDES:
Are you trying to tell me that there's a day that's both old and new?

STREPSIADES:
Of course there is! It's the day when my creditors will file their court deposits.

1172: Presumably the actor playing Pheidippides has changed his mask and now resembles the students met at line 133, with a pallid complexion and gaunt features.

PHEIDIPPIDES:
Then, they'll lose their money, won't they? There's no way that one day
can suddenly become two days, is there?

STREPSIADES:
Isn't there?

PHEIDIPPIDES:
Of course not. I mean that's like saying that a single woman could be both
a young girl and an old woman at exactly the same time.

STREPSIADES:
But it's the law.

PHEIDIPPIDES:
No, no, no. They've obviously completely misconstrued the law.

STREPSIADES:
What does the law really mean, then?

PHEIDIPPIDES:
Solon, the elder statesman, was essentially a benefactor of the people, correct?

STREPSIADES:
What's that got to do with the old-and-new day?

PHEIDIPPIDES:
He was the one who decreed that there should be two days
set aside for the issuing of court summonses, and that all deposits
must be lodged on the new day.

STREPSIADES:
Then why did he add the old day too?

1187: Solon was a sixth-century Athenian statesman, lawgiver, and poet. He abolished the practice of placing a free man in slavery for the nonpayment of debts. He was widely regarded as a wise benefactor and founding father of the Athenian state.

PHEIDIPPIDES:
My dear fellow, to give the accused the opportunity to settle out of court
one day prior to their scheduled trials. Then they would avoid harassment
by their creditors until the actual morning of the new day.*

STREPSIADES:
If that's the case, why do the court officials receive deposits
on the old *and* new day instead of just on the new day?

PHEIDIPPIDES:
Isn't it obvious, they're double-dipping.
They're just like the festival taste-testers*
filching a foretaste of the fees as fast as is feasible!

STREPSIADES:
Ha ha! You poor fools! You don't stand a chance! Look at you simpletons sitting
out there, just begging to be ripped off by us members of the intelligentsia!
You're dunderheads, clods, and empty vessels, nothing but a herd of sheep!
It is time I serenaded this splendid good fortune
with a nice hymn in honor of me and my son.

(Strepsiades breaks into song.)

"O, Strepsiades, you are the lucky one
So fortunate and so wise,
You've raised a fine, upstanding son."
Thus my friends will eulogize.

When they find out I have a winner,
You'll see the jealousy on their faces,
So let's celebrate with a great big dinner
Before you argue all my cases.

1213: It is not known where the creditors enter from, possibly from behind the scene building and onto the stage from stage left. An entrance from the orchestra wings would have taken too long.

(Exit Strepsiades and Pheidippides through the stage right door. Enter First Creditor and a witness.)

FIRST CREDITOR:
So what's a man supposed to do, throw his own money down the drain?
Not likely, I shouldn't have felt so embarrassed, I should have just said no
right when he asked me for the loan, then I wouldn't be in this mess.*

(Addressing the witness)

And I wouldn't have to waste your time dragging you all the way down here
to witness a summons for money that was rightfully mine in the first place.
Both ways I lose, either my money or the good will of a neighbor.
It's no good worrying about it, I have my duty as a true Athenian,
I must go to court. I hereby summon Strepsiades to appear in . . .

(Enter Strepsiades from the stage right door.)

STREPSIADES:
Who is it?

FIRST CREDITOR:
. . . in court on the old-and-new day.

STREPSIADES:
Did you hear that? He's summoned me on two different days.
Why, pray, are you summoning me?

FIRST CREDITOR:
You owe me twelve hundred drachmas. You borrowed
the money to purchase that dapple-gray horse.

STREPSIADES:
A horse! Did you hear that? Everyone knows that I can't stand horses.

1225: The same amount entered in Strepsiades' ledger as "owed to Pasias" (line 23). The First Creditor may indeed be Pasias in person.

FIRST CREDITOR:
You made a sacred oath before the gods that you would repay me.

STREPSIADES:
Indeed I did, but you see, that was before my lad Pheidippides had gone and learned the unbeatable Argument.

FIRST CREDITOR:
I see, and I suppose now you think you can simply forgo your debts?

STREPSIADES:
Don't you think it's reasonable that I receive some benefit from his education?

FIRST CREDITOR:
Well then, if that's the way you want it. Are you willing to refute your oath before the gods while standing on sacred ground?

STREPSIADES:
Which particular gods?

FIRST CREDITOR:
Zeus, Hermes, and Poseidon.

STREPSIADES:
Of course! I'd even pay three obols for the privilege.

(The First Creditor is shocked and angry, becoming agitated and animated.)

FIRST CREDITOR:
By all the gods! May you be damned for your blasphemy!

(Strepsiades grabs hold of the First Creditor and pats him on the belly.)

STREPSIADES:
You know if we were to split you open and rub you down with salt, your belly would make a lovely wineskin.

FIRST CREDITOR:
How dare you!

STREPSIADES:
It'd hold at least four jugs' worth.

FIRST CREDITOR:
By Zeus almighty, by all the gods, you'll never get away with this!

STREPSIADES:
Ha, ha! That's a good one that is, "by all the gods!" Don't make me laugh!
Those of us "in the know" realize that Zeus is just a joke.

FIRST CREDITOR:
I'm telling you, soon enough, you'll pay for this. Just tell me one thing,
do you have any intention of paying what you owe me?

STREPSIADES:
Hang on, I'll let you know . . .

(Strepsiades runs inside the stage right door.)

FIRST CREDITOR:
(To the witness) What's he up to now? Do you reckon he's going to pay me?

(Strepsiades comes out again holding a kneading board.)

STREPSIADES:
Where's that man demanding money? Right then, tell me what this is?

FIRST CREDITOR:
That? It's a meal-kneader, of course.

STREPSIADES:
And you have the gall to ask me for money! How could you be so stupid?

1239: This seemingly nonsensical diversion into pure physical comedy may actually be a comic reference to Strepsiades' abortive attempts to grasp the concepts of "measures" taught by Socrates (lines 641–45).

You won't catch me parting with a single obol to such a moron.
You're the one who "needs the fee," it's obviously a "fe-meal kneader."

(Strepsiades tries to dismiss the First Creditor.)

FIRST CREDITOR:
I take it that you have no intention of paying your debt.

STREPSIADES:
Not likely, now turn around, get off my doorstep, go on, piss off!

FIRST CREDITOR:
I will go, straight to the court to lodge my deposit.
I'll see you prosecuted if it's the last thing I do!

(Exit First Creditor and Witness.)

STREPSIADES:
You'll just be adding that to those twelve hundred drachmas and increasing
your losses. Will you people never learn?
I feel sorry for him really, I mean, imagine not knowing your gender!

(Enter Second Creditor.)

SECOND CREDITOR:
Oh, no! No!

STREPSIADES:
Ah!
What now! Who the blazes is this chap, warbling dirges?
Looks like he's wandered away from a scene in a tragedy.

SECOND CREDITOR:
Why do you care to know my name? I am doomed, doomed!*

1261: The Greek names Carcinus here, a tragic dramatist who had won first place at the City Dionysia in 446. See *Wasps*, note on line 1502.

STREPSIADES:
Well go and be doomed somewhere else, will you!

SECOND CREDITOR:
Oh, heartless demons, oh calamity that destroyed my chariot!*
Oh, Pallas Athena, you have brought me rack and ruin!

STREPSIADES:
The true tragedy is how you're mutilating those lines.

SECOND CREDITOR:
You may mock me, sir, but all I want is for your son to repay the money that he borrowed from me, particularly in light of my recent hapless misadventure.

STREPSIADES:
What money?

SECOND CREDITOR:
The money that I lent him.

STREPSIADES:
Oh dear, I can see that you're in a bit of a mess.

SECOND CREDITOR:
I was rounding a bend and fell out of my chariot.

STREPSIADES:
Out of your mind, more like! I think you're the one who's "round the bend," coming here spouting gibberish.

SECOND CREDITOR:
It is not gibberish, I just want to be repaid!

STREPSIADES:
You're clearly quite insane, a lost cause, I'm afraid.

SECOND CREDITOR:
What do you mean?

STREPSIADES:
I believe that you have been knocked senseless, your brain's addled.

SECOND CREDITOR:
And I believe that I'll be seeing you in court, by Hermes,
if you don't pay me back the money that I'm owed!

STREPSIADES:
Tell me something, when Zeus makes it rain, do you believe that he sends
fresh water each time, or that the sun absorbs the moisture from the earth,
reclaims it, and sends it back down again in the form of a rain shower?

SECOND CREDITOR:
I have absolutely no idea, and I don't see what it has to do with . . .

STREPSIADES:
Well how can you justify reclaiming your money if you
don't understand the rudiments of meteorology?

SECOND CREDITOR:
Listen, if you can't handle the whole payment this month,
then how about just paying me the interest?

STREPSIADES:
What do you mean, "interest"? I'm not in the least bit interested in your problems.*

SECOND CREDITOR:
I mean the charge on the loan that increases in size
from day to day and month to month as time flows on by.

STREPSIADES:
That's all very well, but do you think the sea
has increased in size at all since olden times?

SECOND CREDITOR:
By Zeus, of course not, it would be against
the law of nature for the sea to change in size.

1281: This parodies the theories of Anaximander, Diogenes, and other natural philosophers.

STREPSIADES:
Well then, you pitiful wretch, if the sea doesn't increase in size with all the rivers flowing into it, who the blazes do you think you are to try and increase the size of your loan! Now bugger off away from my house, or you'll get a damn good prodding!

(Strepsiades calls inside his house.)

Boy! Bring me my cattle prod!

(A slave rushes out of the stage right door with a cattle prod.)

SECOND CREDITOR:
Help! Somebody witness this!

(Strepsiades starts prodding the Second Creditor.)

STREPSIADES:
Giddy up! Get up there! Get going before I brand your horse's arse!

SECOND CREDITOR:
This is outrageous! I protest!

(Strepsiades continues his assault.)

STREPSIADES:
Giddy up! Move it! Or I'll make a gelding out of you!

(The Second Creditor flees offstage, and Strepsiades calls out after him.)

Oh, you can move quickly enough when you want to! You can take your
horses and your chariot wheels and stick them where the sun don't shine!

(Exit Strepsiades through the stage right door.)

CHORUS:
Depravity often proves a fatal attraction
That can drive an old man to distraction.

1297: The Greek has *kentron* ("goad" or "point"), which has phallic connotations and is also employed in *Wasps* (lines 225, 408, 115).

This one thinks he can evade his debts,
So he'll push his luck and hedge his bets.
But we all know that one day soon,
There will come an end to this honeymoon,
That will force our sophist roughly back
From his latest wicked track.

For he will discover presently
The consequences of his desperate plea.
For his son has learned the wily art
Of successfully arguing the unjust part.
He defeats all opponents however strong
Even when his case is plainly wrong.
But I have a feeling that these disputes
Will make him wish that his son was mute!

(Enter a disheveled Strepsiades running out of the stage right door.)

STREPSIADES:
Oh! Oh!
Help me! Friends, relatives, citizens, help!
Come quickly! I'm in terrible danger! Please!
I'm under attack, he's pummeling my head,
gashing my cheeks! Help me! Help me!

(Enter Pheidippides from the stage right door, looking very smug.)

You monster! You would dare to strike your own father?*

PHEIDIPPIDES:
That's right, old man.

STREPSIADES:
You hear that? He even admits to it!

PHEIDIPPIDES:
Freely.

STREPSIADES:
You're despicable, a father beater and a criminal!

PHEIDIPPIDES:
Oh, say those things again, more, more.
You know how I just love to be insulted.

STREPSIADES:
You filthy arsehole!

PHEIDIPPIDES:
Please, keep showering me with roses.

STREPSIADES:
You would dare to raise a hand against your own father?

PHEIDIPPIDES:
Of course I would by Zeus, and moreover I was perfectly
justified in giving you a beating, as well.

STREPSIADES:
You little bugger! How can striking your own father ever be right?

PHEIDIPPIDES:
I'll prove it to you, by arguing my view, and I'll win too.

STREPSIADES:
You'll never win on this point. It's impossible!

PHEIDIPPIDES:
On the contrary, it'll be a walkover. So, decide
which of the two Arguments you want to present.

STREPSIADES:
Which two Arguments?

PHEIDIPPIDES:
The Superior or Inferior.

STREPSIADES:
It's unbelievable, and to think it was I who had you
educated to argue successfully against Justice.
But there's absolutely no way that you're going to be able
to convince me that it is right for a son to beat his own father.

PHEIDIPPIDES:

Oh, but I shall convince you. In fact, you'll be so convinced once you've heard
me out, that you'll have nothing at all worthwhile to say on the matter.

STREPSIADES:

Go on then, let's hear what you have to say for yourself, I can't wait.

CHORUS:

Old man, it's time you started thinking
About what you need to say to win,
He would not be quite so arrogant
If he did not have an argument.
So be aware of his self-assurance,
It is the reason for his insolence.

CHORUS:

Please tell the chorus how you came to be involved in this dispute.
Tell us in your own words what actually happened.

STREPSIADES:

Oh, I'll tell you all right, you'll hear every sordid detail of this horrible squabble.
We were inside enjoying a nice dinner when I asked him to fetch his lyre
and sing us an after dinner song. I suggested he do a bit of "Hark the Hallowed Ram
Was Shorn" by Simonides, but he would have none of it. No, he told me that strumming
a lyre and singing at dinner parties was "terribly passé" and said that only old women
grinding barley at the stone sing those kinds of songs anymore!*

PHEIDIPPIDES:

Yes, and that explains why you received a thrashing. Who do you think you are,

---

1356: Simonides (c.556–468) was a prolific poet who created choral lyrics, dithyrambs, laments, and victory songs.

ordering me to croon some monotonous old song like a chirping grasshopper?

STREPSIADES:
That's exactly the kind of talk he was spouting inside, and what's more,
he even had the gall to announce that Simonides was a terrible poet!
I just couldn't believe my ears. Well, I swallowed my anger, for the moment,
and asked him ever so nicely to pick up the myrtle bough and recite a little
Aeschylus for me, and do you know what he said! "Oh yes, Aeschylus, surely
the foremost of all poets at being loud, pompous, bombastic, and inaccessible."
Well, I nearly had a heart attack I was so angry at him, but yet again, I curbed
my fury and said calmly, "Why don't you come up with some of that clever
modern stuff, something from one of those fashionable poets you're always
going on about." And with that he blurted out some disgusting lines from Euripides,
about a brother and sister going at it together! Well, that was it, the last straw,
I could contain myself no longer, and I let him have it, I told him
just what I thought and it wasn't pretty either, what's more he answered
me back with some of the foulest language I have ever heard. At that moment
he leapt to his feet and weighed into me, first pushing and shoving, then he grabbed
my throat and started shaking me and punching and kicking. It was terrible!

1365: Aeschylus (525/4–456/5) was one of the most famous and respected Athenian tragedians.

1370: This tragic dramatist (485/4?–407/6) was a contemporary of Aristophanes. This could be a reference to Euripides' *Aeolus* (fr. 14–41), the brother being Macareus and the sister Canace.

PHEIDIPPIDES:
I was well within my rights to punish you, after you dared to insult a gifted man like Euripides.

STREPSIADES:
Gifted! He's just a . . . No, you'll only lay into me all over again.

PHEIDIPPIDES:
And I'd be justified too, by Zeus!

STREPSIADES:
How would you be justified? You insolent ruffian, have you forgotten who raised you?
I was the one who had to listen to your lisping baby talk, when you went "wu-wu!"
I knew what you wanted and would fetch you something to drink. Then you would go
"foo-foo!" and daddy here would get you some bread. And when you cried "poo-poo!"
it was me who would pick you up, take you outside, and let you do your little doo-doos!
But you, on the other hand, couldn't care less about my needs. Why just then, when you
were strangling me, I was completely ignored, even though I was screaming that I was
about to shit my pants, you just kept right on throttling away. You literally squeezed
the crap out of me, and I did my poo-poo right there and then!
It's a disgraceful way to treat your dear old dad.

CHORUS:
The hearts of the young are all a flutter
To hear what words this lad might utter
To justify such disrespect
Could ever be deemed correct
For such an outcome would surely mean
That an old man's hide's not worth a bean!

CHORUS:
Now, you mover and shaker, you maestro of modernity, it is your turn.
You must persuade him to accept your point of view.

PHEIDIPPIDES:

Let me first say how pleasurable it is to be acquainted with modern ways and intelligent
notions, for it enables one to disdain conventional practices from a superior vantage point.
When I filled my brain with only the mindless thoughts of horse riding I could hardly even blurt
out three words without making some stupid mistake. But thanks to my adversary here,
who saw to my education, I now possess a keen intellect and am proficient in finite conception,
subtle argument, and detailed contemplation. In effect, I believe that I have the necessary skills
to fully demonstrate that it is perfectly justified to discipline one's own father.

STREPSIADES:

I wish you'd go back to your horses, by Zeus! I would much rather have to pay
for a four-horse chariot team than run the risk of sustaining bodily harm every day!

PHEIDIPPIDES:

If I may be allowed to return to the point in my argument from where I was so rudely
interrupted. Tell me this, did you ever have occasion to beat me when I was a child?

STREPSIADES:

Yes, but it was always for your own good. I had your best interests at heart.

PHEIDIPPIDES:

Then surely it is justified for me to beat you for your own good, if, by your definition,
"having someone else's best interests at heart" means to beat them? How is it justified
that your body should be protected against beatings but mine not? Is it not true that we

are both free men? "Suffer the little children, do you think the father should not?"
No doubt you will attempt to defend yourself by stating that it is quite legitimate for
this kind of punishment to be meted out to children, and yet, I would say that the
elderly are living a "second childhood." This being the case, surely it is only right
that the elderly should be chastised more severely than the young, as they should
have certainly learned right and wrong after a lifetime of experience.

STREPSIADES:
There's not a place in the world where it is legitimate for a son to beat his father!

PHEIDIPPIDES:
But it is men who make legislation, men just like you and me. In past times,
one man simply persuaded another that this was the way things should be.*
Therefore what is preventing me from similarly stating a new "law" for times to come
specifying that sons should be permitted to beat their fathers in return?
"This will not be retroactive legislation, and all claims for compensation for blows
previously sustained will not be considered and shall hereby be stricken from the record."
Examine chickens and other such farmyard animals, you will see that they freely
attack their fathers, and how are they so very different from us?
Except, of course, that they refrain from drafting statutes.

1414: This is a parody of a line from Euripides' *Alcestis* (691) originally produced in 438 (***1414 Alcestis**).

1426: A lampoon on the legal language found in contemporary Athenian decrees.

1428: See *Birds* lines 1349–50.

STREPSIADES:
If you're so keen to take after farmyard fowl, why don't you start eating chicken shit and roosting on a perch in the hen house?

PHEIDIPPIDES:
Sir, your analogy is hardly relevant, and I am sure Socrates would agree with me.

STREPSIADES:
Then stop hitting me, otherwise you'll come to regret it.

PHEIDIPPIDES:
And why would that be?

STREPSIADES:
Well, when you have a son of your own,
you'll not have the right to beat him, as I did you!

PHEIDIPPIDES:
But what if I don't have a son, then I would have suffered
for nothing, and you'll be laughing at me from beyond the grave.

(Strepsiades addresses the audience.)

STREPSIADES:
You know what, friends, he does have a point, and it seems
only proper that we give the young the benefit of the doubt now and again.
I suppose it's only reasonable that we should suffer a little if we step out of line.

PHEIDIPPIDES:
And another thing . . .

STREPSIADES:
No! I can't take it any more!

PHEIDIPPIDES:
Just listen, perhaps it will make your suffering seem not so bad.

STREPSIADES:
What are you talking about? Nothing could comfort my pain.

PHEIDIPPIDES:
I shall beat Mother just as I beat you.

STREPSIADES:
WHAT! What are you saying? This is going from bad to worse!

PHEIDIPPIDES:
But I can use the inferior argument to defeat you on this very subject.
I can prove that it is right to beat one's mother.

STREPSIADES:
And what then?
What then? I ask you!
You're all doomed!
You're going to throw yourself into the abyss.
You, Socrates, and that damned Inferior Argument!

(Strepsiades looks up and calls out.)

Clouds! This is all your fault, you're responsible!
I trusted you, I believed in you!

CHORUS:
You brought this trouble on yourself when you took
the twisting path of wickedness and deceit.

STREPSIADES:
But why didn't you tell me that in the first place?
I'm just a simple old yokel. You lured me into this mess!

CHORUS:
But we always do this.
When we discover a mortal who becomes
enamored by vice, we drive them to despair.
That is how we teach man to have proper respect for the gods.

STREPSIADES:
Oh, Clouds, you've treated me harshly, but you're right,

I should never have tried to get of out paying my debts.

(To Pheidippides)

Come on, my lad, let's get even with Socrates and Chaerephon,
those villains, it's high time they met their makers!
Let's pay them back for the vile way they deceived us.

PHEIDIPPIDES:
But I must not offend my teachers.

STREPSIADES:
Yes, yes, and "we venerate Zeus protector of fathers."

PHEIDIPPIDES:
Just listen to you, "father Zeus." You're so old fashioned!
Zeus doesn't exist.

STREPSIADES:
Yes he does.

PHEIDIPPIDES:
No he doesn't. "Zeus has been overthrown, Basin is king now."

STREPSIADES:
He hasn't been overthrown, I was misled by this basin.

(Indicating the wine basin set on a stand outside the Pondertorium.)

Oh, what a stupid wretch I am, to believe that a piece
of clay pottery could ever be a god!

PHEIDIPPIDES:
I've had enough of you. You can rant and rave to yourself. I'm not listening!

1469: This is more than likely an unknown quote from a tragedy referring to Zeus Patroos, the protector and patron god of fathers.

(Exit Pheidippides into the house, through the stage right door.)

STREPSIADES:

Oh, I must have been completely out of my mind,
to think I rejected the gods because Socrates told me to.
Unbelievable! What was I thinking? Dear, dear Hermes,*
take pity on me, please be kind, don't destroy me now.
I know I behaved like a raving maniac, but it was all because of them
and their philosophical drivel. I need you now, help me, tell me what
can I do to redeem myself? Should I file a lawsuit against them?
What? What can I do?

(Strepsiades suddenly realizes what he must do.)

Yes, that's it, that's exactly right,
I'm not going to fiddle around with lawsuits, no, I'll burn
those babbling bastards out, that's what I'll do! Xanthias! Xanthias!
Come here at once and bring the ladder and an axe!

(A slave comes running out of the stage right door with a ladder and an axe. He lays the ladder on the scene building.)

I want you to climb up onto the roof of the Pondertorium
and do a hatchet job on their roof, and if you care anything
for your poor old master, you'll really bring the house down
on those charlatans. Light up a torch and hand it to me!*

(Xanthias hands him a flaming torch.)

Now it's my turn to call in the debts, those colossal cheats
are going to pay dearly for what they put me through!

*(Strepsiades and Xanthius climb up onto the roof of the scene building.)**

STUDENT:

Oh! Oh!

STREPSIADES:

"Come torch, send on your mighty blaze!"

(Enter a student from the stage left door hatch, who sees Strepsiades on the roof.)

STUDENT 1:
You there! What are you up to?

STREPSIADES:
I'm demonstrating to your rafters the finer points of my axe!

*(Enter another student from the window.)**

STUDENT 2:
Ahhh! Who set our house on fire?

STREPSIADES:
You should know, you thieves, you lot stole his cloak!

STUDENT 1:
You'll kill us all! Kill us all!

STREPSIADES:
Well at least you're right about that, as long as I don't
get carried away with my axe and come a cropper!

(Enter Socrates from the window.)

SOCRATES:
You up there, whatever do you think you are doing?

STREPSIADES:
I am "walking the air to look down on the sun!"

(Enter Chaerephon from the stage left door.)

CHAEREPHON:
Ahhh! Help! I'm suffocating!

SOCRATES:
What about me? I'm going up in smoke!

STREPSIADES:
It serves you right for daring to think that you could snub the gods

and spy on the moon when she's all exposed. Outrageous!
Chase then down, smash bash and crash them! We'll teach them
a hundred lessons, but most of all never to offend the gods above!

(Exit Strepsiades and Xanthias into the Pondertorium.)

CHORUS:
And now it's time we closed this play
We've performed enough for you today!

(Exit the chorus rapidly offstage.)

–END–

Clouds: Endnotes

Stage Direction: Strepsiades. The name means "son of Twister" and becomes appropriate through the course of the play as Strepsiades attempts to "twist" his way out of his debts. For the meaning of "Pheidippides" see the note on line 66.

Stage Direction: Asleep. Strepsiades and his son may be lying on the *ekkyklema*—the moveable platform that either revolved or was trucked from the central doorway. If this was the case, it could have been withdrawn at some point during the opening scene once both characters were awake.

8: Enemy territory. Shortly after the original production of *Clouds* in March of 423 B.C.E., Athens and Sparta settled on a one-year truce. One of the terms was that neither party should receive deserters. Previously, runaway slaves had been granted immunity if they reached enemy territory.

24: Taken for a ride. The Greek has "the horse with the *koppa* brand." Koppa was an old letter of the Greek alphabet that had fallen out of use by the fifth century but could still be found as a brand mark for livestock. Aristophanes creates a pun on *koppa* and *koptein* (to strike/knock) with the next line, which reads, "I would rather have knocked my eye out with a stone."

38: Bed bailiffs. The Greek names the Demarch, the highest elected official presiding over one of the 139 demes, the small administrative areas that formed Attica. The deme had its own assembly and local government and the Demarch was responsible in administering the collection of debts.

48: Little lady. The Greek has "all Coesyrated," a reference to Coesyra, another prominent member of the Alcmaeonid clan. She is named as an aristocrat in Aristophanes' *Acharnians* (line 614).

52: Aphrodite all over and everywhere Eros. The Greek has "All Colias and Genetyllis." Colias was a promontory near Phaleron where a sanctuary of Aphrodite, the goddess of love, was located. There is also a pun on *Kôlias* (Colias) and *kôlê* (penis). Genetyllis was a sacred spirit associated with Aphrodite and lovemaking.

55: Whacking it. A sexual double entendre for excessive sexual intercourse, extravagance, and the wasting of wealth (Henderson 1991, pp. 171–72).

70: Drive a chariot. Such a scene is depicted on the Parthenon frieze (South frieze slab XXX, Boardman *GS2* fig. 96.7). Pindar celebrated the victory of Megacles in a chariot race at Delphi held in 486 in his Seventh Pythian Ode.

83: God of horses. As well as being the god of the sea and the "earth shaker," Poseidon was known as "Hippios," the god of horses. This cult was quite widespread in Greece, and he was often depicted with horses or riding a chariot. In myth Poseidon is often credited with fathering the horse (Burkert 1985, pp. 136–39).

98: Casserole dish. The Greek has "baking cover," a clay covering used to bake bread and heated by stacking hot coals around it. The comic playwright Cratinus attributed this analogy of the universe to the philosopher Hippon (fr. 155). It is also found in *Birds* lines 1000–1. (For a pictorial representation of a baking cover see Sparkes and Talbot, figs. 36 and 37.)

103: Barefoot. In Plato's *Symposium* (220b) Alcibiades tells how Socrates went barefoot even in the bitter cold of Thrace when they served together during the Potidaea campaign in 431. Also in the *Symposium* (174a) Apollodorus tells of how he saw Socrates wearing sandals and describes this as "an unusual event." Socrates explained that he was going out to dinner and wanted to look his best.

104: Chaerephon. He was lampooned for his pallid, sickly appearance which earned him the nickname of "the living dead" or "the bat" (*Birds* lines 1296 and 1564). No written works by Chaerephon have survived, but he is famous for asking the oracle at Delphi if there was anyone wiser than Socrates (Plato *Apology* 21a). He died shortly before the trial of Socrates in 399. He also appears as a witness in *Wasps* (line 1408).

113-14: Superior and Inferior Arguments. The origin of this notion may be the sophist Protagoras (490–420) who authored a treatise called "Controversial Argument" that set out how to turn the weaker argument into a strong and winning defense. Protagoras was credited with being the first philosopher to charge fees for teaching rhetoric, taking advantage of the new Athenian democratic institutions where political dominance was secured by the mastering of oratorical skills. This new command of public speaking taught by the sophists had caused a sensation in the Assembly in 427 when Gorgias of Leontini (483–376) delivered a speech championing his city's cause against Syracuse. His use of new oratorical techniques stunned the Athenian citizens and enabled him to remain in Athens teaching these methods. According to Plato, Socrates refuted these very lines and used them as an example of the falsehoods spoken about him by the Athenians (*Apology* 18b and 19b).

145: One flea foot. The close attention paid to the movements of a flea lampoons the sophists and in particular, Socrates' methodology whereby concepts and notions would be expounded, questioned, and analyzed in minute detail. (See lines 740-42.) Socrates himself admitted that his methods were often misinterpreted, and this led to a degree of confusion and hostility (Plato *Apology* 23a).

151: Booties. The Greek has simply "Persians," a type of soft boot worn by women (see Brooke, pp. 73–74).

174: Speckled gecko. In Plato's *Symposium* (220d), Alcibiades tells how Socrates would spend hours standing in one spot considering a problem. In this particular instance, while on active military duty in Potidaea, he stayed in one place all day and all the following night, much to the amusement of his fellow soldiers who camped out to watch him. Likewise, the philosopher Thales was said to have been so preoccupied with gazing up at the sky that he fell down a well and killed himself (Plato *Theaetetus* 174a). The relevance of the gecko joke was unearthed by Carl Anderson in *Classical Philology* 93.1 (1998): 49.

179: Wrestling school. In Plato's *Symposium* (217c) Alcibiades describes how as a young man, he would encourage Socrates to visit him at the gymnasium. See Plato's *Lysias* (203a) for an account of Socrates visiting the wrestling schools.

186: Walking wounded. The Greek has "Spartans we captured at Pylos, after spending a year in our jails." An Athenian force under the command of Cleon and Demosthenes had defeated the Spartans stationed at Sphacteria, near Pylos, two years earlier in 425. The Athenians refused all representations to free them, stating that they would be held until a peace agreement was reached, or killed if Attica was invaded (Thucydides 4.37-41).

188: What lies beneath. This was one of the charges brought against Socrates at his trial. "Socrates is guilty of criminal meddling, in that he inquires into things below the earth and in the sky" (Plato *Apology* 18b).

201: Astronomy. Socrates himself did not seem to hold astronomy in particularly high regard (Plato *Republic* 527d), although there where notable contemporary practitioners in Athens who were linked to the Sophistic movement such as Hippias of Elis and Diogenes of Apollonia.

203: Landlords. The Greek has "cleruchs." These were landlords who had confiscated land allotted to them by the state. In 427 the Athenians successfully put down the revolt of Mytilene (in modern day Lesbos). The land was confiscated and distributed by lot to Athenian citizens who became absentee landlords, receiving rent from the remaining locals (Thucydides 3.50).

Stage Direction: Enter Socrates. Socrates appears suspended over the stage by means of the *machina* (stage crane). He is seated on a board slung at each end by ropes that look like a rack used to dry fruit and vegetables.

223: Ephemeral. The Greek term *ephêmeros* means "a life worth but a day." The same term is found at *Birds* line 687 and Plato's *Laws* 11.923a.

225: Look down on the sun. To most Greeks the sun was Helios, a god, and not a natural element. Socrates is reported by Plato (*Apology* 19c) to have referred to this scene at his trial where he describes his portrayal in "that Aristophanes play where Socrates was shown whirling about announcing that he is walking in the air and all sorts of other nonsense that I know nothing about."

236: A good brainwashing. The Greek has Socrates comparing the effects of the earth on his mind to the growth of watercress. Strepsiades responds, "So thought draws moisture to watercress?"

246: Pay you. Several notable sophists were paid substantial fees for their educational services. In Plato's *Apology* (20a), Socrates denies ever charging a fee for teaching and names Gorgias of Leontini, Prodicus of Ceos, Hippias of Elis, and Callias of Paros (who, according to Socrates, was paid more than the other three combined) as all having received payment for teaching. Socrates does not condemn this practice but makes it clear that the assumption that he made money from his pursuits is false.

249: Byzantine. The Greek has "Do you use those iron bars from Byzantium?" This was a Greek colony on the site of modern day Istanbul, and it used large, heavy iron bars as currency. Iron bars were also thrown into the sea to seal oaths. This form of coinage was common in many Greek states in the archaic period. The Spartans also used such currency, apparently to discourage the accumulation of wealth (Plutarch *Lycurgus* 9). Interestingly Plutarch comments that due to the worthlessness of this iron currency, imports to Sparta were virtually halted, and therefore "no instructor of rhetoric ever set foot on Spartan soil."

257: Make a meal out of me. The Greek has "make an Athamas out of me." Athamas was a legendary Boeotian king who married Nephele ("Cloud"). He had two children by Nephele, Phrixus and Helle, and went on to marry Ino, who became jealous of her semidivine stepchildren. Ino devised a false prophecy which demanded their deaths to curb a famine. Nephele saved her children by means of flying them off on a golden ram. Helle fell into the sea, giving her name to the Hellespont, but Phrixus was taken to safety in Colchis. Athamas was then offered for sacrifice in their place and in some versions rescued by Heracles. Sophocles had presented two tragedies named *Athamas;* one apparently contained a scene depicting Athamas standing by the altar of Zeus, wreathed for sacrifice. Walter Burkert (1983, pp. 114–115) finds a link between the Athamas story and weather magic, which would help explain the relevance of this reference in foreshadowing Socrates' notions of weather, clouds, and Zeus.

260: Rattling castanet. The same term is used of Odysseus' speaking skills in Euripides' *Cyclops* (line 104).

262: A good dusting. The fine flour that "baptizes" Strepsiades is both a parody of initiation rites (new members of the Orphic cult were sprinkled with chalk), and a further joke on the finite nature of sophistic inquiry.

292: Thunderclaps. The theatre at this time may have been equipped with a thunder machine which was used at this point. The use of such a machine called a *bronteion* is suggested by the scholia. However, the style and tone of the choral song could well have created a similar effect (Dover 1968, note on 292).

300: Cecrops. He was sometimes depicted as half man/half serpent, an allusion to his origins from the land (see *Wasps* lines 437–40). Athens was known as the land of Cecrops, and the audience gathered in the Theatre of Dionysus to watch *Clouds* were seated on the southeastern slope of Cecrops' rock, more commonly known as the Acropolis.

325: Left and right. The Greek has "coming from the sides," a reference to the actual entrance of the Cloud-chorus from the *eisodoi* (wings) to the left and right. Aristophanes uses this as a pun in *Birds* (lines 195–96) at the entrance of the chorus.

331–34: Sophisticated scholars. In the Greek the list starts with "Prophets from Thurii." Thurii was an Athenian colony founded in 444/3 in south Italy near the city of Sybaris. The "prophet" probably refers to Lampon who was in charge of settling the colony (see *Birds*

*522 **Lampon**). The "atmospheric therapists" may be a reference to Hippocrates of Cos for whom the Hippocratic oath is named. He was certainly a contemporary of Socrates, and some of his medical theories seem to have been based on those of Diogenes of Apollonia. Atmospheric conditions and the nature of the air were regarded by many medical practitioners at this time as having an effect upon the health of the body (Plato *Symposium* 188a-b). For "long-haired loungers, etc.," the Greek has *sphragidonuchargokomêtas*, an Aristophanic creation meaning something like "long-haired-lazy-signet-ring-wearers." These kinds of convoluted comic coinages are often found in Aristophanes such as "Cloudcuckooland" (*Birds* line 819) . The term used here either applies to the well-to-do young gentlemen who sought instruction from the sophists or is a reference to long fingernails, implying the general unkempt state of the men being described. The list concludes with a comic description of dithyrambic poets, composers of choral songs in honor of Dionysus that were often accompanied by a circling or spiraling dance. The traditional construction of the dithyramb was by a system of cyclical strophic responsion. Aristophanes uses similar "airy" terms for his portrayal of the dithyrambic poet Cinesias in *Birds* (lines 1372–1409).

351: Simon. The name Simon is found only in Comedy. A fragment from Eupolis' *Cities* (fr. 218) names him in the context of embezzlement.

362-63: The way you strut. In Plato's *Symposium* (221b) Alcibiades refers to these lines from *Clouds* as being an accurate description of Socrates' behavior during the Athenian forces' withdrawal from Delium in 424.

378: Necessity. *Anankê* was an important element in pre-Socratic theories and can be found in the works of Parmenides, Empedocles, Leucippus, and Democritus. *Anankê* was also a powerful force in tragedy: Aeschylus told of Agamemnon "strapping himself to the yoke of Necessity" when compelled to sacrifice his daughter (*Agamemnon* line 218).

380: Celestial Basin. The *dinos* or mixing bowl was a large basin that stood on a stand (see Boardman *ABFV*, fig. 187, for a pictorial representation). The *dinos* took a central position in the organization and proceedings of the symposium. This was a drinking party frequented by the Athenian intelligentsia, where Socrates and his contemporaries were depicted as meeting and engaging in intellectual discourse (Plato's *Symposium*). *Dinos* also meant spin or whirl, the word being applied to the basin because of its function for mixing wine (the heavy Greek wine was diluted with water). The term is used by Plato (*Phaedo* 99b) to describe how the earth stays in place beneath the heavens. *Dinos* was also used in a similar descriptive context by Empedocles and Democritus. Hence the joke works three ways in *Clouds*:

(1) As a philosopher's term for a natural phenomenon: "the whirling of the celestial *dinos* (vortex)" (line 380).

(2) As a joke on the drinking habits of the sophists: "*Dinos* (wine basin) is king now!" (line 828).

(3) As a household object used as an religious idol (lines 1472–74).

For another view of the role of the *dinos* see Bowie 1997.

407: Spontaneous flame. Both Anaximander and Anaximenes speculated that thunder and lightning were caused by the force of the wind blasting out of thick clouds. Anaxagoras, followed by Democritus, advanced the theory that it was friction that created lightning bolts.

508: Trophonius. The terrifying aspect of entering the shrine of Trophonius was the descent where the initiate plunged through a small aperture, propelled by the suction of a mystical wind (also described by Pausanias as *dinos*). Mention of Trophonius is doubly apt. He was said to have been swallowed by the earth after a botched attempt to steal from one of the Delphic treasuries, and his rites were also connected with issues of memory, forgetfulness, and knowledge. The whole process is vividly described by Pausanias (9.39.5–14), and referred to in Euripides' *Ion* (line 300).

539–40: Cheap laughs from the children. Children in the audience are referred to in Aristophanes' *Peace* (line 50) and *Ecclesiazusae* (line 1146). However, it is not known if children where actually in attendance at the theatre or if these remarks were aimed at the "childish" members of the audience. The costuming of *Clouds* would have almost certainly included a phallus, but Aristophanes may be alluding to a more grotesque type of appendage preferred by other "cruder" comics. He may be simply poking fun at his own conventions as many of the elements he refutes here actually occur in the course of the play.

541: Bald men. Aristophanes himself seems to have been bald (*Knights* lines 550, *Peace* lines 767–73), and Socrates may have been portrayed as a bald or balding character (he would have been in his forties when *Clouds* was staged). Alcibiades in the *Symposium* refers to Socrates as resembling the satyrs Silenus and Marsyas, both of whom are regularly portrayed as balding characters (for images of balding satyrs see Trendall and Webster, figs. 11, 7–10). It is also not unreasonable to presume that Strepsiades himself would have been presented in a bald mask to mark his advanced years.

543–45: Oh! Oh! *Clouds* opens with the cry *iou! iou!* (oh! oh!). Strepsiades calls it out again at line 1321 when attacked by his son, and a student makes the same cry being hotly pursued by Strepsiades carrying flaming torches.

554: A disgusting imitation. Ian Storey has found thirteen close resemblances between the structure and content of *Knights* and the surviving fragments of *Maricas* (Storey in Sommerstein et al., 1993, pp. 383–84). Eupolis' *Maricas* featured a foreign streetwise slave who represented Hyperbolus just as Aristophanes' Paphlagonian slave represented Cleon in *Knights*.

584: "Such sheets of fire." Originally a quote from Sophocles' *Teucer* (fr. 578), "Amid the lightning came the rolling thunder."

617–19: Lunar cycle. Each Greek city-state utilized its own dating system although they were all based on the lunar cycle. In Athens there were twelve months, each named after a festival. The year started with the first new moon after the summer solstice, and each subsequent month was marked by the falling of the old moon, indicating the end of one month, and the rising of the new moon, indicating the beginning of another. Therefore, Athenian months lasted twenty-nine or thirty days. The last day of the month was called the "old-and-new day." It seems that Athenian officials could adjust the calendar to suit particular civic needs such as the postponement or rescheduling of festivals, therefore causing the calendar to fall out of synchronization with the moon (Burkert 1985, 225–6).

632-33: Into the light. Socrates' language is still that of initiation rites. Strepsiades emerges into the light from the secret interior of the Pondertorium. After leaving the cave of Trophonius (see ***508 Trophonius**), the knowledge seeker was sat on the "throne of remembrance" and questioned by the priests on the nature of what he had learned (Pausanias 9.39.13). The actions of Socrates and the references to Strepsiades' memory, or lack thereof, closely resemble these rites.

651: With your fingers. The Greek has *kata daktulon,* which means "by the fingers." At some point this became a technical term for the measurement of rhythm. Strepsiades misunderstands and either makes a masturbation joke or gives Socrates "the finger" by way of a commonly understood obscene gesture.

659: Correct gender. This is very close to Plato's *Euthydemus* (277e); "First of all, as Prodicus says, you must learn the correct use of words." Both Prodicus and Protagoras were concerned with the "correct" usage of words and categorized them according to gender (Plato *Cratylus* 391c, Aristotle *Rhetoric* 3.5–1407b).

671: Meal-kneader. For a pictorial representation of a *cardopus* see B. A. Sparkes 1962, p. 126 and Plates IV 4, VII 3 & 4. A *cardopus* is also mentioned in Plato's *Phaedo* (99b) as being used to describe the earth as a flat board or trough supported on a cushion of air.

676: By the back door. The Greek has "He kneads his dough in a round pestle." Dover takes this to mean that Cleonymus is so cowardly that he is forced to masturbate for sexual pleasure (Dover 1989, p. 139). Henderson sees an allusion to anal intercourse, focusing the joke on Cleonymus' "womanly" aspects (Henderson 1991, p. 200) This is closer to the sense of the scene, which lampoons the sophist's concerns with the correct use of gender in grammar.

766. The healers. The Greek *pharmakon* ("healer") is also the term used for the Thessalian witch at line 749. Healing, magic, and sorcery were all closely connected. Glass was a rare and expensive commodity at this time.

845: Legally incompetent. Plato describes a court action whereby the head of a family could be judged to be of "unsound" mind and responsibility for all property be handed to the next of kin (*Laws* 929 d and e) . Xenophon states that Socrates was accused of encouraging the young to use this law against their fathers and then goes on to say that Socrates was adamantly opposed to such action (*Memorabilia* 1.2.49).

862: Festival. This was the Diasia, a family festival where gifts were exchanged. This reference to Pheidippides being given a cart at an early age shows his fascination with chariots beginning in childhood. Such as scene is depicted on an Attic red figure Aryballus with a group of boys playing with toy chariots (Boardman *ARFV1*, fig. 318.2).

870: Grasp your own tackle. A much debated pun based around the Greek *tribôn* ("well worn" or "well known") and *kremasta* ("tackle" or "hanging ropes"). *Tribein* (to rub/chafe) has sexual connotations as a byword for masturbation (Henderson 1991, p. 176 and Aristophanes' *Wasps* line 1344) which is fully exploited in the character of the Triballion ("Jerkoffalot") in *Birds* (lines 1565–1684). *Kremasta* is used of Socrates hanging in the air at line 218. Rope is also used in a sexual sense at *Wasps* (lines 1342–44). Hence Pheidippides turns Socrates' innocent remark into a rude retort.

876: A talent. Prodicus was said to charge fifty drachmas for a course in the correct use of words, only one twelfth of a talent. There is no evidence that Socrates ever taught Hyperbolus or even charged fees, something he denies vigorously in Plato's *Apology* (19e). This joke seems squarely aimed at Hyperbolus who was frequently lampooned for his lowly origins. The huge sum of money demanded for his training is a comic indication of the amount of work it took to turn him into a presentable orator.

Stage Direction: Enter the Superior Argument. It is not known how the two Arguments were costumed. The scholia state that they are made to resemble a pair of fighting cocks, but there is no reference in the text to this. Costume that represented each character's generation would be appropriate. It may have been that the actor who played Socrates also played the Inferior Argument after a quick mask and costume change.

905: Locking up his father. The position of the father in the Attic household was held to be supreme, therefore offenses by a child against his father were considered to be a very serious breach of moral code. Zeus overthrew his own father, Cronus, to gain the supremacy of heaven, and he chained him up beneath the earth (Hesiod *Theogony* 73). In Aeschylus' *The Furies,* the Furies use this same argument against Apollo and Orestes: "You say that Zeus has higher regard for a father's fate / and yet he placed his own father, Cronus, in chains" (lines 640–41).

908: Queer. The Greek term *katapugôn,* a derivation of *pugê* (arse), was used to describe passive homosexuals. However, it seems that it can also be used as a general term of abuse (Henderson 1991, p. 210), and could also be applied to women (Dover 1989, p. 143).

922: King of the scroungers. The Greek has "Telephus the Mysian." *Telephus* was a tragedy staged by Euripides in 438. The central character was the king of Mysia, an area in the northwest of Asia Minor (modern day Turkey), and he appeared onstage dressed in rags as a beggar. This device of clothing tragic characters in rags was apparently introduced by Euripides, and he is chastised by Aeschylus in Aristophanes' *Frogs* as "the inventor of beggars and stitcher of rags" (lines 842 and 1063–64).

923: Sycophantic sayings. The Greek has "Pandeletean sayings." Pandeletus is found only here and in a fragment of Cratinus' *Cheirons* (fr. 242). The scholia lists him as a sycophant and a politician with an odious reputation. He was probably active several years prior to the original production of *Clouds.*

984: Sacrificial beef. This refers to the Buphonia, the sacred sacrifice of a bull to Zeus as part of the Diplolieia festival. Evidently this ancient ceremony had become disdained by the youth of Athens who preferred the dramatic and athletic competitions that were part of other Attic festivals.

990: Manly meat. The Greek has *kôlê* (ham), a euphemism for "penis" (Henderson 1991, pp. 20, 129 n. 100). The Superior Argument regards the young as too weak too lift a warrior's shield and not used to being naked in public due to lack of regular training in the gymnasium.

1012–14: A strapping body. This is a vivid description of the "ideal" male form in Athenian art to the mid-fifth-century B.C.E. This type of male figure can be seen on vase paintings and sculpture of the period, and the male form is discussed at length by Dover (1989, p. 125).

1069: She ran out on him. As with most Greek myths there are different versions of the Peleus and Thetis story. One has Thetis leaving Peleus after he had rebuked her severely (Sophocles *Fr.* 151). Apollodorus of Rhodes (3.13.6) relates how Peleus chastised Thetis for questioning his actions in holding the infant Achilles over a fire to burn off his mortality. Euripides' *Andromache* (1231–83) has the couple reunited, the aged Peleus is given immortality, and they live together in the house of Nereus, Thetis' father, beneath the sea.

1075: Human nature. The conflict between *phusis* ("nature/ spirit") and *nomos* ("custom/laws") was much debated at this time (Plato *Republic* 1. 388 ff., *Gorgias* 482e). It was introduced during the Melian Dialogue (416) as reported by Thucydides (5.105.2) and the "force of nature" argument used to justify political and military conquest.

Stage Direction: Barley. It is not known what was given to Socrates; the scholia write that it was a small sack of barley, although the chorus have mentioned this as an opportunity for making money (line 811), it is clear that Strepsiades is destitute from the evidence of the opening scene (line 29). The offering of such a paltry gift would therefore be an appropriate joke at this point.

1154–66: Then be it known. In the Greek this is a parody of contemporary tragedy. The first two lines are lifted from a play called *Peleus*, by either Sophocles (*Fr.* 491) or Euripides (*Fr.* 623). The final lines are from of Euripides' *Hecuba* 171–74.

1195: The new day. Pheidippides uses his new education to twist the meaning of the old-and-new day. He explains that the old day was set aside for settlements, while the new day was when the debts where actually due and could not be demanded until then. He therefore disputes the validity of a system that has confused this and only marks one day for the collection of debts. Strepsiades, suitably befuddled, asks why the courts are allowed to collect on two separate days (the old *and* new day), and Pheidippides replies that they are obviously cheating and this makes any claims against his father through the courts invalid.

1199: Festival taste-testers. According to Athenaeus (4.171c), these where the priests who presided over the Apaturia. This was a local three-day festival organized by each *phratry* (brotherhood). The dining on the first day may have been an exclusive affair and only open to high officials. The second day was the time of the sacrifices and feasting, and the third day was when the infant boys where registered to eventually become full members of the *phratry*. Fathers were required to donate part of their individual sacrifices to the priests, and this may be the practice that Strepsiades is referring to. The actual date of the festival also seems to have been somewhat flexible as long as it fell some time in the month of Pyanepsion (Parke 1997, pp. 89–93).

1216: In this mess. Most lending in fifth century Athens was between private citizens and not through banks or institutions. A primary source for the borrowing of funds would be family friends and neighbors (*philia*), who would have felt obligated to lend money if they themselves had it to spare. This was tied with Athenian concepts of reciprocity and gift giving that helped cement bonds and relationships within the community as a whole (Millet, pp. 109–26).

1262–64. Doomed, doomed! These lines and the following two spoken by the Second Creditor (1264–65) are from *Licymnius,* by Xenocles (fr. 2). Xenocles was a tragic playwright and the son of Carcinus (see the footnote on line 1261). These lines were originally spoken by Heracles' mother, Alcmene, on hearing the news of the death of her brother Licymnius at the hand of Tlempolemus. The word "chariot" was probably substituted for "brother" or "loved one" from the original lines now lost.

1287: Interested. The Greek for "interest" is *tokos,* a word that may have its origins in animal husbandry and farming. Farmers without sufficient land to graze their herd would pay a neighbor for grazing rights to his land by offering him a share in the increase of the herd in the form of the newborn calves. In the Greek, Strepsiades retorts, "And what kind of animal might this interest (*tokos*) be?" Plato's *Re-*

public (507A) contains a similar pun on the word *tokos* in the context of collecting interest.

1325: Strike your own father? The charge of "father beating" was regarded as a particularly vile crime and a slanderous statement under Athenian law (Lysias 10). A law attributed to Solon protected parents from maltreatment by their sons. Under the terms of the law, designed to protect the elderly, sons were expected to provide food and housing and refrain from using any kind of physical assault.

1358: Those kinds of songs. In Plato's *Protagoras* (347a–e) Socrates describes how the guests at a dinner party refuse to hear a song by Simonides about King Pittacus. They profess that gatherings accompanied by music and singing are the preserve of men who do not possess the intellects to converse intelligently. Plutarch reports Thales having heard women at the grinding stone singing a repetitive song about Pittacus (*Dinner of the Seven Sages* 14).

1414: *Alcestis*. In this play Admetus is saved from death by the self-sacrifice of his wife, Alcestis, who offers to die in his place. The distraught Admetus turns on his elderly father, Pheres, and cannot understand why he did not offer to die in her place. The quote used is from Pheres' response to his son. He states that he is a free man, and he reminds his son of his fatherly duties. He then tells his son that he values his life, even though he is old and says, "You relish the light of the sun, do you think your father does not" (*Alcestis* line 691).

1422: The way things should be. These views are reflected in Xenophon's *Memorabilia* (1.2.40–47), where Alcibiades is featured asking Socrates about the nature of law.

1478: Hermes. A representation of Hermes in the form of an angular column with a phallus and head of the god stood at points of transition such as crossroads and thresholds of houses (Boardman *GS1*, fig. 169). There may have been such a "Herm" standing outside the stage right door, in contrast to the basin at the stage left door.

1490: Light up a torch. Torches were a regular feature at the end of Old Comedy, and even though Aristophanes had promised in the parabasis that he would not use them (line 543), here they are. They are also found in *Wasps* (line 1331) and *Ecclesiazusae* (lines 978, 1150) and may have appeared in the celebration scenes in *Peace, Birds,* and *Frogs.*

Stage Direction: Climb up. A similar scene is found on a mid-fourth-century Paestan bell-crater where one comic character climbs a ladder to a woman in a window and another holds a flaming torch (Green & Handley 1995, fig. 31).

Stage Direction: Enter another student. Sommerstein (1982, note on line 1497) suggests that this could be Chaerephon. For an opposing view see Dover (1968, note on line 1493). The argument hinges on the distribution of parts and the fact that certain manuscripts affiliate some lines to Chaerephon while others do not. Chaerephon does make a fleeting appearance as a witness in *Wasps* (line 1412), and it would be hilarious to see the pasty-faced and lurking Chaerephon flushed out into the open by the smoke. This is possible with Aristophanes' four speaking actors if the students and Socrates do not come out of the house but either pop their heads out of windows or open a part of the door, revealing only a mask. This would let one actor quickly play two characters with a swift mask change. As Chaerephon was often presented in the guise of death (Aristophanes' *Birds* 1564), this would have a double dramatic impact on the end of the play. This staging would also allow two actors to play all the parts of the characters in the Pondertorium, negating the need for an extra to play Xanthias.

Wasps

Procleon and the chorus leader from *Wasps*. Aquila Productions, London 1994

Wasps: Introduction

Wasps is rather like *Knights* (424), in that the action and the "great idea" operate within a metaphorical setting. Here we get two metaphors, in fact: first, the addiction of the old Procleon to jury duty—several times this is described as a "disease"—and second, the image of the old jurors as swarms of wasps, complete with stings. The setting throughout is the house of Procleon and his son, Contracleon, who wants to remove his father from what he will describe in the agon as part addiction and part exploitation and to install him in a comfortable life at home. The house is tightly sealed up and guarded by a pair of less than watchful slaves and their master, who will try to prevent the old Procleon from escaping to his morning routine at the law courts.

The first two-thirds of the comedy flows neatly from this initial premise, falling into two movements. First, we get the prologue (1–229) with the comical attempts of Procleon to escape through every opening of the house, followed by the entry of the chorus and its exchanges with the captive Procleon (230–394), a knock-about scuffle between father, son, and chorus (395–525), and the formal agon (526–759) in which the father argues that a juror's life is to be envied, that it is full of advantages and is in fact comparable to the power of Zeus, while the son, speaking in the crucial second position, shows that the jurors are, in fact, exploited by the demagogues who care little for the mass of Athenian citizenry. His arguments convince the chorus, but not his father, and a compromise is reached, that his father may fulfill his jury duty *at home,* trying offenses around the household. Here we get the second movement

(760–1008), the wonderful trial of the dogs, where for the first time Procleon acquits (accidentally) a defendant and thus brings his career as a juror to an end.

After the parabasis (1009–1121), a typical Aristophanic effort from the 420s with the parabasis proper (1014–59) speaking directly for the poet and the syzygy (1060–1121) developing the imagery and character of the wasps, the direction of the play changes abruptly and becomes a social comedy about class and age as Contracleon attempts to dress up his father, take him out in polite company, and instruct him in proper behavior at a symposium. Of course, this all fails miserably and riotously, and the drunken old man dances off triumphantly at the end.

Wasps has three major themes: current politics, the law courts, and the generation gap. First, it is an intensely political comedy, perhaps the most political of the eleven extant plays. From the very start, politics and politicians, especially the demagogues, pervade the comedy. The 420s had seen the advent of the demagogues in Athenian politics, men such as Cleon and Hyperbolus, men of the mercantile class who had made their money rather than inherited it and who were now seeking political power. They were Athenian chauvinists who favored a strong hand on the empire—Cleon first appears in Thucydides (3.35) as the champion of strong retaliation against the rebels in Mytilene—and who saw the war with Sparta as an inevitable step in the advancement of Athens. Comedy portrays these men as lower-class workers in the marketplace—Cleon, for instance, as a tanner (see 39 "your dream stinks ... like a tannery"), whereas he probably owned the tannery; as aliens masquerading as citizens; as exploiting the people for their own profit; and as employing the tactics of fear, violence, and bribery.[1]

The dreams of the slaves at 14–53 are each set in a public space, and each features a demagogue in animal form. The trials imagined at 240, 288, 590ff., 894ff., and 947 are all political trials; charges of tyranny abound in the exchange before the agon (486ff.), and Contracleon's rebuttal of the advantages of the jury system is conducted exclusively in political terms. The antepirrhema of the parabasis (1102–21) explores the political images of wasps; the symposium at 1220ff. consists of Cleon and his cronies, and finally at 1284–91 the

---

[1] On the comic picture of the demagogues, see W. R. Connor, *The New Politicians of Fifth-Century Athens* (Princeton 1971) 168–75.

poet thumbs his nose at Cleon one last time. When we learn at 133ff. that the main characters are named "Procleon" and "Contracleon," we suspect that we are in for a politically charged comedy, and we are not disappointed. The establishment of a law court at home turns neatly on the familiar anthithesis of *oikos/polis* ("home/city") in Greek drama.

Second, *Wasps* has much to do with the law courts and the Athenian legal system. Much of the play will be mysterious without some understanding of the way in which Athenians conducted legal matters. This is all presented in full by MacDowell[2]; I shall give only the highlights that relate to the play. The jury system lay at the heart of the Athenian democracy. Jury panels were large, at least two hundred, often five hundred (hence "we swarm" at 1107); verdicts were decided by majority vote, and there was no appeal of a jury's verdict. Each year a pool of six thousand jurors was selected for service at the various courts; jurors had to be over thirty, but comedy depicts them as very old men. There is probably some truth here since younger men would be engaged in trade, commerce, or the military, and the three obols pay per day, although little more than minimum wage, would be welcome to elderly men with little financial support. The humor lies in Procleon pretending that his minimal pay makes him a somebody. Trials were presided over by a magistrate, but he was not a judge with a knowledge of law, more of a referee in the antagonistic system that prevailed. There were no lawyers for the defense nor prosecuting attorneys; trials were conducted by the individuals involved. The prosecutor was a private citizen who had to prove his allegation; the defendant spoke in his own defense. Witnesses could be called for either side (see the kitchen utensils at 962), and a time limit was kept by a water clock (93, 857). Jurors voted by pebbles deposited in urns—hence Procleon's need for a beach at 110 and his profession of love for the urn at 99 (see also 854, 990). After a guilty verdict, each side would propose a penalty—see Plato's *Apology* for the most celebrated instance—and the jurors would vote by marking a short or long line on a wax tablet, short for the lesser penalty. At 108 Procleon has so much wax embedded under his nails that it is clear that he has never voted the short line.

Finally, we have the theme of the relationship between father and

---

2 MacDowell (1978); useful summaries can be found at MacDowell (1971) 1–4 and Sommerstein (*Wasps*) xvi–xviii.

son.[3] There was nothing unusual about an elderly father relinquishing control of the home to his son; Homer's *Odyssey* shows this clearly in the case of Odysseus and Laertes. What makes this comedy work is the reversal of roles and attitudes. The old man wants to leave home to indulge his addiction; the son acts as a stabilizing force as he wants only to keep his father in comfortable retirement. How often has a parent said, "I want only what's best for you"? But here it is the son who voices this wish at 503–7 and 737–42 ("I will give him everything he needs/all the pleasures of the old"). In the episodes we see the son showing his father how to dress properly and behave in good company, and at 1335ff., the poet reverses the roles in wonderful fashion—the old man is speaking to the flute-girl:

> You be nice to me, and as soon as my son dies, I'll buy your freedom, then we can be together forever . . . I'm not in control of my assets . . . I'm so young at heart that I'm under constant supervision. It's my son, you see. He's got my best interest at heart, really, I mean I am an only daddy.

Such a theme was not new in comedy. *Clouds* explored the same area with the father going to study unsuccessfully with Socrates and Aristophanes' lost first comedy, *Banqueters,* featured a father and two sons ("the righteous boy and the little bugger"—*Cl.* 529). Just as a willful youth cannot be restrained, so the old father here runs riot.

The principal matter for discussion about *Wasps* is whether Aristophanes is being serious, and if so, about what. Is he really out to "get" the jury system, and if so, does this reflect a political stance? Several critics have thought so, among them de Ste Croix who looks at the frequent jokes in Aristophanes about juries and concludes that "very little of this is funny, except to someone who sees the whole system as a form of popular tyranny, and is out to discredit it by ridicule" (362).[4] On this reading, *Wasps* becomes a clever satire on the legal system, and by extension an attack on the democracy. The problem here is that this is comedy first and foremost and that Procleon is too sympathetic to carry a satirical message; he may be an

---

3 See D. F. Sutton, *Ancient Comedy. The War of the Generations* (New York 1993), especially 17–26.

4 Others who see the poet as attacking the law courts, and by extension the democracy, are Cartledge 50–53 and Konstan 27.

outrageous rogue, but he is a lovable one. If Aristophanes were out to pillory the jury system, he would not have made the old men so sympathetic. I suspect that all the jokes about law courts and jurors are the exploitation of a self-stereotype. Athenians would cheerfully admit their fondness for lawsuits; this is part of their self-image. So when Strepsiades says at *Cl.* 208, "This can't be Athens! Where are all the jurors and law courts?" this is not serious satire but comic stereotype. After all, the best Jewish jokes are told by Jewish comedians, or Scottish jokes by Scots.

It is much more likely that we have political satire in *Wasps*. On this reading, it is not the legal system itself that is the problem, but the exploitation of it by the demagogues.[5] It is they who have turned it into a tyranny, especially Cleon who had recently raised the jurors' pay and who considers himself their patron (see 242). Politicians in the 420s would use the law courts as part of political tactics, taking opponents to court and making their careers by prosecuting major public figures. The real venom in this play is reserved for the demagogues, not the jurors; this is especially clear at 655–724. This fits well with Aristophanes' caricature of the demagogues in other comedies (especially *Acharnians*, *Knights*, and *Frogs*) and with the moderate right-wing bias that de Ste Croix and others have detected in his comedy. But again we must be careful. Demagogues were something new in Athenian politics in the 420s, and comedy's distorted portrait of Cleon may owe more to a current stereotype than to personal vendetta, but on the whole I agree with MacDowell in seeing the play as less of an attack on the jury system and more as a continuation of comedy's caricature of the demagogues.

Two points about Cleon: In one sense the play can be seen as "waiting for Cleon."[6] He is, of course, the sea-monster in the dream at 31–41, and the two main characters bear the names of Pro- and Contracleon. At 409ff., the boys are sent to fetch Cleon, and we wonder when he will arrive. But when he does arrive, it is in the most unexpected guise, as "the hound from Cydathenaeum" (902) in the trial of the dogs, yet one more example of the animal imagery that dominates this play. Second, the dogs in the trial represent real political antagonists. "Dog" in Greek is *kuon*, very close to "Cleon," and (surprise) Cleon's deme was Cydathenaeum; the other dog,

---

[5] This view is best outlined by Murray 69–84 and MacDowell (1995) 175–9.

[6] On the portrait of Cleon in *Wasps*, see Storey (1995).

Labes ("Grabber") from Aexone, is Laches, a political opponent of Cleon, from the deme Aexone, who had served as a general in Sicily in the mid–420s—hence the Sicilian cheese that he is alleged to have filched. Cleon was known for his loud voice; the verbs *krazein* ("scream") and *boan* ("shout") are often applied to him, and thus there is excellent humor in presenting him as a howling dog.[7]

Two further matters can be considered. First, what about the last scenes, which have little to do with what went before? The political comedy has given way abruptly to social humor, and modern readers, raised on the unity of the plot, want the whole play to be tied up at the end, and are confused by the new turn in the action and by the lack of a definitive ending. But Aristophanes and his audience were not so wedded to linear plots, and the reversal of roles has been part of the comedy from the start. Vaio has argued that there are themes in common between the two parts of the comedy, wine and drinking, thieving, contests (with Procleon winning in the second part where he had lost in the first), but whether these hold the play together is debatable.

Then who is the main character in the comedy? Or, to ask two further questions, who is "right" and who is "wrong," and where does the audience's sympathy lie? Some regard Procleon as the principal (indeed only) comic character; he is the lovable clown, the irrepressible rogue, the juror-in-the-box who cannot be contained or restrained.[8] Certainly he is amusing and sympathetic, and his final scenes are a great tour-de-force, but in terms of the plot and the agon he is in the wrong, and Contracleon is meant to succeed with the chorus and audience in his camp. To some, Contracleon is either a boring nonentity or a sinister advocate of right-wing feelings, and is ignored in the appreciation of the comedy. In their view Procleon has exchanged one master (the demagogues) for another (his son) and would be better off relaxing at home, while others run the state. He has merely traded in one disease (trialophilia) for another (carousing), and in the end the juror today will become tomorrow's defendant.

I do not share this ironic and negative view of *Wasps* or of Con-

---

[7] Thus there is a nice moment at 922 when Procleon says, "the facts are positively screaming at you." There is evidence also that Cleon portrayed himself as "the watch-dog of the people"; see Storey (1995) 16.

[8] This is particularly true of the studies by Whitman 143–66, Reckford 219–81, and Bowie (1993) 78–101.

tracleon. The comedian has structured the play so that we are on his side throughout the early scenes, the agon, and the trial of the dogs. In the later epsiodes he will take the role of the straight-man to his outrageous and comical father, but by then the political point has been made. I would call attention first to 650ff., where Contracleon all but identifies himself with the comic poet in his attempt "to cure the city of one of her most vile afflictions," and then to 1463–73 where he gets a marvelous sendoff from the chorus ("in our eyes he's a wonderful son/ wise and loving and tender"). In Greek his qualities are *philopatria* ("love of father") and *sophia* ("wisdom"); the former can also mean "love of country," and "wisdom" is a quality the poet often imputes to himself. I suggest that in *Wasps* the poet identifies himself with Contracleon, the dutiful son correcting an aberrant father, be it an old juror or the city of Athens.

The hypothesis suggests that Aristophanes finished second with *Wasps* at the Lenaea of 422 while Philonides was victorious with *Proagon* ("Preview"), Leucon being third with *Presbeis* ("Ambassadors"). But Philonides is known to have been a producer for Aristophanes (*Banqueters, Frogs*), and whenever *Proagon* is cited, it is always attributed to Aristophanes. It seems that Aristophanes wrote both comedies and thus found a way to win two prizes at the same festival in 422. *Proagon* seems to have been a play about the theatre—the *proagon* was the preview held two days before the City Dionysia—and to have featured Euripides as a character (see Σ *Wasps* 61). So when at *Wasps* 61 we hear that "we will not be taking the piss out of . . . Euripides—well, not this time anyway," there is a neat intertextual reference, with Aristophanes denigrating a rival who is fact himself.[9] *Wasps* is also Aristophanes' first production since the "failure" of *Clouds*, and he twice reminds the audience of their lack of critical taste (54ff., 1043ff.). *Wasps* positively seethes with comic power and personal jokes, as if the poet were trying to make up for his recent disappointment.

I.C.S.

[9] I owe this suggestion to Toph Marshall of Memorial University.

Wasps: Cast of Characters

SOSIAS	a slave in the house of Contracleon
XANTHIAS	a slave in the house of Contracleon
CONTRACLEON	a wealthy young Athenian
PROCLEON	his elderly father
WASP CHORUS	twenty-four elderly impoverished Athenian jurors
BOY	the poor young son of the chorus leader
BOYS	three poor young boys who accompany the chorus (mute)
MIDAS	a slave in the house of Contracleon (mute)
PHRYX	a slave in the house of Contracleon (mute)
MASYNTIAS	a slave in the house of Contracleon (mute)
CLEONHOUND	a household dog
LABES	a household dog (mute)
DARDANIS	a flute girl (mute)
MYRTIA	a baking woman
CHAEREPHON	a well-known philosopher (mute)
INJURED MAN	an Athenian assaulted by Procleon
WITNESS	his witness (mute)
CRAB DANCERS	the three sons of Carcinus (mute)
CARCINUS	an Athenian sea captain (mute)

Wasps was first produced by Aristophanes in 422 B.C.E., at the Lenaea festival in the city of Athens. An adapted stage version of this translation received its first public performance by the Aquila Theatre Company at the Place Theatre, London, England, in November 1993, directed by Peter Meineck and Robert Richmond.

Wasps

SCENE: *A house in Athens.*

(Two slaves, Sosias and Xanthias, are asleep on stage. Sosias wakes up, walks over to Xanthias, and kicks him.)

SOSIAS:
Xanthias, you idiot! What are you doing?*

XANTHIAS:
I'm learning how to relieve the night watch.

SOSIAS:
You'll be learning how to take a beating if the master catches you!
Don't you realize what kind of monstrosity we're guarding?

XANTHIAS:
I just want to "send my cares away, afore the break of day."

SOSIAS:
Then "venture forth," I won't stop you (*yawning*),
But I must admit, I feel like taking a sweet little nap myself.

**:* (An asterisk refers to an endnote, found at the end of the play.)

5: The high style of this line suggests a parady of an unknown quote from tragedy or poetry.

(Sosias falls asleep, but soon begins to toss, turn, and babble, waking Xanthias.)

XANTHIAS:
What is wrong with you? Are you having a seizure, is it the Corybantic frenzies?

(Sosias wakes with a start.)

SOSIAS:
Huh! No, no, the spirit of sleep came to me, it was a visitation from Sabazius.

XANTHIAS:
The only visitation you had, mate, was to the one you made to the tavern!
But then, I have been known to participate in the worship of the grape myself.
And while we're on the subject of "Eastern influences" *(he tips his wine flask),*
I just had an amazing dream sneak up on me like a Persian invasion.

SOSIAS:
I don't believe it! Me too, it's unbelievable!
Go on, tell me your dream first.

XANTHIAS:
I saw a massive eagle swoop down into the marketplace
and snatch a poor defenseless chicken in its fierce talons.
Up, up into the sky went the eagle, soaring high.
And then it turned into Cleonymus and dropped its load!

8: A cult sacred to Cybele with rites that involved wild ecstatic dancing (***8 Corybants**).

9: A god of wine and/or sleep, originally from Phrygia, a region of modern day Turkey (***9 Sabazius**).

13: The Persians were regarded as an aggressive and deceitful enemy.

19: A politician known as the "Shield Dropper" because of his alleged cowardice in battle (***19 Cleonymus**).

SOSIAS:
Ha, ha! That's a good one. I know a great little riddle about Cleonymus.

XANTHIAS:
Let's hear it then.

SOSIAS:
It's perfect for a drinking party.
Name me a creature that shrieks, shakes, shits, sheds, and shoos,
on land and sea, all at the same time!

XANTHIAS:
What a thought! I hope my dream doesn't spell bad luck.

SOSIAS:
Don't worry, it's perfectly harmless.

XANTHIAS:
Harmless? A dream about a man shedding his weapon!

SOSIAS AND XANTHIAS:
(Clutching their private parts) Owww!

XANTHIAS:
Anyway, tell me about your dream.

SOSIAS:
It was huge and political. It will really rock the boat.

XANTHIAS:
Well don't go overboard. Just tell me what you saw.

SOSIAS:
The night had just begun and I was dreaming away.
I saw a flock of sheep huddled together in the assembly up on Pnyx hill,

---

32: The meeting ground of the Athenian citizen assembly.

they all had walking-sticks and were wearing threadbare and filthy old cloaks.*
And these poor sheep were shaking with fear and being shouted at by an enormous,
gluttonous whale with a voice like the squeal of an aggravated pig!

XANTHIAS:
(Pinching his nose) Phooey!

SOSIAS:
What's wrong?

XANTHIAS:
Stop! Stop! Please Stop!
Your dream stinks . . . like a tannery!

SOSIAS:
And this revolting whale had a set of scales and was weighing meat.

XANTHIAS:
By the gods! He's butchering the state and living off the fat of the land!*

SOSIAS:
And I saw Theorus sitting underneath the whale,
except he had the crest of a rook! Then young Alcibiades
turned to me and said, in his own lisping little way,
"What a thight, can you thee? Theorus has a wook's cwest!"

39: This is a reference to Cleon, the most prominant politician at this time. He was said to have risen from the lower classes, and his family may have run a tannery, an operation that produced a terrible smell (***39 Cleon**).

42: A minor politician in the circle of Cleon. Aristophanes portrays him as a fraud, a liar, and a braggart.

43: A young aristocrat who was beginning to make his mark in the Assembly. He went on to become a general and a prominent politician.

45: Alcibiades had a lisp and pronounced his "R's" as" L's." In Greek the word "crow" (*korakos*) spoken with this lisp would sound like the word "flatterer" (*kolakos*).

XANTHIAS:
More like a "crook's quest," if you're talking about Theorus!

SOSIAS:
Don't you think that's bizarre, Theorus turning into a rook?

XANTHIAS:
No, not at all, in fact it's a very good sign.

SOSIAS:
How come?

XANTHIAS:
Because your dream showed Theorus turning from man to bird,
so there can only be one interpretation of your vision;
Theorus is going to "foul his own nest," "be given the bird," and "croak!"

SOSIAS:
Brilliant! You should go into business interpreting messages from "the other side."
I could keep you on a retainer of two obols a day, then hire you out.

XANTHIAS:
It's time I told the audience what's going on.
I need to introduce the show.
Now you shouldn't expect anything too highbrow from us,
but you're not going to get any of that disgusting stuff lifted
off the Megarians either. We haven't got a pair of slaves
wandering around handing out nuts, and you won't see Heracles

---

51: The Greek has "Go to the crows!" a proverbial phrase meaning "Go to hell!"

54: Two obols was the daily fee paid to the poorest citizens when they served as rowers in the Athenian navy.

58: The city of Megara lay to the west of Athens. Megarian comedy seems to have been regarded as cheap and vulgar.

59: The hero who became a demigod after completing his famous labors. Heracles was often a figure of fun in comedy and lampooned for his gluttony.

getting robbed of his dinner. We will not be taking the piss
out of that great tragic dramatist, Euripides—well, not this time anyway,
and we are certainly not going to be having another go
at that most beloved of political figures, Cleon.
No, what we've got here is just a little story, but with a moral,
something we can all understand. Don't worry, it won't go over your heads,
but it will be on a higher level than those other disgusting, obscene farces.*

(Xanthias points to Contracleon, who is asleep on the roof.)

See him, that big chap, sleeping up there on the roof?
That's our lord and master, and he has ordered us to keep guard
over his old dad, who he's locked up inside the house.
The old man is suffering from a very rare and strange illness,
in fact it so rare that you would never be able to guess it
unless we were to reveal it to you.

(Xanthias challenges the audience.)

Go on, guess, I dare you.

(Sosias has descended from the stage and crossed the orchestra, and is now roaming in the audience.)

SOSIAS:
Amynias here thinks that he's a compulsive gambler, a "philocubist!"

XANTHIAS:
By Zeus! you'd better throw again. He must be thinking of his own addiction!
But he's right about one thing, the name of this malady does have a "philo" in it.

(Sosias moves to another member of the audience)

61: Euripides (485/4?–407/6) was a famous Athenian tragic playwright (***61 Euripides**).

75: A general and politician. Comedy portrayed him as a corrupt effeminate braggart, a freeloader, and a gambler.

SOSIAS:
Dercylus thinks that he's a wine-lover, a "Philotippler!"

XANTHIAS:
I don't think so. That's a very noble ailment, and only the very best people suffer from it!

(Sosias seeks out another audience member.)

SOSIAS:
Nicostratus reckons he's addicted to making offerings and being a compulsive xenophile.

XANTHIAS:
If Nicostratus wants to offer himself and love his guests, that's his business,
but it's not what's wrong with our chap. You are all clutching at straws.
You'll never get it, so I suppose I'll just have to tell you myself.

(Shouting to the audience) Quiet there at the back, please!

Our master has been stricken with a terrible affliction,
namely he is a "trialophile"—addicted to litigation, serving on a jury
and passing judgment! He absolutely loves it, can't get enough of it!
You should hear him moaning if he doesn't get a seat on the front bench!
He doesn't get a wink of sleep at night, and even if he does nod off
for a little, his mind takes wing and goes on its own flight of fancy
hovering around the court water clock. He's so used to clutching*
a voting pebble that he wakes up in the morning with his fingers

---

79: Dercylus is unknown.

81: A general during the Peloponnesian War.

88: The various Athenian courts were served by large citizen juries, chosen by lot from volunteers and numbering anywhere from two hundred to five hundred. See the introduction, pp. 127–28.

94: Jurors registered their verdicts by dropping a pebble or mussel shell into one of two large urns, designated "guilty" and "not guilty."

stuck together as if he's sprinkling his incense in honor of the new moon.
If he's out and about and sees some graffiti, you know the sort of thing,
"Demos the son of Pyrilampes has a sexy little bot,"
he writes underneath, "Not half as sexy as the voting urn's slot."

One morning the cock crowed a little later than usual, and he went around
claiming that the councilors had bribed it so he would miss their audit!*
What's even worse, every single night he gobbles down his dinner,
puts his shoes on, and runs off down to the courtroom so he can sleep right
outside the door, clinging to the notice board like a limpet.
That way he's one of the first in line when they select the jury.
Mind you, he's a mean old bastard, this one, every time they get a conviction
and the jury are asked to set damages, he always goes for the maximum,
scratching the longest line in his wax tablet. He comes home each day
with enough wax under his fingernails to fill a beehive.
He's so paranoid that he'll run out of voting pebbles to drop in the guilty
urn that he's got his own private beach piled up in his room.
"Such is his infatuation, but when his love is chided, he judges all the more."

95: Athenians marked the start of the month by making small offerings on their household altars.

97: Pyrilampes was Plato's great uncle and stepfather. His son Demos was renowned for his good looks (***97 Pyrilampes and Demos**).

98: Voting urns were covered with a wicker lid with a hand-sized slot to keep the ballot secret.

107: The longer the line a juror drew in the wax, the more severe he assessed the penalty.

111: A parody of a line from Euripides' *Stheneboea* (***111 Stheneboea**).

So in desperation we've locked him in the house, and we slaves are standing
guard to make sure he doesn't try and make a break for it.
It's the son I feel sorry for, he's taking all this very badly.
At first he tried to persuade his old dad to stop wearing that filthy
old peasant cloak and stay indoors, but to no avail.
Then he gave him a ritual bathing and had him purified, but it was still no good.
Next, he took him to visit the priests of Dionysus who whipped
him up into a Corybantic frenzy. But that didn't cure him either;
he just ran off to the court, chanting away, banging his little drum,
and joined a jury at the courthouse hearing a case!
Nothing seemed to work, so out of desperation he sailed his father across
to Aegina Island and had him spend the night in the temple of Asclepius.
But come first light, there he was, back in Athens, standing outside the courthouse!
Well, since then we decided to keep him shut up in the house, but he kept escaping,
crawling through the water pipes or nipping out a little hole, so we have stopped
up all the chinks with rags and filled in all the gaps. Then we discovered
him knocking pegs into the courtyard wall and scuttling up onto the roof
like a pet jackdaw. So, we've put nets right across the yard.
It's our job to patrol the perimeter of the house to make sure he stays put!*

You'll never believe what the old codger is called—Procleon,
I swear it's true! And his son here is named Contracleon.

117: The short coarse woolen cloak is a badge of class pride for Procleon and a hideous social embarrassment for his son (***33 Cloaks**).

118: The Greeks believed that madness was a kind of religious pollution (***118 Purification**).

125: A healing deity with a sanctuary on Aegina, off the coast of Attica in the Saronic Gulf (***125 Asclepius**).

He's a bit stuck up, likes to live the good life and . . .

(Contracleon wakes up and calls down from the roof.)

CONTRACLEON:
Xanthias! Sosias! Are you two asleep?

XANTHIAS:
Oh no!

(Xanthias kicks Sosias.)

SOSIAS:
What! What!

XANTHIAS:
Contracleon's woken up.

CONTRACLEON:
Quickly, one of you run around to the back!
Father's gone into the kitchen, and he's scurrying around like a mouse.
Make sure he doesn't try and disappear down the plug hole in the sink!

(Exit Sosias running around the back of the scene building.)

(To Xanthias) You keep watch on the door.

XANTHIAS:
Yes, master.

(A rumbling is heard from inside the house.)

CONTRACLEON:
By Poseidon! Whatever is that noise coming from the chimney?

(Enter Procleon, emerging from the chimney pipe on the roof of the scene building.)

(To Procleon) What are you doing? Who are you?

PROCLEON:
I'm just a little puff of smoke.

CONTRACLEON:
Smoke? From what kind of wood?

PROCLEON:
Sycamore.

CONTRACLEON:
More like Sycophant! That's a load of hot air, and it would choke anyone.
You get back inside this minute! Where's that chimney cover gone to?

(Contracleon forces Procleon back down the chimney and puts the cover over.)

You get back inside, blast you! I'll make sure you never try this one again
by putting a block of wood over the cover. *(He does so.)*
I'd like to see you try and get out of there. That idea of yours
went up in smoke. To be known as the son of a puff, what a drag!*

PROCLEON:
(Banging on the door from inside) Boy!

XANTHIAS:
He's banging away at the door! *(He leans up against it.)*

CONTRACLEON:
You'll have to take the force of his thrusts!
I'm on my way down to help.
Keep your eye on the lock and watch the bolt,
make sure he doesn't try to chew my knob.*

(Procleon appears at the window.)

PROCLEON:
What the hell are you doing? Can't you see? I'm trying to get to court.

143: God of the sea and the most important patron of Athens after Athena.

147: A man who sought to profit by collecting incriminating information for use in prosecutions.

Let me out, you bastard, otherwise Dracontides will get off!

XANTHIAS:
Oh bloody hell! What does it matter?

PROCLEON:
You don't understand! I had my fortune told at Delphi, and it said that if I acquitted anybody I would shrivel up and wither away to nothing.

XANTHIAS:
(Clutching his private parts) OOHHH! Apollo save us! What a prophecy!

PROCLEON:
Come on, you've got to let me out, I'm bursting!

XANTHIAS:
Not for all the fish in Poseidon's sea.

PROCLEON:
Right, you asked for it! I'll just have to chew through the net with my teeth.

XANTHIAS:
But you haven't got any teeth.

PROCLEON:
By all the gods! I'll kill you! You little bastard, someone get me a sword, quickly!
No, better still, bring me my juryman's wax tablet.

(Contracleon has now come down from the roof and joins Xanthias.)

157: There are four men known as Dracontides. All of them held political offices (***157 Dracontides**).

159: The sanctuary to Apollo and seat of his priestess, the Pythia, who pronounced sacred oracles (***159 Delphi**).

161: Apollo was the god of prophecy and healing.

CONTRACLEON:
He'll do himself a mischief if he's not careful.

PROCLEON:
No, no I won't, I just want to take the donkey to the market and sell him as an all-inclusive deal, including panniers, it's market day today.

CONTRACLEON:
Couldn't I sell it for you?

PROCLEON:
Not half as well as I could.

CONTRACLEON:
Exactly! I could do it twice as well.

PROCLEON:
What? All right, then, if you insist, bring the donkey out.

XANTHIAS:
That was a good one, he's fishing to get out. He's a slippery customer, this one.

CONTRACLEON:
Well, I didn't take the bait, I can see just what he's up to. I think I'll get the donkey myself just in case the old man tries to nose his way out.

*(He goes in and leads out the donkey, which refuses to move and brays loudly.)**

Come on, Neddy, move! What's the matter? Are you sad that you're going to be sold today? Come on. What are you groaning for? Anyone would think that you had Odysseus hanging down there.

180: Homer's hero, who blinded the Cyclops and escaped from his cave by hiding under a sheep (*Odyssey* 9.424–63).

XANTHIAS:
By Zeus! He has got someone down there!

CONTRACLEON:
Nonsense, let me see.

XANTHIAS:
It's not nonsense. Come here and have a look.

(Contracleon examines the donkey.)

CONTRACLEON:
What's going on, who's down there?

PROCLEON:
No one, by Zeus!

CONTRACLEON:
No one? And where are you from, "Mr. No one"?

PROCLEON:
I'm from Ithaca, the son of Flee-on-an-ass.

CONTRACLEON:
Well "Mr. No one," there's no way you're getting away with this. *(To Xanthias)* Pull him out from under there!

(Xanthias pulls Procleon out from under the donkey.)

Ugghhh! You disgusting old man. Just look where he's stuffed himself! This must surely be the first time a donkey has ever given birth to a complete ass!

185: Odysseus had told the Cyclops that "no one" was his name. When he blinded the creature, the other Cyclopes came running to his aid and shouted into his cave demanding to know who was hurting him. The Cyclops gave the famous reply "No one," and his neighbors went away, leaving the path clear for Odysseus to escape.

187: Ithaca was the island home of Odysseus, off the northwest coast of Greece.

189: The Greek *klêtêr* could mean both "donkey" and "server of a summons."

PROCLEON:
I'm warning you, I won't go without a fight!

CONTRACLEON:
You'd be flogging a dead horse.

PROCLEON:
It'll be donkey's years before you ever stop me!

CONTRACLEON:
You're as stubborn as an old mule and twice as rotten.

PROCLEON:
Rotten, me! I am certainly not, by Zeus! I'll have you know
that I am regarded by some as quite a dish, and very tasty.
Perhaps you would like to sample a prime upper cut of matured juryman!

(Procleon takes a hopeless swing at Contracleon, misses, and falls on the floor.)

CONTRACLEON:
Get back inside, and take this stupid "donkey" with you!

(Xanthias pushes Procleon and the donkey back inside.)

PROCLEON:
Help! Help me! Fellow jurors, Cleon, help!

(Xanthias slams the door shut.)

CONTRACLEON:
You can shout as much as you like, but the door stays shut.
(To Xanthias) Pile up a heap of stones against the door!

(Xanthias runs stage left.)

Put the knob back in the hole!

(Xanthias runs stage right.)

192: The Greek has "a donkey's shadow," an expression meaning something not worth fighting for (***192 Donkey's shadow**).

Wedge that plank of wood against the door!

(Xanthias runs stage left.)

Roll that big grinding stone . . .

(Something falls on Xanthias' head.)

XANTHIAS:
Oww! By all the gods! A clod of earth just fell on me!

CONTRACLEON:
Perhaps there's a mouse scuttling about in the eaves.

(Procleon pokes his head out of a hole between the wall and the roof.)

XANTHIAS:
That's no mouse, that's a house-juror, and he's trying
to squeeze out from under the roof tiles!

CONTRACLEON:
By the gods! He thinks that he's a sparrow!
He's going to take flight any minute! Where's my net?

(Contracleon shoos his father back inside.)

Shoo! Shoo! Get back! Shoo! By Zeus, I'd sooner join the army
and freeze on the frontier, than keep watch on my father.*

XANTHIAS:
Look, we've shooed him back inside; he's not going to get out again.
Can't we have some rest and relaxation time?
We need some time off for a little nap. Please.

CONTRACLEON:
Don't be stupid! The other jurors will be here any minute now
to call on father and take him off to court with them.

XANTHIAS:
But it's only just starting to get light!

CONTRACLEON:
Then they must be running late this morning.

They usually get here just after midnight,
carrying lamps and warbling those sickly old
Phoenician-Phrynichus-phrases!

XANTHIAS:
I'll go and get some stones to throw at them. That should keep them away.

CONTRACLEON:
No, you idiot! You can't provoke these old fellows,
it would be like stirring up a wasps' nest. Every single one
of them has a sharp sting poking out of his backside,
and they're not afraid to give you a damn good poking either.
They bumble and buzz and come at you like sparks from a fire.

XANTHIAS:
Don't worry about it boss, I've got enough stones
to scatter any old swarm of jurors *(yawns).*

*(Xanthias and Contracleon sit down by the door and soon fall asleep. Enter into the orchestra the chorus of old men walking with sticks and being led by a group of boys carrying lamps.)**

CHORUS:
Come on! Step lively, keep up, Comias, you're too damned slow,
you used to be as tough as old boots in the old days,
now even old Chariades is overtaking you,
and he's about as slow as one of my bowel movements.
Ah, Strymodorus of Conthyle, my fellow juryman,
is Euergides here? Have you seen Chabes of Phyla?
Here we all are then, all that's left of the old battalion.

220: A tragic dramatist active in the late sixth and early fifth century. He had produced a play called *Phoenician Women* (***220 Phrynichus**).

230: These names are not identifiable contemporary characters but suitable titles for a chorus of old men.

234: A rural *deme* (small district) in the east of Attica.

235: A deme a few miles to the northeast of Athens.

Those were the days standing side by side on guard at Byzantium.
Do you lads remember the night we "liberated" that baking woman's
bread-board and used it for firewood? I can still taste the porridge
that we made that night. Ah, those were the days!
Come on! Hurry up! Laches is up in court today, and he's got
plenty of money stashed away. Cleon, our glorious leader,
told us to arrive in plenty of time with three days' rations
of mean spirit, so we can really punish him for his crimes.
Let's get going, brother jurors, it'll be daybreak soon.
Keep those lamps burning and an eye out for stones,
we don't want anyone having a nasty accident.

BOY:
Careful daddy, watch out for the mud.

CHORUS:
Pick an old stick up off the ground and have a fiddle with the wick.

BOY:
It's all right. I'll give the wick a pull with my finger that'll get it up.

CHORUS:
Who taught you to do that? Don't jostle the wick!
You know full well that oil is in short supply, stupid!
You're not the one who gets stung with the high price of the stuff!

BOY:
I'm telling you, by Zeus, if you don't stop shaking your fists
and moaning on at us, we'll pinch your wicks and you can find your

---

237: Byzantium (modern day Istanbul) was captured in 476 by the Athenians after a short siege. This would make the chorus around seventy-five to eighty years old (***237 Byzantium**).

241: A general and political rival of Cleon's (***242 Laches**).

244: Athenian servicemen called up for active duty were required to bring three days' field rations with them.

252: A common euphemism for sexual impotency, but also a serious comment. The Spartans had recently destroyed valuable Attic olive groves, causing an acute oil shortage (***246 Lamps**).

own way home. You can fumble around helpless in the dark, sloshing along in the mud with your tails between your legs!

CHORUS:
I'll have you know that I frequently punish bigger men than you, my lad . . .

(As he brandishes his walking stick at the boy, he slips and falls over.)

Argh! Now I really am "muckraking."*

(As the other chorus members help him up)

I'll give it four days at the most, then the god
will send us some rain, he's bound to.
Our wicks are moldy, and that proves that there's
a shower on the way. It'll soon be fertile again,
and make everything nice and fruity. We should get
some north wind, and there's nothing like a good hard blow!

(They arrive at Procleon's house.)

That's strange, this is Procleon's house and he's
not here yet. It's not like him to miss a trial.
He's usually first to join our little swarm,
singing his little heart out, with a touch of Phrynichus.
I know, let's give him a tune, he'll get all excited
when he hears us singing sweetly to him.
That's bound to get the old geezer outdoors.

(The chorus breaks into song.)

Can you hear us calling? Join us now.
It's time you made an exit.
Did you lose your shoes in the dark,
Have you sprained your little digit?
Can you hear us calling? Come on down.
We're all outside your door.
Have your ancient joints all seized up?
Are your bollocks big and sore?

For he is the firmest of us all,
They'll never make him bend.
Try as they may to talk him round,

He'll beat them in the end!

And when they beg for mercy, he stands alone,
He lowers his head as if in pity, and says:
"You'd have more luck getting blood out of a stone!"

Could it be what happened yesterday
Has made him somewhat sick,
When we sat and heard the testimony
Of that slippery little snitch?
He told that Samos was revolting
And so he nearly got away.
Perhaps that's why Procleon's sulking
And not coming out today?

Come on then, we've a case from Thrace,
We mustn't let him loose.
There's a greedy traitor on the docket,
Let's go and cook his goose!

Come on, boy! Keep moving.

(The music changes.)

BOY:
Dear father, dear, dear father
Will you buy me something nice?

CHORUS:
Of course I will, my boy,
*Some lovely knucklebone dice,**
Hours of boyhood pleasure
At a very reasonable price.

283: An island off the coast of modern day Turkey. Samos rebelled against the Athenian-led Delian League in 440 (***283 Samos**).

288: A region to the north of Greece and the site of recent military and diplomatic action (***288 Thrace**).

BOY:
No, father, no, by Zeus
*I would love to taste a fig.**

CHORUS:
Go hang, you little bastard!
You're a greedy, selfish pig.

BOY:
If you take that tone, I'm going home!

CHORUS:
Fuel, food, and grain I have to buy
On the little that they distribute.
A family of three needs to be fed,
While you're enjoying forbidden fruit!

BOY:
But father, how will we buy lunch?
For I've had a horrible thought:
what if the Archon decides today
*Not to convene the civil court?**
What will we do if you don't get paid,
Cast adrift on the waters of hell?

CHORUS:
You can moan and you can groan,
because you'll get no dinner as well!

BOY:
"Oh why, oh why was I ever born!
*Mother, poor mother, what did you do!"**

CHORUS:
She brought you into this old world
To give me the pain of feeding you!

BOY:
*Oh, my poor little, useless sack,**
A dangling testament to forced cutbacks!

(Procleon appears at the window of the house.)

PROCLEON:

Friends, it's been so long,
I heard you through my cranny,
But I cannot join your song
For a slave acts as my nanny.

Please get me out of here,
I want to go to court with you.
I miss my jury so dear
I've got some serious harm to do!

Oh, Zeus of mighty thunder,
Make me a puff of smoke,
Like Proxenides the boaster
As hot air always floats.

Or turn me to a creeping vine,
Like the son of verbal shite,
I'll lie and crawl and then I'll climb,
Take pity on my plight.

Or fry me with your thunder-flash
And set the heat to broil,
Pick me up, blow off the ash,
And dip me in boiling oil.

But forget all that and be a rebel,
Turn me to stone—a voting pebble!

(The chorus calls out to Procleon.)

CHORUS:

Who is keeping you shut up in there?

324: "Smoke" was used to denote someone who was boastful, rather like the English "windbag" or "hot air."

325: Also called a boaster in *Birds* (line 1126). His position in Athenian society is unknown.

328: Amynias (note on line 74) is called this at line 1267, as is Aeschines (note on 458) at lines 1459 and 1243.

Tell us! We're your friends.

PROCLEON:
Shhh! It's my son. But keep your voices down,
he's just over there, asleep.

CHORUS:
You silly old fool!
Why is he doing this to you?
What's he trying to do?

PROCLEON:
He won't let me be a juror any more; he says I'm not allowed to do any harm
to anyone. He says that he'll wine and dine me if I give it all up, but I don't want to!

CHORUS:
How dare he do that to you! The bastard!
Who does he think he is—this damn Demagogocleon!
He just can't bear to hear the truth.*
It's a conspiracy! A plan to overthrow the democracy!
You need to find a way of getting down
from there without him knowing.

PROCLEON:
There's no way out, you try and think of one, I've tried everything. I'm desperate
to get to court and go round the back of the notice boards holding my voting pebble.

CHORUS:
Couldn't you find a little hole that you could squeeze through?
Then, you could slip away dressed in rags like wily Odysseus.

PROCLEON:
They've bunged up all the holes. That would be like trying to crawl up a gnat's ass,

---

349: Jurors passed behind the court notice boards to cast their votes.

what do you think I'm made of, feta cheese? You'll have to think of something else.

CHORUS:

Do you remember back in the old days, the army, the Naxos campaign?
You pilfered those kebab skewers and shimmied down the side of the wall.

PROCLEON:

Yes, I remember, but so what? I was a young man in those days,
fast on my feet with sticky fingers. I was at my peak,
and there were no guards prowling around so I could get
away really easily. I'm under siege here, surrounded by hordes
of soldiers, drawn up ready for battle, armed to the teeth.
They're watching all the escape routes, and there are two of them
right by my back door who can't wait to give me a damn good skewering!
There's no way I can weasel my way out of here.

CHORUS:

You've got to come up with something soon,
my poor little bee, it's starting to get light.

PROCLEON:

I suppose I'll just have to try and nibble my way through this net.
May Dictynna forgive me for making a mess of her mesh!

CHORUS:

That's what I like to hear, fighting talk!
Commence nibbling!

PROCLEON:

Sshhh, keep quiet! We don't want Contracleon to catch us at it.

354: Naxos is an island of the Cyclades in the Aegean Sea. It tried to secede from the Delian League around 469 and was forced into subjugation by an Athenian blockade (***354 Naxos**).

368: A goddess of wild animals and hunting, often identified with Artemis.

(He chews through the net.)

I'm through! Keep an eye out for Contracleon.

CHORUS:

Don't you worry about him, old son,
if he so much as farts we'll make him wish
that he'd never been born.
That man will rue the day
he tried to trample on the sacred
decrees of the two goddesses!

CHORUS:

Tie a rope around your middle and lower yourself out the window
Now, do as Diopeithes, trust in Zeus, and, Procleon, come on down!

*(The stage crane line is lowered in front of the window, and Procleon puts the harness around his waist.)**

PROCLEON:

All right, all right. But hang on, what'll I do if one of those two idiots
spots me on the way down and tries to reel me back inside?

CHORUS:

Stop worrying! We'll rescue you, won't we lads? They'll never be able
to keep you in against your will, not up against our "hearts of oak."

PROCLEON:

Right, I'll do it. But if anything should happen to me on the way down,
then recover my body, mourn for me, and bury me . . . outside the law court.

CHORUS:

Nothing's going to happen to you, I promise, it'll be easy.

378: Demeter and Kore, the deities that presided over the sacred Eleusinian Mysteries (***1363 The Mysteries**).

380: A politician and oracle interpreter. His name can mean "believe in Zeus" (***380 Diopeithes**).

Now pray to your ancestral gods and lower away!

PROCLEON:
Great Lycus of the law courts; it is to you I cry.
You are my neighbor and my hero and love the same as I.
You cherish the sound of defendants wailing at their fates.
And, hence, you set up home just by the courthouse gates.
Take pity on your servant here as he prepares to make his fall.
And I promise never to shit or piss against your sacred wall.

(Procleon lowers himself out of the window.)

CONTRACLEON:
Xanthias! Wake up!

XANTHIAS:
What, what is it?

CONTRACLEON:
I thought I heard voices floating around.
Make sure father's not trying to crawl out again, will you?

(Xanthias sees Procleon suspended above him, on the rope.)

XANTHIAS:
He's not crawling, he's falling! He's climbing down a rope!

CONTRACLEON:
You crooked old codger! What are you doing! You stay right there!
Xanthias, climb up after him and beat him with the harvest wreath.*
He might ease his oars when he feels the stroke of a birch branch.

(Xanthias takes the harvest decoration from the door, climbs up the rope, and starts to swipe at Procleon. Meanwhile, Contracleon runs in the house and climbs to the window, where he tries to pull his father in.)

388: The patron gods of an individual family. Procleon prefers gods associated with the law courts.

389: An Athenian cult hero who evidently had a shrine overlooking one of the law courts (***389 Lycus**).

PROCLEON:

Help! Help! Anyone prosecuting a case this year, Help!
Smicythion! Teisiades! Needanobol! Keepsmefed!
I need you now! Help! Stop them pulling me back inside!

CHORUS:

Delay no more, let your anger rise,
This man has disturbed our wasps' hive.
Our stinging passion has been provoked,
Thrust on in, stand by to poke!
Stick it to them hard and fierce,
Have your pricks all poised to pierce!

(The chorus addresses the boys.)

Hold our coats boys and run to town,
And go fetch Cleon to our showdown.
Tell him there's a man who hates the state,
And he's going to suffer an ugly fate.
For he has had a despicable thought,
That we should never go to court!

(During the choral song, Xanthias climbs up the stage crane line and beats Procleon while Contracleon pulls him back inside the house. Xanthias follows, climbing in through the window. At the end of the song, they appear at the door with Procleon in the clutches of Xanthias.)

CONTRACLEON:

My dear fellows, will you kindly stop droning on and listen to the facts?

CHORUS:

We'll keep droning on all the way up to high heaven, by Zeus!

CONTRACLEON:

I can assure you, gentlemen, on no account will I release this man.

401: Probably comic distortions of the names of real prosecutors or sycophants.

CHORUS:
This is outrageous! Appalling! Bare-faced dictatorship!
Oh Athens, my city! The sites that fear us! The shites like Theorus!
And any other brown-nosed creep that crawls for the cause!

*(The chorus has thrown off its cloaks to reveal wasplike costumes consisting of yellow and black striped tunics and large stingers protruding from the choristers' backsides.)**

XANTHIAS:
Heracles! They've got stingers! Look, master!

CONTRACLEON:
The same ones that shafted Philippus, the son of Gorgias, at his trial.

CHORUS:
And you're next in line for a damn good shafting! *(Shouting to the Wasps)*
ATEEEN SHUNNN! Left wheel! By the center, forward march!*
Present stingers! Close ranks there! Hold the line! Wait for it!
Let your passion swell. Stand by to swarm into the attack!

(The chorus forms up in military ranks and points stingers at Contracleon and Xanthias.)

XANTHIAS:
It's not looking so good, master, I don't rate our chances in a fight with this lot, and I don't like the look of those great big pricks!

CHORUS:
Let that man go free. Otherwise, you'll wish you were
a tortoise with a solid shell for a hide!

PROCLEON:
Come on then, my old jurymates, my lovely little angry wasps!

418: For Theorus see note on line 42.

421: Philippus was probably a sycophant or prosecutor and an imitator of the oratorical techniques of Gorgias, a famous teacher of rhetoric from Leontini in Sicily.

Poke your points up their arses! Give their fingers a nasty jabbing!
Stick your stingers right in their eyes!

(Contracleon calls on his house slaves to help.)

CONTRACLEON:
Midas, Phryx, come out and help us! And bring fat Masyntias too!

*(The three slaves come charging out of the house.)**

You keep hold of him, otherwise I'll put you back in chains and stop
your meals. Don't worry about this lot, they may make a lot of noise,
but it's all just fizz and splutter. There's no lead in their pencils!*

(Contracleon, Xanthias, and Masyntias run into the house, leaving Procleon in the clutches of the two remaining slaves.)

CHORUS:
Let him go or I'll stick my prick in you!

PROCLEON:
Oh Lord Cecrops, human above the waist but all snake below,
how can you bear to watch me being manhandled by these barbarians,
When I've worked my fingers to the bone, beating their blasted arses!

CHORUS:
Oh, there's nothing worse than old age! How miserable it is to be elderly.
Just look at those slaves laying in to their poor old master.
To think of all he's done for them, how quickly they forget his generosity;
the lovely secondhand donkey jackets he bought them, those nice
sackcloth tunics, with all those holes for ventilation. How thoughtful!
Those dashing dog-skin hats, and all the care he lavished on their feet to keep

---

433: The three slaves all have Phrygian or Eastern names, from areas under Persian control. The ensuing scuffle is a comic reenactment of the battle of Marathon (***711 Marathon**).

438: A mythical ancient king of Athens, often depicted as half man, half snake, and viewed as one of the original Athenians (***438 Cecrops**).

them warm in winter.*

(As the slaves kick Procleon)

Look at them, no respect for old . . . shoes. Disgraceful!

PROCLEON:

Let me go, you thug! You've got a short memory, you ungrateful bastard.
Don't you remember when I caught you pilfering those grapes? I tied you
to the olive tree and gave you a man-sized seeing-to. The whole district
was jealous of you, and you never showed the slightest bit of appreciation.
Come on you two, quickly, let me just slip away before my son comes out again.

CHORUS:

Just you wait! You two will pay dearly for this.
You'll soon find out about the consequences of messing
with sour-faced, sharp-tempered old geezers like us!

(Contracleon, Xanthias, and Masyntias reemerge from the house.)

CONTRACLEON:

Pound them, Xanthias! Beat those wasps away from the house!

(Xanthias starts swatting the wasps with a broom.)

XANTHIAS:

Here I go!

CONTRACLEON:

(To Masyntias) You there! Give them something to choke on! Smoke them out!

(Masyntias brandishes a smoking firebrand.)

458: Portrayed as a boaster who made frequent false claims regarding his financial standing (see *Birds* line 822).

XANTHIAS:
Buzz off! Get away! Shoo! Shoo! Piss off!

CONTRACLEON:
Smack them! Swat them! If only we had Aeschines the boaster to stink them out with some of his bullshit.

(The wasps fall back.)

XANTHIAS:
I knew smoke would work! They're retreating.

CONTRACLEON:
Lucky for us they know only those sickly sweet songs by Phrynichus.
Those pointed tunes and sharp chords of Philocles would have finished us!

CHORUS:
It's very obvious to the working class
That a dictatorship has come to pass.
Examine him closely and you will find
That tyranny has taken us from behind!
From our city's laws he shuts us out,
But we'll not heed this long-haired lout!
He flouts the law without explaining facts,
He's a treacherous, oppressive autocrat!

CONTRACLEON:
Listen, let's stop fighting. Can't we have a sensible, civilized dialogue without all this screaming and shouting?

CHORUS:
A dialogue? With you? An enemy of the people's democracy!
A royalist! A consorter with Brasidas the Spartan!

461: For Phrynichus, see note on line 220.

462: The nephew of Aeschylus and a tragic dramatist.

475: A leading Spartan general, who was active in Thrace at the time *Wasps* was performed (***288 Thrace**).

You must be joking! You woolly-tasseled, unkempt radical.

CONTRACLEON:
I'd be better off without a father than having to launch
an armada against this lot each and every day.

CHORUS:
You don't know your onions, mate! We haven't even started yet.
Just you wait until the prosecutor gets you in court,
then we'll be using words like "CONSPIRACY!"
(The whole chorus chants.) CONSPIRACY! CONSPIRACY! CONSPIRACY!

CONTRACLEON:
In the name of heaven! Why can't you lot just go away and leave me alone,
or am I doomed to stand here arguing for the rest of the day?

CHORUS:
You won't budge me, mate! Not while there's still a breath in my body.
I can spot a conspiracy to establish a "TYRANNY" when I see one!

TYRANNY! TYRANNY! TYRANNY!

CONTRACLEON:
Oh for goodness, sake! Everything's a "conspiracy" or a "tyranny"
with you lot. If anyone disagrees with you over even the slightest
little thing, then it's a "tyranny." That particular coinage hasn't been used
in Athens for the last fifty years, and now it's cheaper than a tin of fish!*

476: Long hair, unkempt beards, and fringes on clothing were all regarded as Spartan fashions and became popular among the upper-class youth of Athens. The working-class chorus sees these traits as marks of pro-Spartan and antidemocratic political views.

483: This and the following "chanting lines" are my own additions from performance.

CHORUS:
TIN O' FISH! TIN O' FISH! TIN O' FISH!

You can't make a move in the market without having it flung at you.
If you should happen to buy some perch from a fishmonger's stall,
the chap next door, selling cut-price whitebait, accuses you of wanting
to eat like a king and calls you a monarchist! Then if you ask
the fishmonger to throw in a couple of free onions, the grocer
pipes up and accuses you of charging the Athenians imperial tribute!
Before you know it, the whole market is calling you a tyrant. It's ridiculous!

XANTHIAS:
You're right. I had the same treatment from a callgirl yesterday.
I went down to the brothel at noon and asked her to get on top for a ride,
and she accused me of trying to jockey the tyrants back into power!*

CONTRACLEON:
I think these people positively enjoy hearing these words.
All because I want my father to give up his early morning-
gallivanting-judging-trumped-up-court cases-and-unsociable-habits,
and live like a gentleman, leading a classy life, just like Morychus.
For this they call me a conspirator and a tyrant-lover!

PROCLEON:
Well, that's exactly what you are, by Zeus! I'm not interested in all your
fancy living. You could offer me a lifetime supply of bird's milk,
but it wouldn't make me give up my juries. You can keep your caviar

---

497: Persian client kingdoms paid tribute to the Great King in the form of a portion of their produce. Athens also received tribute from the allied states of the Delian League (***1102 An empire made**).

506: A wealthy, high-living, effeminate Athenian, the very opposite of Procleon.

509: A proverbial expression for expensive and rare luxuries (see *Birds* lines 734 and 1673).

and salmon; just give me a nice juicy lawsuit, stewed and seasoned.

CONTRACLEON:
Yes, I know, it's obvious, you're used to that way of life now.
But, father, just control yourself for a while, keep quiet, and listen
to me. I think you'll agree that you really are quite mistaken.

PROCLEON:
Mistaken, to be a juror?

CONTRACLEON:
More than mistaken, those men that you revere so highly are laughing
at you behind your back. You're a slave and you don't even know it!

PROCLEON:
Me, a slave? I don't think so. I am the master of all I survey.

CONTRACLEON:
You think you are, but in reality you are just a servant. Athens profits from
the entire Greek world, but tell me, father, just what do you get out of it?

PROCLEON:
All right, I'll tell you, but I want these gentlemen *(pointing to the chorus)*
to judge between us.

CONTRACLEON:
I agree. (*To the slaves*) Let him go.

PROCLEON:
Somebody get me a sword, because if you beat me in this debate,
I'm going to fall on my blade and end it all.*

CONTRACLEON:
Really? But what if you should lose and then break your promise?

PROCLEON:

Then I will never toast good fortune and drink neat jury pay again.

CHORUS:

Now, you represent the old school,
Your duty's clear—to beat this fool.
Use skill and cunning like a sly old fox.

PROCLEON:

Someone run and fetch my large lunchbox!
But what kind of opponent will I face?

CHORUS:

A youthful upstart, a hotshot ace!
It's artful arguments you must make
So concentrate, for all's at stake.
In your own hands you hold your fate,
By heaven, you must win this debate!
He'll never beat you, have no fear.

CONTRACLEON:

I'll keep notes of everything I hear!

PROCLEON:

But what if he does win this contest?

CHORUS:

Then he'd have proved that his way's the best,
And all us elders will have no more use.
They'll put us out to grass, by Zeus!
And when we walk by huffing and puffing,
They'll say "Old farts!—Good for nothing!"
In the old folks' march as an afterthought,
Like useless statements, thrown out of court.

525: At a symposium a draft of unmixed wine was drunk after the toast to good fortune. This was one of the most savored parts of the entire evening. Procleon's "unmixed wine" is his jury pay.

544: Older Athenians marched in special group as part of the Panathenaea festival (***544 The old folks' march**).

It's up to you, Procleon. You must defend our majestic power.
Summon every oratorical skill you possess and take heart.

PROCLEON:
Right then, let's get started. I will prove to you that our powers are equal
to those of any king. Name me a single living creature that is happier,
more envied, pampered, and feared than a juror? You can't.
As soon as I jump out of my bed in the morning, I find a line of great big men
waiting for me outside the court. As I walk past, one of them places his soft
hand in mine, a hand fresh from being dipped into the public funds!
Then they all bow and scrape and plead with me like a bunch of suppliants;*
"Honorable father, I beg you, if ever you yourself pilfered a bit of petty cash
or stole some of the change when you were out shopping for the office, I beg you,
show some mercy!" All this from a man who would have never had known of my
existence, if I hadn't acquitted him the last time he was up on a charge!

CONTRACLEON:
I'll note that down: "suppliants at the bar," very interesting.

PROCLEON:
Then after all their fawning and crawling, and their feeble attempts to curtail
my anger, I enter the courtroom. Once I'm inside, I forget all the promises
I've just made, and I sit there listening to their pathetic excuses.
Any excuse to get off! There's nothing they won't say or do to win a jury over.
Some of them moan on and on about being poverty-stricken and pile on the misery
to the point where they actually say that they're as poor as us jurors. Unbelievable!

Others tell us stories or a funny little fable from Aesop, and then there are those
who deliver a few gags to get us laughing and on their side. "Ha, ha, ha!"
If all that doesn't work and we're still not persuaded, out come the damn kids,
up on the stand beating their heads in unison, and crying their little hearts out.
What an awful row! Then their father approaches the bench, shaking in fear
as if I were a god! He pleads with me to pass his audit, and says, "If you like
the sound of a little bit of lamb, pray, take pity on the cries of my poor son."
But if he thinks that I prefer a nice cut of pork, then he begs me to be persuaded*
by his daughter! Well, after that, I might relent a little bit—but not that damn much!
Now that's what I call real power, it makes mere wealth seem worthless!

CONTRACLEON:
(*Writing*) "Makes mere wealth seem worthless." Now, tell me, father,
what benefits do you receive from your so-called "Sovereignty over Greece."

PROCLEON:
We get to check the manhood of the naked boys when they're up for registration!
If we have, say, the actor Oeagrus up before us on a charge, then we don't let him off

---

566: Aesop was a former slave famous for his animal fables, which he composed in the early sixth century B.C.E.

578: Disputes over the citizen registration of eighteen-year-olds were settled in court. This involved a naked inspection to determine maturity.

579: Oeagrus is known only from this reference.

unless he recites the best bits of *Niobe*. If a musician wins a case, then we get
him to put on his strap and play us a lovely little tune as we're leaving the court.
Then there are those cases where a man dies leaving only a virgin daughter. We don't worry
about whether his will names a husband to inherit his wealth. No, we just break the
seal open and give her to the suitor who puts up the best performance in court.*
Of course you mustn't forget the fact that we can't be held accountable afterward,
if something goes wrong, not like the magistrates and other public officials!

CONTRACLEON:
Well, I have to agree that it is quite an achievement not to be held accountable.
But you really shouldn't be fiddling with a virgin's will at your age.

PROCLEON:
There's something else! When the Council or the People's Assembly can't come
to a decision on an important case, they hand the miscreants over to the jurors.*
Then we get that poofy Scythian prosecutor, Euathlus or even kiss-arse-onymus,
"the shield-dropper," saying they will always be loyal to the people and fight

---

580: Niobe boasted that she was a better mother than the goddess Leto, who then sent her son Apollo to kill her children. Both Aeschylus and Sophocles had produced a tragedy based on this myth.

581: The player of the *aulos,* a twin-piped reed instrument, wore a strap to hold his cheeks in place (***581 Aulos**).

587: The position of juror was not an elected public office and therefore not accountable to any kind of official scrutiny.

592: Euathlus was known to have prosecuted Protagoras the sophist for heresy.

for our democratic rights. Also, no one would ever dare to try and pass a motion
in the People's Assembly unless they've made provisions to have an early recess
in the courts. Then we get dismissed nice and early after just one case.
Then there's Cleon, the great bellower himself, he loves us, we're the only
people he doesn't bite chunks out of. He protects us, holds us in his arms,
keeps the flies off us. Which is more than you've ever done for your poor old dad!*
What about Theorus, what a man! Is he a man? Anyway, he is always
crawling on in to give our boots a good licking, or scratch our backs.
Just think of all these wonderful things you're depriving me of, and you said
that you were going to prove that I was a slave!

CONTRACLEON:
You can go on talking about it as much as you like, but I'll prove that you're
just a dirty old arse, and no amount of your so-called power will wipe you clean!

PROCLEON:
I know! I know! I'd forgotten something. What about my pay, eh?
That's the best thing of all. When I get home with my money, they can't get enough
of me. First of all, my daughter washes my feet and gives them a massage.
Then, she kisses me and whispers sweet nothings into my ear, "Daddy, dear daddy."
All the time she's using her tongue to try and fish my three obols out of my mouth!

597: Cleon was said to have possessed an incredibly loud voice which he used to great effect in the assembly.

600: For Theorus, see note on line 42.

610: Greeks often carried small coins in their mouths.

Then the wife comes running out of the house and offers me all manner
of delicacies and sweet things, telling me to "have a little nibble of this my dear"
I love all that. And, I don't have to rely on you and that damned slave of yours
to feed me either, miserable bastard. When he eventually deigns to bring me
my supper, all he does is mutter rude remarks under his breath, I've heard him!
If I get hungry, I've got my own defense against a sudden attack of hunger.

(He produces a squashed cake from under his cloak.)

If I don't get a drink, I've got my own little "donkey,"
and when I pour myself a tot, it even brays.

(Procleon takes his wine flask and squeezes some wine out of it, which makes a farting sound.)

So (*faaaart*) to your fancy wine basin!

(Procleon takes a drink of wine and bursts into song.)

Zeus-like power is in my grasp,
And I am viewed in equal wonder.
A noisy courtroom people pass,
And say, "By Zeus! What a thunder!"

Verdicts flash like a lightning zap,
Defendants quake at what I'll do.
Great men shudder and rich men crap.
So I am not at all afraid of you!

617: A small flask with large handles that resembled donkey ears, or a small wineskin (***617 Little donkey**).

618: Either the gurgling of the wine pouring from the clay spout or the noise made when the wineskin was squeezed.

619: This was a *dinos*, used for mixing wine at a symposium, the intellectual drinking parties frequented by Contracleon.

630: Procleon compares his power as a juror to that of Zeus, king of the gods, who controls thunder and lightning.

(The chorus joins in singing Procleon's song.)

CHORUS:
A beautiful speech, so much grace,
Superb words put him in his place.
A better argument he won't find,

PROCLEON:
And he thought he would strip my vines!
Now he knows that he's beat for sure.

CHORUS:
You said it all, there is nothing more!
Such forceful language and fine debate,
As a public speaker you are first rate!
I swell up with pride at your conquest,
I feel like a juror on the Isle of the Blessed.
And now the score stands at one to nil.

PROCLEON:
He's nervous now, he can't stand still!
He has the look of a beaten man.

CHORUS:
It's obvious you've wrecked his plan.
He can only weave a web of lies,
because his ways we all despise.
He'll not be able to soothe our rage,
our terrible anger will last for days!

(The chorus addresses Contracleon.)

CHORUS:
You've got a huge millstone around your neck, my lad.
Perhaps you think it will grind down our anger?

634: A rustic expression that means an easy victory.

640: The legendary place where heroes live in happiness and luxury for all eternity.

CONTRACLEON:

Gentlemen, I hope you will understand what a difficult task it is for me to stand
before you and attempt to cure the city of one of her most vile afflictions.
It will require a degree of skill and intelligence far beyond the ability of, say,
the average comic poet. Nonetheless: "Our father who art the son of Cronus . . ."

PROCLEON:

Stop! There's enough "Old fathers" here already. You have to prove that I'm a slave.
Get on with it, otherwise I'll damn well kill you myself right where you stand!
I suppose I'll be barred from the sacrificial feasts after that. Never mind.

CONTRACLEON:

All right, daddy, listen, and please stop frowning at me. I want you to quickly add up,
not with your counters, by hand, how much tribute Athens receives from the allied states.

(Procleon starts to calculate.)

Then add all the tax revenue, the one percent sales tax, the legal fees and fines, the revenue
from the mines,

(Procleon works feverishly to keep up.)

the market tax, harbor duties, state rents, and government confiscations.*
What's the grand total?

(Procleon looks up, completely confused.)

652: An old invocation found in Homer. Cronus ruled heaven before being usurped by his son Zeus.

653: A murderer was polluted by the blood of his or her victim until ritually purified.

Nearly two thousand talents a year!*
Now take out of that the amount of pay given to the jurors each year, let's see, six thousand jurors* . . .

(Procleon goes back to calculating.)

"This Athens, this teeming womb of jurors,"*
. . . that makes about one hundred and fifty talents.*

(Procleon looks up, astounded.)

PROCLEON:
What? Do you mean to tell me that our pay doesn't even amount to ten percent of the state revenue!

CONTRACLEON:
That's correct.

PROCLEON:
So where the hell does the rest of the cash go?

CONTRACLEON:
You know, the "I-will-never-betray-the-Athenian-rabble-and-I'll-always-
fight-for-the-plebs" people. The very same people you choose to rule over you!
But you've been had, hoodwinked with all their clever talk. They go around
threatening the allies, saying that they will unleash their thunderous speeches and
move to have them overthrown, if they don't pay them a bribe worth fifty talents.*
Meanwhile, you lot seem quite content to gnaw at the bones of your own empire!
The allies take one look at you and see a common rabble feeding on the swill,
slopping out of a voting urn. You're nothing to them, just slaves to the system.
But you should see the gifts they give to these other fellows, caviar, fine wines,
cheese, expensive carpets, honey, sesame cakes, lovely soft pillows, libation bowls,

superb clothes, jewelry, and drinking cups. Everything a man could possibly need
to stay healthy and be wealthy! And what do they give you? You who won it all in
the first place battling on land and sweating at the oar. I doubt that they would
even give you a clove of garlic to season a measly bowl of fish stew!

PROCLEON:
You're right! Only yesterday I had to send for three garlic bulbs from Eucharides.
But where's all this leading? I'm getting fed up with you!
You said that you were going to prove that I am a slave.

CONTRACLEON:
Surely it is complete slavery for all these men and their lackeys to have prime
government posts and get huge fat salaries, while you lot roll over with pleasure
at your paltry three obol dole? Which, I might add, is money that you earned
in the first place, rowing, battling, and scrapping for the state. You go running
from pillar to post whenever they snap their fingers! What really gets my goat
is when I see some dimwitted young poofter, like the son of Chaereas, come
mincing up, wiggling his little arse, and start bossing you around, telling you when
to be in court and saying, "If any of you are late, then you won't get your three obols."

678: The luxurious lifestyle of the demagogues conflicts with the poverty of the elderly jurors, who fought for the empire in the first place.

680: Garlic was a cure for a sore anus. Procleon quips that he was forced to get his garlic from Eucharides, a known homosexual playboy (***680 Eucharides**).

688: This character is unknown.

He still gets his prosecutor's fee, a whole drachma, whatever time of day
he decides to swan in. They're all in it together, defenders and prosecutors.
If the accused offers a bribe, they split it fifty-fifty, and rig the whole thing.
Just like a couple of lumberjacks sawing down a tree, one pulling the case
his way, the other yielding and letting it go, and you lot are so enamored by the
court cashier that you can't see what's going on right under your noses!

PROCLEON:
I cannot believe they'd do that to me. You're really rocking the boat
and churning things up. I'm all at sea!

CONTRACLEON:
Just imagine how wealthy you and all the people would be, if it wasn't for these
rabble-rousing politicians herding you about like cattle. The Athenians control
a huge amount of cities, reaching from the Black Sea, all the way to Sardinia,*
but you get absolutely nothing, except that pitiful jury pay that you draw.
Even that they feed to you in little drips, a day at a time, just barely enough
to live on, because they want you poor and hungry. Why? So you'll never bite the hand
that feeds you, and come running whenever they need to savage one of their enemies.
It's a dog's life! If they really cared about the people, they could easily provide
every citizen with a good living. There must be at least a thousand states that pay*
us tribute, all they would have to do is make each one care for twenty Athenians,

---

691: There were six obols in a drachma.

and you'd have twenty thousand of the working class feasting like kings.*
Just think, the finest meats, fresh cream, herbs and spices. You'd enjoy a life
worthy of this land and her victory of Marathon. Instead, you get in line
for the man with the obols, like a bunch of olive-picking field hands!

(Procleon starts to wither.)

PROCLEON:
Good gods! What's coming over me? I'm starting to feel numb.
I can't keep my sword up. I feel all limp!*

CONTRACLEON:
But look what happens when they get frightened that they're exploiting you too far.
What do they do? They offer you the lands of Euboea and promise to hand out fifty
bushels of wheat per man. But it never turned up, did it? All you got was five bushels,
and you had to suffer the indignity of proving that you were a true citizen. What's more,
they gave you only a handful a day, and to cap it all, it wasn't even wheat, it was barley.
Don't you understand now? That's why I've been locking you up, I want to look after you.
It should be me who feeds you. I don't want those politicians taking advantage
of my father, and making a fool out of you with their overblown oratory.
I'll give you anything your heart desires, you only have to ask for it.

711: The battle of Marathon in 490 was a stunning victory by the Athenian infantry over the vastly superior Persian invaders (***711 Marathon**).

716: The long island which lay to the northeast of Attica and was a major grain producer. In 446 it revolted from Athenian control and was reconquered by Pericles, who parceled out the land to Athenian citizens (***716 Euboea**).

But no more milk of courtroom blindness!

CHORUS:
It was a wise man who once said, "you should never decide until you have heard both sides of the argument." We have made up our minds that Contracleon* is the clear winner. We will lower our shafts. Our anger has abated!

(The chorus breaks into song and addresses Procleon.)

CHORUS:
Be persuaded by his words,
Don't be a stubborn old fool.
Bend your stiffened manhood,
He's giving good advice to you.

He's been blessed by some god,
I wish that I had such a boy.
It is your welfare he has at heart,
His loving care you will enjoy.

CONTRACLEON:
I'll give him everything he needs,
All the pleasures of the old;
Warming porridge, leather coats,
Soft blankets to keep away the cold.

He looks so down, he makes no sound.
This behavior is very silly,
For I'll bring him ladies of the night,
*To stroke and rub his willy!**

CHORUS:
It's no surprise he has just lost
What once was his obsession.

724: The Greek has "Paymaster's milk to drink." An ironic variation on the expression "bird's milk" (see note on line 509).

He's heard good sense, was he wrong
To enjoy a legal profession?

Was he persuaded by your speech?
Did the truth seem very strange?
Either way, we heard him say,
That if defeated, he would change.

PROCLEON:
(In a high tragic style) "Woe is me! Woe is me!"

CONTRACLEON:
What are you shouting about now?

PROCLEON:
"Your promises mean naught to me,
for there, there is where I long to be.
The only place to which I am devoted,
where the herald cries who has not voted!
At the voting urns where the jurors stop,
I am the last to let my pebble drop!"

(Procleon prepares to fall on his sword.)

"Jurors, thy soul's flight,
If it find heaven, must find it out tonight."*

(He botches his "suicide" attempt.)

I am the "soul" survivor!

(He tries again.)

"Make way thou shady thickets, let me pass!"*

(He falls flat on his back.)

I've come a cropper and fallen on my arse!

Oh Heracles let me never be forced to serve on the jury
that finds my beloved Cleon guilty of theft!*

757: Procleon responds in the manner of a Euripidean tragic actor.

CONTRACLEON:
Come, father, by all the gods, please, will you take my advice?

PROCLEON:
What advice? You can say whatever you like, except just one thing.

CONTRACLEON:
And what might that be?

PROCLEON:
I won't ever give up my jury work, never! Over my dead body!

CONTRACLEON:
All right, all right, if you won't give it up, why not stay at home and judge,
at least then you won't have to walk all the way to the courthouse every day.

PROCLEON:
Judge cases at home? What cases? What are you talking about?

CONTRACLEON:
You can do exactly the same here as you do in court. For example, say one of the
housemaids has been secretly going "in and out," you could seize her "assets,"
that'd be nice, wouldn't it? That's all you lot think about in court anyway.
If it's a nice day, you can sit out in the sun and fine the accused in "fine" weather.
If it's snowing, you can sit by the fire and listen to "heated" debates, and if it rains,
you can stay inside and put the defendants in "deep water." Best of all, if you happen
to sleep in one morning, then there won't be any court clerk to stop you getting
to the bench, it will be entirely up to you when to convene the court.

PROCLEON:
Now that I like!

CONTRACLEON:
If you get one of those boring old defense speeches droning on and on,
you won't have to go hungry, chewing up your tongue and the poor old defendant.

PROCLEON:
Eh? How will I decide cases properly if I'm eating food all the time?

CONTRACLEON:
Oh, you would be a far better judge. After all, you must have heard the saying,
"the proof of the pudding is in the eating." You can "chew the facts"
and then make them "eat their words!"

PROCLEON:
You know, this is starting to sound pretty good. But tell me one thing,
where will I get my pay from? Eh?

CONTRACLEON:
From me.

PROCLEON:
Fine, that means I might get the full amount for once and not have to share it
with anyone else. Do you have any idea what that tight old bastard Lysistratus
did to me one time? The court paid us, but they didn't have the right change, so they
gave us a one drachma coin to split. Well, we went down to the fish market
to get change, but that cheating old shit put three fish scales in my mouth,
instead of the obols I should have had. Well, I didn't realize until I caught a whiff

---

788: Lysistratus appears in a number of Aristophanes' plays, where he is portrayed as a pauper and a practical joker.

of them, damn things stank, I nearly puked! So I had a right go at him.

CONTRACLEON:
Oh yes, so what did he say?

PROCLEON:
"You must have the guts of a goat to have eaten away your cash so fast."

CONTRACLEON:
Can't you see what a great idea this is?

PROCLEON:
Yes, it's beginning to make a lot of sense. All right, I'll do it!

CONTRACLEON:
Wait here, and I'll go and get everything ready.

(Contracleon runs inside.)

PROCLEON:
Do you see that! Who'd have thought it! I had heard that
the Athenians were given an oracle that said one day
they would judge their cases at home, and now it's come true!*
Everyone will soon have their own little law courts in the yard,
just like those little shrines of Hecate we have out front!

*(Contracleon returns with the slaves carrying various household articles.)**

CONTRACLEON:
Right then, what do you think about this? I've brought everything
I promised and a few little extras to make you really comfortable.

(Contracleon hangs up a small jug.)

804: An underworld goddess of witchcraft, curses, and transformation. Her shrines stood on boundaries, usually where a smaller road joined a larger one or at the end of a path leading to a house (***804 Hecate**).

First things first, let me hang a jug on this little knob so that you can relieve yourself during the proceedings.

PROCLEON:

That's good thinking, that is, son! You've discovered the perfect cure for a full bladder. Just what an old man like me needs.

*(Contracleon sets down a brazier and sets a pot on it.)**

CONTRACLEON:

Here's a nice warm fire and some lovely lentil soup to keep you going.

PROCLEON:

Brilliant! Now if I'm sick, I can still get paid, and all the time I'll be here at home, slurping down lentil soup!

(Contracleon puts the cock up on a perch.)

What's the cock for?*

CONTRACLEON:

He's here to wake you up in case you nod off during a defense speech.
He'll be the first to spot a cockeyed defense!

PROCLEON:

There's something still not quite right.

CONTRACLEON:

What! What!

PROCLEON:

We need the shrine of Lycus, the juryman's patron hero.

CONTRACLEON:

Eh . . .

*(He takes a large amphora, turns it upside down, and places it on the ground.)**

819: For Lycus, see note on line 389.

Look! There he is!

(Procleon gets up to inspect the upturned amphora, which looks decidedly phallic.)

PROCLEON:
Lord Lycus! Firmest of all the heroes. How hard you look today!

CONTRACLEON:
I think he looks like Cleonymus, personally.

PROCLEON:
Another dickhead. Hey, Cleonymus, we've found where you dropped your weapon!

CONTRACLEON:
Come on, daddy, sit down so we can call the first case.

(Procleon rushes back to his seat.)

PROCLEON:
Our first sitting! I'm ready, come on, come on!

CONTRACLEON:
Well now, let's see, who can I call first? Who has been misbehaving lately?
I know! Thratta didn't polish my valuables very well the other day . . .*

PROCLEON:
STOP! You'll be the death of me, you will! How can anyone charged with an offense
possibly make a defense if we haven't got a fence in the first place? It's the first
of all the sacred objects that are revealed to us as we enter the court.

822: For Cleonymus, see note on line 19.

831: Procleon treats the courthouse as if it were the site of a sacred mystery cult. At Eleusis, the rites involved having a number of sacred objects revealed during the course of initiation (***831 Sacred objects revealed**).

Contracleon:
By the gods! You're right, it's not here.

Procleon:
It's all right, I will fix it!

(Procleon runs inside the house.)

Contracleon:
He's really hooked on this whole courtroom thing.

(Enter Xanthias.)

Xanthias:
That bloody dog! I'm sick of it!

Contracleon:
Whatever is the matter now?

Xanthias:
It's that dog of ours, Labes! He's just stormed into the kitchen,
grabbed a great big piece of Sicilian cheese, shoved it in his huge
hungry chops, then ran off, and scoffed the lot!.

Contracleon:
Wonderful! We have our first case, The Household versus Labes the Dog.
Xanthias, you'll have to act as the prosecuting counsel.

Xanthias:
We've already got a prosecutor. The other dog involved in this affair, is on record
as stating that he will pursue legal proceedings personally, should it go to trial.

837: Labes means "grabber" and is a play on the name Laches, the general who was accused by Cleon of embezzling from the Sicilian cities (see note on line 241).

842: This dog will actually resemble Cleon, who had made his intention to bring charges against Laches widely known (see note on line 241).

CONTRACLEON:
Excellent! Have them both brought before the court.

XANTHIAS:
I'm on my way.

(Procleon comes dashing out of the house carrying a small wicker fence.)

CONTRACLEON:
What have you got there?

PROCLEON:
It's the pigpen for the swine we sacrifice to Hestia.

CONTRACLEON:
But you can't use that! It's sacrilege!

PROCLEON:
Oh, don't be so pigheaded, I just wanted to go the whole hog.
Come on, let's get started. I'm dying to fine someone!

CONTRACLEON:
I'll just go inside and fetch the charge sheets to post on the board.

(Contracleon goes into the house.)

PROCLEON:
Well, hurry up! You're wasting the court's time, you are!
I can't wait to run my fingers through that lovely soft wax!

(Contracleon dashes out of the house with some wooden chopping boards.)

844: The goddess of the hearth and home.

845: The pig was a common sacrifice, and, when butchered for household consumption, would presumably be first offered to Hestia. Contracleon assumes that the pigpen also belongs to Hestia and that it is sacrilege to use it for any other purpose.

CONTRACLEON:
Here we are, notice boards!

PROCLEON:
Right! Call the first case!

CONTRACLEON:
Call the first case!

PROCLEON:
Who's up first, then?

CONTRACLEON:
Shit! I've forgotten the voting urns.

(Contracleon starts running toward the door.)

PROCLEON:
Shit! But hang on. Where are you off to now?

CONTRACLEON:
To get the voting urns.

PROCLEON:
Don't worry, I've got a pair of beakers that will do nicely.

(He gives the two beakers to Contracleon.)

CONTRACLEON:
Right, we've got everything we need, we can start the proceedings.
No, wait! What about the court water clock?

PROCLEON:
(Pointing to his chamber pot) Well, what do you think that is, then?
It's a perfect water clock. When I've filled it up, the case is over!

CONTRACLEON:
I have to admire your resourcefulness, like a true Athenian.
Quickly, someone bring out the sacred fire, and the myrtle

857: See (***93 Water clock**).

wreaths. Make sure you remember to fetch the incense. Let us pray to the gods before we begin.*

(The chorus accompanies the rites with a hymn as Contracleon performs the sacred rites.)

CHORUS:
Say your prayers, bless the peace,
The fighting's over, the war has ceased.
You've made a treaty good and strong,
We'll sing its praises with this song.

CONTRACLEON:
Let no ill words be spoken here.

CHORUS:
*Oh, Lord Apollo have Good Fortune guard**
This makeshift court in this front yard.
May we discover much to commend,
And may our wanderings come to an end.

Praise Apollo!

CONTRACLEON:
Our master who art in heaven,
Apollo be thy name,
thy courtyard come
to this father's son.
Give us this day new holy rites,
and forgive dad his hardheartedness,
as we give his soul some sweetness from us.
Lead him not into litigation
and deliver him from malice.
Find him some kind wisdom
to tolerate the sad stories,
and never sting ever again.

CHORUS:
Let us join together in asking that this new institution
founded here receive all blessings from on high.

All of us endorse your plan,

It's clear you love the common man.
A better democrat we've never met
At least among the younger set.

CONTRACLEON:
All jurors are requested to be seated in the courtroom. Latecomers will not be admitted once the speeches have commenced.

PROCLEON:
Who is the accused? I can't wait to convict him!

CONTRACLEON:
Order! Order in the court of the reading of the charges! The dog from Cydathenaeum
hereby brings a suit against one Labes of Aexone for the illegal and solitary
consumption of one Sicilian cheese. The prosecution proposes
that the maximum penalty should be imposed, namely the sycamore collar.*

PROCLEON:
No! No! A dog's death if he's found guilty.

CONTRACLEON:
The defendant, Labes, will stand before the court.

*(Enter the first dog, Labes, from the house.)**

PROCLEON:
This one's a villain if ever I saw one. He looks like a right thug.
And he won't get around me with that stupid grin of his.
Where's the hound from Cydathenaeum? Call the other dog.

*(Enter the second dog, Cleonhound.)**

895: Aristophanes plays on the similarity between *kleôn* ("Cleon") and *kuôn* ("dog"). Furthermore, Cleon was from the *deme* (district) of Cydathenaeum (as was Aristophanes).

896: Laches was a member of the deme of Aexone.

CLEONHOUND:
Ruff! Ruff!

CONTRACLEON:
Present!

XANTHIAS:
This one's just as rough as Labes, all he's good for
is barking at people and licking plates clean!

CONTRACLEON:
Silence in the court! *(to Cleonhound)* Be seated! Proceed with the charges.

PROCLEON:
Now seems a good time to have a little slurp of soup.

(Procleon takes a gulp of soup, but when Cleonhound starts shouting, he spits it out in shock.)

CLEONHOUND:
MEMBERS OF THE JURY. YOU WILL NOW BE FULLY AWARE OF THE CHARGES
I AM BRINGING AGAINST THE DEFENDANT SEATED BEFORE YOU.
HE HAS WILLFULLY COMMITTED THE MOST HEINOUS OF CRIMES NOT JUST
AGAINST ME, BUT IN SO DOING, AGAINST THE ENTIRE HOI POLLOI!
FOR THIS VERY DOG DID "SICILICIZE" AN ENORMOUS QUANTITY OF CHEESE,
THEN SCURRIED OFF TO A DARK CORNER WHERE HE WOLFED IT ALL DOWN!

PROCLEON:
By Zeus, he's plainly guilty! Just a minute ago the dirty dog
belched at me, and there was a disgusting smell of cheese!

911: The Greek has *katesikelize,* a comic invention derived from the name Sicily.

CLEONHOUND:

AND WHAT'S MORE, THE SAID DOG FAILED TO SUPPLY MY GOOD SELF
WITH AN APPROPRIATE SHARE OF THE AFOREMENTIONED CHEESE!
MEMBERS OF THE JURY, I PUT IT TO YOU, WHO IS GOING TO LOOK AFTER
YOUR INTERESTS UNLESS A PROPER SHARE IS FIRST GIVEN TO ME,
YOUR WATCHDOG?*

PROCLEON:

I certainly didn't get any, neither did the people.
This defendant is really in the soup now!

(Procleon tries to take a slurp of soup, but Contracleon grabs his arm.)

CONTRACLEON:

For god's sake, father, don't prejudge the poor fellow.
Wait until you've heard both arguments and then decide.

PROCLEON:

My dear boy, it's an open-and-shut case, the facts are positively screaming at you.

CLEONHOUND:

YOU MUSTN'T ACQUIT HIM! YOU CAN'T! HE'S A MONOGUZZLER,
HE MAKES A DOG'S DINNER OUT OF EVERYTHING! HE CRUISED
AROUND THE KITCHEN ISLAND BITING CHUNKS OUT OF THE RIND.

PROCLEON:

And I haven't even got a pot to piss in!

925: A large mortar for grinding and food preparation. In profile it would have resembled the triangular shape of Sicily (***925 Mortar**).

CONTRACLEON:
Yes you have, I gave you one.

CLEONHOUND:
CONVICT HIM! THIS HOUSE IS NOT BIG ENOUGH FOR TWO THIEVES!
I'M NOT GOING TO WASTE MY DOG BREATH BARKING OVER NOTHING!
IF I DON'T GET A CONVICTION, YOU'RE NEVER GOING
TO HEAR ANOTHER DAMN WOOF OUT OF ME!

PROCLEON:
Bravo! Bravo! That's quite a lot of felonies you've charged him with.
He's obviously an absolute scoundrel, there's no doubt about that!
(to the cock)
What do you think, Rooster? Look, by Zeus! He's winking at me.*
I've a willing cock! Bailiff! Get me the court water clock.

CONTRACLEON:
You're quite capable of doing that yourself. I'm calling the witnesses.

(Procleon takes the chamberpot, walks upstage, turns around, and urinates into the pot.)

The defense for Labes calls the following witnesses:
Big Dish! Grinder! Cheese grater! Griddle! Honey pot!
And any other little pieces with burnished bottoms!*

(to Procleon) Have you finished? Good, now sit down and stop running about.

(Procleon runs back to his seat.)

PROCLEON:
(Pointing at Labes) I know someone else who'll have the runs before long.

CONTRACLEON:
Will you stop being so bad tempered and strict with the poor defendants?
You just can't wait to get your teeth into them, can you?
Labes, take the stand and make your defense.

(Labes takes the stand but remains silent.)

Why don't you speak? Come on, get on with it!

PROCLEON:
He's obviously got nothing to say.

CONTRACLEON:
I've seen this kind of thing before. It happened to Thucydides
at his trial, sudden acute paralysis of the jaw, quite painful really.
(To Labes) Get out of the way, I'll conduct the defense.

(Labes steps aside.)

Ahem! Members of the jury, it is a difficult task to defend the honor
of a slandered dog. However, I must remind you of his previous good character
and extreme bravery demonstrated while chasing away hostile wolves.

PROCLEON:
That's a load of old bollocks! He's a thief and a conspirator!

CONTRACLEON:
Not at all, he is a dog of the highest pedigree.
He is quite skilled at rounding up great multitudes of sheep.

PROCLEON:
That's no use at all if he goes and keeps the all the cheese to himself.

CONTRACLEON:
No use? But he stands and fights for you, and guards the door. He's a top dog,
his character is quite unblemished. If he did commit one small indiscretion, then
I ask the court to show leniency. He never had the opportunities that others were

---

946: Not the historian, but a political enemy of Pericles who was ostracized (banished by popular vote) for ten years in 443 (***946 Thucydides**).

given, he comes from a deprived kennel, he never even learned to play the lyre.

PROCLEON:

As far as I'm concerned, I think it was a great pity that he learned to read and write, then he wouldn't have been able to submit false accounts to the court!*

CONTRACLEON:

Sir, please hear the testimony of my first witness. Cheese grater, take the stand.

*(The cheese grater takes the stand.)**

Please answer clearly. I understand that you acted for my client in the position of treasurer, is that correct?

(The cheese grater nods.)

And am I correct in assuming that your gratings were properly distributed to the troops?

(He nods again.)

He says they were.

PROCLEON:

He's lying! I'm sure of it. Step down!

(The cheese grater leaves the stand.)

CONTRACLEON:

Members of the jury, I ask you to show compassion for those afflicted by misfortune. While Labes leads a dog's life, out on active service, living off old bones and rotten fish, this lapdog *(pointing to Cleonhound)*, this horrendous hound, skulks at home and snatches a hefty share of whatever anyone

---

959: The education of a refined young Athenian gentleman included music tuition.

else brings into the house. And if he doesn't get what he wants, he bites!

PROCLEON:
Oh No! This can't be happening! I'm starting to go all soft! This is terrible!
It's the sickness dreaded by all jurors: I'm actually being persuaded!

CONTRACLEON:
I beg you, show mercy on this poor dog, please, dear father, don't order
him to be put down. Where are his children? *(Some puppies are brought out.)*

PROCLEON:
No! Not the damn kids!

CONTRACLEON:
Come here, you poor little puppies, and plead to the jury, come on, beg!
Pray to him, let him see your tears and hear your whimpers.

(The puppies surround Procleon and whimper pathetically.)

PROCLEON:
(In tears) Step down, step down, step down, step down.

CONTRACLEON:
I'll step down, though I hope I will not join the ranks of the many men
who have heard those words before me. For they rested their cases
sure of an acquittal only to be deceived and handed a conviction.

PROCLEON:
(Still sobbing) It's that damn soup! It's so hot that it has
brought tears to my eyes. It's not good for an old man like me
to fill up on piping hot lentil soup, it makes everything all mushy.

972: Cleon had recently served as a general in 424–23 and had spent most of this time in Athens (***39 Cleon**).

977: See lines 568–69.

CONTRACLEON:
So are you going to let him off, then?

PROCLEON:
That's a hard one, that is.

CONTRACLEON:
Come on father, this is a golden opportunity to turn to better ways. Here, just take this little pebble in your hand, close your eyes, nip over to the second urn, and acquit him. It's that easy!

(Procleon makes his way downstage to where the two beakers are standing and then suddenly reels back.)

PROCLEON:
NOOOO! I can't! He's not the only one who never learned to play the lyre!

(Contracleon takes his arm and leads him. Meanwhile, Xanthias switches the beakers.)

CONTRACLEON:
Come on then, I'll help you. I know a nice shortcut to the voting urns.

PROCLEON:
(Arriving at the urns) Is this the guilty urn?

CONTRACLEON:
That's right.

PROCLEON:
In it goes then. *(He drops the pebble into the acquittal urn.)*

(Procleon returns to his seat.)

CONTRACLEON:
(*Aside*) Got him! He's voted "not guilty." At last!

PROCLEON:
Well, what's the result?

CONTRACLEON:
Hang on, we've got to wait for the vote count.

(Contracleon tips out the beakers.)

Labes, you are hereby acquitted of all charges!

(Procleon faints, and Cleonhound storms off in disgust.)

Father! Father! What's wrong! Oh my gods! Get some water!

*(Xanthias throws the contents of the chamber pot in Procleon's face, and he comes around.)**

PROCLEON:
Blughhh! Tell me the truth, son, he wasn't really acquitted, was he?

CONTRACLEON:
Yes he was.

(During the next few lines the slaves clear the court props, and Labes is led off.)

PROCLEON:
Then I'm finished!

CONTRACLEON:
Don't worry, father, here stand up.

(Contracleon helps his father to his feet.)

PROCLEON:
I can't bear it, to have such a thing on my conscience, I had a man brought
up before me on a charge and . . . and . . . I let him go! How did this happen to me?
Oh great gods above, you must forgive me, I didn't know what
I was doing. It was just a momentary lapse of character. Ohhh!

CONTRACLEON:
Don't be upset, father, I'll look after you now. There's a great big world out

there just waiting for you, and I'm going to be your guide, I'll take you
everywhere; high-class parties, dinners, the theatre. It'll be nothing but
pleasure from now on, and just think, you won't ever be tricked and laughed at
by Hyperbolus again. Come on, what are you waiting for? Let's go!

PROCLEON:
All right, son, if you say so.

CHORUS:
Good luck, wherever your journey may take you.

(Exit Procleon and Contracleon.)

[Parabasis]*

(The chorus addresses the audience.)

CHORUS:
Now hear this message loud and clear,
You many thousands gathered here.
We only hope you'll recognize
That the coming words are very wise:
A stupid crowd might not heed our call,
But we know that's not like you at all!

CHORUS:
Now heed me, all you people, it's high time you heard the simple truth.
The author of this magnificent play needs to speak to you, to tell you his message.
He speaks directly to you, through me, and he tells me that you have been bad, really,
really bad! You've done him an awful wrong, especially after all the wonderful things

---

1007: At this time a prosecutor in the courts and still fairly young. He went on to succeed Cleon as the most prominent politician in the assembly and was often vilified in comedy.

he has given you. Yes, I know in his early days he had to work in secret, unseen,
playing second fiddle to other dramatists. Just like the prophet Eurycles, who speaks
through others, he too got under their skin, and true comic genius was heard.
Then on that great day he ventured forth, alone into the fray, riding his own chariot
of comedy and holding the reins of his personal team of thoroughbred muses.
And he won great honor, the likes of which had never before been awarded to any one man.
And when he reached this pinnacle of greatness, was he arrogant? No. Did you see
him mincing around the gymnasium, making passes at all and sundry? No. Did this man
ever take a bribe from a spurned lover, to send up his little fancy boy on this very stage? No!*
He would never stoop so low as to prostitute the muse! And when he produced his own
great plays, did he attack mere men? Of course not! Like the mighty Heracles, he challenged
the greatest monsters in our land. Alone he stood his ground against the saber-toothed beast,
whose eyes shot terrible rays like those of the searing doggie-style star.
Yes, the beast, with the hundred-headed serpent of flattery crawling in its hair,

---

1019: A spirit that spoke prophecies through men rather like a medium at a séance. He was said to inhabit men's bellies (***1019 Eurycles**).

1020: Aristophanes' first three plays, *Banqueters* (427), *Babylonians* (426), and *Acharnians* (425), were all produced by Callistratus. For Aristophanes' early career under Callistratus' patronage, see General Introduction.

1031: This monster is Cleon, who appears to have tried to sue Aristophanes over his play *Babylonians* (426). Aristophanes likens himself to the hero Heracles fighting for his satirical rights (***39 Cleon**).

1032: This is Sirius, the dog star. It was said to bring the fierce heat of summer. However, the word *kunos* (of the dog) is replaced by *kunnês,* the name of a well-known Athenian prostitute.

licking its arse with those slithery, forked tongues. Yes, the beast, with it's heinous roar,
the stench of a rotten seal, the arse of a camel, the looks of a Lamia,
and huge, dirty, great, unwashed . . . BALLS!

Yet he defied all these terrors and resisted all temptation. He fought the good fight for
you and still does so today. Last year he attacked the demons, plagues, fevers,
and nightmares that came by night to throttle your fathers and choke your grandfathers,
with their subpoenas and writs, their affidavits and summonses. Yes, they preyed on you!
You poor harmless, peace-loving people, until you could take no more and you begged
the state for protection! But it was he who delivered you from those curses and purged*
this land of ours from evil, and what did you do in return? You shunned him! Denied him!

YOU LET HIM DOWN WHEN HE NEEDED YOU THE MOST!

Last year he tried to sow a crop of new ideas,

BUT YOU JUST DIDN'T GET THE MESSAGE, DID YOU?

He himself will swear by Dionysus and pour countless libations that no one
had ever seen a better comedy. You should feel shame! Shame on you!
Let's face it, people, no intelligent person will think badly of our author
for being so far ahead of his field that his new concept crashed!

(The whole chorus sings.)

1035: This child-devouring hermaphrodite was originally a mortal woman who was punished by Hera for an affair with Zeus.

1038: In 423 Aristophanes produced *Clouds* at the City Dionysia.

1046: *Clouds* placed third at the City Dionysia in 423.

So in future my friends
You should open your minds
And accept the poet's ideas.

You should listen and learn
And perhaps you might find
Wisdom can last many years,

Just like clothes in a trunk
Packed with a fresh lime.
New concepts will wear
For a very long time!

(The music changes and the chorus sings again.)

In days of old, way back when
We danced with pride and fought like men,
Women ached, virgins quaked,
And wondered when we'd come again!

(Each chorus man thrusts his phallus.)

Though our joints are knackered our bones are old
Our virile spirit has not gone cold.
Back in our prime, we'd win every time,
But we're still strong, still manly, still bold!

The youth of today don't carry spears,
They're poofters, pansies, and queers!
They haven't a care and wear rings in their hair,
We'd still whip 'em in spite of our years!

LEADER:

I'm sure that some of you have been sitting there wondering why I am dressed in this wasp costume. I am sure you would also love to know the reason why we have these stings.

"For I can easily school him, even if he had no skill before."

1057: Athenians stored clothes away with citrus fruit to keep them fresh and the moths away.

1074: A parody of a quote from Euripides' *Stheneboea* (*Fr.* 663), "A poet in fact is schooled by love, even if he had no skill before."

Those of us who sport this handy little addition to our backsides
are very proud to be called native Athenians, a hardy breed
that has time and time again come to its country's rescue whenever
trouble is on the horizon. When those Persian barbarians came to
sack and burn our beautiful city and to smoke us from our nests,
we flew into angry action and swarmed to get our weapons.
We were there to meet them at Marathon! "Shield and spear in hand,"
standing fast in line, buzzing with rage and swelling with manly pride!
Their arrows blotted out the sun from the sky, but we were helped
by our patron goddess, Athena, who sent her sacred owl to fly over
our ranks and bring us luck. By nightfall we'd forced them back.
Then we made a beeline for them, jabbing them up their baggy Persian
fancy pants, stinging their cheeks, their eyebrows, and their arses!
And to this day the barbarians to the East still say,

"Osh kallucj jeratshup ugraxzumthrum sheetarpus nuk!"

Which means, "There is nothing more manly than an Attic wasp!"

(The chorus sings again.)

When I was still a strapping male,
The fiercest foes I would assail.
To foreign shores we'd pull our oars,
To every place our ships would sail.

1079: The Persians had fought the Athenians on two notable occasions: the battle of Marathon in 490 (***711 Marathon**) and the battle of Salamis in 480.

1081: A quote from the tragedy *Momus* (fr. 29) by Achaeus.

1085: The owl was the patron bird of Athena and symbol of Athens. At the battle of Salamis against the Persian navy in 480 an owl had appeared just prior to the Athenian's successful attack.

1087: Trousers or britches were not worn by the Greeks, who ridiculed their Eastern neighbors for their ostentatious clothes (***1087 Fancy pants**).

1089: An additional line from performance used for comic clarity and credited to Robert Richmond.

We never paid honors to a clever speech,
We rewarded the man with the best oar-reach.
We heard no denials, sat through no trials,
Just wondered where our ship would beach!

And all the Persians we chased and fought,
Taking enemy towns and foreign ports.
An empire made, the tribute paid,
*Then stolen by the young in court!**

LEADER:

Whichever way you look at it, we are just like wasps. For a start, no living creature is more angry and savage once provoked, or harder to pacify than we are. We are a lot like wasps in other ways too, we all swarm together in groups as if we were going to our different nests, buzzing to the Archon's jury, swarming to the fraud trials, or nesting in the Odeon courtroom, packed around the walls like grubs in their cells. Our economy is resourceful, too; we sting everybody to make a living! It's true, like all wasps colonies, we too have our drones. Some of them are sitting out there now. They don't have a sting, they just lounge at home eating their way through our hard-won tribute without working for it. And that's what makes us really angry! To think that there are some people among us who shirk their duties to the state, and avoid joining the service. They're just guzzling up our pay, when they've never even lifted an oar, raised a spear, or suffered a single blister to defend our city. I think it's high time we had a new ruling: "Any citizen found not to possess a sting in full working order will no longer receive the daily dole of three obols in state benefits!"

1107: The Archon's court was primarily concerned with cases involving orphans, inheritance, and family disputes.

1108: The fraud trials were presided over by eleven officials and held in a smaller roofed building in the Agora. The Odeon was the large roofed auditorium built by Pericles and situated next to the Theatre of Dionysus at the foot of the Acropolis. It is not known which court convened there.

*(Enter Procleon and Contracleon from the house. Procleon is clutching his old motheaten cloak as Contracleon is carrying a bundle.)**

PROCLEON:
I will not take it off! Not as long as I've breath in my body!
We served, side by side, it virtually saved my life protecting
me from the northern onslaught of the invading . . . wind!

CONTRACLEON:
I'm just trying to do something special for you.

PROCLEON:
No, by Zeus, I don't want anything special! Last time we had
"something special" it was that fancy grilled fish you served me,
cost me an entire day's jury pay to get the puke stains out!

CONTRACLEON:
Oh, come on, you said you were in my hands now, I'll look after you.
Just try it. You never know, you might like it.

PROCLEON:
Well, what do you want me to do then?

CONTRACLEON:
Just throw away that filthy old cloak . . .

(Contracleon manages to remove his father's cloak.)

. . . and put on this nice new robe!

(Contracleon puts the old cloak aside and unwraps the bundle.)

PROCLEON:
Damn kids, you raise them, feed them, educate them,
then as soon as they're old enough, they try and smother you!

CONTRACLEON:
Oh, stop babbling and just put it on.

(Contracleon holds up a huge woolen cloak with large tassels.)

PROCLEON:
In the name of all the gods! What is this terrible thing?

CONTRACLEON:
It's a Persian robe.

PROCLEON:
It looks more like a Persian rug!

CONTRACLEON:
Well, you've obviously never been to Sardis, have you? It's the latest thing there,
but of course you'd know that if you bothered to keep up with the latest fashions.

PROCLEON:
Fashion! I don't know anything about that. I'll tell you this much, it looks like
the kind of thing that poof Morychus would use to cover his "equipment!"*

CONTRACLEON:
Oh father, this was woven in Ecbactana!

PROCLEON:
Exactly! We all know the Persians like fuzzy sausages!

CONTRACLEON:
Really! Father, you're impossible. This is a quality garment,

---

1137: Contracleon is holding a *kaunakes,* a long heavy winter coat covered with woolen tassels and worn in the East.

1140: A city in Lydia (western Turkey), a major commercial and political center. Athenian ambassadors had recently visited the city to negotiate with the Persians.

1143: The capital city of the Median kingdom and a royal residence of the Persian king. It was located on the Iranian plateau near modern day Hamadan.

1144: The woolen tassels hanging from the coat resemble sausages.

handmade be the locals, a very expensive Persian weave.
This coat alone must have used a talent's worth of wool, easily.

PROCLEON:
Then they should've called it a "waste-coat," shouldn't they? Not a Persian robe,
the amount of perfectly good wool thrown away to make this damn monstrosity!

CONTRACLEON:
Stand still and let's just put it on.

(Contracleon puts the coat on Procleon, who runs off, throwing it down.)

PROCLEON:
I'm not wearing that, the blasted thing stinks!

CONTRACLEON:
Please, father, just put it on!

PROCLEON:
No I won't! I'm not going to be accused of being a turncoat!

CONTRACLEON:
Please, father, please, please please PLEASE!

(Procleon finally relents and petulantly holds out his arm.)

PROCLEON:
I'll be roasted alive in that thing, it's like an oven!

CONTRACLEON:
Come on, Daddy. *(Contracleon puts the coat back on his father.)* There we are.

1147: A wild exaggeration, as a talent was an enormous amount of money equivalent to 36,000 obols. A talent was also a unit of weight, but this would still be an enormous amount.

PROCLEON:
Make sure you've got a fork.

CONTRACLEON:
What for?

PROCLEON:
So you can serve me up when I'm poached.

CONTRACLEON:
Right, let's get these awful shoes off you, and get your feet into these lovely Spartan booties.

(Contracleon takes a pair of tall boots out of the bundle.)

PROCLEON:
What! Are you seriously expecting me to put on "enemy footwear"?

CONTRACLEON:
Just stop moaning and put this on.

PROCLEON:
(He does so.) To think that I will be standing on Spartan territory!

CONTRACLEON:
Now the other one.

PROCLEON:
No! You can't! Not this foot! One of its toes is particularly anti-Spartan.

CONTRACLEON:
Can't be helped now *(he puts the boot on).*

PROCLEON:
Oh woe is me! Now I won't have a single blister to show the lads and keep me company in my old age.

1159: High leather boots tied with straps (***1159 Spartan booties**).

CONTRACLEON:
There, now let's see "The Walk."

(Procleon performs a ridiculous walk.)

No! No! No! Put a little panache into it:
some style, sophistication, sensuality!

(Contracleon demonstrates an affected walk across the stage.)

PROCLEON:
I'll give it a go.

(He mimics Contracleon's movements, but without any subtle grace.)

Oh yeah, a man could get used to used to this.
Who do I remind you of?

CONTRACLEON:
Someone who's having hemorrhoid treatment!*

PROCLEON:
I really am trying to get the arse wiggle right.

CONTRACLEON:
Right then, to work! Now if you're going to be socializing with wealthy,
educated people, you'll have to learn a few witty anecdotes.

PROCLEON:
That's all right, I know loads.

CONTRACLEON:
Like what?

PROCLEON:
I know, the one about the farting Lamia!
And the one about what Cardopion did to his old mother with his . . .

1177: For the Lamia see note on line 1035 (***1177 Farting Lamia**).

1178: Cardopion is not known.

CONTRACLEON:
No! Please not that kind of stuff, all those legends are very passé now,
I mean something contemporary, a story about your family, nice and homely.

PROCLEON:
I know some nice homely stories. What did the ferret say to the mouse when . . .*

CONTRACLEON:
(Enraged) NO! You stupid, uneducated shit! *(checking himself)*
Eh . . . said Theogenes, rudely rebuking the manure gatherer.
You can't talk about rodents in the company of great men!

PROCLEON:
Well, what sort of stories should I tell, then?

CONTRACLEON:
Impressive stories, you know the sort of thing, "When I was on
diplomatic duty with Androcles and Cleisthenes . . ."

PROCLEON:
(Laughing) Diplomatic duty! Me? The only diplomatic duty I've ever been on
was to Paros . . . rowing the galley for my two obols navy pay.

1184: A leading political figure and opponent of Cleon who was satirized for his excessive boasting, overindulgence, and obesity (***1184 Theogenes**).

1187: A politician who was satirized as being an ex-slave and a vicious prosecutor. Cleisthenes was frequently portrayed in Aristophanes' plays as a beardless, effeminate man.

1189: An island of the Cyclades in the Aegean Sea which paid tribute to Athens (***1102 An empire made**). Lower-class Athenians served as rowers in the navy and were paid two obols per day.

CONTRACLEON:

Well, tell them how you once saw that great old wrestling champion,
Ephudion, beat Ascondas at unarmed combat.
Tell them what a fine figure of a man he was with his shock of white hair,
his superb muscles, powerful glistening thighs, a chest like armor.

PROCLEON:

Steady on, son! You're letting your emotions run away with you.
How could he possibly compete in the unarmed combat if he was wearing armor?

CONTRACLEON:

It was a poetic metaphor, that's the kind of talk these clever fellows
like to hear. Tell me this then, if you were out at a society party and you
were drinking with a group of complete strangers, what would you tell
them was the most daring and bravest exploit of your youth?

PROCLEON:

My bravest exploit? I know! That time when I went out alone on a dangerous midnight
raid and "liberated" several important implements from old farmer Ergasion's vineyard.

CONTRACLEON:

So that's where you got those vine-props from! No, something heroic, like how you once
hunted down a ferocious boar, or won a hare-coursing tournament, or when you ran in
the torch-race. Try to think of the most outstanding moment of your entire youth.

1191: A champion fighter in the *pankration*, a fight where virtually every manner of unarmed combat was allowed. Nothing is known of Ascondas.

1201: Ergasion means "farmworker." Procleon is talking about vine props which he stole from a vineyard.

1204: All gentlemanly pursuits. The torch-race was an event at a number of Athenian festivals including the Panathenaea.

PROCLEON:
An outstanding moment? Let me think, I know! When I was a big young lad,
I took on Phayllus, the famous runner, and I beat him too.

CONTRACLEON:
You beat Phayllus?

PROCLEON:
Only just though, by two votes. I sued him on obscenity charges!

CONTRACLEON:
I give up! Come over here and practice your recline, let's see if you can learn
how to behave at a symposium and engage in refined intercourse.

PROCLEON:
Recline? How am I supposed to do that?

CONTRACLEON:
Gracefully.

PROCLEON:
Like this?

*(Procleon throws himself onto the couch.)**

CONTRACLEON:
Absolutely not!

PROCLEON:
Show me then.

CONTRACLEON:
Bend gracefully at the knees and pour yourself elegantly and gently onto the cushions.

1207: A famous Athlete from Croton in south Italy. His name became a by-word for speed. Aristophanes puns his name with "phallus" (***1207 Phayllus**).

(Procleon tries to copy Contracleon's movements.)

Now look around the room and compliment the host on the ornaments . . .

PROCLEON:
Your wife has a lovely set of jugs!

CONTRACLEON:
. . . Then gaze up at the ceiling, admire the tapestries on the walls.

(Procleon swings around upside down at an impossible angle and looks up.)

Bring out water for our hands!

(Xanthias comes out of the house with two water bowls.)

Now we dine, now we wash our hands again, and now we toast the gods.

(He demonstrates.)

PROCLEON:
Was it my imagination, or did we just eat dinner?

CONTRACLEON:
The flute girl begins to play, you are drinking with Theorus, Aeschines, Phanus, Cleon, and a funny little foreign chappy sitting next to Acestor. Now in all this distinguished company, do you think that you are capable of joining in the singing?

1207: An extra line from performance to help with Procleon's punchline.

1216: An added line from performance. Procleon is making a complete hash of his attempts to behave in the appropriate manner.

1220: Cronies of Cleon. For Theorus see note on line 42. For Aeschines see note on line 459. Phanus was a supporter of Cleon and assisted in his prosecutions.

1221: Acestor was a dramatist. He is described as a social parasite, a crawler, and of foreign descent (see *Birds* line 30).

1222: This was the *skolia,* a symposium game where guests would sing one or two lines on a theme and then pass to another guest who would add another line or two and so on.

PROCLEON:
Oh yes, I like a good drinking song.*

CONTRACLEON:
Right then, pretend I'm Cleon and I start off with *Harmodius.* Do you know it?

PROCLEON:
I do.

CONTRACLEON:
Right, you pick it up from me:

"Never did an Athenian deserve so much credit . . ."

PROCLEON:
"Nor was there ever such a thieving little shit!"

CONTRACLEON:
You can't sing that! You'd be killed in the uproar. Cleon would threaten to ruin you, destroy your property and have you kicked out of Attica.*

PROCLEON:
Well, if he threatens me, I'll just give him another little song,

"Don't you try to unbalance our city.
*Absolute power corrupts absolutely!"**

CONTRACLEON:
Well, what are you going to do if Theorus, lying at Cleon's feet, takes hold of his right hand and sings,

"My friend, you should remember the fable of Admetus

1224: The famous "Tyrant Killer." He and Aristogeiton assassinated Hipparchus, the brother of the Athenian tyrant Hippias in 514 (***1224 Harmodius**).

1238: Admetus was the mythological king of Pherae in Thessaly. His wife, Alcestis, was rescued from the underworld by Heracles, who was repaying him a debt of guest-friendship.

*And try to show respect to worthy men like us."**

PROCLEON:
I'll just give him a bit of this,

"Those who try to straddle the classes
*Usually end up falling right on their arses!"**

CONTRACLEON:
What about Aeschines, he's regarded, mainly by himself, as an extremely
talented musician and a very learned man, he'll sing:

"I journeyed far to Thessaly
The wealth is hard to surmise,
And Cleitagora came with me . . .

PROCLEON:
"I wish he'd stop telling those lies!"

CONTRACLEON:
I suppose you're as ready as you'll ever be. Right then, we're off
to Philoctemon's house for a dinner party tonight.
Xanthias, pack some party snacks. We're going to need plenty of
food in us if we're going to be spending the night drinking.

PROCLEON:
No, no, I don't approve of drinking. We all know what guzzling wine leads to:
nighttime disturbances, fighting, smashing up people's property, and to top it all,
a hefty fine to pay in the morning, and I'm not just talking about the hangover!

1247: The name of a female poet either from Thessaly or Sparta and the title of a drinking song. There seems to have been a courtesan of the same name, and Aristophanes may be exploiting this (***1247 Cleitagora**).

1250: The name means something like "lovemystuff." But it may also have been the name of a wealthy Athenian.

CONTRACLEON:

Not if you're drinking with real gentlemen. These men can placate anybody.
Either you learn how to say just the right words to calm them down,
or you tell them a witty story, one of Aesop's fables for example, or a story
from Sybaris, some witty little anecdote you picked up at the party.
All you have to do is make a joke out of the whole episode and the victim
will forget all about it, go on his way, and leave you in peace.

PROCLEON:

I'll have to learn a lot of these anecdotes, then, if I want to get off my fines
when I do some serious damage to something. What are we waiting for? Let's go!

(Exit Procleon, Contracleon, and Xanthias offstage.)

[Second Parabasis]

I always thought that I was wise
In full possession of every wit,
I never dreamed I would eulogize
Amynias and his bullshit!

But I have to say he takes the cake,
When it comes to devil may care,
He has Leogoras serve him steak,
And he wears a bow in his long hair!

1259: A Greek city in south Italy that became a byword for the corrupting influence of wealth and overindulgence. Hence "Sybarite stories" were fables about foolish and indulgent human acts.

1267: For Amynias, see note on line 75.

1268: A distinguished Athenian of great wealth who served as a naval commander and ambassador, known for extravagant hospitality and a perfect host for the freeloading Amynias (***1268 Leogoras**).

He eats like Antiphon, it's plain to see,
But his noble front's a farce.
He let us down in Thessaly
Because he's really working class!

For we cannot have the Athenian presence
Represented by men who eat like peasants!

It is Automenes we should congratulate
For fathering sons who are all first rate.
The eldest could not have climbed any higher
With those beautiful tunes he strums on his lyre.
The middle boy is a genius for his age,
What a wealth of talent he brings to the stage.
But the best is Ariphrades, the last you bore,
For this boy really knows how to treat a whore!

(The chorus leader addresses the audience.)

LEADER:
I would like very much to take this opportunity to set the record straight.
Some of you apparently believe that I reached an out-of-court settlement
with Cleon after the pre-trial hearing, when he viciously attacked me
and showered me with abuse. Some of you out there, actually thought that it was
funny to see him banging away at me, huffing and puffing and shouting

---

1270: The wealthy orator and speech writer, executed in 411 for his involvement in the antidemocratic coup.

1273: It seems that Amynias managed to get himself appointed to an important embassy to Pharsalos, a major city in Thessaly.

1275: Automenes is not known.

1278: This is a man named Arignotus.

1282: Possibly a comic dramatist. Described in comedy as a man with a fondness for cunnilingus (***1282 Ariphrades**).

1284: Here Aristophanes uses the parabasis to address the audience via the chorus leader.

his mouth off. Perhaps you think that he successfully managed to put the squeeze
on me and wring out my best gags. Well today I've had the last laugh, the comic's
revenge. I've pulled the rug from right under him. How's that for sour grapes!

(Enter Xanthias, running from offstage.)

XANTHIAS:

I wish I was a tortoise, with a nice hard shell for a skin,
bloody clever bastards those tortoises are, they have the sense
to wear protective clothing to deflect the blows. I've been beaten
black and blue with that damned walking stick of his!

CHORUS:

What's up, laddie?
Did you get a beating for being a naughty boy?

XANTHIAS:

It's the old man, he's completely out of control! He's getting
himself into all kinds of trouble. He's turned into the biggest old
soak in the whole city. He drunk them all under the table, and that's
quite a feat considering the company he was keeping, Hippyllus,
Antiphon, Lycon, Lysistratus, Thuphrastus, and all those mates
of Phrynichus! Complete hooligans! But he was the most depraved
of the lot. They served a wonderfully refined dinner with some
delicious wine, but he just guzzled it all down. Then he jumped up
and started prancing around, laughing, burping, and farting at everybody
like there was no tomorrow! He made a complete ass of himself.
Then he started beating me with his damn stick, shouting, "Come here,

---

1291: Cleon may have sued Aristophanes after *Knights* in 424, where he was portrayed as a slave. If, as this passage implies, some sort of agreement was reached where Aristophanes would refrain from attacking Cleon, it is gleefully and artfully broken with *Wasps* (***39 Cleon**).

1302: For the guests at Philoctemon's party, see ***1302 Company he was keeping**.

boy! Boy! Boy!" At that point Lysistratus piped up and told him that he
looked like a Phrygian who had found his fortune, or a pig in clover.*
Well, the old man made his own comparison and replied that Lysistratus
resembled a locust who had just lost his wings or the actor Sthenelus
pruned of his props. Would you believe it, everyone applauded in approval,
all except Thuphrastus who made a face like a bulldog chewing a bee.
So Procleon rounded on him and said, "Who the blazes do you think you are!
You babbling buffoon, arse-licking whoever happens to be flavor
of the month!" And so he went on and on, insulting all and sundry, telling
rude stories, making sick jokes, it was really embarrassing I can tell you!
Then, when he was so drunk he could hardly see, he decides to set off
for home, knocking over anyone he happened to meet on the way.
(Seeing Procleon coming) No! Here he is now! I'm off before
I get another beating!

*(Enter a drunken Procleon holding a torch and accompanied by Dardanis, the dancing girl. He is being pursued, and there is a great deal of shouting and crashing coming from offstage.)**

PROCLEON:
Get out of the way!
Get back!
Clear off!

1312: A favorite entertainment at a symposium was the comparison game, where each guest would try to outdo the others with witty and acute observations.

1313: Sthenelus was a tragic dramatist and actor. Aristotle described his work as "lucid but ordinary"(*Poetics* 1458a.18–21).

I'll barbecue the lot of you like a load of whitebait!
Piss off!
Bugger off!

PURSUER:
You just wait, I'll have you in court I will,
and I won't be the only one round here
tomorrow with a summons!

PROCLEON:
Bollocks to your summonses!
You're so old-fashioned!
You can stuff your summonses where the sun don't shine!
I can't stand even to hear the word "courthouse."

(He nestles his head on the girl's breasts.)

These are the only kind of jugs that get my vote.
Juryman? What's a juryman? Never heard of it.
Now piss off and leave me alone!

(He leads the girl toward the house.)

Come on, my little love-toy, this way. Hold onto this bit of rope.

(Procleon holds out his phallus for Dardanis and leads her to the house.)

Careful, it's a bit old and frayed, but it can still take a good hard pull.

(They arrive at the door.)

You see how much I care about you, stealing you away from those horrible
men at the party just as they were about to stick their—HIC! BURP!
Well anyway, I think it's time I was given a nice little thank you present for
my trouble don't you? Come on darling, I'm getting old, I need a hand every
now and then. Come on, give it a little kiss, it won't bite.

(Dardanis laughs.)

Oh, you promised! Don't let me down now, that would be a really low blow,
although I'm sure you're quite the expert when it comes to "low blows!"
I'm a respectable upright man. You're making this very hard for me, my dear.
I'm obviously going to have to be very firm. I tell you what, my little honey-pot,
you be nice to me, and as soon as my son dies, I'll buy your freedom, then we
can be together forever. I'm really quite well endowed, but I'm not in full
control of my assets, they haven't fully matured yet, neither have I really!
I'm so young at heart that I'm under constant supervision. It's my son,
you see, he's a bit of a short-tempered-tight-arsed-parsimonious-prick.
He's got my best interests at heart, really, I mean I am an only daddy,
and he doesn't want me turning into a senior delinquent.*

(He sees Contracleon heading toward him.)

Here he comes now! Here, grab hold of this torch and stand really still, and
keep your mouth shut. I know that's difficult in your profession,
but please! I'm going to play a little joke on him, just some
harmless boyish banter. The same kind of thing he did to me
when I went off to be initiated in the Mysteries.

(Dardanis takes the torch and strikes a pose as Contracleon enters.)

CONTRACLEON:
You dirty old pervert! Well, you've really done it now, haven't you?
You might as well nail down the lid of your own coffin!

1354: It was customary for elderly Athenians to pass their estates on to their oldest son and put themselves in their care.

1363: Masked characters set on the initiates journeying to Eleusis and performed acts of comic buffoonery (***1363 The Mysteries**).

As Apollo is my witness, you'll never get away with this!

PROCLEON:
Oh, I can just see you prosecuting a nice court-case with such relish.

CONTRACLEON:
I'll give you a dressing-down! You can't go around stealing dancing girls from parties!

PROCLEON:
Dancing girl? What dancing girl? You're off your damn donkey, you are, talking rubbish like that. And don't look so grave.

CONTRACLEON:
Well, who's this then? It's Dardanis from the party.

PROCLEON:
No it's not. It's a lamp stand. I found it in the marketplace.

CONTRACLEON:
A lamp stand?

PROCLEON:
Yes, latest model, beautiful, isn't it?

(Contracleon points to Dardanis' vagina.)

CONTRACLEON:
Well, what's this black patch in the middle, then?

PROCLEON:
It's the resin, leaves a terrible stain, you know.

(Contracleon feels Dardanis' backside.)

CONTRACLEON:
And what's this lump at the back? Feels like a bottom to me.

1372: The procession of the initiates to Eleusis was accompanied by torch-bearers (***1372 Lamp stand**).

PROCLEON:
Is that all you ever think about! It's just a knot in the wood.

CONTRACLEON:
Knot, my arse! *(To Dardanis)* You come with me.

(Contracleon grabs Dardanis and starts to lead her off.)

PROCLEON:
Oi! What are you doing?

CONTRACLEON:
I'm confiscating this girl, you silly old fool, you wouldn't
remember how to do it anyway, you're past it.

(Dardanis frees herself and runs offstage.)

PROCLEON:
Oh really? Well let me tell you about the time I was on a state mission to the
Olympic Games. I saw Ephudion wrestle Ascondas, and do you know
that old fighter had some lovely moves. He pulled his arm back like that . . .

(He puts Contracleon into a half-nelson.)

turned him round like that . . .

(He spins Contracleon around.)

and smacked him in the nose like that!

(He punches Contracleon, who falls down.)

And the moral of the story is,
never underestimate the old, or you just might end up with a black eye!

CONTRACLEON:
(Dazed) Well, you certainly know your Olympic Games, that's quite clear.

1383: See note on line 1191.

(Enter Myrtia, the baking woman, with Chaerephon.)

MYRTIA:
You must help me! That's him *(pointing to Procleon)*,
that's the man who attacked me and poked me with his torch!
He knocked all the bread off my tray. Ten obols worth,
and four more in damages, at least!

(Contracleon picks himself up from the floor and confronts Procleon.)

CONTRACLEON:
That's marvelous, that is! Now we're going to have all kinds of trouble,
not to mention the lawsuits, all because of you and your damned drinking!

PROCLEON:
Don't worry about it, there's no problem, remember, I can "pacify
the victim with a few choice words, or a witty story." I'll sort her out.

MYRTIA:
By the two goddesses, you won't get away with it,
I'm from a respectable citizen family,*
and I'm going to sue you for ruining my stock!*

PROCLEON:
Madam, I would like, if I may, to tell you an amusing little anecdote.

MYRTIA:
Don't you try any funny business with me, old man.

PROCLEON:
Ahem. One fine evening Aesop was on his way home
from a dinner party when he was barked at
by an annoying female mad dog.

(Procleon draws Myrtia towards him in order to shout in her ear.)

"BITCH!"

(Myrtia, stunned, jumps backward and knocks Chaerephon to the ground.)

—Said Aesop . . .

"Bitch, why don't you stop yapping at me and just go,"
just go and buy some more flour and bake some more damn bread!"

(Procleon falls about laughing, as Chaerephon picks himself up.)

MYRTIA:
How dare you laugh at me, on top of everything else you've done. Right, you asked for it, I summon you to appear before the market inspectors for causing criminal damage to my stock,*
and I've got the philosopher Chaerephon to act as a witness.

(She grabs Chaerephon and pushes him toward Procleon.)

PROCLEON:
No, wait! I've got another one for you. Once the great poet Simonides was competing against that young upstart Lasus.
And do you know what Lasus said to that? "I'm not in the least bit interested."

(Procleon pushes Chaerephon, who falls once more to the ground.)

MYRTIA:
Right, that's it!

(Myrtia storms offstage, dragging Chaerephon with her.)

PROCLEON:
And you can tell that great poofter Chaerephon to piss off as well, witnessing a summons for women! Don't you go dragging him into it,

---

1408: Chaerephon was a philosopher and colleague of Socrates, frequently lampooned for his deathly pale appearance.

1409: Simonides (c. 556–468) was the famous dithyrambic poet from Ceos (***1409 Simonides**).

1410: Lasus was a dithyrambic poet from Hermione and a younger contemporary of Simonides. Both men were invited to Athens by the tyrant Hipparchus, and it is likely that they would have been competitors.

he reminds me of a white-faced Euripidean heroine, like Ino.

CONTRACLEON:
Oh no! Now there's someone else coming,

(Enter an injured man wearing a bloody bandage on his head and clutching the wound. He is accompanied by a silent witness.)

and he's brought a witness!

INJURED MAN:
Oh my bloody head. Old man, I summon you to appear in court on a charge of common assault.

CONTRACLEON:
Assault? That's a criminal charge. *(To the man)* Oh no, please don't summon him! By all the gods don't! I'll pay you compensation, name your price.

PROCLEON:
No, I'll settle this with him myself. I admit I may have had a bit of a go at him.
(To the man) Come over here, I'll tell you what, if you let me tell you how much I should pay in settlement, we can be friends in the future, or would you rather set the damages yourself?

INJURED MAN:
You make the offer, I don't want all the palaver of legal proceedings.

PROCLEON:
Ahem. A man from Sybaris happened to fall from his chariot and hurt his head
really badly. You see the thing was that this man wasn't a very good driver.
Well, his mate saw him lying there and said, "Men should stick to their own trades."

1414: The daughter of King Cadmus of Thebes. Hera turned Ino into a sea monster, and she was connected with initiation rites. She was a frequent character in drama.

1427: See note on line 1259.

So piss off to doctor Pittalus and stop bothering me!

CONTRACLEON:
(To Procleon) I just can't believe you!

INJURED MAN:
(To the witness) Did you hear what he just said to me?

(The man and the witness start to exit.)

PROCLEON:
Hang on! A woman from Sybaris was once sold a chipped bowl*
—a punch bowl!

(Procleon punches the Injured Man.)

INJURED MAN:
Owww! *(To the witness)* Did you witness that?

PROCLEON:
A witness, exactly! That's just what this woman needed, so she went
running around trying to find one. But she was wasting her time because
the bowl seller just said, "You're a crackpot and that's a crock of crap!"
And here's a chip off the old block . . .

(Procleon delivers a swift head butt to the man, who falls over onto the witness.)

INJURED MAN:
(Picking himself up off the floor) I'll see you in court!

(Exit Injured Man and Witness.)

CONTRACLEON:
By Demeter! I've just about had all I can take from you!
I'm taking you back inside.

(He picks up Procleon.)

1430: Pittalus was one of the physicians employed by the state to treat citizens.

PROCLEON:
(Struggling) What are you doing!

CONTRACLEON:
You're going back inside! At the rate you're going, there won't be enough
people left in Athens to serve as witnesses in all your court cases.

(Contracleon starts to exit carrying Procleon.)

PROCLEON:
Aesop was once accused by the Delphinians . . .

CONTRACLEON:
I'm not in the least bit interested!

PROCLEON:
Of stealing a sacred libation bowl belonging to a god,
and he told them this story about how a beetle . . .

CONTRACLEON:
Sod you and your damn beetles!

(Exit Contracleon and Procleon into the house.)

(The chorus sings.)

CHORUS:
A miraculous reversal of fortune—
I can only envy Procleon's fate,
He's abandoned those crusty old habits
And is thoroughly bang up to date!

A new leaf the old man's turned over,
Modern ways of refinement and taste,

1446: According to legend, Aesop was sentenced to death in Delphi. He told the Delphinians a fable of an eagle who devoured the young of a beetle. Zeus was protecting the eagle's eggs on his lap, but the beetle flew around the god's head, until, exasperated, he jumped up to swat the pest and the eggs were dropped and smashed—the moral of the story being that the weak can always wreak their revenge on the strong.

I hope he'll adopt this fresh lifestyle,
Let it not have all been just a waste.

For old folks are always set in their ways,
It is often just too hard to change,
Though many have come to see better days
By accepting what's novel and strange.

But it is Contracleon we must applaud.
It was he who had the foresight,
Such sense, passion, and fortitude—
His gentle heart proved a real delight.

It's true we're completely converted,
In our eyes he's a wonderful son,
Wise, loving, and tender,
The most dutiful child bar none!

He successfully argued and criticized,
His point of view he did justify,
For he wanted his father civilized
*To become a social butterfly!**

(Enter Xanthias from the house.)

XANTHIAS:
Dionysus! It's a bloody madhouse in there! I think someone must have wheeled
in a demon when no one was looking. All Hades has broken loose!
It's that old man, he got his first sniff of wine for years and got so excited, cavorting
around to all that piped party music, that he's been up all night singing and
dancing, if you can call it that. What a godawful row! He's been doing those ancient
dance routines, you know, the ones Thespis used to do back in the old days.

1479: According to tradition Thespis was the father of Athenian tragedy and the first winner of the City Dionysia in 534.

He reckons he's better than any of the modern tragic performers, says they're a load of old farts, and what's more, he's threatened to come out here and prove it!

PROCLEON:
(From within) "Who guards the courtyard gate?"

XANTHIAS:
This is rapidly going from bad to worse.

PROCLEON:
"Get thee hence and unbar thy doors!"

(Enter Procleon from the house, dressed in a lurid costume and gyrating to ridiculous dance movements.)

Watch, as I dazzle you with my bump and grind!

XANTHIAS:
Not likely mate! You've lost your mind!

PROCLEON:
I twist my frame to a surging swing,
My backbone coiled into a spring,
The nostrils flare, my body's in motion . . .

XANTHIAS:
I think you need a medicinal potion!*

PROCLEON:
Phrynichus quivers like a frightened cock . . .

XANTHIAS:
Let's throw some stones to make him stop!

PROCLEON:
I kick, do the splits, and kick again!

XANTHIAS:
He'll give himself a nasty sprain!

PROCLEON:
I gyrate my hips to a feverish peak!

XANTHIAS:
Just listen to those old joints creak!

PROCLEON:
Hence I dance to overwhelming acclaim . . .

XANTHIAS:
Now I'm certain, he's quite insane!

PROCLEON:
Now then, I need to make an announcement:
Are there are any performers of tragedy in the audience today
who seriously believe they could better my own stunning performance?
If so, let them take the stage for a dancing match with me! Any takers?

XANTHIAS:
Here's someone now.

*(Enter a dancer dressed in a crab costume from offstage.)**

PROCLEON:
What in the name of the gods is that?

XANTHIAS:
It's the son of Carcinus, the crabby old seadog.

PROCLEON:
He won't take long to crack. A little twist and a couple
of right hooks will have him out of his shell in no time!

(Enter a second crab dancer.)

1502: A tragic dramatist who also served as a naval commander. He was nicknamed "Sealord" because of his naval exploits, and his name meant "crab." He had at least three sons who were said to be small men.

XANTHIAS:
Hold on, what's this! Another damn crustacean! His brother.

PROCLEON:
I'll make a meal of him!

(Enter a third crab dancer.)

XANTHIAS:
We've really got crabs now! That's three to stuff.

PROCLEON:
Who's this crawler? Crab or creepy-crawly?

XANTHIAS:
It's the little shrimp of the family. The small fry
who thinks he's a dramatist.

PROCLEON:
Now that is a tragedy. We must thank Admiral Carcinus for sharing
his fine little nippers with us. He is surely the most "un-shellfish" of men.
And now I will take to the dance floor and show them my moves.
Xanthias! Get the pot boiling with plenty of salt water for my victory feast.

CHORUS:
Move back! Stand clear! Let us give them some ground.
Let's keep well out the way when they start whirling around!

*(Procleon and the three crab dancers perform their frenetic dance as the chorus sings.)**

Come on then, children of Admiral Crab,
Swirl through the sand and leap high with a jab!

1505: One of Carcinus' sons, Xenotimus, became a shipowner. Another was named either Xenarchus or Xenocleitus.

1511: This is Xenocles, who followed in his father's footsteps and became a dramatist.

Shimmy the shore with your crabby gyrations,
Show us your moves, you brother crustaceans!

The crab legs rotate and the circle is formed,
And the Phrynichus high kick is deftly performed.
Flailing limbs whizzing upwards so fast,
Force our dear audience to let out a gasp!

So dance round in a circle and give us a twirl,
Give your belly a good slap and make yourselves swirl!
For the king crab is coming, the lord of the sea,
To dance with his sons and sing a shanty!

But now it is time to finish our play,
With an ending that's never been done in this way.
I am sure this theatre has seen every outrage
*Except a chorus dance right off the stage!**

–END–

Wasps: Endnotes

1: Sosias. A name used by both Athenians and slaves. It may have been a Greek version of a name from Thrace, the area to the north of Greece covering the territory of modern day Bulgaria, northern Greece, and parts of northwestern Turkey. The Greeks regarded Thrace as primitive and uncivilized and a source of slaves.

2: Xanthias. The name Xanthias means something like "fair headed" and seems to have been a common name for slaves of European origin. Aristophanes features a slave named Xanthias in both *Clouds* (line 1485) and *Birds* (line 656), and a slave called Xanthias is a main character in *Frogs*. Douglas Young's "Sandy" Brown from his 1959 Scots version of *Frogs, "The Puddocks,"* is a good modern translation of the name.

8: Corybants. These were divine spirits associated with Cybele, the Eastern mother goddess. The rites connected with this cult involved wild ecstatic dancing, which drove the participants into a kind of frenzied madness and a trancelike state. The exhaustion induced by the wild dancing of the Corybantic rites were said to lead to a purging of the insanity (Burkert, 1985, p. 80). Plato describes the Corybantic rites as a treatment for mental sickness in *Laws* (790d).

9: Sabazius. An Eastern god from Phrygia, who may also have been worshipped in Thrace. Sabazian rites spread to Athens at the end of the fifth century, and their illicit nature and popularity among women and slaves has led to identifications with Dionysus, the god of wine and revelry. Aristophanes mentions Sabazius again in *Lysistrata* (line 388) in the context of reveling women.

19: Cleonymus. An Athenian politician ridiculed for his obesity, effeminacy, and idle boasting, in addition to his cowardly behavior (*Clouds* lines 353–54 and *Wasps* lines 592 and 822–23). He was often called "the shield-dropper," because in Greek hoplite (infantry) warfare the large heavy round shield would be the first article the retreating soldier would discard in flight. The original pun here is based around the Greek word *aspis*, which can mean shield, snake, and stomach. The eagle is described as swooping down to catch a snake, which then turns into Cleonymus and is promptly dropped. See Storey in *Rheinsiches Museum* 132 (1989) 247–61.

33: Cloaks. This was a short cloak made of coarse worn wool, hence its name, *tribôn* which also has the sense of "well worn." It was particularly favored by the lower classes for its cheapness, although the fashion originated with the Spartans (Plato *Protagoras* 342c). Socrates is described as wearing one in Plato's *Symposium* (219b).

39: Cleon. Cleon rose to political prominence resisting Pericles' defensive policy during the earlier stages of the Peloponnesian War against Sparta in the 430s. Prior to Cleon, Athenian politicians had been from aristocratic families and had risen up through military and civil postings. Cleon made his name as an effective and bombastic speaker in the assembly and law courts and relied on the support of the lower classes. He passed various measures to appease the ordinary people including raising jury pay from two to three obols a day, the raising of tribute paid to Athens from the members of the Athenian-led Delian League (***1102 An empire made**), and the ruthless subjugation of league member states that attempted to leave. See *Wasps* introduction, pp. 126–30, for the contentious relationship between Cleon and Aristophanes.

41: Fat of the land. A pun on *dêmós* (fat) and *dêmos* (people). Cleon is envisioned setting classes against each other.

61: Euripides. The comic dramatist Callias staged *Men in Fetters* portraying Euripides dressed as a woman, and there were more than likely many more productions, now lost, that featured this famous dramatist. Euripides appears in Aristophanes' *Acharnians* (lines 395–479) produced in 425, and he was a main character in Aristophanes' *Thesmophoriazusae* (411) and *Frogs* (405).

66: Obscene farces. Aristophanes presented his plays as part of a dramatic competition between the works of three comic playwrights. This competitive spirit permeates his plays including this reference to his comic rivals (see also *Clouds* line 525). At the Lenaea in 422 when *Wasps* was staged, Aristophanes received the second prize, with Philonides winning with *The Preview* and Leucon in third place with *Ambassadors*.

93: Water clock. This was the *clepsydra,* which comprised two large vessels, one with an outlet at the base placed above the other. At the beginning of a speech the first vessel would be filled with water, and at the start of a speech it would be allowed to flow into the other. When it had drained dry, the speech had to come to an end. For a reconstruction of such a water clock see Camp 1990 (fig. 85).

97: Pyrilampes and Demos. Pyrilampes was a well-known Athenian and lived from c. 480 to c. 420. He was the greatuncle of Plato and became his stepfather by his second marriage to his own niece, Perictione. He was an associate of Pericles and known for his good looks. His son, Demos, had his father's looks, and in Plato's *Gorgias* (481d) Callias is said to be in love with him.

100: Audit. Athenian citizens who held public positions were subject to an audit after a term in office. This process involved an examination by a group of auditors selected from the members of the *boule,* the 500-member council that served to oversee the functions of the state and advise the citizen assembly. Once this audit was completed, it went to the law courts, which would either pass it or prosecute the particular magistrate for corruption. However, a private citizen could also bring a charge against a magistrate, and this too was heard in the law courts.

111: Stheneboea. This tragedy dramatized the plots of the Lycian princess Stheneboea against the Greek hero Bellerophon after she unsuccessfully tried to seduce him (Collard et al., eds., *Euripides, Selected Fragmentary Plays,* vol. 1, pp. 79–97).

118: Purification. This could take the form of a blood sacrifice, the sprinkling of powders, fumigation, or abrasion with soil or barley husks. The most common form of purification was ritual bathing where the patient was bathed in springwater or seawater as a physical and mental "washing away," rather like a modern baptism.

125: Asclepius. The son of Apollo who possessed the medicinal powers of his father. There was no cult site of Asclepius in Attica until 420–419, and his famous sanctuary at Epidaurus in the Argolid was off limits to Athenians due to the Peloponnesian War. The nearest temple to Asclepius was located on the Athenian island of Aegina. Asclepius was said to cure sickness by a period of incubation in his sanctuary which involved a ritual purification and a night spent either in the temple itself or in the sanctuary grounds (Burkert 1985, pp. 267–68).

132: House. An internal courtyard open to the sky was a feature of many Athenian houses (Camp 1990, fig. 127). The slaves have covered the whole courtyard and the windows with nets.

152: Son of a puff. The Greek has "This is terrible. People will think that I am the son of old Smoky now!" "Smoke" was a common byword for a braggart like the English "hot air" or "windy."

155: Chew my knob. Sexual puns abound in this scene. *Thura* (door) was a common euphemism for both the vagina and the anus (Henderson 1991, pp. 27 and 199), *Piezô* (press) can also mean to penetrate (Henderson 1991, p. 176), and the *balanos* (the bolt of a lock) was a common name for the penis (Henderson 1991, p. 119).

157: Dracontides. There are at least four contemporary individuals named Dracontides known in the latter part of the fifth century B.C.E.: A high-ranking public official who is mentioned in a treaty between Athens and Chalcis, a general who served in 433–32, an Athenian who suggested an audit of Pericles' directorship of the public purse, and a certain Dracontides of Aphidna, a town in Attica, who opposed the democracy in 404 and was a member of the Thirty.

159: Delphi. Situated on the slopes of Mt. Parnassus to the northwest of Attica in the Phocis region, Delphi was the seat of the Pythia, the priestess of Apollo who pronounced oracles said to be the word of the god. More often that not, these oracles were ambiguous and vague and required interpretation by priests and prophets (see *Birds* 959–992 for a comic portrayal of an oraclemonger). The correct interpretation of oracles was hotly debated, and Greek cities would regularly consult them on a number of important matters. Procleon's belief that he has a divine sanction to convict criminals is probably an example of how an oracle could be twisted and turned to suit many given situations.

Stage Direction: Donkey. Real animals do seem to have been used in Greek drama for tasks such as pulling chariots into the orchestra, and it is not out of the question that an actual donkey could have been used. But the logistics of moving the animal into the scene building and having it cooperate and coordinate with the fast-paced stage action make it unlikely. This donkey could well have been a variation on the pantomime horse made up of two actors, one standing to represent the animal's head, chest, and front legs, the other representing the hindquarters in a crouching position. The donkey is wearing panniers, which would presumably disguise Procleon hanging underneath. An Attic black figure amphora from the mid sixth century shows a chorus of men riding on the shoulders of performers dressed as horses with equine masks and tails (Boardman, *ABFV*, fig. 137). All the escapes are absurdly ridiculous and easily thwarted by Contracleon, therefore, the more ridiculous the portrayal of Procleon's escape under the donkey, the higher the comic value.

192: Donkey's shadow. This was a proverbial expression that according to the scholiast, came from a story about a man who had rented a donkey. While on his way to market he stopped and rested from the hot sun by sitting in the donkey's shadow. The owner of the donkey protested that the renter had hired only the donkey and not the shadow and promptly sued him.

210: Frontier. The Greek has "I'd be better off in Scione." This was a city in Pallene situated on the southwestern promontory of Chalcidice to the north of Greece. The city had rebelled against Athenian control in 423 and was subsequently attacked and blockaded by an Athenian force. At the time *Wasps* was staged there was a tenuous one-year peace in force between Athens and Sparta, making the Scione blockade the only current military action (Thucydides 4.134.1).

220: Phrynichus. Aristophanes alludes to the mellifluous tone of his songs as "honey-sweet" here and in *Birds* (lines 748–51). One of Phrynichus' most famous plays was the *Phoenician Women,* staged in Athens at some point between 478 and 473. This play told the story of the defeat of the Persians in 480 at Salamis and Plataea by a predominantly Athenian force. Aristophanes here describes the songs the chorus sing as "Sidonian," named for the chorus of Phrynichus' play. Sidon was a city in Phoenicia under Persian control. These old songs which celebrated the Athenian victory over superior Persian forces would have been appropriate material for the wasp chorus of elderly ex-citizen servicemen.

Stage Direction: Enter the chorus. A chorus of twenty-four old men dressed in long shabby cloaks and walking slowly, some with walking sticks, enters the orchestra. They are led by a group of boys carrying small oil lamps. The exact number of boys who accompany the chorus is not known, although some scholars have proposed that there are four (MacDowell, note on 229). There may have also been four members of the choral "advance party" in *Birds* (note on 268).

237: Byzantium. In 478 the city was taken from the Persians by an allied Greek force led by the Spartan general Pausanias. The Greek forces included a squadron of thirty Athenian warships (Thucydides 1.94). Pausanias was recalled from Byzantium to answer charges that he collaborated with the enemy and was behaving in a manner more befitting a Persian monarch than a Spartan commander. Pausanias was convicted only of minor charges and returned to take control of Byzantium at his own expense. The Athenians, enraged at this behavior, deployed a force under Cimon in 476 and after a short siege, which is probably the action the chorus is referring to, drove him out (Thucydides 1.131). The reference to the Byzantium action is dramatically important on two counts; it marks the age of the chorus as around seventy-five to eighty, and reminds the audience that the Byzantium incident was one of the factors that led to the transfer of leadership of the league of Greek states unified against Persia from Sparta to Athens. This confederacy was to become the Delian League and ultimately the Athenian empire. The events that the chorus and Procleon refer to throughout the play were all important in the formation of Athens as a leading Greek power.

242: Laches. Instrumental in a one-year peace treaty between

Athens and Sparta in 423, which was in force at the time *Wasps* was performed and the subsequent Peace of Nicias in 422–21 (Thucydides 4.118 and 5.43). It appears that Cleon had made it known that he would press charges against Laches, accusing him of embezzlement while commanding a naval squadron in Sicily. It is possible that this was part of a wider political strategy to discredit the Athenian politicians who supported the peace treaty. Aristophanes returns to this subject with the dog-trial scene later in this play (895–98). In Plato's *Laches* the general is portrayed as a sober, unpretentious man. Plato notes that Laches was older than Socrates, which would have made him around 50 in 422.

246: Lamps. The lamp referred to was a small hand-held, hollow oval made from terra cotta with one funnel for the wick and another for the olive oil which would be poured inside. The wick would slowly draw up and burn the oil. The more the wick was exposed, the faster and brighter it would burn (American School 1959, fig. 61). The attention paid to the lamps serves a double function: it displays the poverty of the old men who become angry that oil should be wasted and is also a running joke based around the common double entendre for finger/penis (Henderson 1991, p. 114)) and wick/penis ("wick" is still a common euphemism for penis in British slang). Scarcity of oil was also a euphemism for impotence and old age (see *Birds* 1589 and note).

259: Muckraking. Athenian households threw their toilet waste into the street at night. "They told them to keep clear! just as if they were throwing the shit out at night" (Aristophanes *Acharnians* 616).

283: Samos. The island state rebelled against the Athenian garrison there after a dispute with neighboring Miletus (440 B.C.E.). Pericles led a naval assault and subsequent nine-month blockade of Samos with over two hundred warships. Eventually the island surrendered. Pericles' famous funeral oration as reported by Thucydides (2.35–46) was in honor of the dead in the Samos campaign and other smaller actions. The scholia reports that secret information was passed to the Athenians by a character called Carystion who was given Athenian citizenship as a reward. The Samos campaign was another important military victory for the Athenians in the establishment of their empire.

288: Thrace. A Spartan force under Brasidas had been operating in the coastal region of Thrace since 424, battling over cities in the region that were under Athenian influence. Although at the time *Wasps* was performed a peace was in force, the Athenians had seen recent action at Scione (see ***210 Frontier**).

293: Knucklebone dice. Children used the knucklebones from the feet of butchered animals as dice for various games.

297: Fig. These figs were freely and cheaply available and a popular treat. They were also a fertility symbol and a euphemism for the sexual organs (Henderson 1991, p. 118).

306: Civil court. Based on the comments of the chorus at line 241 we can assume that they are referring to the court of the *thesmothetai* where cases involving embezzlement were heard. This court would have had its own presiding magistrate (Archon). Evidently the jurors were expected to come and assemble at the relevant court without knowing for sure if the court would convene or not. This choral interchange between father and son clearly shows the absolute dependence of the old men on jury dole for their economic survival.

312: "Mother, poor mother . . .": The scholia notes that this is a quotation from Euripides' *Theseus,* which was originally spoken by the children chosen to be sacrificed to the Minotaur on Crete (Euripides fr. 385).

315: Sack. Presumably the boy carries a cloth bag which he had hoped to fill with groceries after his father had been paid his jury dole. This also continues the comic sexual double entendre.

344: The truth. The Greek has "The truth about the navy!" Athens' dependence on rowers drawn from the lower classes for military security gave the ordinary citizen a legitimate share in the government of their state and hence the development of the radical Athenian democracy in the fifth century. The maintenance and outfitting of specific vessels was financed and supervised by individual wealthy men from the upper class (*trierarchs*). The chorus is insinuating that Contracleon is antidemocratic and therefore refuses to accept that Athens is dependent on its lower classes. Public attendance at the theatre was in itself a manifestation of the Athenian democracy, and it appears that declarations against tyranny were issued to the audience between shows (see *Birds* 1074 and note).

354: Naxos. Sometime around 469 Naxos seceded from the Athenian dominated Delian League and was forced into subjugation by a blockade. After capitulating, Naxos become in effect a subject state of Athens and lost a great deal of political autonomy (Thucydides 1.98). This was one of the first members of the Delian League to come under direct Athenian control, and its mention here is yet another example of an important battle fought by the chorus members in the establishment of Athenian imperial power.

380: Diopeithes. Aristophanes refers to him as a religious fanatic (*Birds* 988, *Knights* 1085). Some years before *Wasps* was staged he tried to pass a motion against astronomers and nonbelievers, which forced the thinker Anaxagoras to leave Athens (Plutarch *Pericles* 32.2–5).

Stage Direction: Crane. Most commentators conclude that Procleon lowers a rope from the window, but it seems more likely judging from the way the scene unfolds that Procleon used the stage crane (*machina*)to lower himself down. This could easily have been maneuvered into position so that the line and harness were dangling before the window. At line 396 Contracleon tells Xanthias that he hears voices "hanging around" and then orders Xanthias to push Procleon back inside. This would strongly suggest that Procleon is suspended midway over the stage and completely helpless in the ensuing comic bedlam breaking out below him.

389: Lycus. Very little is known of Lycus. He may be the same Lycus who was the son of Pandion, an Athenian hero and enemy of Theseus associated with the development of the Eleusinian Mysteries (Pausanias 4.1.6). For the possible role of Lycus as a deity connected with initiation see Bowie 1993, pp. 91–93).

398: Harvest wreath. During the fall harvest festival, the Pyanopsia, Athenian boys went from door to door offering blessings and leaving a bough of the olive or the laurel tree which was then hung on the door. This *eiresiônai* was dedicated with colored wool and fruits, and small jars of wine, oil, and honey and would stay on the door throughout the year dedicated to Apollo (for a sculptural representation see Parke 1977, pl. 32). The combination of Procleon's prayer to Lycus and the use of the *eiresiônai* to beat him back inside may well be comic variations on ritual practice associated with childhood rites of passage and the initiation of boys. (For *Wasps* as a play dealing with "reverse initiation" see Bowie 1993, pp. 78–102.)

Stage Direction: Stingers. It is usually assumed that the chorus members have some kind of sting attached to the rear of their costume which is revealed at this point. Sommerstein (*Wasps* note on 423) feels that the chorus must have been able to bring their stings to the front in order to charge effectively as their words in 428–55 show that they can see what is happening and are therefore not running backwards. But it is not inconceivable to assume that the chorus would have used the phallus to represent a sting. It would be very easy to pull the appendage back between the legs to create the impression of a sting. It would also solve the problem that arises if the sting is always present and separate from the phallus, that is, how to successfully hide it from the audience without its distorting the line of the cloak. Certainly the language of "stinging" is rendered in sexual terms, extracting an enormous amount of comic mileage from jokes based around penetration (lines 431–32). It also seems from the text that the sting/phallus is erect and dangerous only when the old men are aroused to anger. This anger and use of the "weapon" is couched in both sexual and military terms (lines 424–45). Visually the link between the obsession of the old men for the courts and potent sexual desire would be marked exceedingly well by using the phallus as the sting. It also makes the threat of a wasp attack all the more threatening to Xanthias and Contracleon as there is the added danger of sexual violation.

423: ATEEEN SHUNNN! Like the chorus in *Birds* (343–51), the old men behave like a well-disciplined group of Athenian hoplite infantrymen and prepare for battle. Whereas in *Birds* the beak is used as a weapon, here it is the sting/phallus. The theatrical chorus may have been recruited from the ranks of Athenian national servicemen. If so, this farcical drill routine would have provided additional comic mileage. (For evidence of young soldiers used in Greek drama, see Winkler, in Winkler & Zeitlin, 1990, p. 20.)

433: Midas, Phryx, Masyntias. This battle between the Wasps, Contracleon, and his slaves is a comic version of the Persian Wars themselves. The slaves are called "barbarians" at 439, and the wasps are smoked out in a parody of the Persian burning of Athens in 480.

436: There's no lead in their pencils! The Greek has "I know all about the sound of a load of old fig leaves!" This is an idiomatic expression denoting an empty threat or lack of sexual performance.

438: Cecrops: The mention of Cecrops here serves two purposes. The first is to maintain Procleon's position of a pure Athenian appealing to one of the oldest Athenians in the face of a barbarian enemy. The second has a pun on the use of the phallus as a weapon. Cecrops is surely the most well endowed of all Athenian deities, with the whole lower part of his body being a serpent. For a pictorial reference see Boardman *ARFV2,* fig. 106). The Greek for "snakelike" is *dracontôdês,* and Aristophanes puns it here in the Greek with Dracontides (***157 Dracontides**).

447: Donkey jackets, sackcloth tunics, dog-skin hats, old footwear. Articles of clothing of the cheapest and crudest quality: a large leather jerkin, a slave's tunic that exposed one shoulder, basic caps, and a pair of hard-wearing and also possibly used shoes.

502: Trying to jockey the tyrants back into power. The Greek has "trying to let Hippias remount." Hippias was the son of Pisistratus and the last tyrant of Athens. He was expelled in 510. The joke here is a play on his name with *hippus,* "horse."

523: Fall on my blade and end it all. The most famous suicide of this type was the death of Ajax as portrayed in Sophocles' *Ajax* and also a popular theme in Athenian art. The Athenian general, Paches, resorted to this end when he was found guilty of impropriety and fell on his sword in court (Plutarch, *Aristides* 26).

544: The old folks' march. The Greek has "We would be known as olive branch carriers." At the Panathenaea festival there was a large parade where the elderly participants would carry an olive branch. Slabs 84–101 of the Parthenon frieze may depict these old men, but the branches either are not shown or were originally bronze attachments that have not survived (Boardman *GS2,* fig. 93a).

554: Suppliants. In times of great distress Greeks would seek sanctuary and support by appealing to a higher authority as a suppliant. Xenophon noted the practice Procleon describes and wrote, "The law (in the courts) depends solely on the ordinary people. Therefore he (the litigant) is obligated to plead with humility in the courts and to grasp people's hands as a suppliant as they go in" (*Constitution of Athens* 1.18).

573: Pork. A common euphemism for the vagina (Henderson p. 21). Aristophanes exploits this sexual pun in *Acharnians* (763-815) where a Megarian passes off two girls as pigs and sells them to Dicaeopolis.

581: Aulos. For a pictorial reference of an aulos player wearing a cheek strap, see Boardman, *ARFV1*, fig. 75.2

585: Will. If an Athenian citizen died and left only a daughter, his estate would pass to the husband of his daughter. If she was unmarried, then either the nearest male relative would have the legal right to marry her or the father could nominate an heir in his will. Cases where the will was disputed were settled in the courts. These wills were sealed in order to deter forgery (Parke 1977, pp. 95–98).

591: An important case. Crimes against the state could be heard either by the assembly or by the courts. Procleon fantasizes that the cases handed to the courts are the ones too difficult to be decided upon by the people. The truth is more likely to have been that prosecutors may have preferred to try certain cases in the courts where the smaller juries could be more easily manipulated.

599: He . . . keeps the flies off us. In *Knights* (60) the Paphlagonian slave representing Cleon performs the same function. Instead of flies here he swats politicians and keeps them away from Demos ("The People").

617: Little donkey. For an Attic black-figure *kantharos* (large wine cup) in the shape of a donkey's head, see Boardman, *ABFV*, fig. 321.

656: Tax revenue. A list, although not comprehensive, of the revenue earned by the state. The tribute received from the allies was by far the largest amount. Each member state of the Delian League paid a certain amount of tribute to Athens depending on its size and productivity. In 425 a decree was passed in the assembly, which may have been engineered by Cleon, significantly raising the tribute amounts to help finance the war against Sparta. A special court with a jury of one hundred was established to reassess the amount of tribute each allied city should pay. Most cities had their tribute doubled by two or three times, and over one hundred cities not previously on the tribute list were added. The income received is estimated at around 1500 talents a year (Meiggs & Lewis 1988, p. 69). There was a one percent tax levied on goods arriving at the port of Piraeus (Xenophon *Constitution of Athens*.1. 17). Court fees were paid by the prosecutor for certain types of cases usually involving the settlement of a financial dispute. These costs were recoverable from the defendant if a guilty verdict was reached. Athens had significant silver deposits in Laurium in the southeast of Attica. In the fourth century these were state owned but operated by private individuals who would pay a fee for a lease (Aristotle *Constitution of Athens* 22.7). This may well have been the case in Aristophanes' day as the mines were an important part of Athenian revenue throughout the fifth century. The other taxes mentioned include import duties, a sales tax on goods sold in the market, rents earned from state lands, and property that was confiscated by the state from criminals.

658: Two thousand talents a year! It is impossible to calculate for certain if this figure is an exaggeration or not. It does seem that although a tribute figure of around 1500 talents was set, that a large amount of it was never collected. Xenophon (*Anabasis* 7.1.27) estimates the state revenue in 431 as around 1000 talents. With the increase in tribute and presumably accompanying tax increases to help finance the war, Contracleon's figure may not have been so very far from the truth

659: Six thousand jurors. This agrees with the figure given by Aristotle (*Constitution of Athens* 24.3).

660: "This teeming womb of jurors." The Greek has "This land has never seen so many," and the quotation is unknown. I have shamelessly adapted a similar quotation from Shakespeare's *Richard II*, "This nurse, this teeming womb of royal kings" (II, I).

661: One hundred and fifty talents. Contracleon seems to be stretching the truth here: 150 talents amounts to 5,400,000 obols which by Contracleon's calculation means that on 3 obols a day, the jurors are serving 300 days a year. But the courts did not convene on religious holidays, nor on days when the assembly met or when a murder trial was in session. Sommerstein (*Wasps*, note on line 663) calculates that this would leave only 225 days in a year available for trials, and even then the courts were not always convened (see line 305). Aristophanes depicts Contracleon as using what was probably an advocate's technique of exaggerating the facts while not exactly lying. It seems enough to convince Procleon, who is enraged that the jurors should not receive even 10 percent of the state income.

670: A bribe worth fifty talents. Contracleon is exaggerating again, as fifty talents was an enormous amount of money. Yet allied states did seek to bribe prominent officials to keep their tribute payments low, and this figure may actually represent the amount of tribute not collected by Athens as a result of this underhand process. Contracleon cleverly creates an image of Cleon and his cronies pocketing this loss of revenue.

680: Eucharides. It has been assumed that Eucharides was a greengrocer and that the joke is based on the use of garlic, which Contracleon uses as an example of poverty as it was cheap and readily available. But line 1172 show that garlic bulbs were used to soothe boils and abrasions of the anus. In addition, the name "Eucharides" means "pleasing" or "engaging" and is found on an Archaic red figure Attic hydria now in the Getty Museum in Malibu as part of an inscription that reads "Eucharides is beautiful." The painting on the vase depicts two naked youths in a courtship scene. It therefore seems likely that Procleon expoits the famous reputation of Eucharides as a male beauty, suggesting that in desperation he is forced to use garlic that has been employed as a balm after homosexual lovemaking.

701: Sardinia. Another case of exaggeration on the part of Contracleon. Athens had recently assessed a number of cities on the Black Sea coast as part of the revision of the tribute lists in 424 (***656 Tax revenue**), but it is not certain that these cities were actually contributing at this point. To the west Athens certainly had allies in south Italy and Sicily, but they were not tribute-paying members of the Athenian League. There is no evidence for any Athenian influence over any cities in Sardinia.

709: Twenty thousand of the working class. There were more like three hundred cities assessed for tribute at this time. The figure of twenty thousand citizens (adult Athenian males) could well be reasonably accurate for the number of *thetes* (lower-class men) at this time.

711: Marathon. The battle of Marathon in 490 was a stunning victory by the Athenian (and Plataean) hoplite infantry over the vastly superior Persian invaders, with reported losses of 6,400 Persians and only 192 Athenians. This victory helped to establish Athens as a military power in the Greek world. However, it seems unlikely (although not impossible) that Procleon or his cronies could have actually served at Marathon as the battle was fought sixty-eight years prior to the performance of *Wasps*. The chorus seem to take every opportunity to mention their past military exploits such as Byzantium in 479 (line 237) and Naxos in 469 (line 354) with no specific mention of serving at Marathon. The battle of Marathon was fought by members of the middle classes who could afford the heavy armor of the hoplite and not the lower classes who served as rowers. Although the chorus says "we were there at Marathon" at line 1081, this seems to be a reference to Athenians in general rather than any specific characters and is in keeping with the style of a parabasis, which is a moment of suspension from the dramatic narrative of the play.

714: I feel all limp! It is not difficult to imagine that Procleon's phallus (perhaps his "sword" here) would be erect as he proudly tells of his powers. Now as his world is steadily being shattered by Contracleon's arguments, the phallus becomes limp again. Alternatively, a sword could be used in a similar phallic manner.

716: Euboea. A major producer of grain. The promise of a grain dole may well have been one of the methods used by politicians to win favor with the people (*Knights* lines 1100–6, *Birds* line 581). Fifty bushels per man is enough to feed a family for a year. Perhaps at some point a promise was made to the people that the land of Euboea would support them. Contracleon's point is that Cleon and his cronies promise the world but fail to deliver, as barley was regarded as an inferior foodstuff to wheat.

726: Both sides of the argument. The originator of this quote is not known, but the sentiments expressed are not unlike the pronouncements of a chorus found in tragedy.

740–42: Rub his willy. With the dropping of his "sword" and the lowering of the chorus' "shafts" Contracleon promises to find alternative and more traditional methods of arousing his father.

756: Jurors, thy soul's flight. The Greek has "Speed thou, thy soul," probably a lost quote from a Euripides play. I have substituted a slightly adapted line from Shakespeare's *Macbeth* (III, 1).

757: Make way thou shady thickets. A quotation from *Bellerophon* by Euripides (fr. 308). "Make way thou shady thickets, let me ruse above the dewy vale."

759: Cleon guilty of theft. Procleon had been beaten by a better argument, and after his comically botched suicide attempt he is forced to fulfill his promise that he will not go to court again. However, he is still a faithful follower of Cleon, and in this respect it is important to distinguish between the argument itself and the content of the argument. The *Agon* was a contest of oratorical skill rather like a debating competition. The loser of the debate does not necessarily have to believe every argument his opponent presented in order to concede a victory, just agree that he has lost to a better argument. Contracleon has not yet healed his father of his obsession for the law courts or his infatuation with Cleon, but he has now won agreement from Procleon that he will cease his escape attempts and place himself in his son's care. Contracleon's arguments do not convince the chorus to stop going to court either; it responds positively to his oratorical abilities and concern of a son for his father. It is clear that the poverty of the chorus members makes them dependent on the jury dole to feed their families, unlike Procleon, who is fortunate enough to have a wealthy son to care for him. Now that Contracleon has managed to convince his father to comply with him, he must move on to the next stage of his "treatment" and break his habitual and damaging tendency of convicting defendants no matter what.

800-1: Oracle. Divine messages and their interpretation played an important part in both the Athenian household and state affairs. The foretelling of future events evidently became quite an industry with oracles being generated and interpreted not only by the large cult sites, such as Delphi and Dodona, but also by individuals claiming to be able to unravel the riddling language of mysteries for a small fee (Burkert 1985, pp. 114–18). See *Birds* lines 959–91 for a comic depiction of such an "oraclemongerer." Perhaps Aristophanes was parodying a famous oracle given to the Athenians, which has been suitably altered to suit the playwright's comic purposes.

804: Hecate. Her worship probably originated in the East, and the earliest reference to Hecate is found in Hesiod (*Theogony* 411 ff.). She was a deity of transformation, and purification ceremonies played an important part in her rites. Appropriately Hecate was associated with the law courts as a goddess who received curses (Mikalson, pp. 76–77) and was depicted sitting in judgment and described as "Preeminent in the Assembly" by Hesiod (*Theogony* 430–31). Interestingly, she also had a strong affiliation with dogs who will be the litigants in this front-yard court. Each month at the new moon, a purification rite was held by the household which involved offering her dog flesh (Parker, p. 358).

Stage Direction: "Courtroom" props. Contracleon brings out a chair for Procleon, probably a chair for himself and something to act as a raised platform for the speakers, possibly an upturned basin. He also has a small brazier, a chamber pot, a cockerel (probably wooden or terra-cotta), a bowl of soup, and two serving cups.

Stage Direction: Brazier. For a pictorial reference of a fifth-century brazier see Sparkes & Talbot, fig. 44.

815: What's the cock for? There is no reason why Contracleon could not have brought out a real cock. However, a "dummy" cock would be more in keeping with the other inanimate objects that go to make up the courtroom and be funnier when Procleon insists that it is winking at him at line 934. Perhaps an ancient precursor of that hardy comic perennial, the rubber chicken. For a pictorial reference of a terra-cotta cock see Higgins, pl. 36 fig. A. Procleon has reason to be suspicious of being handed a cock as this was often a love gift to a young man from an older admirer. Perhaps Aristophanes intended this as a visual role-reversal joke. For a pictorial reference of such a gesture see Boardman, *ARFV*1 fig. 373.

Stage Direction: Amphora. It is uncertain exactly what Contracleon used to represent the image of Lycus. It has been suggested that Contracleon makes one of the slaves sit on the altar and that this slave is not wearing a phallus, hence the gags that follow. It is clear from the text that whatever device is used, it must be large and bulbous to represent the obesity of Cleonymus, perhaps somewhat phallic in appearance and having no protruding objects that could be mistaken for a phallus or a weapon. I suggest that a large upturned amphora performs the task adequately and feel that an inanimate object would be more comic than an actor.

828: Thratta. The Greek has "Thratta burned a pot the other day." Burning and burnishing were euphemisms for sex (Henderson 1991, p. 143).

831: Sacred objects revealed. The rites at the Eleusinian Mysteries involved having a number of sacred objects revealed during the course of initiation (***1363 The Mysteries**) Procleon's spiritual enlightement comes from his attendance at the courts, and the court fence would be the first thing he saw on his way in.

862: Let us pray. All essential elements for religious rites. The incense would be frankincense or myrrh, which would give a distinctive aroma to the ceremony. The myrtle wreaths would be worn on the heads of the participants, and the fire would burn to represent purity and to receive offerings. This kind of rite was probably not an element of courtroom procedure but an inaugural sacrifice for this new "courthouse."

868: Lord Apollo. A prayer to the god of healing, as he is being asked to make Procleon more temperate toward the defendants and thereby assist in the cure that Contracleon is attempting to effect.

898: Sycamore collar. The Greek has "figwood collar" from *sukinos*, "figwood," sounding like *sukophantês*, "sycophants," the despised men who made their living bringing charges and accusations against people in court.

Stage Direction: Enter Labes and Cleonhound. Labes may have been played by one of the slaves in a dog mask which could well have been fashioned to represent Laches. Labes never speaks, which may be a comment on the tendency of Athenian law courts to try defendants in their absence or the fact that Laches himself stayed silent on the matter in question. Cleonhound was played by an actor possibly wearing a similar doglike mask to Labes with features resembling Cleon.

916: Your watchdog. This portrayal of Cleon as a watchdog, guarding the interests of the people, is also found in *Knights* (lines 1017–24). Cleonhound's accusations reveal the real reason for his prosecution—that he was not given a cut of the stolen goods.

925: Mortar. For a pictorial reference see Sparkes & Talbot, fig. 34. Labes, prowling around the mixing bowl and chewing at the rind of the cheese, is compared to Laches sailing around the cities of Sicily (most of the major settlements were located on the coast) and extracting tribute to pay for an Athenian naval operation, which he then allegedly kept (Thucydides 3.86). The use of the mortar to grind grain may also hint at the purpose of Laches' mission, which was to prevent Sicilian grain exports from making their way to Sparta and her allies.

934: He's winking at me. The fact that the cock is winking at Procleon may be a reference to certain individuals leading the jury to make a decision favorable to their own political agenda.

937–39: Witnesses. A collection of household utensils are called for. There is also a sexual pun here as a "scalded pot" and many other kitchen implements such as bowls, ladles, and cheese graters carry sexual overtones (Henderson 1991, pp. 142–43). The cheese grater was a flat grater with a handle carved in the likeness of crouching animals. Judging by the reference in Aristophanes' *Lysistrata* (line 896), "cheese grater" may have come to be a euphemism for a sexual position.

946: Thucydides. A political enemy of Pericles who was eventually ostracized (banished by popular vote) for ten years in 443. He returned to Athens and was prosecuted by Euathlus (see line 592). Aristophanes refers to this trial in *Acharnians* (lines 703–712) where the chorus complains of the unfair nature of the proceedings.

961: False accounts. Presumably Laches would have already had an audit following the completion of his command in Sicily two years earlier. At that time he would have submitted accounts to the relevant court for scrutiny. Procleon assumes that these must have been false accounts. For the administration of official audits see MacDowell (1978), pp. 170–72.

Stage Direction: Cheese grater. The cheese grater is also a non-speaking role, which suggests that it could be played in a number of ways. Either a real cheese grater was placed on the witness stand and held by one of the slaves, or one of the slaves was dressed in some sort of simple costume or mask that represented a cheese grater.

Stage Direction: Chamber pot. There is superb comic value in throwing the chamber pot over Procleon to revive him. This gag is set up at the introduction of the chamber pot at line 858, reinvested with a humorous toilet joke at 936 and finally fulfilling its logical comic potential here.

Stage Direction: Parabasis. The parabasis was the moment within the play when the action is temporarily suspended and the chorus addresses the audience, often seemingly voicing the opinions of the author himself. For the structure of the parabasis, see Dover 1972, 49–53; for its dramatic function see McLeish, pp. 91–92.

1019: Eurycles. For a reference to this strange spirit see Plato *Sophist* 252c.

1027: This very stage? A fascinating insight into the background of some of the quite vicious personal attacks found in Old Comedy. Here Aristophanes rejects the notion that he could be induced to include a scandalous reference in one of his plays in return for a monetary payment. It is possible to infer from this that such practices must have occurred from time to time, making a seat in the theatre at a performance of an Athenian comedy a very dangerous place to be indeed.

1042: You begged the state for protection. The Greek has "you went to the Polemarch." This was the third highest of the nine ruling archons with particular power over legal and religious matters. The investigation into non-Athenians also came under his jurisdiction (MacDowell 1978, pp. 24–26, 76 , and 79).

1087: Fancy pants. For a pictorial reference to Persian dress on a fifth century cup, see Boardman, *ARFV1*, fig. 279.

1102: An empire made, the tribute paid. The Greek forces routed the Persians both at sea at Salamis and on land at Plataea (480). They then launched a seaborne assault on Cape Mycale (479) and captured Sestos (478). These events seriously weakened Persian control over the Greek cities in Asia Minor to the point where many rebelled and asked Athens for protection. This was the origin of the Delian League, which gradually became the Athenian "empire," made up of tribute-paying allied states. Yet again the chorus sings of how it (and those of its class) was instrumental in the decisive actions that built Athens into a leading power. Now it laments the loss of its hard won wealth by the younger generation.

Stage Direction: Bundle. For a pictorial reference to such a stage property on a fourth century south Italian Phylax vase, see Trendall & Webster, pl. IV, 35.

1143: Cover his "equipment." This is a reference to the *sagma*, a soft cloth cover for a shield (for a pictorial reference see Sparkes 1975, pl. XIII). The joke here may have to do with Morychus' large belly (Greek *aspis* can mean both "shield" and "belly"), which needed covering by a huge coat such as the one Contracleon is holding up.

1159: Spartan booties. For a pictorial reference, see Brooke, fig. 38.

1172: Hemorrhoid treatment. The Greek has "Someone who has dressed a boil with garlic." A garlic bulb was used as a balm for a sore anus (see also ***680 Eucharides**).

1177: Farting Lamia. Aristophanes uses this image again in *Ecclesiazusae* lines 76–78.

1181: What did the ferret . . . Procleon has no fear when it comes to telling a good bawdy and thoroughly offensive joke, and this is an integral part of his character that both attracts and repels at the same time. The dramatic image of the elderly uttering offensive remarks and being tolerated by society is still a common comic device.

1184: Theogenes. Mentioned in *Birds* (line 822) as a boaster. He took part in a fact-finding mission to Pylos in 425 and was later one of the official witnesses to the Peace of Nicias in 421 (Thucydides 5.19).

1207: Phayllus. This famous champion in the pentathlon and the stadion (the two hundred-yard dash) had a statue erected in his honor at Delphi in recognition of his victories at the Pythian games (Pausanias 10.9.1). He was also known to have commanded one ship that came from Italy to fight on the Greek side at Salamis in 480 (Herodotus 8.47). In *Acharnians* (line 214) the name Phayllus is also used proverbially for speed.

Stage Direction: Onto the couch. At a symposium, guests reclined on couches covered with elaborate rugs while they ate and drank. There are many images of symposia on vase paintings which depict men reclined on couches, especially on vessels for wine and drinking cups (Boardman *ARFV2,* fig. 153). There is no suggestion that real couches are in use on stage during this scene; either the guests simply lay out on the ground or used chairs pushed together. Chairs or stools may have been used in the courtroom scene and could be available.

1223: I like a good drinking song. The Greek has "Oh yes, and I'm a lot better than any old Diacrian." Diacris was the name of one of the three regions allotted to the Attic Leontis tribe. Evidently the Diacrians were famed for their singing.

1224: Harmodius. Plotted with his friend Aristogiton to kill the tyrant Hippias. The plot failed and they were executed, but they did succeed in killing Hippias' brother, Hipparchus. The emerging Athenian democracy made heroes of these young men, erecting a statue with an epigram by Simonides and naming them the "tyrant killers." For copies of this group see Boardman *GS2,* figs. 3–9. The choice of this song, celebrating Athens first "democrats," is not accidental here, and a passionate supporter of the democracy like Procleon would be sure to know it well.

1231: Kicked out of Attica. Contracleon's strategy emerges. He has succeeded in debating his father into cooperating with him and to stop trying to escape, and he has successfully duped him into acquitting a defendant in court. Now he must show Procleon the luxurious lifestyle that his beloved leaders live and the arrogant manner with which they behave. Contracleon's suggestion that Cleon would behave like a tyrant and expel Procleon from the city is met by righteous democratic indignation from his father.

1235: Absolute power corrupts absolutely. An adaptation of a quotation from the lyric poet Alcaeus, who was active in the late seventh and early sixth century (fr. 141. 3–4). The original line may have been directed at Pittacus who ruled Mytilene in Lesbos (Alcaeus' home city) in the early sixth century. This reference to a tyrant is pointedly addressed to Cleon.

1239: Worthy men like us. This is the first line of a song attributed to Praxilla of Sicyon (fr. 3). She composed dithyrambic poetry and hymns as well as songs.

1242: Right on their arses! The Greek has "It is not possible to play the fox or to befriend both sides at once." The author of this line is not known. Again this is a remark aimed at Cleon and his attempts to curry favor with the aristocratic class of Athens.

1247: Cleitagora. This name is also used as a title of a drinking song in *Lysistrata* (line 1237), and the scholiast there states that she was a Spartan poet. An Attic red figure hydria dated 450–30 in the University of Mississippi Museum (1977.4.98) depicts two women with the inscription, "Cleitagora is beautiful." This may be evidence for a contemporary courtesan sharing the same name.

1268: Leogoras. He served as the commander of an Athenian naval force during the Corcyra engagement in 433 (Thucydides 1.51) and was the chairman of an Athenian embassy to the king of Macedonia in 426. His son was the orator Andocides, and he tells of how his father was one of the men charged with the mutilation of the Herms and the profanation of the Mysteries in 415 (Andocides, *On the Mysteries*).

1282: Ariphrades. Aristotle mentions an Ariphrades in *Poetics* (1458b.31), and this may well be the same man. Aristophanes mentions his sexual habits in *Knights* (lines 1274–89) and *Peace* (line 885).

1302: Company he was keeping. From what is known about these men, it may be that they had oligarchic tendencies. In this respect the symposium may have been more than just an opportunity for socializing and used as a covert gathering of political allies at night and behind closed doors in stark contrast to the open air mass public meetings of the assembly and the courts (see Bowie 1993, p. 99).

1311: Pig in clover. The Greek has "A donkey in a field of barley."

Stage Direction: Dardanis. Guests at a symposium would have been entertained by dancing girls and flute players, and it seems likely from the text that Dardanis is at least semi, if not completely, naked and would have probably been played by a woman.

1358: Senior delinquent. More comic role reversal. Procleon has been reborn and initiated into a new way of life, and so he imagines himself as a young man with Contracleon as his father. For a full discussion of *Wasps* in terms of a play dealing with rites of passage and initiation, see Bowie 1993, pp. 78–87.

1363: The Mysteries. The important stages of an Athenian's life were marked by sacred rites such as the naming day, initiation from child to adult, the acceptance into a clan, marriage, religious enlightenment, and the funeral. Procleon may well be referring to the process of transformation from juror to a young-at-heart party goer as some kind of reverse initiation. Alternatively this could be a comic reference to Eleusinian Mysteries, the secret initiation rites in honor of Demeter and Kore, which promised spiritual enlightenment and an afterlife. Comic banter was an integral part of the initiation process as it is with new recruits in the armed forces and inexperienced workers today. The initiates attending the Mysteries endured similar treatment, crossing the many bridges that spanned the small streams encountered on route from Athens to Eleusis. Masked characters set on the initiates and performed acts of comic buffoonery known as *gephyrismoi.* The fact that Procleon attempts to pass Dardanis off as a torch also points to the torchlight procession of the initiates to Eleusis (Burkert 1985, 285–90).

1372: Lamp stand. The Greek has "torch." This kind of long torch was made by bundling strips of wood and tying them together. A torch of this type is depicted on a relief from Eleusis dated around 440–30, which shows Demeter handing the gift of corn to a young

Triptolemus, who is accompanied by Kore/Persephone holding a torch (Boardman *GS2*, fig. 144).

1397: A respectable citizen family. The Greek has "I'm the daughter of Ancylion and Sostrate!" Hence Myrtia proudly announces that she is from a citizen family.

1398: I'm going to sue you. There are no another accounts of women actually launching legal proceedings at this time, and it may have been that Myrtia needed the attendance of a male citizen not only to act as a witness but also to assist her in serving the summons. At line 1413 Aristophanes ridicules Chaerephon for attempting to witness a summons on behalf of a woman, which raises the question of its legality.

1408: Market inspectors. The *agoranomoi,* appointed to oversee the conduct of business in the two main markets of Athens and Peiraeus (Aristotle *Constitution of Athens* 51.1).

1409: Simonides. See *Clouds* line 1356 and note.

1435: A chipped bowl. The Greek has "a woman from Sybaris happened to break a jar."

1473: A social butterfly. At first sight this choral song may seem out of place thematically as the chorus sings of the affection of the son to his father and of its hopes that he will enjoy his new lifestyle. The audience have just witnessed Procleon out of control and an infuriated Contracleon resorting to locking him back up in the house. Hence, we are right back where we started at the beginning of the play. This song is deeply ironic and has great comic value. Douglass Parker's 1962 translation of *Wasps* (Ann Arbor) divides the song into eight stanzas broken by stage directions denoting scenes of destruction, father beating, and general mayhem coming from the house.

1489: A medicinal potion. The Greek has "Have a drink of hellebore!" Hellebore was a plant, and a tonic made from it was used as a cure for insanity.

Stage Direction: The crab dance. This seems to have been a whirling, frenetic, high-kicking affair. The dance itself may well have been a visual metaphor for the "moral" of the play tantalizingly mentioned by Xanthias at line 64. In *Peace* (line 1083) the oraclemonger Hierocles tells Trygaeus "You can't make a crab walk straight," evidently a common saying meaning that a creature's essential nature cannot be changed. Procleon has been exposed to a whole range of "treatments" to stop his excessive behavior, yet at the close of the play we find him as irascible and energetic as ever. The wild crab dance is an expression of the indomitable will of this old Athenian and a celebration of his essential spirit, which for better of worse will always prevail.

1537: Dance right off the stage. It is impossible to know for sure if this claim is true. Of the comedies we have staged prior to *Wasps*, *Acharnians* does end with a song, but it cannot be ascertained if it was accompanied by a dance. *Knights* closes with character dialogue, leading some to assume that the end has been lost. *Clouds* seems to have been revised sometime after *Wasps*, although it may well have ended with a dance. Perhaps Aristophanes means that it is the first time a chorus has actually exited, singing and dancing, rather than completing the last song and having the show brought to a close onstage. This would certainly make for an energetic finale, suggesting that the crab dance will break out of the confines of the theatre and continue on into the streets of the city of Athens itself.

Birds

Heracles, Poseidon, Jerkoffalot, and Prometheus from *Birds*. Aquila Productions, London 1997

Birds: Introduction

Birds is one of Aristophanes' two great comic masterpieces—the other being *Frogs*—yet at the Dionysia of 414, it finished second to Ameipsias' *Komastai* ("Revellers"). It is the longest ancient comedy that we have, but so good is the humor and the comic invention that we do not notice its length. This is Old Comedy at its most imaginative, and Aristophanes at his very best.[1]

Two elderly Athenians, Peithetaerus ("Makemedo") and Euelpides ("Goodhope"), have left home fed up with the problems of home, particularly Athenians' love affair with the law courts (29–47). Their mission: to find Tereus, a figure of myth with an Athenian connection who has become a bird (the Hoopoe), and to ask him if in his travels he has seen a comfortable place where they might live.[2] They want to go to the birds, and in fifth-century Greek, "to go to the birds" was "to go to hell." The play opens in a trackless waste where in the prologue (1–208) they encounter, in a familiar door scene, first the Hoopoe's servant and then the Hoopoe himself,

---

[1] My comments here are expanded from my entry on *Birds* in the *Reference Guide to World Literature* (Detroit 1995) 67ff.

[2] Tereus (the Hoopoe) is an odd character. He married an Athenian woman and was the subject of tragedies by Sophocles (100ff.) and Philocles (281), but in *Birds* he has changed from the wicked barabarian in a grizzly story to a happily married bird. On Sophocles' lost play, see A. Kiso, *The Lost Sophocles* (New York 1984) 57–84, and the fragments in H. Lloyd-Jones, *Sophocles* vol. III (Cambridge MA 1996) 290–301. See also Dobrov (1993).

bearing some signs of his avian transformation. At line 162 Makemedo has an inspiration, and the "great idea" is born: to found a city in the sky among the birds from which to rule all men and cut off all worship to the gods.

The Hoopoe enthusiastically summons the chorus of Birds (229–62), each one representing a different bird—the parodos (267–304) must have been spectacular!—who respond initially with great hostility and threats toward the humans, whose kind has been killing and eating birds for millennia (305–450). There is no contest in *Birds*; rather, Makemedo uses the format of the agon (451–636) to make his two points to the birds: (a) that they once ruled the universe before the gods, and (b) that they can rule again by adopting his scheme. His proposals are accepted enthusiastically, and the humans are invited inside the house of the Hoopoe.

For the first time in the surviving plays, the chorus does not speak for the poet in the parabasis proper (685–737) but remains in its character of birds, and sings a marvelous parody of creation myths from Hesiod and the Orphic tradition. After the parabasis (678–801) the new city is now in place; all it needs is a name, and the winning choice has entered the English language, "Cloudcuckooland" (802–61). Three sets of episodes follow, which show Aristophanes at his most inventive. First a series of "experts" arrive (862–1057), wanting to be in on the creation (a priest, a poet, an oracle-mongering prophet, an inspector, Meton the astronomer and city-planner, and a decree-selling lawyer); they are driven off in the usual manner of intruders. The second series (1119–1469) features the goddess Iris (the rainbow), who is threatened with physical and sexual violence, and then three Athenians who want to be part of this new order (a father-beating youth, Cinesias the poet, and an informer). The first is cleverly dissuaded, while Cinesias and the informer meet the usual fate of intruders. It is in the final sequence (1494–end) that Aristophanes' imagination reaches its height. First Prometheus sneaks in under an umbrella to report that the gods are about to capitulate and that an embassy is on its way to talk peace; Makemedo must hold out for "the Divine Princess" as his wife. Her identity is not specified, but her description at 1537–41 sounds rather like Athena—presumably the poet could not take the dangerous step of marrying the comic hero off to Athens' virginal patron. Then the embassy arrives (Poseidon, a good upper-class god, Heracles, the one-time human who cares only about food, and a barbarian god who cannot speak Greek). The negotiations proceed smoothly for

Makemedo, who at the end of the play celebrates his marriage to the Divine Princess and, thus, Makemedo becomes the new ruler of the universe. Not bad for an elderly Athenian who just wanted to get away from it all!

How are we to interpret this marvelous fantasy? Critics usually fall into one of three camps: (1) that the play is an outstanding piece of comic fantasy, (2) that his creation of the city in the clouds is a reaction to or commentary on certain current events and personalities, and (3) that the comedy is intentionally ironic, showing the extent to which megalomania will run.[3] Those who favor the second cite the Athenian massacre of the men of Melos (416/5), the launching of the great expedition to Sicily in the spring of 415, or the religious and political scandals of 415 that had shaken Athens and driven many prominent Athenians into exile, including the charismatic and notorious Alcibiades. Thus the play is an "escape," in which the poet "turned away from the realities of public life" (Murray 137), or an exploration of the theme that Athens' problems are "rooted in the sophistic delusion that Man himself can somehow become God" (Hubbard 182). The exuberant tone at the end masks an essential irony, that "Cloudcuckooland" is a scheme gone awry, like the massacre at Melos or the unnecessary Sicilian campaign, which would end in total disaster the next year.

Even if one does not stress such contemporary issues behind the comedy, one can still read the play as ironic. Critics have observed that as Cloudcuckooland develops, it begins to seem more and more like Athens—one cannot escape Athens, only re-create it. The birds, it is noticed, have merely exchanged one set of rulers for another, and we see at 1583–85 certain rebellious birds being roasted at the stake for crimes against the state, a treatment that Makemedo promised to outlaw at 524 ff.[4] Finally, that a mere human can threaten a goddess with rape, marry a divine princess who sounds rather like Athena, and replace Zeus as supreme ruler of humankind seems to be *hybris* just waiting to be punished. Makemedo "has no

---

[3] MacDowell (1995) 221–28 has an excellent summary of current approaches; also good are Sommerstein (*Birds*) 1–5 and Dunbar 1–6.

[4] Bowie (1993) is particularly adamant on this point, "as in *Wasps*, dissatisfaction with democratic action leads to a tyranny of a worse kind, because it is that of one man, but Philocleon's pales beside Peisetaerus'" (176).

purpose but power," and Cloudcuckooland is "a pipedream Utopia . . . a visible parody of the Athenian Empire" (Arrowsmith 10).

But the tone of the whole play is not obviously satirical. As MacDowell (1995) puts it, "for the Athenian audience the first sight of the play was the only sight" (p. 223), and the ending should be taken as exuberant fantasy rather than irony. The Sicilian expedition is nowhere mentioned,[5] apart from one casual allusion (147) to the state galley popping up in strange places to recall an Athenian (this alluding to Alcibiades' recall from Sicily), and if "allegory" is to work, it must be made clear—as the poet does with Cleon in *Knights* and *Wasps*. Sommerstein (*Birds* 1–6) makes the good point that the spirit in Athens in 414 was not one of fear or apprehension, but of optimism and bellicosity—there was nothing an Athenian could not do—and *Birds* harmonizes well with the public mood as recorded by Thucydides (6.8–32).

There have been other ways of approaching the play that stay away from a political or an ironic reading and seek to find deep levels of meaning, often with an almost metaphysical symbolism. Thus for Whitman the comedy is an elaborate statement of the "Anatomy of Nothingness"—the universe is created by Love from a wind-egg (696)—and for Reckford comedy is like Love, able to create a splendid fantasy from chaos. Hoffmann argued that Aristophanes is parodying poems about the battle between the gods and the Giants; *Birds* is thus a sophisticated literary creation. But one must always be careful in attributing such depths to Aristophanic comedy. His plays were intended to be popular and imaginative fantasies, creations for the moment, the humor immediate, sometimes trivial and foolish. There is no hint in *Birds*—as there is in *Acharnians, Wasps,* or *Frogs*—that here is a comedy with a "message" or a "point." It is safer to read the comedy as a wonderful fantsay on "going to the birds," a variation on the theme of utopia ("no place" or "good place"), a *topos* that goes back to Homer and Hesiod. Here the imagery of wings and flying brilliantly embellishes this wish-fulfillment, and "the charm of *Birds* is that it is a dramatization of dreams come true" (MacDowell [1995] 228).

I.C.S.

---

[5] Some have tried to see *Birds* as a detailed political allegory of the Sicilian expedition (Süvern, Katz, and Vickers), but these impress the reader only with their ingenious arguments.

Birds: Cast of Characters

GOODHOPE	an Athenian
MAKEMEDO	an Athenian
SECRETARY BIRD	servant to the Hoopoe
HOOPOE	Tereus, once king of Thrace
CHORUS	of birds
PRIEST	from Athens
POET	from Athens
PROPHET	from Athens
METON	an Athenian mathematician
INSPECTOR	from Athens
LAWYER	from Athens
MESSENGER	a bird
GUARD	a bird
IRIS	the rainbow goddess
MESSENGER 2	a bird
MANES	a servant
YOUTH	from Athens
CINESIAS	a dithryrambic poet
INFORMER	from Athens
PROMETHEUS	a Titan
POSEIDON	god of the sea
JERKOFFALOT	a Triballian god
HERACLES	a demigod
DIVINE PRINCESS	daughter of Zeus
HERALD	a bird

Birds was first produced by Aristophanes in 414 B.C.E., at the Dionysia Festival in the city of Athens. This translation was first presented by the Aquila Theatre Company, receiving its first U.S. public performance at the Morton Theatre, Athens, Georgia, in February 1997 and its first U.K. public performance at the Pleasance Theatre, London, November 1997, directed by Robert Richmond and produced by Peter Meineck.

Birds

SCENE: *A mountainous landscape, desolate and miles from anywhere.*

*(Enter two older men, Makemedo, who has a jackdaw perched on his arm, and Goodhope, who is likewise carrying a crow.They are accompanied by two slaves carrying their baggage and a variety of baskets, pots, and pans.)**

GOODHOPE:*
(To his jackdaw) What was that? Straight on, over by that tree?

MAKEMEDO:*
(To Goodhope) Oh, damn you! This one keeps croaking "go back."

GOODHOPE:
You stupid idiot. What's the point of wandering about, up and down,
backwards and forwards on this wild-goose chase? It's hopeless.

MAKEMEDO:
I must be an idiot, letting a crow persuade me
to go trudging around in circles, mile after mile.

---

*: (An asterisk refers to an endnote, found at the end of the play.)

GOODHOPE:
Then I'm a moron, letting a jackdaw persuade me
to go about wearing my toenails away to nothing.

MAKEMEDO:
I wonder where on earth we are? Do you think we could find
the way back to our country from here?

GOODHOPE:
I don't think even Execestides could do that.

MAKEMEDO:
Hell!

GOODHOPE:
You go there if you want, but don't expect me to follow!

MAKEMEDO:
That bird-bartering bastard at the market. It's all his fault!
Flaming Philocrates, the filthy fraudster!
He swore these birds would lead us to Tereus,
the Hoopoe-Bird who turned from flesh to fowl.
One obol for that jerk of a jackdaw there*
and three for this clueless crow, and all we've
found so far is peck marks on our fingers!

(To the crow, who stands still, open-beaked)

What are you gawking at? You are leading us right over those rocks,
there's no sign of any road over there.

11: Public office could be held only by full citizens who could prove that both their mother and father had been born in Attica. There seems to have been some doubt as to Execestides' lineage.

14: Philocrates was a bird seller and is mentioned only here and at line 1077.

15: The legendary king of Thrace raped Philomena, the sister of Procne, his Athenian wife. In revenge Procne killed their only son, Itys. The gods turned Tereus into a hoopoe, Procne into a nightingale, and Philomena into a swallow (***15 Tereus**).

GOODHOPE:
Nothing, by Zeus, there's no way through there.

MAKEMEDO:
This crow's trying to tell us the way,
he's definitely croaking on about something, by Zeus!

GOODHOPE:
What's he saying about the way?

(Makemedo is struggling with his crow.)

MAKEMEDO:
Oww! He's telling me the way he likes to nip my fingers!

GOODHOPE:
Look at us, what a pair of idiots,
all we want is to "get the bird"
and we can't even do that!

(To the audience)

Yes, gentleman, I'm sick as a parrot.
We both are, but not sick like Sacas,
He's not a native though he'd love to be.
No, we're true citizens born and bred,
honored members of both tribe and clan.*
But we want to be as free as the birds,
so we've upped and flown our country's coop.
It's not that we hate our city, not at all,
its a magnificent land, where all are free . . .
to come to court and pay their fines!
Take the cricket. For one month, maybe two,
he sits up in a fig tree and chirps out his song,
whereas your average Athenian wastes a lifetime
sitting in court chirping on and on and on.
That's why we are on this journey, kitted out

27: The Greek has "go to the crows!" which is akin to "go to Hell!"

30: The nickname of Acestor, a tragedian who was rumored to be of foreign descent. Sacas was the Persian name for a Scythian.

with these pots, baskets, and myrtle boughs.
We're in search of a land free from hustle and bustle*
where a man can just settle down and rest.
So our expedition is in search of Tereus, the Hoopoe,
with all the flying about he's done he'll know
just where to find such a city . . .

MAKEMEDO:
Hey, look!

GOODHOPE:
What is it?

MAKEMEDO:
Look at my crow!

(The crow is looking up in the air.)

GOODHOPE:
My jackdaw's staring up at something as well.
It looks like he's pointing up to the sky.
There must be birds around here, let's make some noise
and see if we can get them to show themselves.

MAKEMEDO:
Try giving that rock a big kick with your foot.

GOODHOPE:
Why don't you bang on it with your empty head, it'll make a lot more noise!

MAKEMEDO:
I know! Pick up a stone and knock it on the cliff.

GOODHOPE:
All right.

42: All items used in sacrificial rites and possibly foundation ceremonies (***42 Rites**).

(He starts pounding on the door of the scene building.)

Boy! Boy!

MAKEMEDO:
What are you doing? Don't go calling the old bird "boy"!
You should summon him by calling, "Hoopoe!"

GOODHOPE:
Coo-ee! Hoopoe! Here Hoopoe, Hoopoe, Hoopoe!
Yoohoo, Hoopoe!

*(Enter a servant bird, who pops his head out of the scene building's window.)**

SERVANT:
Who are you to yoohoo, the Hoopoe?

*(They reel back in terror. Makemedo loses control of his bladder and Goodhope his bowels as their birds fly away.)**

GOODHOPE:
Apollo help us! Look at the pecker on this bloke!

SERVANT:
Oh no! Nestrobbers!

MAKEMEDO:
Hang on, that's not a very nice thing to say!

SERVANT:
I've nothing to say to you men.

MAKEMEDO:
But, eh . . . but we're not men.

SERVANT:
Well, whatever are you then?

(Makemedo shakes out his legs.)

MAKEMEDO:
Eh . . . I'm a Yellow-streaked Dribbler, a Libyan species.

SERVANT:
There is no such bird.

MAKEMEDO:
Hey, if you don't believe me, take a look at my feet.

(Makemedo points to a puddle of urine, and the servant bird turns to Goodhope.)

SERVANT:
And you, what species of bird are you?

(Goodhope is wiping his backside.)

GOODHOPE:
I am a brown-rumped turddropper from Phartia.

MAKEMEDO:
What about you then, what in the name of the gods are you?

SERVANT:
Isn't it obvious? I am a Secretary Bird.*

GOODHOPE:
You mean you're bottom of the pecking order?

SERVANT:
No, not really. When my master got his wings,
I signed up for the feathers too, so I could stay on,
attending to his needs. I'm the Hoopoe's personal assistant.

MAKEMEDO:
We know what kind of "personal assistance" you give, mate!

65: Apparently, they were so shocked at the sight of the secretary bird that Makemedo has urinated and Goodhope has "shit himself."

SERVANT:
Well, he was a man once. He still has certain longings.
If he fancies a little bit of fish to nibble,
I run down to Phaleron and get him a nice dish.
When he wants to lick up some soup, I run and grab
a couple of big jugs so he can dip his ladle.*

MAKEMEDO:
Oh, I see, you're a swift. Why don't you run inside,
and get your master, and be "swift" about it!

SERVANT:
No, no, no, no, no! He's taking a nap
after lunching on myrtle and gnats.

MAKEMEDO:
So? Go and wake him up!

SERVANT:
All right, all right, just for you, I'll wake him,
but I warn you, he's not going to be very happy about it.

(Exit Servant through the window.)

MAKEMEDO:
Good riddance! Scared me half to death, the bastard.

GOODHOPE:
Bastard. He scared my jackdaw away.

(Makemedo points to Goodhope's backside.)

MAKEMEDO:
You mean you got scared and dropped your load.

(Goodhope points to a puddle at Makemedo's feet.)

77: The old harbor of Athens.

88: The Greek has "you let your jackdaw go," a play on words between *koloios* ("jackdaw") and *kolon* ("anus").

GOODHOPE:
Where's your crow then? You relieved yourself of it, didn't you?

MAKEMEDO:
I certainly did not!

GOODHOPE:
Well, where is it then?

MAKEMEDO:
It pissed off.

GOODHOPE:
I'm relieved to hear of your bravery, my friend!

(From offstage)

HOOPOE:
Unbar the hedgerow, I am coming out!

*(Enter the Hoopoe through the doors, clearly a man wearing a bird-mask with a long bill and a large crest. Makemedo and Goodhope fall about laughing.)**

GOODHOPE:
Heracles! What kind of creature is that?
Just look at his plumage and that great triple-crest!

HOOPOE:
And you are?

MAKEMEDO:
Gods! It must have taken all twelve Olympians
to have done that to you!

89: *korônê* ("crow") was a euphemism for the penis.

92: More word play. Here the Greek *apeptato* ("fly away") implies *apopatein* ("defecate").

94: The hoopoe bird has a distinctive crest (***Stage Direction: Hoopoe**). Military commanders wore a triple crest on their helmets, and this may allude to Tereus' former status as a king.

HOOPOE:
I do hope you are not ridiculing my plumage.
Remember, strangers, that I was once a man.

GOODHOPE:
We're not laughing at you.

HOOPOE:
What then?

GOODHOPE:
It's that beak. It looks ridiculous!

HOOPOE:
You can blame that damned playwright, Sophocles.
He did this to me in that dreadful tragedy of his, *Tereus*.

MAKEMEDO:
So you're Tereus. Are you really a bird, or do you just strut like a peacock?

HOOPOE:
I am indeed a bird.

GOODHOPE:
Well, what happened to all your feathers then?

HOOPOE:
They fell out.

GOODHOPE:
Have you been unwell?

HOOPOE:
Don't be absurd. Everyone knows that birds molt
in the winter. Come spring and they will all be back.*
Now then, who exactly are you?

101: Sophocles had produced a tragedy on the theme of the Tereus/Procne myth called *Tereus*.

MAKEMEDO:
We're humans.

HOOPOE:
And where are you from?

MAKEMEDO:
From the land of beautiful battleships.

HOOPOE:
You're not jurors, are you?

GOODHOPE:
No, not at all, in fact you might call us juryphobes.

HOOPOE:
I didn't think they had that species in that particular region.

GOODHOPE:
Oh, there's a few, out in the country. They're very rare.*

HOOPOE:
Why have you come here, gentlemen?

MAKEMEDO:
We wanted to get together with you.

HOOPOE:
Whatever for?

MAKEMEDO:
Because once you were a human, just like us,
because you were plagued by debts, just like us,
because you hated paying them, just like us.
But then you turned from man to bird and winged it
over land and sea, a bird's-eye view you might say.
I mean, you've walked on the wild side.

109: The Athenians were famed for their love of litigation and their huge citizen juries (see *Wasps*, introduction, pp. 125–31).

We thought that you might be able to help us.
That in all your flying about, you may have come across
a nice soft and woolly city where two tired men
can snuggle up and live in peace and tranquility.

HOOPOE:
So you are seeking a place greater than Athens?

MAKEMEDO:
No, not greater—softer. A city tailormade just for us.

HOOPOE:
Perhaps you are looking for an aristocracy?

MAKEMEDO:
No thank you! I've had enough of those farty windbags!*

HOOPOE:
Well, what kind of city do you want to live in?

MAKEMEDO:
A place where the worst thing that could possibly happen,
would be to wake up in the morning and find all my mates
crowding round my door with party invitations saying:
"By Zeus! Get up! Get washed and dressed! Give the kids
a bath! We're having a wedding feast, no excuses!
And you'd better make sure you turn up, otherwise
we won't be around to help when you're in a fix."

HOOPOE:
By Zeus! I can see you know all about suffering.

(To Goodhope)

132: Guests at a wedding ceremony were required to purify themselves with a ritual bath and then dress in new robes.

134: A twist on the Greek concept of reciprocity. Normally friends (*philoi*) of the family would be repaid with their support by invitations to ceremonies. But in Makemedo's dream city he would be shunned if he failed to partake in the feasting.

And what about you?

GOODHOPE:
Oh, I'm after the same kind of thing.

HOOPOE:
Such as?

GOODHOPE:
A place where the father of some pretty young boy
would come up to me and complain saying "Hey, twinkle-toes,
That's no way to treat my son, he told me that you bumped
into him outside the gym and you never tried to give him a little kiss
or a cuddle, and what's more, you didn't even bounce his balls!
And you call yourself a friend of the family!"

HOOPOE:
Oh dear, you really do love trouble, don't you?
I think I know just the place, a lovely little
Arabian resort on the Red Sea.

GOODHOPE:
Good gods, no! Nowhere near the sea. I don't want
an Athenian battleship like the *Salaminia* turning up
one morning, carrying a cargo of court summonses.
Is there a city in Greece you could recommend?

HOOPOE:
What about the city of Lepreus in Elis?

145: A region renowned for its opulence. In the fifth century this was the body of water that makes up the Arabian Gulf, the Arabian Sea, and the Indian Ocean.

147: One of the fastest ships in the Athenian navy, often used for important diplomatic missions. Only nine months before *Birds* was staged the *Salaminia* was sent Sicily to recall Alcibiades to stand trial in Athens.

148: A city in the western region of the Peloponnese on the borders of Messenia and Elis.

GOODHOPE:
Ugh! Sounds bit infectious to me. I'd never be able to forget
Melanthius and his acne, makes me itchy just to think about it!

HOOPOE:
You could settle down with the Opuntii in Locris.

GOODHOPE:
Opuntius! That one-eyed, big-beaked swindler!
You couldn't pay me to live with him.

MAKEMEDO:
So what's it like living with the birds then?
You'll know all about that.

HOOPOE:
Oh, it's not bad at all. For a start, birds don't need money.

GOODHOPE:
I suppose you just put it on your bill!*

HOOPOE:
We just swan around nibbling on sesame seeds,
myrtle berries, poppy seeds, and mint.*

GOODHOPE:
What a life, like being on an everlasting honeymoon!

MAKEMEDO:
That's it! That's it!
I've got it! What a brilliant idea, the power you could hold!
If only I could persuade the birds to do it . . .

151: A tragic playwright often vilified for his effeminacy, sexual perversions, and expensive tastes. Here his apparent skin problems are being derided with a pun on Lepreus (from *lepra*, "scabby").

152: Opus was a city in the eastern Locris region in central Greece near the straits of Euboea.

154: Opuntius may have been an Athenian sycophant (an accuser) nicknamed Raven for his huge hook nose.

HOOPOE:
Make me do what?

MAKEMEDO:
Well for starters, I would make you take some advice.
I mean, stop flapping around with your beaks open,
look at you! Everyone thinks that birds are stupid.
Back in Athens birds aren't worth a hoot.
If we see someone running about like a headless chicken,
we call him bird-brained, a cock-up, or Teleas the flighty.

HOOPOE:
By Dionysus, you are quite right! But what would you have us do?

MAKEMEDO:
Found your own city.

HOOPOE:
Found a city! The Birds?

MAKEMEDO:
You really are a bird of ill omen, aren't you, Hoopoe?
Look down there.*

(The Hoopoe looks down across the orchestra.)

HOOPOE:
I'm looking.

MAKEMEDO:
Now look up there.

(He looks up into the sky.)

HOOPOE:
Looking.

170: A politician who served as secretary of Athena's treasury. Comic playwrights portrayed him as morally corrupt and unreliable.

MAKEMEDO:
Look about, crane your neck.

(He performs a ridiculous head-twisting movement.)

HOOPOE:
I just hope I don't do myself an injury twisting around like this.

MAKEMEDO:
What do you see?

(The Hoopoe, Makemedo, and Goodhope look out over the orchestra.)

HOOPOE:
Clouds and a great deal of sky.

MAKEMEDO:
Exactly, that's the pole of the birds.

HOOPOE:
What do you mean, "pole"?

MAKEMEDO:
It is quite simply the place of polarity and everything
passes through it, hence, it is called a pole.
The pole needs a policy, so colonize it, build walls,
police the pole, and the pole becomes a polis, the polorized polity!*
Instead of grubs and grasshoppers you'll master
all mankind, and if the gods kick up a fuss, you can starve
them out with your very own Melian siege.

HOOPOE:
How?

179: The Greek word *Polos*, punned here with *polis* (city), has several interlinked meanings, such as "axis," "vault of the earth," and the center of a threshing floor (***180 Pole**).

186: A small island state in the Cyclades that was besieged by Athens in 416 and starved into submission (***186 Melos**).

MAKEMEDO:

Because you will inhabit the space between Heaven and Earth.
Look, if I wanted to go from Athens to Delphi, I would have to pay
the Boeotians to cross their territory. Now, when mortals sacrifice
to the gods, the smoky savor has to pass through your territory
in order to reach up to heaven. If the gods refuse to pay tribute,
then you just stop the smoke and starve them out. Do you get it?

HOOPOE:

Oooh! Oooh! I just love it!
By all the nets, traps, and snares of this good earth,
I've never heard such an exquisitely clever idea!
Let us build this City of Birds together,
that is, if the other birds agree, of course.

MAKEMEDO:

But who will put it to them?

HOOPOE:

You will! Don't worry, I've taught them to speak.
They used to twitter away like, well, like birds, but not any more.

MAKEMEDO:

How are you going to call them together?

HOOPOE:

Simple! I'll just quickly slip in the bush
and rouse my lovely little Nightingale.
They'll all come flocking
when they hear our birdcall.

188: The shrine of Apollo and location of his oracle, situated to the northeast of Athens in the foothills of Mt. Parnassus.

189: A region to the north of Attica. The Boeotians had placed restrictions on other Greeks crossing their territory, which was essential for delegates wanting to visit the Panhellenic shrine at Delphi.

192: The smoke from burnt sacrificial offerings rising to heaven was said to form a holy communion between mortals and gods.

MAKEMEDO:
My dear Hoopoe, what an excellent idea.
Quickly, pop in the bush and get your wife,
I can't wait to see the Nightingale aroused.*

(The Hoopoe begins to sing.)

HOOPOE:
Come my darling, rise from slumber,
Fill the air with your holy number.
Cry the keen from lips divine,
Sing for Itys, both yours and mine.
Pour forth the melody, honey-sweet,
Raise the warble, chirp the tweet.

*(The Hoopoe is joined by the Nightingale.)**

Through the leaves the song is loose,
Pure notes reaching the realm of Zeus.
Golden-haired Apollo hears her sing,
And to this lament plucks his strings.
Heavenly chords from his ivory lyre,
Inspire the gods, the immortal choir.
Singing together, one voice for all,
Blessed gods cry the hallowed call.

GOODHOPE:
By Zeus, what a heavenly sound!
She's filling the whole bush with her honey.

MAKEMEDO:
Hey!

GOODHOPE:
What?

MAKEMEDO:
Keep quiet.

222: This is the *ololugmos*, a shrill, piercing cry, usually made by women at the climax of a sacrifice or at the height of emotion.

GOODHOPE:
Why?

MAKEMEDO:
The Hoopoe's getting ready to sing again.

HOOPOE:
Epopoi! Popopopopoi! Popoi!
Io, io! Ito, ito, ito, ito!

To me, come to me feathered friends, to me, to me,
Nibblers of freshly plowed fields, come and see.
You several species that on barley corn chew,
Come seed-pecking flocks and hear this news.
Fly quickly, little chirpers that scuttle to and fro,
Come here all those that thread the furrow.
Between the parted ruts, they twitter all,
So come to the sound of your blissful call:

Tio, tio, tio, tio, tio, tio, tio, tio!

Those who like to visit gardens, nestling there,
You ivy-branch peckers must hear of this affair.
You hill-dwellers that chew the olive dear,
Suck up your strawberries and wing it here.

Trioto, trioto, totobrix!

Those who pierce the marshy gullies,
Swallowing down the gifts so lovely,
Those comely, moist meadows of Marathon,
Haunt of the partridge, the speckled hen.

Those who swoop the swelling sea,
Bring the kingfisher and come to me.
Come and learn this revolutionary news,
You crane-necked birds must hear these views.

Come and hear this sharp old man,
Hear his thoughts and test his plan.
What he is saying is so radical,

*Come and hear, come one and all.**

Come, come, come, come, come!

Torotorotorotorotix!
Kikkaboo, kikkkaboo!
Torotorotorolililix!

MAKEMEDO:
See any birds yet?

GOODHOPE:
No, by Apollo, I have not, and I've been standing here
the whole time gaping up at the sky.

MAKEMEDO:
Looks like the Hoopoe was wasting his time,
banging away in the bush like a yellowhammer.*

HOOPOE:
Torotix! Torotix!

(Enter a bird onto the roof of the scene building.) *

MAKEMEDO:
Look! Over there, there's a bird coming!

GOODHOPE:
By Zeus, it's a bird! What kind do you think it is? A peacock?

MAKEMEDO:
The Hoopoe will know.

(To the Hoopoe)

What kind of bird is that?

269: Very rare and exotic birds in Athens. Makemedo and Goodhope may never have actually seen one, but only heard about their fantastic plumage. It seems clear that this first bird is spectacularly costumed.

HOOPOE:
Oh that's a very rare marsh bird, you certainly won't see him every day.

MAKEMEDO:
Phew! It's gorgeous! Flaming red.

HOOPOE:
Precisely, he's a flamingo.

GOODHOPE:
Will you look at that!

MAKEMEDO:
What?

(Enter a second bird on the scene building roof.)

GOODHOPE:
Here comes another bird!

MAKEMEDO:
By Zeus! You're right, he looks like something from a Greek tragedy,
"Who can this poet-prophet be, hillock bird prancing daintily."

HOOPOE:
He is known as the Iranian fowl.

GOODHOPE:
The Iranian fowl? Lord Heracles! How did he get here without a camel?

MAKEMEDO:
Here's another one, look at that huge crest!

272: The flamingo was known in Greece but was fairly rare.

276: The quotation is from Aeschylus' *Edonoi*, originally referring to Dionysus, dressed in ornate Lydian robes.

277: An unknown species, but evidently rare and exotic. Romans later used the same term for the peacock.

(Enter another Hoopoe on the scene building roof.)

MAKEMEDO:
Hold on, that's another Hoopoe! I thought you were the only one.

HOOPOE:
You are quite right, he is a Hoopoe. He's my grandson actually,
the son of Philocles' Hoopoe—and what a "tragedy" that was!
It's just like any noble family, Hipponicus was called the son
of Callias, and his boy, Callias, the son of Hipponicus.

MAKEMEDO:
I see, so this bird's a Callias, but where are all his feathers?

HOOPOE:
He's well-bred, so he's regularly roasted in court,
and has plenty of hens yanking his feathers and getting him plucked.

(Enter a fourth bird on the scene building roof.)

GOODHOPE:
Poseidon! Here's another, what a color!
What's that one called?

HOOPOE:
That is the yellow bellied gobbler.

MAKEMEDO:
What! There's another beside Cleonymus?

282: A dramatist and nephew of Aeschylus, who staged a version of the Tereus story in his *Pandionis* tetralogy (***282 Philocles**).

283: Members of the aristocratic Ceryces family. The excessive lifestyle of Callias was the subject of the comedy *Flatterers* by Eupolis, staged in 421 (***283 Callias**).

286: *Ptera* ("feathers" or "wings") was a euphemism for "penis" (***286 Ptera**).

289: A politician lampooned for gluttony and cowardice. A soldier fleeing from battle would discard his helmet with its distinctive crest (see *Wasps* ***19 Cleonymus**).

HOOPOE:
It can't be Cleonymus, he hasn't thrown away his crest.

MAKEMEDO:
Why do these birds have such big crests on their heads,
are they planning to enter the Armor Race?

HOOPOE:
No, no, they use the same tactic as the Carian Hill-Fighters,
After all, crests make combat safer.

(Makemedo sees the bird chorus in the wings of the theatre.)

MAKEMEDO:
Poseidon! Look there. I've never seen such a "fowl" collection of birds!

(Enter the chorus of birds from the offstage orchestra entrances, left and right.)

GOODHOPE:
Lord Apollo, what a flock! There are so many flapping about,
I can hardly see the wings!*

MAKEMEDO:
Look, there's the partridge!

GOODHOPE:
A grouse, by Zeus!

MAKEMEDO:
A mallard duck!

292: The *diaulos,* a footrace, consisting of two lengths of the stadium. In certain versions of this event the competitors ran in full armor, including crested helmets.

293: Caria was a mountainous region of southwestern Asia Minor (modern day Turkey). The Carians lived in fortified hilltop cities.

298: The Greek has *kerulos,* which was a mythical bird that according to legend was carried on the back of the kingfisher. Aristophanes puns *kerulos* with *keirein* ("to cut hair").

GOODHOPE:
And there! A kingfisher hen.

MAKEMEDO:
What's that one right behind her?

HOOPOE:
I believe it is the shaveling.

GOODHOPE:
You mean there's a bird who shaves?

HOOPOE:
Surely you know Mr. Sparrow the barber?
Here comes the owl.

MAKEMEDO:
Fancy that! Bringing owls to Athens.

HOOPOE:
Jay, turtle-dove, lark, warbler, pipit, pigeon!
Vulture, hawk, ring-dove, cuckoo, redshank, firecrest!
Purple gallinule, kestral, little grebe, bunting, lammergeyer, woodpecker!

(The chorus of twenty-four birds fill the orchestra.)

GOODHOPE:
Oh, wow! Billions of birds!

MAKEMEDO:
Oh wow! What a row! So much fowl!
Just look at them, scuttling about, clucking and chattering away.

GOODHOPE:
Oh dear, I don't think they like the look of us.

300: Sporgilos was evidently the name of an Athenian barber. It was also a colloquialism for "sparrow."

302: Athenian coins had a picture of an owl on them, the patron bird of Athena and the symbol of Athens.

MAKEMEDO:
They're staring right at us, gawking, and I don't like the look of those peckers.

GOODHOPE:
Me neither. I'm scared.

(Makemedo and Goodhope hide behind the Hoopoe's wings.)

CHORUS:
Who-who-who-who called us? What is it? Where is he?

HOOPOE:
Here I am, I called, your trusty old friend the Hoopoe.

CHORUS:
Tch-tch-tch-tch-then speak, Hoopoe, what is it you have to tell us?

HOOPOE:
Something wonderful, for the good of us all,
two fine-thinking gentlemen have come to me . . .

CHORUS:
Where? Why? Who?

HOOPOE:
I was telling you that two esteemed old gentlemen have come to me,
from the realm of the humans with the promise of a preeminent plan.

CHORUS:
You fool! You have just laid the greatest blunder since I was hatched!
What are you saying?

HOOPOE:
Have no fear, listen to me.

CHORUS:
Hoopoe, what have you done?!

HOOPOE:
I have merely taken two bird fanciers under my wing.

CHORUS:
What! You admitted two men?

HOOPOE:
Yes indeed, and it was my pleasure.

CHORUS:
You mean to tell me they're here, now!

HOOPOE:
Oh yes, look.

(He reveals Goodhope and Makemedo, cowering.)

CHORUS:
Caw! Caw!
Catastrophe! Treachery and treason!
Our feathered friend calls an open season.
Once he dipped his pecker in our fields,
And yet our ancient tenets he now yields.
The sacred Bird Laws have been transgressed,
The Hoopoe has fouled his very own nest.
Those evil humans snare us in their trap,
Our eternal enemies have put us in a flap!

We will deal with you later, Hoopoe.
Now for these two old men, the penalty is clear:
Peck them to death! Tear them to shreds!

MAKEMEDO:
Ahhh! We're finished!

GOODHOPE:
This was your cockeyed scheme right from the start!
Why did I ever let you talk me into leaving home?

MAKEMEDO:
Well, you bloody followed me!

GOODHOPE:
Our goose is cooked! I want to cry.

MAKEMEDO:
No chance, mate, not once these birds have pecked your eyes out.

*(The chorus maneuvers into military formation.)**

CHORUS:
ATEEEN SHUNNN!
Forward! Charge! To bloody battle! Attack!
Advance with wings extended, push them back!
Maneuver in a circle, cut off their retreat!
They're cowering like cowards, howling in defeat.
Soon enough they'll feel the anger of our beaks,
there'll be no hiding place among the shady peaks.
No refuge on the gray seas, no cloudy sanctuary,
you two men have had it, there's no escape from me!

Let's not delay any longer, let's prick them and pluck them!
Where's the commander? Have him lead the right wing!

(The chorus closes in on Makemedo and Goodhope, who are trapped with their backs to the scene building.)

GOODHOPE:
I've had enough of this! I'm off!

MAKEMEDO:
Chicken! Stand and fight like a man.

GOODHOPE:
No way, we'll be sitting ducks!

MAKEMEDO:
You'll be a dead bloody duck if you don't listen to me!

GOODHOPE:
What can we do?

352: This is the *taxiarch*, the commander of a line of hoplites (infantry). Hoplites would be drawn up in lines and advance together against the enemy, pushing until one line gave way and scattered in defeat.

(Makemedo throws him one of the pots he has been carrying.)

MAKEMEDO:
Our only chance is to stand and fight!
Here, stick this pot on your head.

GOODHOPE:
What good will that do?

MAKEMEDO:
Birds don't like cooking pots.

GOODHOPE:
But what about their horrible sharp talons?

MAKEMEDO:
Get one of those skewers and hold it like a spear.

GOODHOPE:
Chicken kebabs! But what about my eyes?

MAKEMEDO:
Cover them with a couple of saucers!

GOODHOPE:
Another bloody tin pot idea, out of the frying pan right into the fire!
But I admire your resourcefulness, you could out-general Nicias!

CHORUS:
Chaaaaarge! Onwards! Give them a taste of cold beak! Come on!
Grab, pluck, claw, and flay them alive! Smash their skillets!

(Just as the chorus charges, the Hoopoe intervenes.)

358: The Greek has "It will keep the owls at bay." This may be an allusion to the practice of placing pots on the roof containing hot coals to deter birds, or that the owl was Athena's symbol and she was also a patron goddess of potters.

363: Nicias was an elected Athenian general and commander of the huge Athenian force then in Sicily.

HOOPOE:

Please! Listen to me! Let us not kill the goose that laid the golden egg. These men have done you no harm, and they're related to my own dear wife.

CHORUS:

What? They're humans, aren't they? Our worst enemies! They're worse than wolves, what other creature treats us so badly?

HOOPOE:

You can't blame them for the accidents of their births. They've come in friendship bearing precious information.

CHORUS:

What can humans teach the birds? They are our natural enemies, our age-old predators.

HOOPOE:

Is it not wise to learn from one's enemies?
Is not an open mind the best defense?
Men do not build walls, towers, and warships*
because of their friends. No, it is enemies
that make them protect their loved ones.
Should we not do the same?

CHORUS:

There's something in what you are saying, Hoopoe. We'll listen to them first. Perhaps we might learn something.

MAKEMEDO:

They're not quite so angry now. Let's inch our way back a bit.

(Goodhope and Makemedo slowly move back.)

HOOPOE:

Moreover, you should do this for me out of gratitude.

368: Tereus' wife, Procne, was an Athenian princess, the daughter of King Pandion.

CHORUS:
That's true, we have always agreed with you, Hoopoe.

MAKEMEDO:
They seem to be settling down,
all right, lower your pot,
but keep your hand on your spearshaft,
I mean your skewer. We must
patrol the perimeter.
Stay alert at all times,
we have to stand firm.

GOODHOPE:
I just hope they don't kill us.
I mean, where would we be buried?

MAKEMEDO:
In the Athenian National Cemetery
at public expense.
Our tombstones will read,
"Here lies a soldier who battled for Greece.
He gave his dear life fighting off Geese."

CHORUS:
Birds! Stand down! Back to the line!
Port your peckers, lower hackles,
ground all grudges in hoplite fashion.*
We must discover who these men are,
why they have come here,
and what they want with us.

(The birds fall back as ordered.)

395: This was the *Cerameicus* (potters' quarter) to the norhwest of the Agora and the location of the best cemeteries of Athens.

399: The Greek has "We died fighting the enemy at Orneae." The city of Orneae was captured and destroyed in 416–15 without any fighting after the pro-Spartan occupants fled. *Orneon* also means "bird."

"Hail Hoopoe, heed our call."

HOOPOE:
I "heed" indeed, and am here to hear.

CHORUS:
Who are these men, and where are they from?

HOOPOE:
They come from the learned land of Greece.*

CHORUS:
What are they doing here?
Why have they come to us birds?

(The Hoopoe pushes Makemedo before the birds.)

HOOPOE:
Passion!
A passion for our way of life,
A passion to be with us,
to live with us, forevermore!

CHORUS:
Really?
So what's this all about, then?

HOOPOE:
Something incredible! Something fantastic!

CHORUS:
But what does this human get out of it?
Trying to feather his own nest, I bet.
He just want to charm us birds off the trees.
He's after a nice little nest egg.

HOOPOE:
No, he will you tell you about a life of bliss,

406: The high style of these lines indicates a parody from tragedy or poetry.

great prosperity, and perfect happiness.
Words fail me, this idea defies description,
but all this is yours, here, there, everywhere.
As far as the eye can see, it is all yours!

(Pointing to Makemedo)

CHORUS:
Is he completely deranged?

HOOPOE:
No, just indescribably clever!

CHORUS:
Inherently wise?

HOOPOE:
Oh yes, and cunning like a fox.
Shrewd, smooth and subtle, a real old hand.*

CHORUS:
So let him speak! let him speak!
I'm all in a flap now,
I want to hear this big idea.

(To the servants)

HOOPOE:
You two slaves, carry this armor back inside
and hang it up in the kitchen by the trivet.
It might bring us luck, or at least a nice stew.

(To Makemedo)

Sir, the floor is yours, please make your case.

MAKEMEDO:
No, by Apollo! Not yet! I want a guarantee,

436: A victorious army would dedicate armor to the gods and hang it in a temple, the origin of the trophy. A trivet was a tripod used for holding a mixing bowl. Greek temples also contained sacred tripods.

from the organ grinders, not the monkey.*
No biting, scratching, grabbing my balls,
or poking those peckers up my . . .

HOOPOE:
Do you mind!

MAKEMEDO:
Nose, I was going to say nose.

CHORUS:
We give our guarantee.

MAKEMEDO:
Swear it! Give me your word.

CHORUS:
All right, I'll swear it, but only if you promise that our little comedy here will win first prize by unanimous vote.

MAKEMEDO:
Agreed.

CHORUS:
And if I break my oath, may I win by just one vote!

(Makemedo shouts out orders to the chorus)

MAKEMEDO:
Squad! Attention! All hoplites stow your equipment
and return at once to barracks.
Stand by for further postings. Dismissed!*

(The chorus sings.)

CHORUS:
Man is a liar, everyone knows it,
Deceitful, crooked, and bent.

446: *Birds* actually came second behind *The Revellers* by Ameipsias.

Tell us your story, we want to hear it,
Could you hold the key to our strength!

We're not the brightest creatures on earth,
Explain it please, if you can.
We want to hear the good things you offer,
Share it, and tell us your plan.

Now speak, human. Let us consider what you are proposing.
Don't worry, we will not be the first ones to breach the treaty.

MAKEMEDO:
By Zeus, I've a "crop" of words you really "knead" to make a "meal" out of!
Just wait until you taste the bread I'm going to break with you.
Boy, fetch me a garland and water for my hands! All please recline.*

GOODHOPE:
Is it dinnertime already?

MAKEMEDO:
No, by Zeus, it is not! However, I am going to deliver a great big, beefed-up
feast of a stampeding speech, and they're going to eat it up.

(Makemedo turns to address the Birds.)

Gentlemen, my heart is full of sorrow for the birds.
You who once ruled as kings!

CHORUS:
Us, kings! Kings of what?

464: Reclining, washing hands, and wearing garlands were all features of the symposium. This, combined with Makemedo's edible metaphors, makes Goodhope think of food.

467: Zeus overthrew his father, Cronus, after a long battle with the Titans. Cronus and the Titans were the children of the Earth (Gaia) and the Sky (Uranus) (***467 Heavenly succession**).

MAKEMEDO:
Kings of everything! Everyone! Kings of Creation!
Kings over Zeus himself! Kings more ancient than Cronus,
more archaic than the Titans, even older than the Earth!

CHORUS:
The Earth?

MAKEMEDO:
Yes, by Apollo.

CHORUS:
By Zeus, I never knew that!

MAKEMEDO:
Because you are uneducated, you have no hustle or bustle.
You've never learned Aesop's fables. He says the lark was the first bird,
born before even the Earth. When her father died, what could she do?
No Earth, so no earth to bury him under. Four days he went unburied,
until she had a brainwave and laid him to rest in her own head!

GOODHOPE:
And that's the origin of the phrase "bird brained!"

MAKEMEDO:
You see, the birds existed before creation, before even the gods.
That means you should have sovereignty. I mean, the eldest inherits, right?

472: The famous sixth-century storyteller from Samos. His animal fables were widely known in Athens.

475: This particular fable attributed to Aesop is unknown, but see ***475 Lark** for a reference to a similar tale noted by Aelian.

476: The Greek has "That's why the lark is buried in Headcrest Cemetery!" *Cephale* was an area of Attica and also Greek for "head."

CHORUS:
By Apollo, he's right!

GOODHOPE:
But you had better keep your beaks sharp. Zeus is not ready
to hand his scepter over to the first little pecker that taps his oak.

MAKEMEDO:
Back in the halcyon days, it wasn't these modern, upstart gods
that ruled mankind, it was the birds! Allow me
to prove my point with an example. Consider the cock.
Long before the Persians had their Dariuses or their Megabozes,
the rooster was king, that's why we still call him the Persian fowl.
I mean, doesn't he strut about all cocksure, like he rules the roost,
and he still wears that big red Persian crown on his head.
Just think of his power! Why even nowadays the cock still commands;
when he "cock-a-doodle-doos," everyone has to jump up out of bed:
blacksmiths, potters, tanners, cobblers, bathhouse managers,
barley traders, lyre-manufacturing-shield-beaters,
they all throw their shoes on and are up and out into the night!

GOODHOPE:
He's right! I lost my best Phrygian woolly coat thanks to a cock!
It was after a family get-together, a name day actually. I had a couple
of drinks to wet the baby's head, and come dinnertime I was fast asleep.
Next thing I know that damn bird pipes up, and I, thinking it was morning,
set off down the Harbor Road in the dead of night. I'd just passed the walls,
when—WHAM! A clothes-thief bashed me and ran off with my coat!

480: The sacred tree of Zeus was the oak, and the Greek woodpecker was known as the "oak-pecker."

484: Both names of Persian rulers. At the time *Birds* was produced, Darius II was king of Persia.

487: The Persian monarch wore a stiffened triple-pronged hat, which is compared to the comb of a rooster **(*487 Hat)**.

MAKEMEDO:
And look at the swallow, he used to be the King of the Greeks.

CHORUS:
All the Greeks?

MAKEMEDO:
King of all the Greeks, and we still kneel before him.

CHORUS:
When?

MAKEMEDO:
When we are waiting for spring and we see the first swallow,
we get down on our knees and give thanks for the end of winter.

GOODHOPE:
I saw a swallow once; it was payday, and I was on my way to market
with a mouth full of obols. I threw myself down on my knees so hard,
that I "swallowed" my bloody cash! I nearly starved that week.

MAKEMEDO:
The cuckoo was king of the Egyptians and the Phoenicians,
when the cuckoo called "cuckoo!" they would all get on the job,
thrusting their tools in the furrows and sowing their wild oats.

GOODHOPE:
So "cuckoo!" is the call for a clipped cock to start thrusting!

MAKEMEDO:
Birds had so much power that in the Greek cities ruled by kings

---

499: The Greek has "kite," which migrated to Greece each spring and was a sign for the end of winter.

504: Greeks often carried coins in their mouths (see *Wasps* line 610).

507: The Egyptians and the Phoenicians practiced circumcision.

like Agamemnon and Menelaus, the monarch always had a bird perched
on his scepter, and it would receive a share of the royal donations too.*

GOODHOPE:
I've always wondered why in tragedy I've seen some of the characters,
like King Priam, come on stage with bird-scepters. It's to keep an eagle eye
on all our corrupt politicians like Lysicrates and see what "donations" they share.

MAKEMEDO:
The eagle! Why he's best proof of all, Zeus, who reigns now, uses the eagle
as his symbol. His daughter, Athena, has an owl perched on her head,
and his son, Apollo, his father's helper, has the hawk.

CHORUS:
By Demeter, you're right! But why do they use birds?

MAKEMEDO:
Why do you think whenever we have a sacrifice, the birds swoop down
and take the offal from the hand of the god? It's the birds that take it to heaven,

---

509: Brother kings who led the Greek forces at Troy and frequent characters in tragedy.

512: Priam was the legendary king of Troy and had appeared as a character the previous year in the produciton of Euripides' *Alexander*.

513: Nothing is known about this character. It is assumed he was a public official or politician.

516: The eagle was associated with Zeus in art and myth. The owl was sacred to Athena, and Apollo is likened to a hawk by Homer (***512 Birds of the gods**).

519: A portion of some sacrifices may not have been burned but placed in the open hand of the cult statue.

they get the first peck. What's more, men used to swear by the birds, not the gods.
Take Lampon the prophet, he still does! When he's working one of his cons,
he doesn't say, "By Zeus," he says, "By Goose!"

Once you were holy, you were lords of this place.
Today you are lowly, you have fallen from grace.

Now they treat you like madmen and villains,
They throw stones and pelt you with shot,
And in temples where you were once worshiped,
They trap you as food for the pot

Caught in a net, snagged by a snare,
Choked by a noose, you haven't a prayer!

Once they've caught you, they take you to market,
Bundled up and forced in a cage.
Poked and prodded, felt up and handled,
Plucked clean, packaged and weighed.

Caught in a net, snagged by a snare,
Choked by a noose, you haven't a prayer!

But you're never just cooked through and eaten,
They baste you in all kinds of sauce.
*Herbs and spices, sweet oils and dressings,**
You're destined to be the main course.

Caught in a net, snagged by a snare,
Choked by a noose, you haven't a prayer!

522: Lampon was a prominent politician and religious authority. He was satirized by the comic playwrights for corruption and begging. The substitution of "Goose" for "Zeus" may be a comment on the reliability of his oracular interpretations (***522 Lampon**).

533: The refrain lines here are not found in the Greek.

CHORUS:

It pains us to know the truth you have told,
Of the honors our fathers once held.
Thrown to the winds, given for nothing,
Once our powers were unparalleled.

But now you have come and our fortune shines.
You're the savior of everything dear.
The trust you possess from those in our nests,
We'll follow you, we will all volunteer.

But what can we do? You must show us, tell us your plan!
Life has no meaning until we recover our ancient sovereignty.

MAKEMEDO:

My plan is to found a city of the Birds
and to encircle the sky between heaven and earth
with massive walls of big, baked Babylonian bricks.

CHORUS:

By Cerbriones and Porphyrion! A city fit for giants! A Babylon of Birds!

MAKEMEDO:

As soon as you have built the walls, you must send a delegation to Zeus
and set out your demands. If he ignores them or refuses to surrender,
declare a holy war, close all ports of entry, and deny them access
through your territory. Visa refused! No more popping down to earth
with their great hard-ons for a quick one with Alcmene,
all Alopes and Semeles are off limits, any infringement of the embargo

---

553: Two of the giants defeated by the Olympians at the battle of the Phlegrian Plain. The porphyrion is also a species of bird.

559: All mortal women seduced by gods. Alcmene was the mother of Heracles by Zeus, Alope was loved by Poseidon, and Semele bore Dionysus, also the son of Zeus.

will result in instant seizure of all offending members!
We'll hit them right where it will hurt them most.
Next, send an ambassador down to earth and inform the humans
that henceforth Birds will take precedence over gods in all sacrifices.
Each god will be assigned an official Bird; hence
Aphrodite will be honored by the cock getting his oats.
A sheep for Poseidon must be accompanied by toasted grains for the duck,
Heracles' honey cakes will be given to the greedy gulls,
And before king Zeus gets his goat, the kingbird, the wren,
will receive a sacrificial gnat, balls and all!

GOODHOPE:
A sacrificial gnat! That's a good one. Thunder now, great Zan!

CHORUS:
But the humans will think we're just a flock of scrawny old jackdaws,
they won't believe we're gods. These wings give us away every time.

MAKEMEDO:
But look at Hermes, he's got wings, and he flies all over the place.
What about the "gilded wings of Victory?" She's got a huge pair!
Then there's Eros who "sets hearts a flutter,"
and Homer says Iris resembles a "trembling dove," so she must have wings, too!

565: The Greek has Aphrodite paired with a *phaleris* ("coot") punning on "phallus."

568: The wren was sometimes named *basiliskos* ("little king").

569: This indicates that the sacrifice was not to be consumed but offered completely to the gods.

570: "Zan" was an archaic word for "Zeus" still in use at Olympia. Its use here may be to make Zeus seem irrelevant and old-fashioned.

573: Hermes was the messenger god, depicted with winged sandals (***573 Hermes**).

574: This is Nike who was always depicted with wings. A golden statue of Nike was held in the right hand of the statue of Athena in the Parthenon (***574 Nike**). Eros was a god of love often depicted with wings (***575 Eros**).

575: A messenger of the gods and goddess of the rainbow.

GOODHOPE:

Yes, and what about Zeus, he'll thunder away and send us his winged thunderbolt!

CHORUS:

But what happens if the humans just don't realize that we're the new gods?

MAKEMEDO:

Simple! We'll raise a regiment of sparrows, deploy them in the fields,
and let them peck away at their seeds until nothing's left.
Then we'll see if the humans honor Demeter at the next harvest festival.

GOODHOPE:

She'll just dole out a "cereal" of excuses.*

MAKEMEDO:

We'll send down the crows to peck out the eyes of the cattle,
then they'll go to Apollo for help, he's their god of healing,
but they won't be too happy when they get his doctor's bill!

GOODHOPE:

Let me know in plenty of time, will you? So I can sell my oxen first.

MAKEMEDO:

But, on the other hand, if they do recognize you as their gods, their Cronus,
Zeus, Earth, and Poseidon, then you must offer them a few benefits.

CHORUS:

What sort of benefits?

MAKEMEDO:

You will send owls and kestrels to wipe out the bugs

580: Demeter was the harvest goddess of cultivation and the principal deity of the Eleusinian Mysteries.

584: A number of doctors were retained by Athens and paid large fees by the state to treat the citizens (***584 Doctors**).

that plague their vines, and thrushes will swoop down
to eat all the maggots and flies that feed on their fruit.

CHORUS:
But how can we make them wealthy? Isn't that what all men pray for?

MAKEMEDO:
Easy! The humans use birds to give them signs, you can show
them where all the good silver mines are, they'll make a killing!
Plus you can predict the best trade routes so there'll be no more shipwrecks.

CHORUS:
How come?

MAKEMEDO:
How do you think humans forecast the weather? They watch the Birds.
You can warn them of any approaching storms and tell them when to sail.

GOODHOPE:
I'm buying myself a cargo ship. I'm off to sea!

MAKEMEDO:
And you can lead them to all the hordes of buried treasure
that their ancestors buried all those years ago.

CHORUS:
Eh?

MAKEMEDO:
You have inside knowledge, you've heard them, when one human asks
another how he found out about something, he says, "A little bird told me."

GOODHOPE:
I'm selling my cargo ship! Give me a pick and shovel, I'm going for gold!

CHORUS:
But what about long life and good health, that is the preserve of the gods?

MAKEMEDO:
You know the way things work on Earth, "If you're wealthy,
you're healthy, and if you're poor, you're at death's door!"

CHORUS:
But how can we guarantee that they will live to a ripe old age,
surely that's up to the Olympians, what's to stop them dying young?

MAKEMEDO:
You'll add at least three hundred years to their lives!

CHORUS:
How come?

MAKEMEDO:
Haven't you heard the proverb,
"The Crow lives longer than you folks,
five ages pass before he croaks."*

GOODHOPE:
Wow! These birds will be better rulers than Zeus.

MAKEMEDO:
Yes, so much better!

Now men have no need of temples,
No monuments built out of stone.
There'll be no great golden doorways,
The birds live in far simpler homes.

Lodged in a bush, perched in a pine,.
Grass for a roost, a nest for a shrine.

As a temple for birds who are proudest,
The olive tree will more than suffice.

Men won't need to journey to Delphi,
And to Ammon they'll not sacrifice.

Lodged in a bush, perched in a pine,
Grass for a roost, a nest for a shrine.

Man will stand among the olives and berries,
Holding barley and a handful of grain.
They'll stretch out their arms for the blessing,
And some wheat will ease all their pain.

Lodged in a bush, perched in a pine,
Grass for a roost, a nest for a shrine.

CHORUS:
Oh! What a transformation, from bitterest enemy to greatest friend!
You've won us over, from now on we're going to listen to you.

We applaud your words, such panache, what flair!
Now take heed and hear what we swear,
If you join forces here with us,
Help us plan and lead the thrust,
With right on our side we will attack
And force the gods to give our scepter back.

You're the brains, we're the brawn. We're ready.
Tell us exactly what it is you need us to do.

HOOPOE:
Yes, yes, to work! To work!
This is no time for twittering about like that nitwit Nicias.

619: For Delphi, see note on line 188.

620: Ammon was an Egyptian deity with an oracular shrine at the Siwa oasis in the desert of modern day Libya (**620 *Ammon**).

639: Nicias was regarded in some quarters as an overly cautious general, especially after failing to capitalize on his initial successful action in Sicily in 415.

Let us go forward together!*
But first please, come up and make yourself comfortable
in my nest, just a few twigs and leaves I threw together,
but it's home. Would you kindly introduce yourselves?

MAKEMEDO:
Of course. My name is Makemedo,
and this is Goodhope, late of Crioa.

HOOPOE:
Pleased to meet you.

MAKEMEDO:
Thank you very much.

HOOPOE:
Shall we go in?

MAKEMEDO:
After you, we'll follow.

HOOPOE:
Come on then.

(They follow the Hoopoe towards the door, and then Makemedo suddenly stops.)

MAKEMEDO:
Hey! Hold water! Back up your oars! Come back here!

(The Hoopoe returns.)

How on earth are we going to be able to live with you?
You birds have all got wings, we can't fly!

HOOPOE:
It's easy.

644: Crioa was one of the *demes* (districts) of Attica.

MAKEMEDO:
Listen up, Hoopoe, I know my Aesop, the fable of the fox and the eagle,
they tried living together too; one was outfoxed, and the other got burned.*

HOOPOE:
Don't you worry. I know of this little root,
one bite and you're as a high as a kite!

MAKEMEDO:
If that's the case, let's go in!

(Calling to the slaves)

Xanthias! Manodorus! Bring the bags!*

CHORUS:
Hoopoe! I'm calling.

HOOPOE:
What is it?

CHORUS:
Please show these men your best hospitality, but first, fetch
the Nightingale, your lovely little muse-inspired songbird.
Please have her come out so we can play with her.

MAKEMEDO:
Oh, yes, yes, by Zeus! Please be persuaded.
Have the little birdie come out of her bush.

GOODHOPE:
By all the gods have her come out!
I'm dying to catch a glimpse of the Nightingale.

HOOPOE:
Well, if that's what you both want, I will be happy to oblige.

(The Hoopoe calls inside the door.)

Procne! Come out and show yourself to our guests!

*(Enter Procne from the door with the twin pipes strapped to her mouth.)**

MAKEMEDO:
Zeus almighty! What a beautiful birdie!
Lovely plump meat, so tender.

GOODHOPE:
I wouldn't mind stuffing that bird!

MAKEMEDO:
What a lovely set of jewels, such a beautiful young thing.*

GOODHOPE:
I'm going to give her a kiss.

MAKEMEDO:
Hold on, you idiot, she's got a pair of skewers for a beak!

GOODHOPE:
It's all right, it's just like eating an egg,
you have to peel the top off first.

(Goodhope attempts to lift the pipes from the mouth of the Nightingale, who quickly jabs them into his face.)

OWWWW!

HOOPOE:
Shall we go?

MAKEMEDO:
Lead on, Hoopoe, and good luck to us all.

(Exit Makemedo, Goodhope, and the Hoopoe through the doorway.)

671: This could refer to the twin-piped aulos strapped to the mouth of the Nightingale.

[Parabasis]

(The chorus sings.)

CHORUS:
Beloved beauty,
Sweet songbird,
Sound this tune for me.
Nightingale,
To me come now,
Let us hear your melody.

The strains of springtime,
The pipes' call so fine,
Uplifting our every line.

Listen you feeble, faint, and frail humans. You weakly specimens fashioned from clay, turning to nothing and falling like dying autumn leaves. Ephemeral, ethereal, immaterial. You mortals are forlorn, flightless, and shadowy forms. Listen to us, the immortal, eternal, perpetual, and celestial. Hear from us the indestructible truth from on high. Be told the genesis of the Birds, the birth of the gods, the origins of the rivers and how Chaos and Darkness came to be. Know the truth and then go and tell Prodicus where to get off!

In the beginning there was only Chaos and Night, black Darkness and vast Tartarus,
there was no earth, no air, and no heaven, and in the infinite hollow of Darkness,

---

686: The Greeks believed that man was first modeled from clay by Prometheus (Hesiod *Works and Days* 77–82).

692: Chaos was the first element of the cosmos and means "abyss" or "gaping hole." "Darkness" is Erebus, son of Chaos and the brother of Night (Hesiod *Theogony* 116).

693: A sophist from Ceos who may have proposed his own radical version of the creation.

694: The bleakest region of the cosmos, lying beyond Chaos. It was here that Zeus imprisoned the Titans.

black winged Night laid the first wind-borne egg. Nurtured by the seasons
it hatched Eros, soaring love high on the wind with his glimmering golden wings.
In turn, Eros flew in by night and lay with Chaos in the vastness of Tartarus
and conceived the race of birds, hatched out into the brilliant new light.
There were no immortal gods until Eros merged the elements together into one,
creating Heaven, and Ocean and Earth, and *then* the race of deathless gods.
Hence we are far more ancient than the blessed gods themselves, and it is clear
that we are the true children of Eros, for like him we fly and we are bound with love.
Consider how many lovely young things have been seduced in their prime
thanks to the gift of a little lovebird. They all resisted at first but,
"Give the gift of a cock, a stork, a shag, or a duck.*
They're bound to say yes and you'll have some . . . luck!"

Just think of all the great gifts we birds give to you humans,
we tell you when it's winter, spring, summer, or fall. You know
just when to sow, because the Crane going to Africa says it's so!*
The Mariner knows to stow away the tiller and take a well-earned
rest, and Orestes knows that he must weave himself a nice warm
coat so he won't catch cold while he's out at night stealing clothes!
When winter's done, the kestrel comes to show the start of spring,
and you know to go and shear the wool from all your flocks of sheep.
Then the time to shear yourselves of winter woollies is marked
by swallows swooping in the sky and the summer wear you go and buy.

697: One of the earliest elements mentioned by Hesiod (*Theogony* 120).

712: The nickname of an Athenian thief who stole clothes, a very serious offense, perhaps named for his mad behavior after Orestes, the son of Agamemnon, who was driven mad by the Furies.

We are your prophets, your Ammon, Delphi, and Dodona, your personal
Phoebus Apollo. It is only after consulting us that you would dare embark
on any task. A voyage by sea, the sale of stock, a marriage in the family.
Birds permeate each and every important aspect of your lives.*
When facing a difficult choice, you say: "A bird in the hand is worth two in the bush."
When embarked on a perilous undertaking, you are "on a wing and a prayer."
When you have achieved something it is "a feather in your cap," a troublesome servant is a "lame duck," an informer "sings like a canary,"
and when you pass away, you are "as dead as a dodo!"

(The chorus sings.)

So, humans, name us as your gods
And inherit musical seers,
Prophetic birds for all seasons,
Free oracles down through the years.

We won't perch on high and snub you,
Looking down from clouds with disdain.
We'll not be like Zeus and sit aloof,
You'll never have cause to complain.

To you and your children hereafter,
We promise a life of great wealth.
Peace, prosperity, and laughter,
Festivities, dancing, good health.

So much rich creamy bird's milk slopping around,
You'll wear yourselves out and need a lie down!

718: Dodona was an oracle of Zeus in northwestern Greece. For Ammon see ***620 Ammon**.

736: The term *bird's milk* was a common expression for the most rarefied of luxuries.

(The flute player joins.)

Muse of the briar,

Tio tio tio tio!

We join your intricate notes
In this glen on a mountain peak,

Tio tio tio tinx!

High on the leafy ash,

Tio tio tio tio!

Coax my throat to quiver
The holy rounds for Pan.
The sacred air for Mountain Mother,

Tototo tototo tototo tinx!

Like a bee tasting honey,
Phrynichus sipped the nectar
To make his sweet ageless song,

Tio tio tio tinx!

Step on up, theatregoers, spend the rest of your days enjoying a life
with the birds, come here and live with us. So many things which
are deemed shameful and illegal by humans are common practice
among the birds. For example, you consider it a great disgrace if a son

---

745: God of the mountains and wild places. He had a cult site in one of the sacred caves on the Acropolis (***745 Pan**).

746: Cybele was an Anatolian mother goddess presiding over fertility and health. She was associated with the mountainous wilds and also gave oracles.

750: An early tragic playwright of the late sixth and early fifth centuries, known for his sweet melodic compositions (see *Wasps* ***220 Phrynichus**).

strikes his father, whereas with us, if a cocky youngling cocks a snook
at his sire and causes a cockfight, it's really quite all right!
If you happen to be a runaway slave, marked with the brand,
we would just call you a speckled swift, and you'd blend right in.
Perhaps you're a Phrygian foreigner like Spintharus, here you would be
just a common pheasant like Philemon the common peasant.
You might well be a slave like Execestides the Carian, we'd name you
the cuckoo, and you could nurture your chicks in another bird's nest.
If the son of Peisias fancies opening the gates to the traitors,
we won't condemn him, for "birds of a feather always flock together,"
it's "water off a duck's back" to us, for even the stool pigeon has his place.

The swans serenade,

Tio tio tio tio!

Winged harmony
Calling out to Apollo.

Tio tio tio tinx!

Flocking to the banks of Hebrus,

Tio tio tio tio!

759: Runaway slaves were branded forever with a mark on their foreheads.

761: Spintharus is unknown, perhaps an Athenian with murky family origins. Phrygia was a large region in Anatolia (modern day Turkey/Iraq). Philemon is unknown; his circumstances may have been similar to that of Spintharus. For Execestides see note on line 11. Caria was a region of southwestern Asia Minor (modern day Turkey).

766: The son of Peisias may be the one-legged shopkeeper referred to at line 1292. The "traitors" were probably those denounced in 415 for their role in the mutilation of the Herms prior to the sailing of the fleet for Sicily.

772: Apollo was said to travel in a chariot drawn by swans from the land of the Hyperboreans in the north to Delphi.

774: A river in Thrace to the north of Greece.

Through the clouds to heaven's heights,
The throngs of beasts are stilled in silence,
The wind drops and the sea is stunned,

Tototo tototo tototo tinx!

The clamor rings through Olympus.
The gods are gripped in awe.
The Graces chime with the Muses
And echo the hallowed call,

Tio tio tio tinx!

Members of the audience, let me tell you something, there is nothing
better than to possess your very own personal set of wings.
Imagine it, when you get a little peckish and bored during the tragedies,
you could fly up out of the theatre, pop back home, have a nice
spot of lunch, and still be back in plenty of time to see us!
What if you're a bit windy, like Patrocleides, and you need the bathroom?
You wouldn't have to hold it in, wriggling about, disturbing everybody,
or worst of all, run the risk of a very nasty accident. No, just do as we
birds do, fly up high in the sky and let rip, you can shit away, come what may!
For those of you who like a bit on the side now and again, wings are great.
If you are having an affair with a married woman and you see her husband*
down in the government seats, you can swoop off, have it off, and be back
before you're missed. You see, these wings are truly invaluable!
Take Dieitrephes, he's got a lovely pair of wings—wicker wings from a wine flask,

---

790: A politician who was called "The Shitter" for apparently suffering a bout of diarrhea while addressing the assembly.

796: A 500-seat section of the theatre was reserved for the Athenian *boule* (legislative council).

and he soared through the ranks, squadron leader, commodore, and marshal.
From a humble unknown basket case to an overblown, strutting peacock.
And it was all because of *wings!*

*(Enter Makemedo and Goodhope from the door, dressed as birds.)**

MAKEMEDO:
Will you look at that! Great Zeus! I can honestly say that I
have never, ever seen a more ridiculous sight in all my life!

GOODHOPE:
What's so funny?

MAKEMEDO:
You are in those wings! What do you look like?
I know, a badly painted decoy duck!

GOODHOPE:
Well, you look like a blackbird with a bowl-cut!

MAKEMEDO:
Well, these comparisons were inflicted on us
"not by another but by our own feathers," to quote Aeschylus.

CHORUS:
So tell us, what do we do next ?

800: A man who climbed through the ranks of Athenian public starting as a manufacturer of basket flasks, which had large handles called "wings." Aristophanes actually calls Dieitrephes a "horsecock" after a mythological creature (***800 Horsecock**).

806: Slaves received cheap "pudding-basin" haircuts, and no self-respecting freeman would wear such a style.

808: From Aeschylus' *Myrmidons* (Fr. 139. 4–5), attributed to Achilles on the death of Patroclus, speaking of an eagle shot by an arrow with eagle-feather flights.

MAKEMEDO:
First of all, we need a grand name for our new city,
then we must make the inaugural sacrifice.

CHORUS:
Yes, yes, you're quite right.

MAKEMEDO:
Now then, let's see, what should we call this new city?

CHORUS:
What about a strong laconic name like Sparta?

MAKEMEDO:
By Heracles! I'm not naming it Sparta. I hate them so much
I won't even use esparto grass for my mattress.

GOODHOPE:
Quite right, I'd rather sleep on the floor.

CHORUS:
Well, what shall we name it then?

GOODHOPE:
Something that sums up this place, the cloudiness,
the airiness, the sheer elevation of it all.

MAKEMEDO:
I've got it! What about "CLOUDCUCKOOLAND!"

CHORUS:
Oh yes! Yes! What a beautiful name, very long, very impressive.

817: A type of grass twisted into twine and used as strapping for a bed.

819: Nephelokokkygia (Cloudcuckooland) contains a second meaning, "Trap for chattering idiots," derived from *Nephelê* (bird-net) and *kokkuges* (chattering idiots) (***819 Cloudcuckooland**).

GOODHOPE:
Yes, Cloudcuckooland, "where Theogenes' cash is not a joke
and Aeschines' wealth won't vanish like smoke."

MAKEMEDO:
I think they'd be better off on the "windy" plain of Phlegra
where the gods out-boasted the entire race of giants.

CHORUS:
What a dazzling city this will be. But which of the gods
will be our patron? Who will wear the sacred robe?

GOODHOPE:
What about Athena of the City?

MAKEMEDO:
And just how will we maintain order in a city where our god
is a woman wearing armor and carrying a spear,
while Cleisthenes sits at home shuffling his shuttle?*

CHORUS:
Then who will guard our citadel?

MAKEMEDO:
The birds, of course! We'll line the walls with fighting cocks,
they're certainly not chickens, they're the chicks of Ares!

GOODHOPE:
The cocks of war! Just right for roosting on rocks.*

821: A merchant, shipowner, and minor politician nicknamed "Smoky" (i.e., "full of hot air") for his vain boasting.

822: A politician also ridiculed for bragging (see *Wasps* lines 459 and 1243).

827: Athena's statue on the Acropolis received a new woven robe every four years during the Panathenaea festival (***Robe**).

831: A character frequently portrayed by Aristophanes as highly effeminate (see *Clouds* line 355).

MAKEMEDO:

(To Goodhope) I need you to flutter off, up into thin air,
and go and help the builders of our wall, there's a good chap.
Make sure they have enough materials, bring them some bricks and mortar,
don't forget to carry a hod, and watch yourself on scaffold,
make sure you don't fall or anything! Stay up there at night
and keep the watch fires smoldering, make sure the sentries
are posted, chime the guard bell, and be certain to do the rounds.

(To the birds)

Send out two messengers, one to the gods on Olympus and one down to the humans.
We need to herald the founding of Cloudcuckooland and deliver our ultimatum.

GOODHOPE:

Hey! What are you going to be doing while I'm working away?

MAKEMEDO:

You must go where you are needed, my dear friend,
and you are needed out there to get all this done.

(As a dejected Goodhope exits)

My work is here, I have to send for a priest, organize
a sacred procession, and sacrifice to the new gods.

(He calls to a servant.)

Boys! Boys! Fetch the basket and the holy water!

(Exit Makemedo through the doors. The chorus sings as the servants bring out a vase of holy water and a basket. The aulos player comes onstage to accompany the chorus.)

CHORUS:

We do agree, we all consent,
The sacred rites we'll implement.
We'll walk in step and sing the hymn,
We will offer the gods a nice victim.
Chapter and verse we will quote,
As we sacrifice a sheep or goat.

Chirp the trill of Apollo's shout,
Have Chaeris get his pipe to play us out.

(Enter Makemedo with the Priest through the doors and into the orchestra to the central altar.)

MAKEMEDO:
What a terrible row!

(To the aulos player)

Will you stop blowing that pipe!

(Makemedo examines the aulos player.)

By Heracles, what on earth is this? I've seen it all now,
a raven, croaking away with a piper's markings.

(Exit flautist offstage.)

Right then, priest, it's time to sacrifice to our new gods.

PRIEST:
Then let us begin. Where is the boy with the basket?

(The servants bring the basket and water jug.)

Let us pray. O Hestia the nestmaker, O holy Hawk of the hearth.
To all the cocks and hens of Olympus. . . .

MAKEMEDO:
Let us pray to the birds of prey, to the Lord of the sea . . . gulls!

PRIEST:
To the Swan of Apollo, to Leto's Mother Goose,
to Artemis the Woodlark . . .

857: Chaeris was evidently a well-known aulos player and is mentioned in several comedies **(*858 Chaeris)**.

861: A reference to the *phorbeia,* the leather strap that was worn by the aulos player to hold his cheeks in place.

865: Hestia was the goddess of the hearth and invoked first in sacrificial rites.

870: For Apollo and swans see note on line 772. Leto was the mother of Apollo and Artemis, the virgin huntress and protector of wild animals.

MAKEMEDO:
. . . no more our virgin matriarch!

PRIEST:
O Sabazius the Oriental Cuckoo, Cybele, Ostrich Mother,
Come now, be here with us . . .

MAKEMEDO:
. . . and bring your fat son, Cleocritus!

PRIEST:
Give your blessing to Cloudcuckooland, bring health and wealth,
keep them all free from harm both here and in Chios . . .

MAKEMEDO:
Not Chios again. It's ridiculous!

PRIEST:
And all you ornithological Heroes, the many Gulls, Vultures,
Buzzards and Crows, the Ravens, Widgeons, Rooks and Pigeons,
The Crossbills, Creepers, Magpies and Wheatears,
The Chiffchaffs and Skimmers the . . .

MAKEMEDO:
Stop! Stop! You idiot! You fool! What the hell are you doing summoning
all these vultures and seagulls to our celebration. Do you think I want
the likes of those filthy, gluttonous birds spoiling the festivities!
Chiffchaff! More like riffraff! Now piss off and take your wreaths
with you! I'll just have to finish the sacrifice off myself.

875: An Eastern god closely associated with Dionysus (see *Wasps* *9 **Sabazius**). For Cybele see note on line 746.

877: Cleocritus was possibly an archon in 413–12. He was ridiculed for his obesity, lowly origins, and sexual perversions.

880: Chios, a large island state off the western coast of modern day Turkey, was an autonomous member of the Athenian League. In recognition of its loyalty it was decreed that all prayers for the welfare of Athens should also mention Chios.

(Exit Priest offstage.)

CHORUS:
It's plain to see that once again
We must now sing another amen.
Retract that hymn we sang sublime,
Recall the gods—just one this time!
Our sacrifice is short on meat,
We've barely got enough to eat.
Our offering is quite forlorn
Just skin and bones, all beard and horn.

MAKEMEDO:
Right then, back to the sacrifice. Let us wing our prayers to heaven . . .

*(Enter the Poet.)**

POET:
Of Cloudcuckooland,
The blessed I sing
Beloved by the Muse,
Hear my hymn.

MAKEMEDO:
By all the gods! Who let him in?

(To the Poet)

And who or what might you be?

POET:
A honey-tongued singer
Of glorious news,
Like Homer before me,
I serve the great Muse.

904: As in the opening line of Homer's *Iliad* (1.1), the poet invokes the Muse.

MAKEMEDO:
In other words, you're a slave with long hair.

POET:
No, a poet par excellence
Come to enthuse,
Like Homer before me,
I serve the great Muse.

MAKEMEDO:
All I can say is the "great Muse" hasn't served you very well, mate!
Just look at the state of you! What cloud did you float in on?

POET:
I came to sing the praises of Cloudcuckooland,
and I have specially composed a number of dithyrambs
and virgin songs in the style of Simonides.

MAKEMEDO:
Really, and when did you write these lovely little ditties?

POET:
Oh, I have been praising this marvelous city for ages.

MAKEMEDO:
That's rubbish, I haven't even finished the inaugural rites,
the place is in its infancy, I've only just named it!

POET:
The word of the Muse
Runs swiftly the course,

911: Slaves wore their hair short (see note on line 806); however, very long hair was fashionable among the rich young men and intellectual elite of Athens. Hair was also worn long by Spartans and those who cared little about grooming.

919: Simonides (c.556–468) was a renowned creator of lyric poetry, dithyrambs, and popular songs. In the late fifth century he had gained something of a reputation for being old fashioned. See *Clouds* 1356.

Faster than even
A galloping horse.

Oh, founder of Etna,
Named for the holy fire,
Just tilt thy holy head,
And this poet's been hired!

MAKEMEDO:
This one's not going to stop bothering me,
unless I give him something to go away.

(To a servant)

Hey! Take off your leather jerkin and give it to this "inspired" poet.

(The servant removes his coat and gives it to the Poet.)

If you're half as numb as your poetry, you'll need these.

POET:
For the sake of my Muse, I'll accept this gift,
My heart will be warm like a cinder.
I'll thank you now, and your spirit will lift
As I recite a few lines of Pindar.

MAKEMEDO:
There's no getting rid of this one!

POET:
He resides with Scythian tribesmen,
With no woven tunic to wear.
His skin is exposed to the elements,
His shivering bottom laid bare!

930: Based on an ode by the lyric poet Pindar (*Fr.* 105a), composed for Hieron the tyrant of Syracuse, who founded a city in 475 B.C.E. near Mt. Etna. Pindar himself despised the notion of the "poet for hire" (*Isthm.* 2.6).

941: The poet continues the version of the Pindaric ode he began at line 926 (*Fr.* 105b).

MAKEMEDO:

You need something to clothe the font of all this "magnificent genius."

(To the slave)

Come on, give him your underwear!

(The slave takes off his underwear and stands naked and shivering as Makemedo gives it to the Poet.)

Here you are, just the thing for man who talks out of his arse. Now be off with you, and don't come back!

POET:

I'm going, and as I depart, I shall create one more great work.

Golden throned Muse,
From this shivery place I go,
Along the many pathways,
Forging through the snow.

Hurrah! Hurrah! Hurrah!

(Exit Poet.)

The nerve! Moaning about the cold after we completely clothed him,
and how, by Zeus, did that pathetic poetic find out about us so fast?
Oh well, he's gone now and on with the sacrifice. Pray, silence!

(To the servants)

Take the holy water and go around the altar again.

*(Makemedo raises the knife to kill the offering. Enter Prophet.)**

PROPHET:

Hold! Stay that blade. Let no harm befall thy goat!

957: Holy water was sprinkled around the altar and on the participants of the sacrifice to consecrate and cleanse.

MAKEMEDO:
Says who?

PROPHET:
Say I, the Pious Prophet.

MAKEMEDO:
Well, "pious" off! There's nothing you can "prophet" from here.

PROPHET:
Sacrilege! You think so little of heaven's decrees?
I bring the voice of Prophet Bacis of Boeotia,
a revelation, a message, a prophecy for Cloudcuckooland.

MAKEMEDO:
It's too late now, you idiot! I've already founded the city.
Why didn't you come earlier?

PROPHET:
I was held back by the power of the godhead.

MAKEMEDO:
Oh, really? Go on then, get on with it, let's hear this oracle of yours.

(The Prophet unrolls a large scroll.)

PROPHET:
"When the wolf packs merge with the flocks of Crows,
where the river of Sicyon and Corinth flows . . ."

963: A renowned seer whose prophecies had been circulating since the early fifth century. The plays of Aristophanes make several references to false prophets and ragtag soothsayers attempting to use Bacis' reputation for their own enrichment (***963 Bacis**).

968: These are both proverbial impossibilities. Wolves would never live with crows in nature. Perhaps this is a reference to Makemedo among the birds. "Between Sicyon and Corinth" meant "nowhere land," as these two cities of the northeastern Peloponnese bordered each other and had no land between them at all (***968 Sicyon and Corinth**).

MAKEMEDO:
Corinth? What's Corinth got to do with me?

PROPHET:
It's a prophetic metaphor of course, it means the air.
The prophecy continues,
"An offering to Pandora you must make
a white fleeced ram, you must take,
and for the bringer of this oracular news,
give a fine cloak and a new pair of shoes."

MAKEMEDO:
It says that I have to give you a cloak and shoes?

PROPHET:
I only interpret the signs. If sir would care to consult the sacred scrolls?

(The Prophet quickly passes the scroll in front of Makemedo, not giving him enough time to read it.)

If I may be allowed to continue,
"And in regard for my prophet's trouble and time,
give him the kidney and a cup full of wine."

MAKEMEDO:
It says you get the kidney, does it? That's the best bit.

PROPHET:
If sir would care to consult the sacred scrolls?

(The prophet swipes the scrolls in front of Makemedo again.)

They continue,

969: Corinth was a longstanding enemy of Athens.

972: Pandora, worshiped as a chthonic goddess, is invoked for comic effect inasmuch as her name means "all-giving."

976: The innards of the sacrificial animal were dedicated to the gods, as was a cup of wine poured as a libation.

978: A parody of a famous oracle foretelling the future success of Athens.

"Heed these words and eagle's wings will bring luck,
dare to ignore them and live life as a duck."

MAKEMEDO:
Is that really what it says?

PROPHET:
If sir would care to consult the sacred scrolls?

(The Prophet starts to swipe the scrolls, but Makemedo stops him.)

MAKEMEDO:
You know, it's funny, but your oracles seem quite different from mine,
and I took these down just as Apollo told them to me:

(Makemedo grabs the scroll.)

"A fraudulent scoundrel you will meet
demanding presents and plenty to eat,
give him no clothing, feed him no meat,
take a stick to his arse, and savagely beat!"

PROPHET:
I can't believe it says that!

MAKEMEDO:
If sir would care to consult the sacred scrolls?

(Makemedo grabs the Prophet and roughly swipes the scroll in front of him.)

It goes on:
"If stories of eagles this faker should tell,
despite Diopeithes and Lampon as well,

979: Instead of "duck" the Greek has "rock thrush," a small insignificant bird that inhabited mountain areas.

987: For Lampon see ***522 Lampon**. Diopeithes was a politician and a religious expert who had proposed a decree against the practices of certain philosophers, such as Anaxagoras, alleged to be working against proper religious law (see *Wasps* ***380 Diopeithes**).

beat him harder and send him to hell!"

PROPHET:
It doesn't really say that, does it?

MAKEMEDO:
I've had enough of you. I'm going to take these damn sacred scrolls and shove them right up your . . .

(The Prophet flees pursued by Makemedo beating him with the scroll.)

PROPHET:
No! Help! Help! Mercy!

(Exit Prophet)

MAKEMEDO:
You didn't predict that, did you? Right then, back to the meat.

(Enter Meton.)

Oh bloody hell! What now?

METON:
I have come here . . .

MAKEMEDO:
"What does this man need of me, why come here with great good speed,"
Which particular tragedy have you swanned in from?

METON:
I have come to survey your skies, measure the air-space,
and calculate subdivided areas for suitable habitation.

993: Meton was a famous Athenian astronomer and mathematician said to have calculated a new lunar calendar. He became involved in scandal involving his attempts to exempt his family from military service (***Stage Direction: Enter Meton**).

994: The Greek has "Why have you traveled this high-booted road?" a reference to the *cothornoi,* the soft high boots worn by tragic actors (***994 Cothornoi**).

MAKEMEDO:
By all the gods! Who is this numbskull?

METON:
I am Meton, Greek astronomer, surely you know of my sundial at Colonus?

MAKEMEDO:
And what's all that stuff you're carrying?

(Meton starts to measure with his instruments.)

METON:
Ah, finely calibrated instruments for the precise measurement of thin air.
For the air in its entirety is not that dissimilar to a baking dish—a crock pot . . .

MAKEMEDO:
More like a crackpot!

METON:
I can simply calculate the trigonometrical divergence of the topographical
plain here, reaching a tangential alignment here. You follow?

MAKEMEDO:
No, I do not!

METON:
It's really quite simple. Now, I envisage, a radial hiatus
for Cloudcuckooland, an orbicular design that becomes a square,

---

1001: The Greek has "baking cover." This was a terra cotta bowl-shaped cover used in the oven to bake bread.

1003: These may have been a large protractor, or a right-angled rule and a huge pair of compasses.

1005: Many fifth-century philosophers such as Anaxagoras, Antiphon, and Hippocrates sought a geometric solution to the problem of constructing a square equal in area to a particular circle.

with circuiting streets surrounding the circumference, and hemispheric centers here, here and here, culminating in ellipsoid curvatures, converging on convex coronas of cyclic, convoluted coils!

MAKEMEDO:
This one's a real Thales!

(Meton continues to measure.)

Hey, Meton, hey!

METON:
What is it now!

MAKEMEDO:
I'm going doing to do you a very big favor because I like you, Meton. If you'll take my advice, you'll be on your way as quick as you can.

METON:
Why, whatever for? Is it dangerous here?

MAKEMEDO:
Well, it's not unlike Sparta, you know. They don't like foreigners very much, and, well,
there's been a serious outbreak of unprovoked beatings all over the place.

METON:
You mean there's been some civil disorder?

1009: Most ancient town planners used a rectangular grid system. The circular design proposed by Meton seems to be purely fanciful and designed to be a ridiculous parody of contemporary civil engineering practices.

1010: A philosopher from Asia Minor who lived in the early sixth century. He was widely regarded as the father of physical science and admired as one of the seven sages.

1016: Sparta would sporadically expel any foreigners living within their territory (***1016 Spartan expulsions**).

MAKEMEDO:
No, by Zeus, not at all.

METON:
Then what is it?

MAKEMEDO:
Well, it's like this; just like you, we've got quite a lot of "rules" ourselves.
One of them says that any fraudster found within the city can be publicly beaten.

(Meton quickly gathers up his instruments.)

METON:
Eh, yes, well I had better be on my way.

MAKEMEDO:
I think your meters just run out, mate! Here's the measure of my city.

(He beats Meton with one of his rulers.)

Calibrate that, you cheating bastard!

(Meton flees persued by Makemedo.)

METON:
Help! Help!

(Exit Meton. Enter the Inspector, dressed in elaborate Persian robes and strutting with great authority. He is carrying a pair of voting urns.)

INSPECTOR:
Where will I find the consuls?

1022: Inspectors were appointed to report on the allied states, regulating tribute payments and implementing legislation (***Stage Direction: Inspectors**). The Athenian *proxenoi* were consuls or envoys who lived in an allied city and represented the interests of Athens. They were an important element in the Athenian domination over their allied states.

MAKEMEDO:
Who's this Sardanapallos?

INSPECTOR:
By the powers vested in me, I hereby announce my election
as external inspector of Cloudcuckooland.

MAKEMEDO:
An inspector! By whose authority?

INSPECTOR:
This illegible Athenian decree makes it so.

MAKEMEDO:
That's not worth the paper it's written on. I tell you what, let's talk turkey:
I'll make a deal with you. I will give you a nice big bribe if you flutter off home.

INSPECTOR:
A marvelous suggestion. In fact, my presence is sorely needed back in Athens,
there are some delicate Persian negotiations I have been assigned to take care of.

MAKEMEDO:
Really? Then I'll pay you off right away so you can get on—a nice back-hander.

(He slaps the Inspector.)

1023: This was the Assyrian king Ashurbanipal (668–c.627), derided by the Greeks for his lavish tastes and extreme Oriental effeminacy.

1025: The Greek has "This wretched paper from Teleas" (for Teleas, see note on line 170).

1028: The Greek has "negotiations with Pharnaces," who was the Persian *satrap* (client king) of Dascyleion in northwestern Asia Minor and an ally of the Spartans.

INSPECTOR:
How dare you! I'm an Inspector, what's the meaning of this?

(He slaps him again, and the Inspector flees)

MAKEMEDO:
It's a slap in the face of democracy!
Now get out of here and take those damned voting urns with you!

(Exit Inspector.)

The nerve of it! Sending city inspectors before there's even a city to inspect!

(Enter the Lawyer carrying scrolls.)

LAWYER:
Article five, section seven, to wit: "Any resident of Cloudcuckooland
found guilty of assault and battery on any full Athenian citizen will . . ."

MAKEMEDO:
Not another blasted bureaucrat with a book!

LAWYER:
Sir, I am an interpreter of decrees, a seller of statutes, a peddler of process,
in short, a lawyer at your service, and I have some nice new laws for you.

MAKEMEDO:
For example?

LAWYER:
According to Athenian directive thirty seven b, subsection four g: All coinage,

---

1035: This is a "Decree-Seller," who peddles copies of state decrees to the litigious Athenian citizens.

weights, and measures of Cloudcuckooland must hereby be brought into accordance
with the coinage, weights, and measures of Olophyxia.

MAKEMEDO:
You're the only "oily fixture" 'round here, mate.

(Makemedo attacks him.)

Sod off back to Athens and find some ambulances to chase!
The last thing I need is a lawyer. All barristers are banned!

(Exit Lawyer. Reenter Inspector.)

INSPECTOR:
I hereby summon Makemedo to appear in court on a charge of assault against . . .

MAKEMEDO:
Ye gods! You're not back again, are you? Get out of it!

(He beats the Inspector away. Exit Inspector. Reenter Lawyer.)

LAWYER:
I'll take the case! According to article five of the Athenian Criminal Code,
any person who seeks to impede, delay or otherwise distract an official of
the Athenian govern . . .

MAKEMEDO:
Not again! If I've told you once . . .

(He beats the Lawyer away. Exit Lawyer. Reenter Inspector.)

1042: A small town in Thrace and an Athenian tribute-paying ally that changed sides to Sparta for a short time in 424–23 B.C.E.

1043: The pun in the Greek is on *Olophuxioi/Ototuxioi,* from *ototoi* meaning "to cry in pain."

INSPECTOR:
I'll see you punished, and what's more I'm suing you for two thousand drachmas!

MAKEMEDO:
Right! That's it! I'm going to smash those damned voting urns of yours.

(He attacks the Inspector as he exits. Reenter Lawyer.)

LAWYER:
I know all about you and your offenses against the state. You were seen
out one night pissing on an Athenian decree tablet! I'll report you!*

MAKEMEDO:
It's time you were permanently disbarred!

(He beats the Lawyer away. Exit Lawyer.)

I've had enough of this. I'm going to take this goat indoors.
I'll just have to finish the sacrifice off inside.

(Exit Makemedo through the doors.)

[Second Parabasis]

CHORUS:
Now all you mortals must sacrifice
To this omnipotent bird-paradise.
To feathered sentinels say your prayer.
We watch your world, we're everywhere.
We'll maximize your bounteous crop,
We'll kill the pests, the blights will stop.
On those seed devourers of voracious jaw
From pod to sod we will declare war.
The ravenous maggots that ruin your fruits,
Destroyers of gardens, flowers, and roots,
All agricultural blights we'll put to flight,
Against horticultural enemies we will fight.
All creeping creatures and crawling things
Will be annihilated beneath our wings.

On this day we publicly denounce our enemies and repeat the state declaration:
"For the killing of Diagoras the Melian heretic,
a reward of one talent. For the death of a tyrant,
even though they are in fact already dead, one talent."
In addition we wish to make our own declaration:
"For the Killing of Philocrates the Bird-Seller, one talent,
if captured alive, four talents." This criminal is known
to string chaffinches up in bundles and sell them, seven
for an obol. He blows up his thrushes for display,
and he tortures blackbirds by shoving their own feathers
up their noses. Not only that, he imprisons poor pigeons,
crams them into nets, and makes them lure other birds into his clutches.
Any of you who might keep birds caged up in your houses,
we hereby order their immediate release. Anyone who fails
to do so will be rounded up by the birds and arrested.
Then we'll see how you like being kept in cages and used as decoys.

Most blessed birds, blissful breed,
What splendid airborne lives we lead.
Come wintertime and we need no cloak,
And we're cool in summer while others roast.
In the rustling leaves we make our home,
In the meadows' blossoming buds we roam
While the cicada sings her heavenly tune,
Beneath sun-filled skies in the heat of noon.
We spend our winters snug in rocky caves,
With mountain nymphs we share our days.

1072: State proclamations and public announcements were made between shows at the festival of Dionysus.

1073: Diagoras was a lyric poet from Melos charged with ridiculing the mysteries. He escaped to Pellene, an anti-Athenian city in the north of the Peloponnese. The Athenians issued a warrant for his death or arrest, which is repeated here.

1074: It seems that there was a tradition of publicly denouncing the Tyrants, even though Hippias, the last of the Athenian Tyrants, had been expelled in 510 B.C.E.

1077: For Philocrates see note on line 14.

When warmth returns with spring's first shoots,
We bask in sunshine and feast on fruits.
Virgin myrtle berries feel our first bite,
In the garden of Graces, to our delight.

We would like to take this opportunity to say a few words to the judges
of this dramatic competition. We want you to know all the wonderful
presents you will receive from us, if you are wise enough to award this play
first prize. Wonderful gifts far greater than anything Paris was offered.
Firstly, you will receive what every judge yearns for the most, namely, owls.
We promise that Laurium owls will come to your home to roost, they'll nest
right in your purses and hatch out lots of brand, spanking new, small change.
We will crown your houses with eagle-roofs, it will be like living in a temple,
and if you are allotted a public office and fancy taking a peck at the petty cash
now and then, we'll give you a sharp talon to help you rake in all that money.
Finally, when you go out for a nice dinner, we'll give you the mouth of a pelican!
However, if you should decide not to cast your vote our way, then beware!
We would advise you to carry an umbrella at all times, like the metal parasols
they put on the statues, for next time you are out and about, strolling along

---

1105: Paris was offered tantalizing gifts by Athena, Hera, and Aphrodite to name her the fairest goddess. He chose Aphrodite, who promised the most beautiful woman. His subsequent abduction of Helen caused the Trojan War.

1107: Laurium, in northeastern Attica, was the location of the Athenian silver mines. For owls on Athenian coins see note on line 302.

1109: The triangular pediments of Greek temples were called *aietoi* (eagles).

in your finest white gown, the birds will shit on you from a very great height!

(Enter Makemedo from the doors.)

MAKEMEDO:
My feathered friends, I am happy to tell you the omens are very good (*burp*).
That's strange, the messenger should be back from the walls by now.
Aha! Here's someone now, wheezing like an Olympic runner!

(Enter a bird-messenger. panting hard.)

MESSENGER:
Whoooo, whooooo, whoooo, whoooo, whe, where is he?
Where's Prime Minister Makemedo?

MAKEMEDO:
Over here!

MESSENGER:
Whoo, whoo wonderful news! The wall, phoooo, the wall is . . . finished!

MAKEMEDO:
Marvelous!

MESSENGER:
And what a whopper of a wall it is! Stupendous, enormous, gigantic!
It is so wide you could yoke two teams of huge, titanic Trojan horses
to a pair of chariots, put Proxenides in one and Theogenes
in the other, and send them thundering along the top of the wall

---

1123: The Greek has "Archon," the chief magistrate of a Greek state. This is the first official title given to Makemedo, although the birds themselves do hand him decision making authority at lines 636–37.

1127: Both men were known to be excessive boasters (for Theogenes see line 821).

from different directions, *and* they would still easily miss each other.

MAKEMEDO:
By Heracles! That wide?

MESSENGER:
Not just wide, but tall. I measured it myself at least a hundred fathoms high!

MAKEMEDO:
By Poseidon! I just can't fathom it! Who ever could have built a wall so high?

MESSENGER:
Birds! The birds built it! There were no Egyptian
pyramid builders, no stonemasons or carpenters.
The birds did it themselves, their own way!
I couldn't believe my eyes when the work started;
thousands of African cranes swooped in with boulders
in their bellies and gave them to the curlews
for carving. The house martins made the bricks,
while river birds brought billions of beaks full of water.

MAKEMEDO:
Amazing! But who brought in all that clay?

MESSENGER:
Hod-carrying herons, hauled up by cranes.

MAKEMEDO:
How on earth did they shovel the clay into the hods?

1129: A similar description of the walls of Babylon is found in Herodotus (1.179.3). The walls of Cloudcuckooland could also allude to the long walls of Athens, between the city and harbor built by Pericles. Thucydides describes the width of these walls as having, "room for two wagons to pass each other" (1.93.5).

1130: Approximately six hundred feet.

1138: The Greeks believed that cranes swallowed stones to provide them with ballast during flight.

MESSENGER:
That was the most astounding thing, the geese shoveled
it into the heron's hods using their wonderful webbed feet.

MAKEMEDO:
Now that's what I call a "feet" of engineering!

MESSENGER:
You should have seen the ducks in their little aprons
laying the bricks, and the swallows flitting about
carrying the plaster rendering in their beaks
and using their tails as trowels.

MAKEMEDO:
It's the birdustrial revolution! Manpower is obsolete!
But who did the wood finishing on the walls?

MESSENGER:
Woodpeckers drove in the nails,
and the woodcocks chiseled the timber,
it sounded like a great shipyard!
Now the walls have great gates and huge bolts,
the wall is manned, the sentries have been posted,
the watchbirds have been given their bells,
and the torch fires on the towers are all burning.
Do you think I can go and have a bath now and get some sleep?
We've done our part, it's up to you now.

(Exit Messenger offstage. Makemedo is struck dumb.)

CHORUS:
What's wrong? Are you surprised that the wall's finished already?

MAKEMEDO:
Mmm, it is absolutely amazing!
It sounds like a "tall" story to me.

(Makemedo sees a bird-guard approaching.)

Hey! look over there, here comes a guard with a message,

Looks like he's performing the war dance!

GUARD:
Oo, oo, oo, oo, oo, oo!

MAKEMEDO:
Whatever is the matter?

GUARD:
It's terrible! There's been a violation of our airspace!
One of the gods has just breezed in through the gates
right under the beaks of the ravens on guard duty.

MAKEMEDO:
"Such fearful, desperate acts we must endure."
Which god was it?

GUARD:
We couldn't tell, it was moving too fast. I'll tell you this much,
he, she, or it was wearing a lovely set of wings.

MAKEMEDO:
Alert the skirmish squadrons!

GUARD:
We've already sent up everything we have,
a whole flight of kittyhawks, an air corps
of cormorants, and our entire tactical
talon group comprising every bird of prey
we could muster, kestrels, vultures, eagles,
buzzards, you name it! The whole sky's a whirl
of rushing wings whistling through the air.
That god must be closing in somewhere nearby!

(Exit Guard offstage.)

1169: The *purrikê* was a dance performed in full *hoplite* (infantry) armor (***1169 War dance**).

MAKEMEDO:
Then this god is going to suffer the slings and arrows
of my outrageous fortune! Call out the guard!
Bring me a sling! A catapult! Anything!

CHORUS:
Prepare for battle, this is War!
Defend the skies that Erebus bore.
Bird 'gainst god for this cloudy home.
Let none pass through our no-fly zone.

Keep watch! Look everywhere!
I can hear the sound of whirling wings.
That air-borne god is right around here somewhere!

*(Enter Iris the rainbow goddess, "flying" on the stage crane. Makemedo has been chasing Iris around the stage and is now out of breath.)**

MAKEMEDO:
Hey You! Whe . . . whe . . . where do you think you're flying? Heave to! Hold fast!

(Makemedo tries in vain to bring Iris to a halt as she swings across the stage.)

Stop fluttering about all over the place! Stop! Halt! Keep still, will you!

(Iris finally come to rest, suspended over the stage.)

Right! State your name, purpose of visit, and country of residence.

IRIS:
I have come from the gods on Olympus.

MAKEMEDO:
State your name! Are you a boat or a bitch?

1190: For Erebus see note on line 692.

Iris:
I am Iris the fast.

Makemedo:
I'll bet you are, my dear. The *Paralus* or the *Salaminia?*

Iris:
What is the meaning of this?

Makemedo:
It's a forced entry! Buzzards stand by to board!

Iris:
I'd like to see you try! How dare you!

Makemedo:
I'll impound you!

Iris:
This is outrageous. I protest!

Makemedo:
So my little bitch, how did you get through? By what passage?

Iris:
Why would I need any sort of "passage"?

Makemedo:
I see, you're going to be like that, are you?
Did you report to the jackdaw at immigration control?
Did you get your passport stamped by the cock?

Iris:
I beg your pardon!

1203: Iris was the rainbow goddess and a messenger of the gods Her Homeric epithet was "swift Iris" (*Iliad* 8.399).

1204: The two fastest Athenian triremes (see note on line 148).

1210: The Greek has *pulos* ("gate"), a euphemism for the vagina. This was doubly offensive because Iris was a virgin goddess.

MAKEMEDO:
So you haven't been properly handled yet?

IRIS:
Are you quite mad?

MAKEMEDO:
Did the stork enter you correctly?

IRIS:
You can be quite certain that nobody has entered me!

MAKEMEDO:
Don't try any of that funny stuff with me, "Wonder Wings,"
you're flying over our airspace without authorization.

IRIS:
Authorization! The gods don't need authorization.

MAKEMEDO:
They do here, by Zeus! You have entered the country illegally,
you are committing a crime just by being here.
You may well say that we're chasing rainbows,
but the law is the law and the sentence is death!

IRIS:
But I'm an immortal, I can't die.

MAKEMEDO:
Don't you go splitting hairs, with me, my dear.
The sentence stands, you'll be put to death.
We can't let you gods just do as you please,
you have to obey the laws too, just like
everybody else. We're in charge now!
Tell me, "Where are you sailing on the breeze?"

IRIS:
I am bearing an important message for mankind from father Zeus:
"Slay your livestock for Zeus the savior,
fill the skies with smoky savor.
Roast the meat, baste and slice,

it's time you mortals sacrificed."

MAKEMEDO:
And to which gods are the humans supposed to make these sacrifices?

IRIS:
To the gods on Olympus, of course!

MAKEMEDO:
I don't think so.

IRIS:
Well, what other gods are there, then?

MAKEMEDO:
Haven't you heard? The birds are the gods of mankind now,
It's the birds that get the sacrifices, not the gods, by god!

IRIS:
You fool, you fool! Test not the mettle
of the dread gods for your people will be crushed
by the hand of Zeus, overthrown by Justice and smitten
in the smoky fire, consigning you to the flames
and incinerating your house with his thunderous bolts!

MAKEMEDO:
Madam, I would greatly appreciate it if you
would be kind enough to stop spitting
and spluttering all over me and shut your blasted mouth!
I'm not some quivering Lydian or Phrygian,
and all this talk of smiting does nothing for me.
If Zeus gives me the slightest little bit of trouble
I'll incinerate his place like "the halls of Amphion"

1246: Both areas of the Near East. The Greeks regarded men from the East as cowardly, superstitious, and effeminate.

1249: A quote from Aeschylus' *Niobe* (*Fr.* 100). Amphion was the husband of Niobe. His house was ravaged by the deaths of his children at the hands of Apollo and Artemis.

with my fire-brandishing eagles. Then I'll send porphorion
birds on up to heaven, and you know the terrible
trouble he had with Porphyrion the Titan, well I've got
six hundred of them here, complete with leopard skins!
You had better do as I say, my girl, or there'll be trouble!
I may be getting on a bit, but I can still sail at ramming speed.
I'll find your sea-legs, splice your mainbrace, and shiver your timbers!

IRIS:
I have never heard such filthy, disgusting language in all . . .

MAKEMEDO:
Flutter off, "rent-a-rainbow!" Shoo! Shoo!

IRIS:
Just you wait until my father hears about this! You'll be sorry!

MAKEMEDO:
He won't say "boo" to a goose!
Go and fire up some younger fellow!

(Exit Iris.)

CHORUS:
To Gods and Zeus we've closed the gate,
No more will they fly through this state.
The smoky offerings men send on high
Will never get through bird-held sky.

MAKEMEDO:
I fear the worst! Where's the messenger
who went down to the humans, is he never to return?

(Enter Messenger 2.)

1253: Porphyrion was the legendary king of the giants who fought against Zeus and the gods, and also the name of a species of the Purple Gallinule (see note on line 553).

Messenger 2:
O Lord Makemedo! O Excellency! O Great Sage!
O wise one, O celebrated one, O suave one,
O blessed one, O smooth one, O somebody stop me!*

Makemedo:
What do you want?

(The Messenger offers Makemedo a golden crown.)

Messenger 2:
Here, take this, it is yours, the golden crown of public opinion
from your adoring populace in honor of your wisdom.

(The Messenger crowns Makemedo.)

Makemedo:
I accept this crown. But why have the humans given me this?

Messenger:
Oh, most wondrous founder of this skyborne city,
your modesty astounds me, that you could even ask
such a question! The humans have gone cuckoo
for Cloudcuckooland! Sir, you are the toast of all mankind.
I mean, what were they before, before you showed them the way,
they were Laconizers! Sparta freaks! Hungry, hairy, hoary
and humming, just like Socrates, going around with Spartan sticks.
But now it's different, they've gone absolutely bird-crazy,
birds are all the rage, and they are emulating every aspect of bird life.
You should see them, dawn breaks and they break into birdsong:
"up with the lark!"—"the early bird catches the worm!"
Then they all fly their coops and flock together amid the papyrus

---

1283: Socrates was often depicted as having a "Spartan" lifestyle. He was known for depriving himself of food and for being unhygienic (see *Clouds* lines 175 and 441–42). Both he and some of his pupils were also said to have admired the Spartan system (Plato *Critias* 52e). The Spartan stick was a type of gnarled walking stick or club preferred by the Spartans. In *Lysistrata* it has distinct phallic associations (991).

sharpening their bills, pecking at laws and perching by the statutes.
Those who have gone really feather-brained are even changing their names,
that one-legged shopkeeper calls himself "Flamingo" now.
Menippus, the horse-breeder, is "Swift." Opuntius the informer,
"Stool Pigeon." Philocles the poet, you know, Aeschylus' nephew,
is now called "Lesser Spotted Warbler." Theogenes is "Little Bustard,"
Lycurgus "Ibis," and Chaerephon the philosopher is "Batty."
Syracosius the politician is now known as "Crow" as he sounds like one,
and Medias, whom you could knock down with a feather, is "Sitting Duck."
And you should hear the music that they are all listening to these days,
every new song teems with birds: nightingales, bluebirds, doves, eagles.
No one can turn out a tune these days without a feather floating about
or something taking wing or wanting to be as free as a bird.
Prepare yourselves for the mass migrations,
there are going to be thousands of humans making

1289: Athenian legislation was carved onto large decree stones, then copied onto papyri and sold (see ***1054 Decree tablets**).

1292: Menippus may have been an Athenian politician, but the scholia mention a connection with horse-breeding. For Opuntius see note on line 154.

1293: For Philocles, see note on line 282.

1294: For Theogenes, see note on 822.

1295: The grandfather of the fourth-century statesman of the same name. This old Athenian family may have had Egyptian roots; hence "Ibis," a bird closely associated with Egypt. Chaerephon was a colleague of Socrates and often lampooned for his unhealthy demeanor and pallid skin. He appears as a witness in *Wasps* (line 1409) and is mentioned throughout *Clouds*.

1296: A politician who had a piercingly loud speaking voice and in the Greek is named "Jay."

1297: A minor politician known for his love of gambling. For "Sitting Duck" the Greek has "Quail," after a cruel game played in Athens where two quails were placed on a board and struck on the head until one of them flinched and lost.

their way up here to earn their wings, and they'll be wanting
beaks and talons too. You had better find some wings
from somewhere to give to all your new immigrants.

(Exit Messenger.)

MAKEMEDO:
Wings! Wings! We need wings and lots of them!

(To Manes the servant)

Come on! This is no time for standing around!
Get inside and fill up all the baskets you can find with wings!
Tell Manes to bring them out here and give them to me.
I must prepare to receive our new colonists.

(Manes walks inside.)

CHORUS:
Now the humans are on their way,
Migrant streams, strong and steady.
To settle among us come what may . . .

(As Manes brings out a very small basket)

MAKEMEDO:
By god, I hope we're ready!

CHORUS:
This blessed place, this city dear . . .

(As Manes slowly goes back inside)

MAKEMEDO:
I wish he'd hurry with that gear!

CHORUS:
This wondrous city of gentility,
Full of wisdom, love, and grace,
Happiness, peace, tranquillity . . .

(To Manes)

MAKEMEDO:
Move! Or I'll punch you in the face!

CHORUS:
Now is the time to bring out the wings,
this opportunity must not pass.
It is up to you to do these things . . .

MAKEMEDO:
I'll kick him up the arse!

(Manes continues to bring out the baskets very slowly.)

CHORUS:
Your slave moves slowly like a mule . . .

(Shouting to Manes)

MAKEMEDO:
Get a move on, you lazy fool!

CHORUS:
You must choose the wings we see.
Inspect each human and take your pick,
For music, sea-travel, or prophecy . . .

MAKEMEDO:
I'll beat this shirker with my stick!

(Enter Youth, singing.)

YOUTH:
If only like an Eagle I could soar
High above the swelling untamed sea
Where breakers crash and waves roar,
If only an Eagle in flight I could be."

MAKEMEDO:
Looks like that messenger was right, here's someone singing about eagles.

1339: This may well be a quotation from Sophocles' tragedy, *Oenomaus* (fr. 476).

YOUTH:
I want to fly like a bird in the sky!

MAKEMEDO:
He'll be wanting a set of wings no doubt.

YOUTH:
Wings, I want wings! I'm for the birds!
I want to emigrate, I like the sound of your laws.

MAKEMEDO:
Which particular laws do you mean, the birds have quite a few?

YOUTH:
You follow the law of nature up here, right?
I mean, it's customary to peck your father and wing his neck.

MAKEMEDO:
Well yes, we do recognize that it's perfectly natural
for a youngling to take a potshot at the old cock.

YOUTH:
Right! That's exactly why I want to live here. I want to strangle
my father and inherit everything he owns!

MAKEMEDO:
I see. But we do have a law that is set down on the sacred
Stork Tablets that states:
"When the young of birds fly the nest
and wing it through the air,
they must swear to do their best
to give their parents care."

YOUTH:
No way! I'm not caring for my old dad when he's past it!
I've wasted my time coming all the way up here!

1353: A comic adaptation of the old codes of the early Athenian statesmen, Solon and Dracon, which were written on wooden blocks and set up on the Stoa Basileius in the Agora in Athens.

MAKEMEDO:

No, not at all. Listen I can tell you've got a heart of gold really.
You've just been led astray, negative influences, a bad childhood.
You're just like a poor orphan chick. I've got just the thing for you,
forget about your dad. If you really want to beat someone up, here, take this nice wing . . .

(Makemedo hands him a shield.)

. . . and put this talon in your other hand.

(He hands him a sword.)

Imagine that this is a nice cockscomb . . .

(He puts a crested helmet on the Youth's head.)

There you are,
Right! You little bastard, you're in the Army now!*
Stand up straight! Stomach in! Chest out!
There's plenty of fighting in Thrace I hear. I'm shipping you there.
Attention! About turn! Quick march! Left right, left right, left right!

(The Youth double-marches offstage.)

YOUTH:

You're right, by Dionysus. It's a life in the infantry for me!

MAKEMEDO:

Off you go!

(Exit Youth. Enter Cinesias the poet, singing and dancing.)

CINESIAS:

Away, away, soaring on the wing to Olympian heights
My melody flitter flutters on its way, here, there, everywhere.

1368: In the spring of 414, a force was being assembled for operations in Thrace, the region to the north of Greece (***1396 Thrace**).

1373: A dithyrambic poet and a contemporary of Aristophanes. Dithyrambs were choral songs accompanied by the aulos, and their performance was an integral part of the festival of Dionysus (***Stage Direction: Enter Cinesias**).

MAKEMEDO:
We're going to need a shipload of wings to elevate this bloke's poetry!

CINESIAS:
My spirit steeled, my body in motion, seeking elusive flight . . .

MAKEMEDO:
Why it's Cinesias, the "talking twig"! Why have you come circling your way up here with your peglegged poetry!

CINESIAS:
Oh, to be a bird in the sky and sing like the nightingale fair.

MAKEMEDO:
Will you stop singing that awful row! Just *tell* me what you want.

CINESIAS:
Oh, for a pair of wings! I want to fly, high in the sky,
then I can swoop up, up, up, and touch the lofty clouds,
and there I'll find the soaring, ethereal, snow-pure verses!

MAKEMEDO:
You mean to tell me that you get verses from the clouds?

CINESIAS:
Of course! The entire art-form is inspired by them.
The most dazzling dithyrambs are vaporous, vacuous,
elusive, misty, wind-wafted, hazy fluff!
You'll know when you hear some. Ahem!

(Cinesias prepares to sing.)

MAKEMEDO:
No, really, I won't!

CINESIAS:
But, by Heracles, you will! Just let me whip through
a cycle of some of my airs for you.

(He starts to sing and dance.)

Wafting gently upon the sweeping breeze
Bird-like clouds sailing through the sky . . .

(Makemedo tries in vain to stop him.)

MAKEMEDO:
Easy oar there, matey!

CINESIAS:
Floating up, blown with breathless ease,
Sped by the wind, the air moves briskly by.

(Makemedo takes a pair of wings from the basket.)

MAKEMEDO:
By Zeus, I've had enough of this!
I'm going to knock the wind out of your sails!

(Makemedo chases him stage left.)

CINESIAS:
Hither I go sped on toward the south,

(Cinesias evades him and runs stage righ.t)

Now thither to the icy north thus I clip,

(Makemedo chases him back to center stage.)

Cleaving sky furrows to the harbor mouth . . .

MAKEMEDO:
I'll "waft these wings" and your arse I'll whip!

(Makemedo beats him with the wings.)

CINESIAS:
I can't believe that you would dare to treat me like this.
I am a highly respected choral director of dithyrambic odes!

MAKEMEDO:
Oh, in that case, you can stay up here with us and train

a gaggle of geese or chorus of crows for Leotrophides.

CINESIAS:
Are you trying to make a fool out of me? I tell you this, sir,
I shall not tire in my quest for wings!
I *will* have wings and soar to the heights of poetry!

(Exit Cinesias. Enter the Informer wearing a tattered cloak.)

INFORMER:
"Whoever can these speckled birds be
That have no debts nor property?
Oh Swallow, Swallow, of you I sing."

MAKEMEDO:
Another bloody immigrant! There goes the neighborhood.

INFORMER:
"Oh Swallow, Swallow, of you I sing . . ."

MAKEMEDO:
Judging by the state of his cloak, he should remember:
"One swallow does not make a spring."

INFORMER:
Is this the place where I can get my wings?

MAKEMEDO:
It is. What do you want?

INFORMER:
"Wings! I must have wings!"

1406: The Greek has "Train a chorus here, for Leotrophides." Leotrophides was a remarkably thin Athenian politician and so the perfect producer for the skinny Cinesias.

1410: The Informer is a sycophant, an individual who sought to profit by collecting information and bringing charges against other parties.

1412: Adapted from a poem by Alcaeus (*Fr.* 435).

1420: Taken from Aeschylus' *Myrmidons* (*Fr.* 140): *"Weapons! I must have weapons!"*

MAKEMEDO:
So you can fly off to your tailor and get a new cloak, I suppose.

INFORMER:
No. I'm a professional bailiff to the island states, a sycophant, specializing
in false testimony, perjury, trumped up charges, and general shit-stirring.

MAKEMEDO:
It's nice to see a man happy in his work.

INFORMER:
I have a particular penchant for provoking lawsuits. That's where the wings
would help, I could easily swoop down on all the allies and deliver my writs.

MAKEMEDO:
Greek island hopping! So a set of wings would increase your efficiency!

INFORMER:
That's impossible! But they would help me give pirates the slip,
and I could fly about unnoticed with the storks delivering newborns,
newborn writs and summonses of course!*

MAKEMEDO:
So that's the sum total of your life, is it? A nice young lad like you,
going around accusing poor foreigners.

INFORMER:
It's a living. I'm not good at manual labor.

MAKEMEDO:
By Zeus! I can't believe that a big strapping young lad like you

---

1421: The Greek has "fly off to Pellana," a city in northern Peloponnese where a heavy woolen cloak was awarded as first prize in the chariot race at the local Hermaea festival.

can't find good honest gainful employment and instead
has to sully himself peddling perjury and serving summonses.

INFORMER:
Look, I came for a set of wings, not free advice.

MAKEMEDO:
But I am giving you wings, with my words!

INFORMER:
What? How can you get wings from words?

MAKEMEDO:
Everyone knows that "words are wings."

INFORMER:
Everyone?

MAKEMEDO:
Listen, I'll give you an example of what I mean.
You've heard the old men sitting around playing checkers
and hanging around the barbers, "That fly-by-night Dieitrephes
and his feather-brained advice, my lad's flown off to ride horses."
Or, "My boy can't keep his feet on the ground either, his head's in the clouds,
and he's decided to become a tragic poet. What a flight of fancy!"

INFORMER:
So you're saying words make wings?

MAKEMEDO:
Right! Words heighten the mind; they let the spirit soar.
Words are morally uplifting, raising standards leading
to the pursuit of higher things. Words of wisdom can wing
you on to a more elevated occupation.

INFORMER:
Sorry, it won't work with me.

1442: For Dieitrephes see note on line 800.

MAKEMEDO:
Why ever not?

INFORMER:
I couldn't disgrace the family name. I come from a long line
of despised sycophants and reviled informers.
Come on, let me have a nice fast pair of wings, the hawk variety,
or the falcon, I'm not fussed. Then I can swoop down to the islands,
deliver a few summonses, whiz back to Athens to get my convictions,
then fly off to the islands again . . .

MAKEMEDO:
Oh I see, you plan to have these foreigners tried and convicted before
they even have a chance to get to the court and make an appearance.

INFORMER:
You've got it.

MAKEMEDO:
And while they're on their way to Athens, you'll be flying back
to the islands to confiscate all their property.

INFORMER:
That's right! I'll be hurtling back and forth like a spinning top.*

MAKEMEDO:
Like a spinning top, really? It's not wings you need, but a good horse . . .

(Makemedo produces a large whip.)

A good horsewhipping!*

INFORMER:
Zeus! He's going to flog me!

1456: Many allied states had their cases heard in Athenian courts, and defendants were forced to travel to Athens.

(Makemedo lashes him with a whip as he darts back and forth.)

MAKEMEDO:
Look, you're "flying" now! Your wings need clipping,
you sycophantic sod!

(Makemedo chases the Informer as he weaves across the stage trying to avoid the lash.)

INFORMER:
Help! Help!

MAKEMEDO:
I'll make you go back and forth like a top!
You'll be whizzing all right, free-falling back to earth,
head first! Happy landings!

(Makemedo whips him off the stage. Exit Informer.)

(To the servants) Come on! let's take these wings back inside.

(Exit Makemedo and servants through the door.)

CHORUS:
We've winged it over some wondrous sights,
And swooped far and wide across the sea,
Yet the strangest encounter of all those flights,
Was to spy the rare Cleonymus tree.

Its heart of oak sits on a foreign plot,
Though its boughs spread far and wide,
It produces such a worthless crop,
Yet has reached enormous size.

It blossoms each and every spring,
Courthouse writs are the fruit it yields.
Come autumn it does a very strange thing,
Turns yellow and scatters shedding shields.

1474: For Cleonymus, see note on line 289.

There is a land of no sunshine,
Where darkness smothers every light,
A dismal hinterland of sunless grime,
Where Heroes dwell in the realm of night.

Yet there was once a golden time,
Before the murky night came down,
When Man and Hero together dined,
And it was safe to walk out of town.

Now if Orestes a man should meet,
While partaking of the nighttime air,
He'll be assaulted right on the street,
Knocked out cold and stripped quite bare!

(Enter Prometheus from offstage in disguise.)

PROMETHEUS:
Gently does it. I hope Zeus doesn't see me.
Psst. Where can I find Makemedo?

(Enter Makemedo from the doors, wearing a nightshirt and carrying a chamber pot.)

MAKEMEDO:
What on earth is this? A walking blanket?

PROMETHEUS:
Shhhh! Am I being followed, can you see any gods around?

MAKEMEDO:
No, by Zeus, who in god's name are you anyway?

PROMETHEUS:
Not so loud! What time is it?

1491: For Orestes the clothes thief, see note on line 713.

1494: A Titan who disobeyed Zeus and gave mankind the secret of fire (***Stage Direction: Enter Prometheus**).

MAKEMEDO:
The time? It's the afternoon. Who are you?

PROMETHEUS:
Is it getting dark yet? How close are we to nightfall?

MAKEMEDO:
You're starting to really piss me off now, mate!

PROMETHEUS:
What's Zeus doing with the weather? Is it clear and sunny,
or cloudy with low visibility? What do you see?

MAKEMEDO:
I can tell you that you'll be seeing stars in a minute!

(Makemedo raises his fist to hit him).

PROMETHEUS:
Oh good, it must be dark already. I'll remove my disguise.

MAKEMEDO:
Why, it's "Our Dear Prometheus"!*

PROMETHEUS:
Shhh! Keep quiet!

MAKEMEDO:
Why?

PROMETHEUS:
Shhh, don't say my name out loud!
If Zeus sees me here, I'm in big trouble.
I've come to let you know how things are up above.

(Prometheus puts up an umbrella.)

Quick, hold this parasol over me.

1509: The parasol may have been a parody of a similar item used in ritual processions (***1508 Parasol**).

(He hands it to Makemedo.)

Now the gods won't see me talking to you.

MAKEMEDO:
That's a good idea, how very Promethean,
quick, nip under the shade. What's the word?

(Prometheus and Makemedo huddle under the umbrella.)

PROMETHEUS:
Listen then.

MAKEMEDO:
I'm listening, go on.

PROMETHEUS:
Zeus has had it.

MAKEMEDO:
What! Since when?

PROMETHEUS:
Since you founded Cloudcuckooland and colonized the sky.
We haven't had so much as a whiff of sacrificial smoke since then;
the offerings from earth are just not getting through.
No succulent thigh bones or tasty titbits, not a sausage!
We're famished! It's worse than the Thesmophoria fasting festival!
It's getting dangerous, those uncouth barbarian gods from the mountains
are howling with hunger and threatening to rise up against Zeus.
He has to get the air embargo lifted and get the sacrifice shipments
flowing on up to heaven again.

MAKEMEDO:
You mean to tell me that there are barbarian gods in heaven, too?

1520: The Thesmophoria was a three-day festival celebrated by married women in honor of Demeter and Kore. On the second day the women fasted.

PROMETHEUS:
Why yes, even barbarians need something to pray to.
How else would Execestides have a family deity?

MAKEMEDO:
And what do you call these barbarian gods?

PROMETHEUS:
They are known as Jerkoffalots.*

MAKEMEDO:
Ooh! Sounds nasty, it must be very *hard* being a barbarian god.*

PROMETHEUS:
I imagine so. Listen to this, Zeus and the Jerkoffalots
have got together to try to sort it all out.
They are sending a delegation down to you to make a peace treaty.
Now, here's what you must do: flatly reject all offers*
that they might make until Zeus gives his word that he will return
the scepter of power to the birds and allow you to marry the Divine Princess.

MAKEMEDO:
Who's the Divine Princess?

PROMETHEUS:
Ah, a beautiful girl, the keeper of Zeus' thunderbolts,
and the key to it all, sound judgment, the rule of law,
common sense, shipyards, political backstabbing,
the government coffers, and, of course, jury pay!

MAKEMEDO:
She holds the key to all of that?

1527: For Execestides, see note on line 11. Athenian families had their own patron ancestral gods, which further proved their qualification for citizenship and office.

1536: An invention of Aristophanes, sharing many of the same attributes as Athena. It is through marriage to this goddess that Makemedo will hold divine power (***1536 Divine Princess**).

PROMETHEUS:

Yes indeed she does, and if you marry her, it will all be yours.
Well, that's my advice, you understand why I had to come and tell you.
After all, I am Prometheus, and I have always liked you humans.

MAKEMEDO:

Yes, you gave us fire, and really stoked up the coals!

PROMETHEUS:

Anyway, I hate all the gods, as you know.

MAKEMEDO:

I gather the feeling is mutual.

PROMETHEUS:

Yes, I'm a proper Timon. I must go, it's getting late.
Hand me my parasol, then if Zeus sees me, he'll think
I'm attending a basket bearer in some festival or other.

MAKEMEDO:

Good idea, and while you're at it, you can be a stool bearer too!
Here, take this, will you.

(Makemedo gives Prometheus his chamber pot. Exit Prometheus offstage. Exit Makemedo through the doors.)

CHORUS:

Where the Shadefoot tribe are seen,
And men take handstand strolls,
There is a lake for all unclean,
Where Socrates saves men's souls.

1549: Timon was a mythological misanthrope who lived as a hermit.

1552: Religious processions included stool bearers and attendants holding parasols (***1552 Stool bearers**). Aristophanes mocks this ceremony by making Prometheus carry out Makemedo's lavatory.

1554: A mythological people who were said to have such large feet they would walk on their hands to protect themselves from the hot sun.

And to this place Peisander came,
His human spirit he tried to find.
He'd spent his soul pursuing fame,
Misplaced his heart and lost his mind.

Like Odysseus he made his sacrifice,
But when the blood was spilled, he fled.
*He hoped a camel would suffice,**
But batty Chaerephon was raised instead!

*(Enter Poseidon, Heracles, and Jerkoffalot.)**

POSEIDON:
So this is the city of Cloudcuckooland. Onward, my fellow delegates.

(To Jerkoffalot)

Holy mackerel! What are you doing? You're all at sea! Put your clothes on properly, at least try and look like a god! You wear a gown like this, draped from left to right.

(Jerkoffalot attempts to rearrange his clothing.)

What are you doing, you idiot! Oh the things we gods must do in the name of democracy; it's totally demeaning. However did you get elected! You really are a fish out of water!

(Poseidon tries to adjust Jerkoffalot's gown.)

Will you keep still!

(Jerkoffalot will not keep still.)

1556: The activities of the philosopher Socrates were frequently lampooned by Aristophanes (see *Clouds*). His concern with the psyche of man is parodied as raising dead souls from the underworld in some kind of dark rite.

1557: A leading Athenian politician who served on the commission responsible for investigating the mutilation of the Herms and prosecuting the perpetrators (***1557 Peisander**).

1561: This choral song was inspired by the account of Odysseus' descent into the underworld in Book 11 of the *Odyssey*.

1564: For Chaerephon, see note on line 1296. Aristophanes often derides the philosopher as looking "half dead."

You are truly the most barbaric
barbarian God I have ever encountered!

(Turning to Heracles)

So, Heracles, What's the plan of action here?

HERACLES:
Listen, Poseidon, my advice is find the little mortal
who started this blockade and then throttle the bastard!

POSEIDON:
Heaven help me! How many times have I got to spell it out?
We have been selected as envoys to treat for peace.

HERACLES:
I'll give him peace, a piece of my club up his . . .

POSEIDON:
Shhh! Here he comes.

(Enter Makemedo from the doors with cooking utensils and some dead birds. His servants bring out some jars and a brazier, which they light.)

MAKEMEDO:
Right then, where's the cheese grater? I need some garlic
and a nice bit of cheese. Time to turn up the heat. Lovely!

POSEIDON:
Greetings, mortal! You are in the presence of three gods.

(Makemedo ignores Poseidon and continues to prepare his birds.)

MAKEMEDO:
Hang on, mate, I'm slicing garlic at the moment.

1580: Makemedo is now cooking the birds in the same way he had so strongly condemned at lines 535–38.

HERACLES:
What kind of meat are you cooking?

MAKEMEDO:
Birds! Birds found guilty of insurrection against the bird democracy!

HERACLES:
Oh, so you put the garlic on before you baste?

MAKEMEDO:
Oh, hello, Heracles. What can I do for you?

POSEIDON:
As the appointed delegates of the gods, we three have been entrusted
with the appropriate power to treat for peace in the matter and . . .

(Makemedo ignores Poseidon and continues to cook.)

MAKEMEDO:
Damn it! There's no olive oil left in the bottle.*

HERACLES:
What a shame, you can't baste birds without a nice drop of extra virgin.

POSEIDON:
We believe that this current crisis serves neither party any useful purpose.
Furthermore, it is the opinion of Olympus that there is much you may gain
from renewed friendly and harmonious relations between us. In particular,
a full and plentiful supply of fresh cool water appropriate to all your birdbath
needs, and the pleasant and fruitful halcyon days of summer to run concurrently.
Zeus has given us full authority to act on his behalf in these matters.

MAKEMEDO:
First of all, I would like to say for the record that it wasn't us who started
this conflict. But we won't dwell on that just now as we want peace, too.

We have just one condition: that our ancient bird rights be restored.
Therefore, Zeus must return the scepter of authority to us, the birds.
If this one small concession is agreeable to you three gentlemen,
then I would be delighted if you would like to join me for a nibble.*

HERACLES:
That gets my vote. Let's eat!

POSEIDON:
You fool! You are nothing but an idiot and a glutton.
Would you give away your father's sovereignty so easily?

MAKEMEDO:
Poseidon, you are mistaken. Can't you see that the gods will actually grow
more powerful by redistributing power to the birds? Think about it.
Whenever it's a bit overcast, the mortals run around under the cloud cover
getting away with all kinds of sacrilege and taking your names in vain.
Now, if we were allies, we could easily solve this problem for you.
Say a mortal swore an oath to "the Raven and to Zeus," and then broke
his sacred vow, a raven would swoop down and scratch his eyes out!

POSEIDON:
By Poseidon! That really would be giving someone the evil eye, wouldn't it?

HERACLES:
You're right there, uncle.

(To Jerkoffalot)

What do you think?

JERKOFFALOT:
Nibblenobble!

1615: Probably this phrase was deliberately delivered as unintelligible nonsense.

HERACLES:
You see, he agrees, too!

MAKEMEDO:
And what's more, just suppose that some mortal
promises to sacrifice a goat to the gods,
then says, "heaven can wait."
We can deal with that little problem, too.

POSEIDON:
And just how would you do that?

MAKEMEDO:
We will wait until our man is preoccupied counting his money
or lying about in a nice relaxing bath. Then, when he least expects it,
we'll send down a bloody great condor to swipe *two* of his goats
and have them flown right up to heaven, double damages!

HERACLES:
He's right, give the birds the scepter.

POSEIDON:
And which way does the Jerkoffalot vote?

HERACLES:
Oi, Jerkoffalot! Cast your vote or get a bashing!

JERKOFFALOT:
Shaggyshaft bang bang!

HERACLES:
You hear? He agrees with me!

1625: Athenian law demanded twice the amount stolen as damages for crimes of theft.

1628: The Jerkoffalot seems to use some broken Greek and say something about a "hairy stick." This may again be sexual comedy and be combined with an obscene gesture with the phallus worn by the actor playing this part.

POSEIDON:
Then I am outvoted. I suppose I must concede.

HERACLES:
Then that's that. *(To Makemedo)* The scepter is yours.

MAKEMEDO:
There is just one more small thing. You can keep Hera,
in fact Zeus is quite welcome to her, but I would just ask
that the Divine Princess become my wedded wife.

POSEIDON:
Preposterous! It's quite obvious that you have no intention
of reaching a settlement. Come on you two, we're leaving!

MAKEMEDO:
OK, if that's the way you want it, makes no difference to me.

(Calling out) Chef! Make sure the sauce is nice and sweet!

HERACLES:
Just hold on a minute there, Poseidon, by god! Do we really
want to fight a war over a single woman? That's ridiculous!

POSEIDON:
Well, what alternative course of action do you propose?

HERACLES:
We should accept the terms.

POSEIDON:
My dear nephew, you really do have the wits of a jellyfish.
It's a red herring, and this fellow's as slippery as an eel.
Don't you realize that if Zeus relinquishes his power
and gives it to these birds, you'll inherit nothing when he dies?
At present, you're his son, and you would stand to get the lot.

1633: Hera was the wife of Zeus and a goddess of women and marriage.

1638: The Trojan War was fought for the sake of Helen.

MAKEMEDO:
Don't take any notice of this old salt, Heracles,
he's telling fish tales again. He's all at sea with the truth.
According to the law, none of your father's property
will go to you, nothing! You won't get an obol, mate,
because quite simply, you're a bastard.

HERACLES:
Are you calling me a bastard?

MAKEMEDO:
Your mother was a mortal, a noncitizen of Olympus,
hence you're a bastard! Why would we call Athena "The Heiress"
if you were Zeus' legal next of kin?

HERACLES:
But what if my father leaves me a nice little nest egg?

MAKEMEDO:
He can't! It's against the law. Poseidon would be the first to contest
the will. He's Zeus' brother and the legal next of kin, so he would get
the lot! You must have heard of Solon's law:
"The legitimate offspring of the deceased will always take precedence
in matters of inheritance over any living illegitimate offspring.
In the event of there being no legitimate offspring surviving the estate,
it shall be shared among the legal next of kin in all cases."

1648: Pericles' citizenship law of 451 stated that citizen rights could be granted only to those men born to both Athenian parents. Having a foreign mother would therefore disqualify a man from citizenship.

1654: Athena may have been the protector of heiresses as one of her cult functions. A woman could inherit her father's estate if he left no male heir; however, the property would be passed to her husband when she was married.

1656: Under Athenian law a father could leave only a very small part of his estate to an illegitimate son.

1660: Solon was an Athenian legislator in the sixth century.

1665: The heiress of a man's estate was required to marry the next closest male relative on her father's side who would then inherit the property. In this case it would be Poseidon as Zeus' brother.

HERACLES:
Leaving me with . . .

MAKEMEDO:
Absolutely nothing! Come to think of it, did Zeus ever induct you as a member of his family clan?

HERACLES:
No, he didn't. I was beginning to wonder.

MAKEMEDO:
Come on, old chap, don't look so sullen. Cheer up!
You can join the birds and live in a land of milk and honey!

HERACLES:
You know, I think you have just cause for your claim.
I've said it all along, let's give him the girl.

MAKEMEDO:
Poseidon?

POSEIDON:
I still say no.

MAKEMEDO:
Then it's up to the Jerkoffalot to break the deadlock. What do you say?

JERKOFFALOT:
Wollowy willy, Princessee birdie bye bye.

HERACLES:
You heard him, he votes for the birds!

POSEIDON:
Listen, small fry, he said nothing of the sort!

1669: Boys were presented to the *phratry* (clan) by their fathers when they reached adolescence. Membership of a clan group was an essential part of proving Athenian citizenship.

1678: This response is slightly more understandable, but it is impossible to determine if he says that they *should* give the princess to Makemedo or that they *should not*.

He's just chitter-chattering like a swallow.

HERACLES:
That's right! He said give her to the swallows.

POSEIDON:
All right! All right! There are other fish in the sea.
I'll abstain. The birds have it.

HERACLES:
We hereby agree to all your demands.
Now come with us up to Heaven, and we'll arrange
for you to pick up the princess and the scepter.

MAKEMEDO:
Great! and these birds I'm doing will be perfect for the feast.

HERACLES:
You go on ahead. I'll just, eh, stay here for a bit
and help do the birds.

POSEIDON:
Do the birds! Is that all you ever think about, Heracles?
Come on, we're all going now before you polish off the lot.

HERACLES:
Aww, I would have really enjoyed it here!

MAKEMEDO:
I'd better go and get my wedding clothes on!

(Exit Poseidon, Heracles, Jerkoffalot from scene building roof, Makemedo and servants through doorway.)

CHORUS:
In the land of Sycophantia,

1693: The white gown worn for festive occasions mentioned at line 1116.

1694: A city on the island of Chios chosen for the wordplay with *phanein* (denounce).

Where the river Clepsydra flows,
Live the evil bombastbellies
Who use tongues to plow and sow.

With the tongue they reap their harvest
Of bitter fruit and sour wine,
Gorgias and Philippus,
A coarse barbarian kind.

Should we tell these bombastbellies
That here in Athens when we feast,
We first perform the sacrifice
And cut the tongues out of our beasts!

(Enter Herald from offstage.)

HERALD:
Hear ye! Hear Ye! All you blessed creatures,
you fortuitous, flourishing, airborne birds!
Please welcome your king to his splendid palace!
He comes, bringing radiant light, sparkling like a star,
shimmering, glimmering, and golden, shining bright!
Not even the sun has ever gleamed with such brilliance!
He comes with his wife of indescribable beauty,
wielding the flashing thunderbolt, winged weapon of Zeus!
The delicate fragrances rise up high to the vault of heaven,
and the pungent aroma of incense is wafted on the breeze.

*(Enter Makemedo, riding in a chariot into the orchestra. He is carrying the thunderbolt of Zeus and is accompanied by the Divine Princess.)**

1695: The *clepsydra* was the water clock used in court to time the length of speeches (*Wasps* ***93 Water clock**).

1697: These "Tongue-to-Belly Men" earn their livings by bringing actions in the courts.

1700: Gorgias was the renowned rhetorician from Sicily who visited Athens many times from around the mid 420s onward and taught new techniques of argument. Philippus is not known but may have been his son or a pupil.

1705: Sacrificial beasts had their tongues cut out prior to their ritual killing at the altar.

Here he comes! Herald him with song!
Let the holy Muse sound her divine, sacred melody.

CHORUS:
Be upstanding for the bride and groom!
Make way, stand clear, let them pass!
Fly round the lucky couple and honor this beautiful bride.
Rejoice in this wedding that does so much credit to our city!

CHORUS 2:
The birds are blessed with great, good fortune!
We must give thanks to this human for our success.
Serenade him with the nuptial song!
Sing the wedding hymn for our lord and his princess!

(The chorus sings.)

Once Zeus and Hera came together
In wedded bliss, joined forever.
And to this day man celebrates
Their holy union tied by the Fates.
And so it is that we now sing
Our song to Hymen, our wedding hymn.
Shimmering Eros held the reins,
Guiding their chariot, on it came.
His glittering wings glowing golden,
To Zeus, the groom, he was beholden.
And so it is that we now sing
Our song to Hymen, our wedding hymn.

MAKEMEDO:
What wonderful music!
What a glorious hymn!

CHORUS:
Then let us glorify the awesome thunder

1734: The wedding of Zeus and Hera was seen as the prototype of all mortal marriages. Prior to an Athenian wedding, the participants made the preliminary sacrifice (*protelia*) to Zeus and Hera, "The Fulfillers."

1736: Hymen was the spirit of marriage.

that shakes the very core of the earth
and the flashing thunderbolts of Zeus
that light up the sky with their dread power!

Powerful, mighty lightning bolt
That shakes the earth with its jolt.
Rumbling thunder beneath earth's floor,
That quakes the world and makes rain pour.
Now Makemedo wields Zeus' power,
To shake the earth and make rain shower.
The princess who sat by Zeus' side
Has now been given as Makemedo's bride.

MAKEMEDO:
Come and join the wedding procession,
my feathered friends, you are all welcome
as my guests in the halls of Zeus
to celebrate my marriage rites.

(Makemedo addresses the Divine Princess.)

Give me your hand, my love,
here, take my wing,
let us lead the dance
as we flutter off together!

CHORUS:
Hooray! Hooray!
Hip, hip Hooray!
Hail to the highest divinity of all!

(Exit all in a procession of singing and dancing.)

–END–

1765: Makemedo is now proclaimed as "highest deity"; however, this does not mean that he has overthrown Zeus. His agreement with the delegation from Olympus is that the birds will rule mankind in conjunction with the gods and act as divine middlemen taking a share of sacrificial offerings but also ensuring that mortals pay proper respect at all times. The sight of an ordinary Athenian elevated to heaven would have been as controversial as it was comical inasmuch as Makemedo's power of persuasion to turn nonsense into reality has reached this absurdist and hilarious pinnacle.

Birds: Endnotes

Stage Direction: Carrying birds. Birds were attributed with powers of divination, a fact much exploited in the humor of this play. Pausanias refers to the foundation legend of Colonides in Messenia and tells of the settlers being guided there by a lark (4.34.8). There are also foundation myths about ravens guiding colonists to Cyrene, Magnesia, Coraces, Mallus, Lyon, and Cardia, and doves to Cumae and Naples. Yet in the fables of Aesop, the crow was regarded as an unreliable auger (*"The croak of the Crow is not an omen"*), and the jackdaw is portrayed as an imbecilic bird (Bowie [1993], pp. 155–56).

1: Goodhope. The Greek has "Euelpides," which means "Son of Good Hope."

2: Makemedo. The Greek has "Peithetaerus," which means something like "Persuader of his Comrades." The similarity between this character's name (first announced on stage at line 642) and Pisistratus, the sixth-century Athenian tyrant, may well have been intentional on the part of Aristophanes. Makemedo is pronounced "Make me do."

15: Tereus. Tereus was the king of Thrace and was married to the Athenian princess, Procne. He raped Procne's sister, Philomena, and to prevent her from revealing the crime imprisoned her and cut out her tongue. Philomena, however, sent a handwoven tapestry to her sister that communicated her plight. In revenge Procne killed Itys, her only son by Tereus, and served up his cooked flesh to his father at a banquet. Tereus discovered what had been done, and in a fit of rage he swore to kill the sisters, who fled for their lives. Tereus pursued them with a double axe, but the gods intervened, turning Procne into the nightingale whose call was said to be for Itys. Philomena became the swallow with its chattering unintelligible call, and Tereus was turned into the hoopoe, a bird that is known for splitting wood with its long sharp bill. The name "hoopoe," or "epops" in Greek, is derived from its call, said to be a searching cry, "pou pou," from the Greek *pou* ("where").

17: Jackdaw. The Greek has "Jackdaw, son of Tharreleides." It is uncertain to whom this refers, possibly a man called Asopodorus who was very small in size. It my also be a reference to an annoying talker.

33: Tribe and clan. The citizens of Athens were organized into ten tribal groups *(phylai)* by the statesman Cleisthenes in 508 B.C.E. The audience may well have sat in these tribal groupings in the theatre. The clan *(gene)* was a family affiliation claimed by Athenians who could trace their line back to old Athenian families, heroes, or cult figures.

42: Rites. These items are all used in sacrificial rites. The pots were used for boiling meat or carrying hot coals to light the sacrificial fire, the basket held the sacrificial knife and other implements, and the myrtle boughs and wreaths were a common feature in many Greek sacred rites.

43: Hustle and bustle. Makemedo and Goodhope are seeking *apragmosyne*—a life free from the hustle and bustle of the city of Athens. However, the very concept of *pragmata* (activity) was often held as an essential and valued element of Athenian culture. Alcibiades is reported by Thucydides (6.18 ff.) as justifying the need for the controversial attack on Sicily by stating that a city that has "hustle and bustle" could find no quicker way to ruin than to suddenly stagnate, and that a city should accept its character and institutions for better or for worse. It is not clear if Aristophanes was alluding to this important speech, made in 415 B.C.E.; however, it is certain that this was a highly charged concept to an Athenian audience in 414.

61: Stage Direction: Window. The servant bird was an actor who must have worn a mask with a huge and threatening beak. There is no other textual reference to his costume. It may have been that the Servant Bird just popped his head from the door or even appeared from one of the windows in the scene building. This would save the opening of the doors for the more dramatic entrance of the Hoopoe.

Stage Direction: Their birds fly away. It is not known if the jackdaw and crow were real birds, which at this point would have been let loose, or some kind of puppet operated by the actors. It seems that the stage actions required of the birds, to look in certain directions and to open their beaks on cue, would dictate that they were more likely to have been stage props.

70: Secretary Bird. The Greek has "Runner-Bird." Perhaps roadrunner is the closest assimilation to the Greek of a species that may have been the plover. There may be a sexual joke here on *trechô* (fast) similar to the pun on Iris' title at line 1203. The secretary bird is a known species and seems appropriate here.

79: Dip his ladle. I have tried to re-create the sexual imagery found in the double entendres in the Greek. The names of sea creatures were used as common euphemisms for the vagina, as were references to bowls and basins in this context. Phaleron was one of the ports of Athens, and like all ports, prostitutes could be found there. It is also a play on words with phallus. Soup was a metaphor for sexual liquids, and *toros* (stirring spoon/ladle) has the sense of "drill" or "penetrate" (Henderson 1991, 124). Therefore the secretary bird is envisaged as feeding the Hoopoe's voracious sexual appetite (***16 Tereus**).

89: Crow. For the sexual connotations of this word see Henderson 1991, p. 20.

Stage Direction: Hoopoe. The hoopoe is a native bird to Greece and much of Europe. It nests at ground level in small cavities, tree trunks, and thickets. The species has a long curved bill and a distinctive crest that can be raised and lowered, with the crest being erect when the hoopoe is excited. It has a light pink/brown plumage with a striking black and white wing pattern. The wings are rounded, and the hoopoe has a black and white banded fan tail. The hoopoe's call is a deep "hoo-poo-poo," and it is often seen perching on bushes, trees, rocks and buildings. It is clear from the text that at least the crest and bill are represented by the mask and costume worn on stage.

105: Birds molt. Real feathers were probably not a part of the hoopoe's costume. A late fifth-century Attic red figure calyx crater in the Getty Museum in California (Boardman *ARFV2* fig. 314) shows a pair of performers dressed in bird costumes. They are wearing tight body stockings painted with dappled markings, large wings, tails, and they wear tufts on their feet. Realistic feathers do not feature as an element in this costuming.

112: Country. Many of Aristophanes' heroes were from the country rather than the city of Athens. Procleon in *Wasps* refers often to his rustic childhood, Strepsiades in *Clouds* complains of his troubles beginning when he marries a woman from the city. The leads of *Acharnians, Peace,* and *Wealth* are all farmers.

126: Windbags. The Greek has "No! The son of Scellias makes me fart!" This refers to the politician Aristocrates, an obvious play on words with aristocracy. He was a prominent Athenian and served as a general. He is mentioned by Thucydides (5.19.2; 5.24.1) in connection with the Peace of Nicias in 421. Farting was also used as a sign of overindulgence by the rich (see Henderson 1991, p. 96).

158: Put it on your bill. The Greek has "you can live without the need for a purse."

160: Sesame seeds, myrtle berries, poppy seeds, and mint. All plants connected with marriage, fertility, and sex. The birds are envisioned leading a carefree innocent existence free to indulge in the simple pleasures of life without ever needing to earn money. This connection between food and sex is the catalyst that provides Makemedo with his idea to found a bird city.

175: Look down there. The Hoopoe's home is established in the scene building, which has so far been depicted as a thicket on the side of a mountain. This agrees with Tereus' mythological home of Daulis, one of the highest cities in Greece on the slopes of Mt. Parnassus. This was a region famed for prophecy and close to Apollo's shrine at Delphi, the most important of all Greek prophetic sanctuaries. Here the Hoopoe is asked to look down from the mountain, where he sees clouds, and to look up, where he sees the open sky.

180: Pole. *Polos* has several interlinked meanings. "Vault of the earth" is the obvious expression Makemedo has in mind. Aristophanes cleverly uses the physical staging conditions of the theatre to create his fantastic domain. *Polos* can also mean the center of a threshing-floor (Xenophon *Economics* 18.8), which was a circular level area found in Mediterranean communities for the threshing of corn. This may well have been the origin of the orchestra, the level dancing ground of the theatre. In the center of the orchestra of the Theatre of Dionysus was an altar. Therefore this pun also invests the orchestra with a sense of place prior to the arrival of the bird chorus.

183: The pole becomes a polis. A clever three-way pun on the word *polos* (for the meaning of *polos* see ***180 Pole**). For "polarity" the Greek has *poleisthai*, meaning "revolve" or "frequented," and *polis* means "city." Using quick thinking and verbal dexterity, Makemedo has made a rhetorical case for the sky becoming a city and manages to persuade the Hoopoe to support his idea.

186: Melos. Melos tried to remain neutral during the Peleponnesian War and refused to pay tribute to the Delian League. In 416 B.C.E., a large Athenian-led force landed on the island and demanded that it become a member. The Melians resisted and were eventually starved into submission during a bitter winter siege. The fate of the Melians was voted on in the Athenian assembly, and consequently the entire Melian adult male population was executed, and the women and children were sold into slavery.

208: Nightingale aroused. More sexual innuendo, this time directed at Procne, who is now the Nightingale depicted as living happily with Tereus as opposed to her mythical fate (see ***15 Hoopoe**).

Stage Direction: Joined by the Nightingale. The song of the nightingale was probably reproduced by the aulos player. The aulos was an oboelike reed instrument, and many vase paintings of the period show an aulos player accompanying dramatic performances. The Getty calyx crater (see ***105 Birds molt**) depicts such an aulos player.

259: Come one and all. The Hoopoe calls the birds from fields, meadows, marshes, and the sea. His song serves to invoke the Greek countryside and the wide variety of birds that live there. However, there is also a definite sexual subtext present in this song, and many of the words employed are sexual euphemisms. This seems designed less as titillation than as an illustration of the carefree, idealistic life of the birds. In this song the two basic hedonistic necessities of sex and food merge into one poetic metaphor. It is sex and food that the gods will be deprived of by the birds' blockade and the potent combination of sex and food that forces Heracles to treat for peace at the end of the play.

266: Like a yellowhammer. *Lochmen* meaning "bush" or "thicket" was a common metaphor for vagina. *Kharadrios* can mean "yell" but derives from "torrent" and can mean any kind of conduit including a penis. It was also the name of the yellowhammer, a small bird that nests in gullies. *Epôze* means "cluck" but sounds like *epôtheô*, "push in." So the line could be understood through double entendre as, "The Hoopoe was wasting his time going inside, pushing his penis in the vagina and yelling out."

Stage Direction: Roof of the scene building. Some scholars (Dover 1972, p.145; Dunbar, p. 230) believe that these first four birds appear on the roof of the scene building, while Sommerstein (*Birds* note on 214) states that they may be musicians who take up position on raised hillocks in front of the stage. The jokes that follow alluding to "crests" and "hill-walkers" point to the fact that they were probably elevated above Makemedo and Goodhope who are now on stage. There does seem to be an advance group of some sort from the main chorus of twenty-four members. It may have been that this first group was more elaborately attired while the chorus members were more simply costumed to enable them to sing, dance, and participate in the stage action more easily. A similar choral "advance party" is found in the boys who lead the chorus in *Wasps* (lines 230–316).

282: Philocles. Presumably Philocles' version of the hoopoe story was regarded as a lesser version than the more famous *Tereus* of Sophocles mentioned at line 100. Aristophanes pokes fun at Philocles' physical appearance and birdlike features at line 1295 and again in *Thesmophoriazusae* at line 168.

283: Callias. The first Callias mentioned lived from c. 520 to 440 and was a wealthy aristocrat who negotiated the Peace of Callias with the Spartans in 448. His son Hipponicus served as an Athenian general and died in 422. His son was also named Callias and lived from

c. 450 to c. 366. He squandered the family wealth on his excessive lifestyle and an assortment of sophistic teachers, prostitutes, and hangers-on.

286: Ptera. Greek homes often had fertility symbols consisting of a phallus with wings attached hanging outside their doors.

297: Wings. The *eisodos* was the entrance to the orchestra from where the twenty-four chorus members dressed as birds are now entering. The English word "wings" for the offstage entrances makes for an irresistible pun.

Stage Direction: Military formation. Like the chorus in *Wasps* attacking Contracleon and the slaves (lines 422–25), the bird chorus here attacks in military formation. For the possible practice of recruiting the chorus from the military see *Wasps* ***423 ATEEEN SHUNNN!**

377: Walls, towers, and warships. A veiled reference to the military policies of Athens. The Athenians linked the harbors of Piraeus and Phaleron to the city of Athens with the Long Walls. The Athenians also put most of their defensive resources into their large fleet, which enabled them to maintain military supremacy over the sea.

403: Hoplite fashion. This is a parody of a military command similar to "Ground arms." Whereas the hoplite was commanded to lower his spear and lay it down next to his shield, the chorus members are ordered to bend their *thumon* (spirit) and lay down their *orgên* (passion). *Thumos* was a euphemism for penis, and the sexual imagery is continued throughout this scene.

409: Learned land of Greece. A similar description is found in Herodotus I.60.3.

430: A real old hand. Aristophanes uses similar language in *Clouds* at line 260.

439: Not the monkey. The Greek has "Unless they give me a promise like the one the knifemaker's monkey made with his wife." This may refer to an unknown fable or be a political/sexual joke.

450: Further postings. These orders would have been familiar to an audience well acquainted with military service. Mobilization orders were posted on the notice boards at the statues of the Eponymous Heroes of the ten tribes of Attica. Some scholars attribute these lines to the chorus leader (Dunbar 1995, note on lines 446–50); however, it is important that Makemedo assumes command of the birds at this point, and these specifically Athenian orders strongly suggest that they are issued by Makemedo.

463: All please recline. The political language of the assembly is mixed with the terminology of the symposium, the dinner and drinking parties frequented by the new Athenian intellectual elite, particularly the sophists and teachers of rhetoric. Both speakers in the assembly and symposium guests wore garlands, and the ritual washing of hands was a normal part of purification rites prior to both activities. However, guests at a symposium reclined on couches, whereas listeners at an assembly meeting would have sat on benches. Makemedo's invitation to the chorus to recline is an indication to the audience that he is about to use the language of rhetoric, which was perceived as being an integral part of a symposium.

467: Heavenly succession. This traditional description of the heavenly succession is found in Hesiod's *Theogony* 133–38. Aristophanes returns to this theme several times throughout *Birds,* in the parabasis at lines 694–703, with the appearance of Prometheus at 1494 (Prometheus helped Zeus defeat the Giants), and throughout the negotiations between the gods and Makemedo at the end of the play.

475: Lark. There is a similar fable noted by Aelian (*On the Nature of Animals* 16.5), who tells the story of a hoopoe from India. A prince was banished with his royal parents, who subsequently died on the long journey they were forced to make. Having no place to bury them, the dutiful son split his own head open with a sword and buried them there. In recognition of this act of piety, the gods turned him into a bird with a great crest.

487: Hat. The triple pronged hat worn by Persian kings is referred to by Herodotus 7.61.1 and seems to have been a version of the Scythian felt hat. Persian rulers are depicted on several vase paintings relating to Athenian drama, and they show the Persian or Phrygian rulers wearing such headgear (Trendall and Webster, figs.

III.1,26 *Phineus*, III.3,34 *Medea*, III.5,6 *Persai*). The Athenian audience would have been familiar with this type of headgear from contemporary tragedy.

510: Scepter. Many vase paintings of the period with dramatic connections and themes depict royal personages holding scepters topped by birds. Agamemnon is depicted on a fourth-century Apulian volute-crater holding such a scepter (Trendall and Webster, fig. III.4,2). Other kings holding bird scepters include Tantalus from Aeschylus' *Niobe* (fig. III, 1,23), Phineus from Aeschylus' *Phineus* (fig. III, 1,26), Proetus from Euripides' *Stheneboea* (fig. III,3,45), and Creon from Euripides' *Medea* (fig. III, 5,4).

512: Birds of the gods. Zeus was associated with the eagle as the king of the birds in art and myth. According to Pausanias (5.11.1), Pheidias' statue of Zeus at Olympia held a scepter crowned by an eagle. The owl was a common symbol of both Athena and the city of Athens. A statue of Athena at Elis had a cock on her helmet, and there may well have been an owl similarly located on Pheidias' statue of Athena in the Parthenon. A gold medallion from Kerch (a Greek city in south Russia) of the fourth century depicts an owl perched on the left cheekpiece of Athena's helmet (Boardman *GS2*, fig. 102). Apollo is likened to a hawk in the *Iliad* (15. 237–38).

522: Lampon. A once-noted political figure who appears as the first Athenian name witnessing the Peace of Nicias in 421 (Thucydides 5.1.2). Some years earlier, in 443, Pericles made him the leader of the Athenian settlement in Thurii in southern Italy. He was often lampooned by the comic playwrights as a corrupt glutton, and the mention of his name here may also carry a second significance as Lampon had also been the founder of a new city.

537: Sweet oils and dressings. The Greek has "They grate cheese and silphium over you and bathe you in oil and vinegar." Silphium was a plant from the area around Cyrene in North Africa between modern day Egypt and Tunisia. This plant is now extinct, but it seems that the root, stalk, and juice were all used as a pungent flavoring. In Aristophanes' *Knights* (424 B.C.E.) Cleon is accused of lowering the price of silphium in order to encourage the jury men to eat it and cause them to fart so much that they would kill each other with the smell in court (lines 894–98). These lines have a more ominous significance as Makemedo cooks "treasonous" birds with the same dressings at lines 1579–85.

573: Hermes. For a representation of the winged sandals of Hermes on an Athenian red figure cup see Boardman *ARFV1* (fig. 88).

574: Nike. The spirit of Victory was a common motif in Athenian art appearing in sculptural relief on the Parthenon and in representations on the temple of Athena Nike also on the Acropolis. Nike's wings are depicted on a red figure vase by the Sotades painter (Boardman *ARFV2,* fig. 106). A comic rendering of Nike is found driving a chariot containing Heracles on an oinochoe by the Nicias Painter (Boardman *ARFV2,* fig. 321).

575: Eros. A calyx crater by the Dinos painter shows a splendid set of wings on the tiny figure of Eros (Boardman *ARFV2,* fig. 179).

584: Doctors. Evidence for state-employed physicians can be found in Herodotus (3.131) and Plato (*Gorgias* 514d–515b). One such doctor, named Pittalus, is mentioned in *Wasps* at line 1432.

609: Before he croaks. The crow was said to live far longer than man. A similar proverb is found in Hesiod (*Fr.* 304).

620: Ammon. Ammon was a shrine in Egypt famous for its oracles. Its importance grew in Greece through trade contacts and the founding of the Greek colony of Cyrene in Egypt. Ammon had recently come to the attention of the Athenians because the controversial young general, Alcibiades, had consulted it on the matter of the Sicilian expedition. He received the prophecy that Syracuse would fall to Athenian forces. Although it became a popular site for individuals to visit in the fourth century, it was consulted only by politicians and prominent citizens at the time *Birds* was produced.

640: Forward together. Sommerstein (*Birds,* note on lines 638–40) assigns these lines to Makemedo, reasoning that the Hoopoe would not announce a rush to action and then immediately procrastinate with an offer of lunch. However, this would seem a good opportunity for a contradictory joke, especially after the reference to the shilly-shallying of Nicias.

653: The fox and the eagle. This fable, attributed to Aesop, is told as follows: The fox and the eagle agreed to form a partnership and live together in a tree. The eagle built his nest in the branches, and the fox made his home between the roots. One day when the fox was out hunting, temptation got the better of the eagle who, using the advantage of his wings, swooped down and stole the fox cubs and ate them in his nest, where the fox could not reach him. The flightless fox could do nothing but shout curses, and the eagle thought that he was safe. The eagle, however, saw some meat on a sacrificial altar, stole it, and took it back to his nest. The meat was still smoldering and his nest caught fire. The eagle's chicks fell out onto the ground into the jaws of the fox, who devoured them before the very eyes of their father.

657: Xanthias! Manodorus! The stage movements of these two slave characters are unclear. It seems that they accompanied Makemedo and Goodhope on their journey, though Aristophanes may be inviting a visual pun on having these characters enter here. If onstage from the beginning, they could have been employed as convenient stage hands.

Stage Direction: Enter Procne. This was probably a nonspeaking actor wearing a bird mask and pretending to play the aulos, a small twin-piped oboelike instrument that was held in place by cheek straps. The real aulos player may well have been onstage but not included in the dramatic action itself. For a pictorial representation of an aulos player wearing cheek straps on a red-figure bell crater by the Cleophon Painter, see Boardman *ARF1*, fig. 174.

670: Beautiful young thing. The Greek has "Look at her lovely gold, just like a virgin!" Young girls of marriageable age in Athens wore gold jewelry during festivals. The Greek puns on *chruson* (gold) and *kusos* (vagina) (Henderson 1991, p. 131).

706: Gift of a cock. Certain species of birds were favored as love tokens. The species mentioned in the Greek are quail, gallinule, goose, and cock. I have amended the list to keep the phallic references. A red-figure cup by the Penthesilea Painter depicts Zeus wooing Ganymede who holds a cockerel as a symbol of male love (Boardman *ARFV2*, fig. 82), and a red-figure cup by the Euaichme Painter shows an older man offering a cockerel to a beardless youth (Boardman *ARFV1*, fig. 373).

710: The crane. Hesiod has a similar phrase: "Mind now, when you hear the call of the crane/Coming from the clouds, as it does year by year:/That's the sign for plowing, and the onset of winter" (*Works and Days* 448–51. tr. Stanley Lombardo).

721: Every important aspect of your lives. Aristophanes puns on the use of the word *ornis* (bird) as a byword for prophetic utterances. In the Greek the list says: *Everything that is important to you in the realm of divination you call a bird: A word of ill omen is a "bird," a sneeze is a "bird," a fortunate meeting, a "bird," a sound is a "bird," a servant is a "bird," and so is a donkey.*

745: Pan. The cult worship of Pan in Athens grew in importance after the battle of Marathon (490), when Pan was said to have appeared and inspired the Athenian army to defeat the Persians. Pan had an important cult site in one of the sacred caves on the Acropolis in Athens.

795: An affair with a married woman. This reference to marital infidelity on the part of a male audience member could be evidence that women were not present in the audience during dramatic performances at this point in the fifth century. For a detailed examination of the scant evidence on this controversial area, see Goldhill, S., "Representing Democracy: Women at the Great Dionysia," in *Ritual, Finance, Politics. Athenian Democratic Accounts Presented to David Lewis.* R. Osborne and S. Hornblower, eds. (Oxford 1994), pp. 347–70.

800: Horsecock. A mythical and fantastic creature half horse/half cock. Aeschylus referred to a "tawny horsecock" in *Myrmidons* (*Fr.* 134) when describing the prow of a ship, and this image is lampooned by Euripides in Aristophanes' *Frogs* (line 933) as old fashioned and unimaginable. For a pictorial representation of a horsecock on the neck of a Nikosthenic amphora see Boardman *ABFV*, fig. 150).

Stage Direction: Enter Makemedo and Goodhope . . . dressed as birds. It seems that the two men still wear the same masks and basic costume, but during the parabasis they have put on wings and some other form of plumage. This may have been something resembling tail feathers and perhaps some form of dressing around the feet. An Attic black-figure oinochoe in the British Museum shows two performers dressed as birds with feathered wings, red crests, and a speckled costume (Green & Handley, fig. 3). The bird costume of the Getty vase is discussed above (see note on line 106). There is, however, a depiction of two performers accompanied by an aulos player simply wearing large heavy cloaks and sporting headcrests to suggest cocks (Pickard-Cambridge, *Dithyramb, Comedy and Tragedy,* 2nd ed., rev. T.B.C. Webster [Oxford 1968], pl. 27). Whatever the exact nature of the costuming here, we can be certain that Makemedo and Goodhope look quite ridiculous in their respective outfits.

819: Cloudcuckooland. For a detailed examination of the double meanings contained in Cloudcuckooland, see Dobrov 1993, p. 192.

827: Robe. The presentation of Athena's new robe is depicted on Slab V on the eastern section of the Parthenon frieze (Boardman *GS2,* fig. 96.19).

831: Shuffling his shuttle. The *kerkis* (shuttle) was the long flat wooden blade used by women to pack the threads of the weft while weaving. It was also a euphemism for penis.

835: Roosting on rocks. The Greek has "Chick of Ares," a phrase that may have had its origins as a Homeric epithet. There may also be a joke here based around the Areopagus, the "Rock of Ares," a site in Athens where a judicial council met to hear cases of homicide.

858: Chaeris. For a detailed discussion, see Taplin 1993, p. 105.

Stage Direction: Basket and water jug. The basket would hold the sacrificial knife and barley for sprinkling over the altar. It was a traditional element of sacrificial rites to keep the blade hidden from view until the moment of the kill. The water was used to anoint the victim and to cleanse the hands of the sacrifice.

Stage Direction: Enter the Poet. The Poet arrives in Cloudcuckooland seeking patronage for his traditional Pindaric odes. It is clear that the Poet is poorly dressed and very cold up on the heights of Cloudcuckooland. Aristophanes is parodying the system of patronage that existed between poets and their benefactors, perhaps thinking of the sixth-century poet Hipponax, who offered prayers to Hermes to protect him from the cold.

Stage Direction: Enter the Prophet. The prophet was a common feature of ancient life and of course, peddlers of fortunes, messages from the "other side," and physic knowledge are still predominant in modern society. This Prophet is a wandering soothsayer going from place to place offering interpretations of omens, rather than an agent of one of the recognized mantic sanctuaries. Like the Poet, the Prophet is also poorly dressed and of a disheveled appearance.

963: Bacis. Bacis' prophecies had been circulating at least since the time of the Persian wars (490–80 B.C.E.), and he is mentioned several times by Herodotus, who even quotes his mantic verses (8.77 and 9.42.2), which are in the same style as those here. The original prophecies of Bacis were said to have been incredibly accurate. It is not surprising to find in Aristophanes, several references to charlatans, false prophets, and ragtag soothsayers attempting to use his reputation for their own enrichment (*Knights* 117–43, 1003; *Peace* 1070).

968: Sicyon and Corinth. A well-known proverbial story told how a man (possibly Aesop) had asked Apollo's oracle at Delphi how he could become wealthy. The oracle replied that he could do so by owning the land between Sicyon and Corinth (Athenaeus 219a). Sicyon lies directly on the borders of Corinth, therefore there is no land to be had there. Diodorus Siculus also reported a similar prophecy given to the Spartan Phalanthos who was asking the oracle where he could live (8.21.3). It seems that the phrase "the land between Sicyon and Corinth" became a common expression for "nowhere land" and in this sense is akin to the whole concept of Cloudcuckooland itself.

Stage Direction: Enter Meton. Meton invented the "Metonic Cycle," which calculated that 235 lunar months equaled 19 solar years. Perhaps this discovery was assisted by his sundial mentioned at line 998. Meton's reputation seems to have become somewhat tarnished around 415 when an apartment complex he owned mysteriously burned down just prior to the sailing of the fleet for Sicily. He then pleaded exemption from military service for his family because of the financial hardship this had apparently caused him. The comic playwright Phrynichus mentions him in a play of the same year as "The one who brought the fountains" (*Fr.* 21), and this may be a reference to his working on the Athenian water supply. Meton was a wealthy man, and presumably in contrast to the first two interlopers, his costume would reflect his more affluent means.

994: Cothornoi. For a pictorial representation of an actor dressed as Heracles wearing these high boots on the Pronomos vase, see Boardman *ARFV2*, fig. 323.

1016: Spartan expulsions. Pericles refers to this practice when comparing Sparta to Athens: "If the Lacedaemonians (Spartans) will cancel their policy of expelling us and our allies as aliens . . . / We leave our city open to all; and we have never expelled strangers"(Thucydides 1.144 and 2.39. tr. P. Woodruff).

Stage Direction: Inspectors. Inspectors were appointed by the Athenian state to maintain control over their allies by reporting the results of their inspections back to Athens, regulating the correct payment of tribute, and implementing appropriate political measures where they saw fit. The text suggests that this character is richly dressed in Persian finery. The appearance of the Inspector before the city has even been properly founded makes for a pointed comment on the policy of Athenian imperialism and Athens' treatment of the allied states. The Inspector arrives carrying two voting urns, the perennial symbol of Athenian justice. The huge citizen juries would cast their votes into either the guilty or the not guilty urn. This symbol of Athenian justice is of course one of the very institutions that Makemedo had wanted to escape.

1054: Decree tablet. Both the city of Athens and her allies had stone inscriptions of Athenian laws set up in prominent places. These were a symbol of Athenian power, and to urinate or defecate on them would be seen as a supreme act of treason. Of course Makemedo has not even finished inaugurating his city, let alone been made an ally, and had decree tablets set up.

1169: War dance. For a visual representation of the Pyrrhic dance on a red figure cup by the Poseidon Painter, see Boardman *ARFV1*, fig. 127.

Stage Direction: Enter Iris. Iris' entrance would have been made on the *machina*, the theatrical crane used in tragedy for the entrance of gods. In the Greek, Aristophanes uses nautical expressions to welcome Iris, as if she were a ship with billowing sales and the machina were a crane unloading cargo. For a depiction of Iris, see Boardman *ARFV1*, fig. 252. Iris' costume would have had wings and a female mask, the role being played by a male actor.

1273: O Lord Makemedo, etc. This kind of excessive praise was frowned upon by ordinary Athenians as the mark of a corrupt Persian ruler. Aeschylus has Clytemnestra welcome Agamemnon home from the Trojan War in similar fashion in *Agamemnon* (lines 895–901).

1367: In the Army now! There was an annual military parade of young men who were ceremoniously awarded their arms by the state after serving one year of their ephebic training. This was held in the theatre, and the audience may well have watched the very same ceremony Aristophanes is parodying on the day *Birds* was performed (Aristotle *Ath. Pol*, 42.2).

1396: Thrace. The Athenian forces sent to Thrace were composed primarily of mercenaries, and with the bulk of the Athenian forces in Sicily, it appears that it was difficult to find recruits. The campaign failed to capture the Thracian city of Amphipolis in the summer of 414 B.C.E.

Stage Direction: Enter Cinesias. Cinesias was evidently a composer of a new form of dithyrambic poetry, which abandoned the traditional repeating structure of strophic responsion for "preludes," which were more emotional and elaborate. Cinesias is portrayed by Aristophanes as quite an unsavory character. He is lampooned not only for his vacuous poetry but also for his personal sexual habits and his tall, thin appearance. He was said to be a sickly man who suffered from diarrhea and dabbled in politics.

1429: Newborn writs and summonses. The Greek has "I could fly unnoticed with the cranes and swallow my lawsuits for ballast." derived from the ancient belief that cranes swallowed stones to help them remain stable in the air.

1461: Spinning top. This type of spinning top was spun using a rope lash which whipped it into a spin. An Attic red figure kylix by the Douris Potter dated 480–70 in the Johns Hopkins University Museum in Baltimore (Hopkins AIA B9) depicts a bearded man and a youth playing with this type of top.

1466: Horsewhipping. The Greek has "Corcyraean wings." Public officials in Corcyra (Corfu) were said to wield large double-lashed wings to keep order in the assembly.

Stage Direction: Enter Prometheus. Prometheus was a Titan who gave the gift of fire to man and was punished for it by Zeus who bound him to a rock, where an eagle came daily to peck out his liver. There are differing myths about Prometheus, but he is always envisaged as a benefactor to mankind. The Athenians held a festival in his honor, the Promethea, which celebrated fire. Hesiod tells the Prometheus story in both *Theogony* (521–616) and *Works and Days* (47–58).

1504: "Our Dear Prometheus." Prometheus, whose name means "forethinker," may well have held a special place in the hearts of Athenians, a people who were proud of their resourcefulness and craftsmanship. This welcome delivered by Makemedo may have been a formulaic greeting from cult practice.

1508: Parasol. In the Scira festival, the priestess of Athena and the priests of Poseidon and Helios walked under a parasol, traveling down from the Acropolis to a sanctuary in Sciron outside the city on the road to Eleusis (Burkert 1985, p. 230).

1529: Jerkoffalots. The Greek has *Triballoi*. The literal translation is "three rubbers." The number three has special significance for sexual potency, and to "three-rub" means to masturbate (Henderson 1991, p. 121). There was also a Thracian tribe who lived in what is now western Bulgaria known as the Triballians, known for their extreme brutality and complete disregard for the rules of hospitality.

1530: Very *hard*. A pun on the word *epitribeiês*, which is usually translated as "may you be crushed!" but *tribê* can mean to "rub" or "wear away." A more accurate translation might be based around the act of masturbation and something like, "Go fuck yourself!" Or "Jerkoff!" (U.S.), "Wanker!" (U.K.). Therefore, a closer translation of the Greek might read: "Oh, so that's where we get the word *wanker* from!"

1534: Here's what you must do. In offering Makemedo covert advice on how to defeat the gods, Prometheus is recreating his mythological role, described in Aeschylus' *Prometheus Bound* (lines 199–223), where he secretly offered Zeus information on how to defeat Cronus and the other Titans.

1536: Divine Princess. There has been much speculation over the identity of this deity and probably rightly so. Aristophanes chooses a particularly vague title and gives her attributions that certainly relate her to known goddesses, particularly Athena, who was known to have held the key to Zeus' thunderbolts and represent wisdom and common sense. However, as is clearly shown by Makemedo's response, she is an invention of Aristophanes for his own comedic purposes.

1552: Stool bearers. The Parthenon frieze (east frieze Slab V) depicts stool bearers as part of a religious procession (Boardman *GS2*, fig. 96.19).

1557: Peisander. After serving on the commission responsible for investigating the mutilation of the Herms Peisander went on to support the overthrow of the Athenian democracy in 411 B.C.E. After the demise of the Oligarchs in 410, he fled to Spartan territory, was condemned to death, and was never heard of again. Aristophanes joked about his obesity and cowardly behavior.

1563: A camel would suffice. Peisander's sacrificial animal resembles him, as the Greeks believed camels were dirty, lumbering, stupid, and cowardly beasts, as well as an animal associated with the Persian enemy (see line 278).

Stage Direction: Enter Poseidon, Heracles, and Jerkoffalot. The delegation of three gods arrives, probably on the scene building roof, the area conventionally reserved for the appearances of gods, although in *Birds*, it may also have been utilized for the appearance of the first four birds at 268. The gods must have been instantly recognizable to the audience. So it seems that Poseidon would wear a bearded mask and carry a trident as he is depicted in vase paintings (Boardman *ARFV2*, figs. 289, 316, 383) and Heracles would wear his lion skin and hold a club (Boardman *ARFV2*, fig. 323). An Athenian terra cotta figurine of a comic character dressed as Heracles from the early fourth century may be the closest archaeological evidence for how Aristophanes' Heracles may have looked on stage. He has a large bearded grotesque mask, the lion skin, and headpiece, and wears the traditional comic costume with phallus. He holds his bow and quiver rather than the club (Green & Handley, fig. 34). We can only speculate as to the costume of the Jerkoffalot except that he is attempting to wear a himation, which was the traditional garb of the Athenian gentleman. His mask may have resembled the crude mask of Satyr plays as depicted on the Pronomos vase (Boardman *ARFV2*, fig. 323).

1589: There's no oil left in the bottle. The language of the scene is charged with sexual double entendres such as "stoke the fire" (Henderson 1991, pp. 47–48). *Krea*, "meat," was often used as a slang word for the vagina (Henderson 1991, p. 144), and "there's no oil left in the bottle" is a euphemistic way of describing Makemedo's disappointing sexual performance due to his advanced years (*Frogs* line 1208, "lost his bottle of oil"). This mixed metaphor of food and sex appears throughout this play with vivid descriptions of the feeding habits of the birds couched in sexual terms (the Hoopoe's song at line 228). Also, it is important to remember that the intention of the blockade was not only to prevent the gods from receiving nourishment from sacrifices from below but to prevent them from having sexual encounters with mortal women. It is possible to imagine that Aristophanes may have even made more of this running theme here by having his "birds" appear as real women dressed in seductive bird outfits. This would put far greater force behind Heracles' reasons for wanting to quickly treat for peace and partake of the feast and the Jerkoffalot's obvious sexual frustrations. Aristophanes uses a similar visual comic device in *Wasps* (lines 1364–80) when Procleon attempts to pass off a dancing girl as a torch.

1602: Nibble. Gk: *aristaô* ("breakfast"/"lunch") is another possible double entendre for the sexual act (Henderson 1991, p. 186).

Stage Direction: Enter Makemedo, riding in a chariot. A chariot or a wheeled cart seems to have been an integral part of Athenian wedding ceremonies (for a depiction of a wedding chariot on a red figure pyxis by the Marlay Painter, see Boardman *ARFV2*, fig. 343). The text suggests that Makemedo and the Divine Princess (played by a nonspeaking actor) rode into the orchestra, taking center stage, with the chorus dividing into two halves and then circling around them.

Appendix: The First Version of *Clouds*

The text of *Clouds* that we possess is not that staged at the Dionysia of 423, which gained the third prize. In *Wasps* and in the revised parabasis of *Clouds* the comedian expresses his displeasure at this result and praises his original version of *Clouds*. If we could be certain whether five comedies or three had been presented, we could more accurately gauge the force of Aristophanes' reaction. Did his excellent comedy finish last of three, or did it get "only the Bronze Medal" in a field of five? In considering the matter of the revision of *Clouds*, the student will want to keep a number of questions in mind. When did Aristophanes make the revision? How extensive were the changes? What in our text belongs to the revised version, and what to the original? How close to production is our text? What are the larger implications for the comedy?

The evidence for the revision comes from a number of sources: Aristophanes' own comments in *Wasps* and in the revised parabasis of *Clouds* (518–62), several references in the scholia to *Clouds* (at 520, 543a, 549a, 553, 591a, 1115a) and at *Wasps* 1038c, one of the hypotheses to *Clouds* (Hypothesis I [Dover]), and finally some fragments assigned by ancient sources to *Clouds*, but which do not appear in the text as we have received it.

Aristophanes tells us about the first *Clouds* twice, first at *Wasps* 1045–50 and later in the parabasis (518–62) of the text of *Clouds* as we have it, where it is clear that we are dealing with a revision—as Dover (*Cl.* lxxx) puts it, a comedy cannot refer to its own failure in the past. However, we should be careful of taking the comedian at face value; of course he will tell us that this was a brilliant comedy that failed to find an appreciative audience and lost to inferior competition. At *Wasps* 1045–50 he describes the play (not named):

> Last year he tried to sow a crop of new ideas,
> BUT YOU JUST DIDN'T GET THE MESSAGE, DID YOU?
> He himself will swear by Dionysus and pour countless libations that no one had ever seen a better comedy. You should feel shame! Shame on you! Let's face it, people, no intelligent person will think badly of our author for being so far ahead of his field that his new concept crashed!

Some believe that the previous lines (1037–42) refer also to first *Clouds*, but "last year" could also signify a comedy at the Lenaea of 423 which was well received and then followed by the "failure" of *Clouds*. I think it safer to identify two productions of 423 here.[1] This theme of novelty and excellence forms the core of Aristophanes' *apologia* at *Clouds* 518–62: "most intellectual of all my comedies" (522), "thwarted by all those hacks" (524), "brand new cutting-edge comedy / every play has something different, something innovative, vivacious, skillful" (547). But he really tells us nothing about the content of the first play or what he is doing differently in the revision.[2]

The scholia do not add a great deal. Σ *Cl.* 552 shows that the ancient scholars knew of only one production date for a *Clouds* by Aristophanes (that in 423); thus the revision was never performed at a festival. Σ *Cl.* 520 tells us that the parabasis was not in the same meter as the original, and Σ *Cl.* 543a that the burning down of the Pondertorium was not in the first version, but this is all that we can glean. The hypothesis, however, gives the most information. The text is difficult and disputed in places; the following is Sommerstein's translation (*Clouds* 4):

> The play is the same as the first, but it has been revised in details, as though the poet intended to produce it again but, for

---

[1] These lines run, "Last year he attacked the demons, plagues, fevers, / and nightmares that came by night to throttle your fathers and choke your grandfathers, / with their subpoenas and writs, their affidavits, and summonses." Then he proceeds, "and what did you do in return? You shunned him!" This suggests that the "plagues, demons," etc., belong to a comedy *before* first *Clouds*.

[2] See Hubbard (1986) for an interesting interpretation of *Cl.* 538 ff. in this regard.

> whatever reason, did not do so. To speak generally, there has been revision in every part of the play; some parts have been removed, new sections have been woven in, and changes have been made in arrangement and in the exchanges between characters. Certain parts in their present form belong entirely to the revised version: thus the parabasis of the chorus has been replaced, and where the just argument talks to the unjust, and lastly where the school of Socrates is burned.

It might seem that the revision was extensive; however, there is much that clearly belongs to the 423 version and which would have been altered or replaced, e.g., the rest of the parabasis (especially 575–94), many personal jokes and contemporary references, like that to the war at line 6. One may agree with Sommerstein (*Clouds* 4) that "the revision does not seem to have been as far-reaching as has sometimes been supposed."

That the parabasis proper (518–62) is new is clear from the text itself; it was Aristophanes' response to the results of the competition of 423. It also allows us to date the revision. At 551-58 we hear that Eupolis was the first to attack Hyperbolus in his *Maricas* (421L) and that thereafter Hermippus and everyone else joined in. At the earliest Hermippus and "everyone else" would have produced their plays in 420, and thus the earliest date for Aristophanes' comments would be 419. He mentions Hyperbolus in the present tense (552, 558), and as Hyperbolus was ostracized in 416, we can assume a lower date of 417/16. Thus the revision of *Clouds* belongs to the years 419–417.

The second section singled out as revised is "where the just argument talks to the unjust." But does this mean the verbal scuffle at 899–948, the speech of Superior Argument at 959–1023, or the agon as a whole? The lack of a choral interlude at 888–889 suggests that the reworking began at that point, and that we have only a remnant of a second parabasis at 1115–30 indicates that material was deleted at the end. It seems likely that the agon as a whole was meant, and the changes may have been considerable. A scholion to *Cl.* 889 says that the Arguments were brought on stage in wicker cages, dressed as fighting cocks. There is nothing in our text to suggest such a presentation, and quite probably this comes from the original play.[3]

[3] Taplin 101–4 suggests that the "Getty Birds" on a late fifth-century vase are in fact the Arguments of the original *Clouds*.

Thus there was an agon between the Arguments in the original version; changes were made, but we cannot determine how sweeping or extensive these were. I cannot agree with MacDowell when he argues that there was no agon in the original.[4]

Finally, there is the altered ending, which may make all the difference. *Clouds* is unusual in that the "great idea" is reversed and indeed repented of at the end. My own feeling is that there was no such retribution in the first play, that Strepsiades was allowed to get away with not paying his debts, and that the audience (or the judges) did not react well to such an antinomian ending. There is in *Clouds* a subtle tension between sympathy for the not-too-bright farmer and appreciation of intellectual ideas; this may not have gone over well with the audience. Aristophanes may have intended an ironic ending for first *Clouds*, but usually the later scenes are indulgent wish-fulfillments, and that is how I expect that the orginal ended. Thus the revision will have included the chorus's change of attitude, the almost Aeschylean admission of *hybris* at 1462–64, and the retribution wrought by Strepsiades upon Socrates.

The actual fragments of first *Clouds* are not many (K–A III.2, fr. 392–401), and only a few are at all significant:

fr. 392—This is the fellow [Socrates] who composes those smart-talking clever tragedies for Euripides

fr. 393—They will lie there like a pair of copulating moths

fr. 394—They [fem.] are gone in anger down the side of Mount Lycabettus[5]

fr. 395—Nor will I put a garland around a drinking-cup

Aristophanes then began to revise his *Clouds* sometime between 419 and 417. The revisions were extensive in that he made alterations in all parts of the comedy, but only three major changes in the text can be documented: the parabasis proper, the contest between the Arguments (and here we do not know how much was altered), and the end of the comedy with its retribution against Socrates. The

---

[4] MacDowell (1995) 136–44.

[5] "They" are certainly the chorus of Clouds; at line 323 of our text they are seen approaching from Mount Parnes.

comedy was nowhere near production when he abandoned the project.[6] The topical allusions and personal jokes of the 423 version are still in the text,[7] as is most of the parabasis. Thus it is dangerous to consider what we have as a complete and integrated text and to treat it in the manner that we do other comedies. Two further questions remain and are perhaps unanswerable: (a) how did a partly revised version survive as a text? and (b) how did it displace the version of 423 that was actually produced?

I.C.S.

[6] Fisher and Kopff, however, maintain that the revision was almost complete and ready for the theatre.

[7] On this see Storey (1993) 78–81.

Works Cited

[Text citations used are placed in square brackets.]

American School of Classical Studies at Athens, *Pots and Pans of Classical Athens* (1959)

J. Barron, *An Introduction to Greek Sculpture* (London 1965)

J. Boardman, *Greek Sculpture. The Archaic Period* (London 1978) [*GS1*]

———, *Greek Sculpture. The Classical Period* (London 1978) [*GS2*]

———, *Athenian Black Figure Vases* (London 1974) [*ABFV1*]

———, *Athenian Red Figure Vases—The Archaic Period* (London 1974) [*ARFV1*]

———, *Athenian Red Figure Vases—The Classical Period* (London 1989) [*ARFV2*]

A. M. Bowie, *Aristophanes: Myth, Ritual, and Comedy* (Cambridge 1993)

———, "Thinking With Drinking: Wine and the Symposium in Aristophanes," *JHS* 117 (1997):1–21

I. Brooke, *Costume in Greek Classic Drama* (London 1973)

W. Burkert, *Greek Religion*, tr. J. Raffian (Oxford 1985)

———, *Homo Necans*, tr. P. Bing (Berkeley and London 1983)

J. McK. Camp, *The Athenian Agora: A Guide to the Excavation and Museum* (Athenian School of Classical Studies 1990).

Collard et al., eds., *Euripides, Selected Fragmentary Plays*, Vol. 1 (Warminster 1995)

G. Dobrov, "The Comic and Tragic Tereus," in *AJP* 114 (1993)

K. J. Dover, *Greek Homosexuality*, 2d ed. (Cambridge, MA 1989)

———, *Aristophanic Comedy* (London 1972)

N. Dunbar, *Aristophanes: Birds* (Oxford 1995)

S. Goldhill, "Representing Democracy: Women at the Great Dionysia," in *Ritual, Finance, Politics. Athenian Democratic Accounts Presented to David Lewis*, R. Osborne and S. Hornblower, eds. (Oxford 1994)

R. Green and E. Handley, *Images of the Greek Theatre* (London 1995)

J. Henderson, *The Maculate Muse*, 2d ed. (Oxford 1991)

R. A. Higgens, *Greek Terracottas* (London 1967)

D. MacDowell, *The Law in Classical Athens* (London 1978)

K. McLeish, *The Theatre of Aristophanes* (London 1980)

R. Meiggs and D. M. Lewis, eds., *A Selection of Greek Historical Inscriptions*, 2d ed. (Oxford 1988)

J. Mikalson, *Athenian Popular Religion* (Chapel Hill and London 1983)

P. Millett, *Lending and Borrowing in Ancient Athens* (Cambridge 1992)

H. W. Parke, *Festivals of the Athenians* (London 1977)

D. Parker, *The Wasps*, in *Aristophanes: Three Comedies*, W. Arrowsmith, ed. (Ann Arbor 1969)

R. Parker, *Miasma, Pollution and Purification in Early Greek Religion* (Oxford 1983)

A. H. Pickard-Cambridge, *Dithyramb, Comedy and Tragedy* 2d ed., rev. T. B. L. Webster (Oxford 1968)

A. H. Sommerstein, *The Comedies of Aristophanes*, Vol. 3, *Clouds*, 2d ed. (Warminster 1984)

———, *The Comedies of Aristophanes*, Vol. 4, *Wasps*, 2d ed. (Warminster 1984)

———, *The Comedies of Aristophanes*, Vol. 6, *Birds*, 2d ed. (Warminster 1984)

B. Sparkes, "The Greek Kitchen" in *JHS* 82 (1962) 121–37

———, "Illustrating Aristophanes," *JHS* 95 (1975) 122–35

I. Storey, "Notus est omnibus Eupolis?" in *Tragedy, Comedy and the Polis*, A. H. Sommerstein et al. (Bari 1993)

O. P. Taplin, *Comic Angels* (Oxford 1993)

A. D. Trendall and T. B. L. Webster, *Illustrations of Greek Drama* (London 1971)

J. Winkler, "The Ephebe's Song: 'Tragoidia' and 'Polis,'" in *Nothing to Do with Dionysos?* J. Winkler and F. Zeitlin, eds. (Princeton 1990)

Further Reading

The bibliography on Aristophanes is immense. The following is intended to guide one's first reading, and to suggest some more advanced and specialized studies for those interested in going further.

Texts

Four overall editions of the Greek text can be mentioned, plus the scholarly editions of individual plays. The Oxford Classical Text of Hall and Geldart, *Aristophanis Comoediae*, 2 vols. (Oxford 1906) is very outdated; a newer version is being prepared by N. G. Wilson. The Budé version of V. Coulon (Paris 1923–) is better, but also in need of replacement. A. H. Sommerstein is editing the comedies with a translation and brief commentary for Aris and Phillips (Warminster 1980–); the series has currently reached *Frogs*. Finally, J. Henderson has produced the first volume (*Acharnians–Knights*) of the long-awaited new Aristophanes for the Loeb Classical Library (Cambridge, MA 1998–).

For the individual comedies the following may be recommended (in addition to Sommerstein):

Acharnians —in preparation for the Oxford/Clarendon series (S. D. Olson)

Knights —in preparation for the Oxford/Clarendon series (J. Henderson)

Clouds —by K. J. Dover (Oxford 1968)

Wasps —by D. M. MacDowell (Oxford 1971)

Peace —by S. D. Olson (Oxford 1998)

Birds —by N. V. Dunbar (Oxford 1995)

Lysistrata —by J. Henderson (Oxford 1987)

Frogs —by W. G. Stanford (London 1963)
by K. J. Dover (Oxford 1993)

Ecclesiazusae—by R. G. Ussher (Oxford 1973)

For the fragments of the lost plays of Aristophanes and the other poets of Old Comedy, the student is now referred to R. Kassel and C. Austin, *Poetae Comici Graeci*, vol. II, III.2 (Aristophanes), IV–VIII (Berlin/New York 1983–).

General Studies

P. Cartledge, *Aristophanes and His Theatre of the Absurd* (London 1990)

K. J. Dover, *Aristophanic Comedy* (London 1972)

E. Handley, "Comedy," in *Cambridge History of Classical Literature*, vol. 1, *Greek Literature*, B. M. W. Knox and P. Easterling, eds. (Cambridge 1985) 103–46

D. M. MacDowell, *Aristophanes and Athens* (Oxford 1995)

K. McLeish, *The Theatre of Aristophanes* (London 1980)

G. Murray, *Aristophanes* (Oxford 1933)

G. Norwood, *Greek Comedy* (London 1931)

F. H. Sandbach, *The Comic Theatre of Greece and Rome* (London 1985) ch. 1–3

R. G. Ussher, *Aristophanes* (Oxford 1979)

Specialized Studies

A. M. Bowie, *Aristophanes: Myth, Ritual, and Comedy* (Cambridge 1993)

C. W. Dearden, *The Stage of Aristophanes* (London 1976)

V. Ehrenberg, *The People of Aristophanes*, 2d ed. (Oxford 1951)

T. Gelzer, *Die epirrhematische Agon bei Aristophanes* (Munich 1960)

J. Henderson, *The Maculate Muse*, 2d ed. (Oxford 1991)

T. Hubbard, *The Mask of Comedy: Aristophanes and the Intertextual Parabasis* (Austin 1991)

L. P. E. Parker, *The Songs of Aristophanes* (Oxford 1997)

K. J. Reckford, *Aristophanes' Old-and-New Comedy* (Chapel Hill 1987)

G. M. Sifakis, *Parabasis and Animal Choruses* (London 1971)

C. H. Whitman, *Aristophanes and the Comic Hero* (Cambridge MA 1964)

B. Zimmermann, *Untersuchungen zur Form und dramatischen Technik der Aristophanischen Komödien* (Königstein 1984–87)

Collections of Essays

G. Dobrov, ed., *The City as Comedy* (Chapel Hill/London 1997)

J. Henderson, ed., *Aristophanes: essays in interpretation*, *YCS* 26 (1980)

E. Segal, ed., *Oxford Readings in Aristophanes* (Oxford 1996)

A. H. Sommerstein et al., eds., *Tragedy, Comedy and the Polis* (Bari 1993)

J. Winkler and F. Zeitlin, ed., *Nothing to Do with Dionysos?* (Princeton 1990)

Visual Evidence

J. Barron, *An Introduction to Greek Sculpture* (London 1965)

J. Boardman, *Greek Sculpture—The Archaic Period* (London 1978) [*GS1*]

———, *Greek Sculpture—The Classical Period* (London 1978) [*GS2*]

———, *Athenian Black Figure Vases* (London 1974) [*ABFV*]

———, *Athenian Red Figure Vases—The Archaic Period* (London 1974) [*ARFV1*]

———, *Athenian Red Figure Vases—The Classical Period* (London 1989) [*ARFV2*]

I. Brooke, *Costume in Greek Classic Drama* (London 1973)

J. McK. Camp II, *The Athenian Agora: A Guide to the Excavation and Museum* (Athenian School of Classical Studies 1990)

R. Green & E. Handley, *Images of the Greek Theatre* (London 1995)

R. A. Higgins, *Greek Terracottas* (London 1967)

B. Sparkes, "The Greek Kitchen," *Journal of Hellenic Studies* 82 (1962) 121–37

———, "Illustrating Aristophanes," *Journal of Hellenic Studies* 95 (1975) 122–35

B. Sparkes and L. Talbot, *Pots and Pans of Classical Athens* (American School of Classical Studies at Athens 1959)

O. Taplin, *Comic Angels* (Oxford 1993)

A. D. Trendall & T. B. L. Webster, *Illustrations of Greek Drama* (London 1971)

Related Studies

W. Burkert, *Greek Religion* [tr. J. Raffian] (Oxford 1985)

———, *Homo Necans* [tr. P. Bing] (Berkeley/London 1983)

K. J. Dover, *Greek Homosexuality*, 2nd ed. (Cambridge MA 1989)

D. M. MacDowell, *The Law in Classical Athens* (London 1978)

R. Meiggs & D. M. Lewis, eds., *A Selection of Greek Historical Inscriptions*, 2d ed. (Oxford 1988)

J. Mikalson, *Athenian Popular Religion* (Chapel Hill/London 1983)

P. Millett, *Lending and Borrowing in Ancient Athens* (Cambridge 1992)

H. W. Parke, *Festivals of the Athenian* (London 1977)

R. Parker, *Miasma, Pollution and Purification in Early Greek Religion* (Oxford 1983)

Significant Articles

A. M. Bowie, "Thinking with Drinking: Wine and the Symposium in Aristophanes," *Journal of Hellenic Studies* 117 (1997) 1–21

C. Carey, "Comic Ridicule and Democracy," in *Ritual, Finance and Politics*, R. Osborne and S. Hornblower, eds. (Oxford 1994) 69–83

G. E. M. de Ste Croix, "The Political Outlook of Aristophanes," Appendix XXIX in *The Origins of the Peloponnesian War* (Ithaca 1972) 355–76

J. Gardner, "Aristophanes and Male Anxiety—The defence of the *oikos*," *Greece & Rome* 36 (1989) 51–62

A. W. Gomme, "Aristophanes and Politics," *Classical Review* 52 (1938) 97–109

S. Halliwell, "Aristophanic Satire," *Yearbook of English Studies* 14 (1984) 6–20

M. Heath, "Aristophanes and His Rivals," *Greece & Rome* 37 (1990) 143–58

M. Silk, "The People of Aristophanes," in *Characterization and Individuality in Greek Literature,* C. Pelling, ed. (Oxford 1990) 150–73

A. H. Sommerstein, "How to Avoid Being a *Komodoumenos,*" *Classical Quarterly* 46 (1996) 327–56

I. C. Storey, "Poets, Politicians, and Perverts," *Classics Ireland* 5 (1998) 85–134

R. Wycherley, "Aristophanes and Euripides," *Greece & Rome* 15 (1946) 98–107

Bibliographies

For further reading on Aristophanes and Old Comedy the student is directed to the yearly surveys in *L'Année Philologique* (*APh*). Most recent studies are well supplied with bibliographies. I would call attention to the extensive bibliography in Sommerstein et al. (1993), the introduction to Segal's *Oxford Readings,* and my own two survey articles, "Old Comedy 1975–1984" in *Echos du Monde Classique* 31 (1987) 1–46, and "Δέκατον μὲν ἔτος τόδ: Old Comedy 1982-1991," *Antichthon* 26 (1992) 1–29.

One final work must be mentioned: E. Csapo and W. J. Slater, *The Context of Ancient Drama* (Ann Arbor 1994), which presents the ancient sources for drama (in translation), a fair and informed commentary, a brief bibliography by topic, and some very useful illustrations.

Suggested Readings for *Clouds*

Commentaries

K. J. Dover, *Aristophanes Clouds* (Oxford 1968)

A. H. Sommerstein, *The Comedies of Aristophanes,* vol. III *Clouds* (Warminster 1982)

Books

R. K. Fisher, *Aristophanes Clouds: Purpose and Technique* (Amsterdam 1984)

M. C. Marianetti, *Religion and Politics in Aristophanes'* Clouds (Hildesheim 1992)

D. O'Regan, *Rhetoric, Comedy, and the Violence of Language in Aristophanes'* Clouds (New York/Oxford 1992)

Book Chapters

The chapters in the following may be consulted with profit; full details are found in the general list of further readings: Bowie (1993) 102–33, Cartledge 22–31, Dover (1972) 101–20, Hubbard 88–112, MacDowell (1995) 113–49, Murray 85–105, Norwood 211–32, Reckford 388–402, Whitman 119–43.

Articles

L. Edmunds, "Aristophanes' Socrates," in *Proceedings of the Boston area colloquium in ancient philosophy* 1 (1986): 209–30

P. Green, "Strepsiades, Socrates, and the Abuses of Intellectualism," *Greek, Roman and Byzantine Studies* 20 (1979): 1–17

J. Henderson, "Problems in Greek Literary History: the case of *Clouds*," in, *Nomodeiktes*, R. M. Rosen and J. Farrell, eds. (Ann Arbor 1993): 591–601

T. K. Hubbard, "Parabatic Self-Criticism and the Two Versions of Aristophanes' *Clouds*," *Classical Antiquity* 5 (1986): 182–97

K. Kleve, "Anti-Dover or Socrates in the *Clouds*," *Symbolae Osloneses* 48 (1983): 23–37

E. C. Kopff, "The Date of Aristophanes, *Nubes* II," *American Journal of Philology* 111 (1990): 318–29

T. Long, "Understanding Comic Action in Aristophanes," *Classical World* 70 (1976): 1–8

M. Nussbaum, "Aristophanes and Socrates on Learning Practical Wisdom," *Yale Classical Studies* 26 (1980): 43–97

K. J. Reckford, "Strepsiades as a Comic Ixion," *Illinois Classical Studies* 16 (1991): 125–36

C. Segal, "Aristophanes' Cloud-Chorus," *Arethusa* 2 (1967): 143–61

I. C. Storey, "The Dates of Aristophanes' *Clouds* II and Eupolis' *Baptai*," *American Journal of Philology* 114 (1993): 71–84

H. Tarrant, "Midwifery in the *Clouds*," *Classical Quarterly* 38 (1988): 116–22

———, "Alcibiades in Aristophanes' *Clouds* I and II," *Ancient History: Resources for Teachers* 19 (1989): 13–20

———, "*Clouds* I; Steps toward Reconstruction," *Arctos* 25 (1991): 157–81

L. Woodbury, "Strepsiades' Understanding," *Phoenix* 34 (1980): 108–27

The following studies barely scratch the surface of the matter of the first version of *Clouds*: Dover (*Cl.*) lxxx–xcviii, Fisher 20–23, Henderson (1993), Hubbard (1986), Kopff, MacDowell (1995) 134–49, O'Regan 133–39, Sommerstein (*Cl.*) 3f., Storey (1993), and Tarrant (1989) and (1991). Fuller citations appear in the list above.

Suggested Readings for *Wasps*

Commentaries

D. M. MacDowell, *Aristophanes Wasps* (Oxford 1971)

A. H. Sommerstein, *The Comedies of Aristophanes*, vol. IV *Wasps* (Warminster 1983)

Books

G. Mastromarco, *Storia di una commedia di Atene* (Florence 1974)

G. Paduano, *Il giudice giudicato* (Bologna 1974)

Book Chapters

The chapters in the following may be used with profit; fuller details may be found in the general list of further readings: Bowie (1993) 78–101, Cartledge 50–53, Dover (1972) 121–31, Hubbard 113–39, MacDowell (1995) 150–79, Murray 69–84, Norwood 222–30, Reckford 219–81, and Whitman 143–86.

Articles

A. M. Bowie, "Ritual Stereotype and Comic Reversal: Aristophanes' *Wasps*," *Bulletin of the Institute of Classical Studies* 34 (1987): 112–25

G. Crane, "*Oikos* and *Agora*: Mapping the Polis in Aristophanes' *Wasps*," in Dobrov (1996) 198–229

A. Crichton, "The Old are in a Second Childhood: Age Reversal and Jury Service in Aristophanes' *Wasps*," *Bulletin of the Institute of Classical Studies* 38 (1991): 59–79

G. H. R. Horsley, "Aristophanes' *Wasps*," in *Hellenika: Essays on Greek History and Politics* (North Ryde, N.S.W. 1982) 69–96

D. Konstan, "The Politics of Aristophanes' *Wasps*," *Transactions of the American Philological Association* 115 (1985): 27–46

K. Sidwell, "Was Philocleon Cured? The νόσος theme in Aristophanes' *Wasps*," *Classica et Mediaevalia* 41 (1990): 9–31

I. C. Storey, "*Wasps* 1284–91 and the Portrait of Kleon in *Wasps*," *Scholia* 4 (1995): 3–23

J. Vaio, "Aristophanes' *Wasps*: The Relevance of the Final Scenes," *Greek, Roman and Byzantine Studies* 12 (1971): 335–51

Suggested Readings for *Birds*

Commentaries

N. V. Dunbar, *Aristophanes Birds* (Oxford 1995)

A. H. Sommerstein, *The Comedies of Aristophanes*, vol. VI *Birds* (Warminster 1987)

Book

H. Hoffmann, *Mythos und Komödie. Untersuchungen zu den Vögeln des Aristophanes* (Hildesheim 1976)

Book Chapters

The chapters in the following may be consulted with profit; fuller details are to be found in the general list of further readings: Bowie (1993) 151–77, Cartledge 60–62, Dover (1972) 140–49, Hubbard 158–82, MacDowell (1995) 199–228, Murray 135–63, Norwood 238–44, Reckford 330–43, and Whitman 167–99.

Articles

E. Craik, "One for the Pot: Aristophanes' *Birds* and the Anthesteria," *Eranos* 85 (1987): 25–34

G. Dobrov, "Aristophanes' *Birds* and the Metaphor of Deferral," *Arethusa* 23 (1990): 209–33

———, "The Tragic and Comic *Tereus*," *American Journal of Philology* 114 (1993) 189–234

T. Gelzer, "Some Aspects of Aristophanes' Dramatic Art in the *Birds*." *Bulletin of the Institute of Classical Studies* 23 (1976): 1–14

J. R. Green, "A Representation of the *Birds* of Aristophanes," *Greek Vases in the Getty Museum* 2 (1985): 95–118

B. Katz, "The *Birds* of Aristophanes and Politics," *Athenaeum* 54 (1976): 352–82

D. Konstan, "A City in the Air: Aristophanes' *Birds*," *Arethusa* 23 (1990) 183–207

H.-J. Newiger, "Die Vögel und ihre Stellung im Gesantwerk des Aristophanes," in *Aristophanes und die alte Komödie* (Darmstadt 1975) 266–82

A. Nicev, "L' énigme des Oiseaux d' Aristophane," *Euphrosyne* 17 (1989): 9–30

D. C. Pozzi, "The Pastoral Ideal in the *Birds* of Aristophanes," *Classical Journal* 81 (1986): 119–29